MAXIMUM VSPHERE™

Maximum vSphere™

TIPS, HOW-TOS, AND BEST PRACTICES FOR WORKING WITH VMWARE VSPHERE™ 4

Eric Siebert

Simon Seagrave

PRENTICE
HALL

Upper Saddle River, NJ • Boston • Indianapolis • San Francisco
New York • Toronto • Montreal • London • Munich • Paris • Madrid
Capetown • Sydney • Tokyo • Singapore • Mexico City

Many of the designations used by manufacturers and sellers to distinguish their products are claimed as trademarks. Where those designations appear in this book, and the publisher was aware of a trademark claim, the designations have been printed with initial capital letters or in all capitals.

The authors and publisher have taken care in the preparation of this book, but make no expressed or implied warranty of any kind and assume no responsibility for errors or omissions. No liability is assumed for incidental or consequential damages in connection with or arising out of the use of the information or programs contained herein.

The publisher offers excellent discounts on this book when ordered in quantity for bulk purchases or special sales, which may include electronic versions and/or custom covers and content particular to your business, training goals, marketing focus, and branding interests. For more information, please contact:

> U.S. Corporate and Government Sales
> (800) 382-3419
> corpsales@pearsontechgroup.com

For sales outside the United States please contact:

> International Sales
> international@pearson.com

Visit us on the Web: informit.com/ph

Library of Congress Cataloging-in-Publication Data

Siebert, Eric, 1966-
 Maximum vSphere : tips, how-tos, and best practices for working with VMware vSphere 4 / Eric Siebert ; Simon Seagrave, contributor.
     p.   cm.
 Includes index.
 ISBN 978-0-13-704474-0 (pbk. : alk. paper)
 1. VMware vSphere. 2. Virtual computer systems. I. Title.
 QA76.9.V5S47 2010
 005.4'3—dc22

                                        2010021366

ISBN-13: 978-0-13-704474-0
ISBN-10:   0-13-704474-7
Text printed in the United States on recycled paper at printed at Courier in Stoughton, Massachusetts.
First printing, August 2010

Editor-in-Chief
Mark Taub

Acquisitions Editor
Trina MacDonald

Development Editor
Michael Thurston

Managing Editor
John Fuller

Project Editor
Anna Popick

Project Management
Techne Group

Copy Editor
Audrey Doyle

Indexer
Larry Sweazy

Proofreader
Beth Roberts

Editorial Assistant
Olivia Basegio

Technical Reviewers
Ken Cline
George Vish

Cover Designer
Chuti Prasertsith

Compositor
Techne Group

CONTENTS

FOREWORD

First of all, I'd like to get this out of the way. If you are standing in a bricks-and-mortar bookstore or even sitting on your couch browsing online and flipping through the first pages of this book, wondering if you need yet another book on virtualization and VMware vSphere, let me reassure you: *Yes, you should buy this book.*

This book is not an introduction and not a tutorial. It is an in-depth reference manual from a hands-on expert and experienced technology writer. It lays out the principles for understanding and operating VMware vSphere and the new features introduced in vSphere 4. The author, Eric Siebert, didn't just kick this out the door; he spent a year gathering tips, tricks, and best practices specific to the new version of vSphere, both from his own experience and from his connections to a wide breadth of other virtualization practitioners, and he has included that wisdom in this book. As an example, the "Building Your Own vSphere Lab" chapter is very useful, comes from this kind of collaboration, and seems to be unique among vSphere books.

> *I'm not going to buy my kids an encyclopedia. Let them walk to school like I did.*
>
> —Yogi Berra

Maximum vSphere™ isn't quite an encyclopedia, but it is a reference book that will spare you from feeling like you've got a long slog each day in your datacenter. Eric Siebert is an active virtualization practitioner and IT professional.

For years, he has also been very active in the online virtualization community, which is how I met him in my role on VMware's social media and community team. Eric is well known for being available to help people in the online world. Eric's main website is called vSphere-land, and Eric is truly the Diderot to this online *encyclopédie,* tirelessly gathering and organizing a taxonomy of virtualization best practices, although unlike his eighteenth century counterparts, it hasn't taken him 20 years to finish.

Writing a book is never easy for the author or the author's family. This is Eric's second book and his commitment to delivering high-quality technical material has never wavered. Eric is known for going both deep and broad on technology. One week Eric might be doing original research for articles on vStorage APIs, and the next he'll be pulling together an omnibus of links from across all VMworld blog and press coverage. Eric's articles in the trade press are always informative. His vSphere-land links and "vLaunchpad" are always a great choice to start investigating a VMware-related topic. This book should act as a great launchpad for your VMware work as well.

We're at an interesting place in the evolution of IT. One of the fascinating effects of virtualization in the datacenter is the blurring of boundaries and breaking down of the specialty silos that have developed in the past few decades—the separate teams for storage, networking, servers, apps, security, and more. All these disciplines are blurring as virtualization upends the traditional datacenter architectures and breaks the correspondence between physical device and function. The virtualization expert needs to bridge all these areas. As one VMware administrator told me, "We're the virtualization team because we already know how to do everything else."

Whether the IT industry is called "cloud computing" or something else entirely once we get there, all signs point to it being a very interesting place indeed. Virtualization is an enabler technology of the cloud, but cloud computing also implies a *consumption model* and an *operations model* in the datacenter. In a few years, your datacenter will be delivering a higher level of service and business value in your organization. Although much of the complexity of the technology stack will be abstracted at that point, IT professionals still will need a solid grounding in the concepts of virtualization and the techniques to design and manage the VMware platform.

The VMware admins I know are a smart, savvy bunch. And I might be biased, but I think their eyes are brighter, their teeth are whiter, and their paychecks are fatter than the average IT professional's. It's a good place to be at the moment. Enjoy the book, and remember to give back to others when they need information as well.

—John Troyer
El Granada, CA

ACKNOWLEDGMENTS

It's been a wild ride these past couple of years trying to keep up with the fast pace at which virtualization has been moving. The blogging community has really exploded in the past year with many new bloggers coming on the scene sharing their knowledge and experience. Social networking websites like Twitter have brought a lot of us together in ways that were previously not possible. As a result, I have made many new friends in virtualization and look forward to making many more.

First and foremost, I would like to acknowledge some of my closest friends in the virtualization community. This includes Ken Cline, a technical reviewer on this book whose vast knowledge and experience continually make me feel like a newbie. Also, some other members of the vBrat Pack, including Edward Haletky, Steve Beaver, Jason Boche, Jase McCarty, and last but definitely not least, John Troyer, who is VMware's head blogger and virtualization evangelist. Special thanks to Vaughn Stewart from NetApp and Greg Schulz from storageioblog.com for reviewing my storage chapter, and to George Vish, who was also a technical reviewer on this book.

I'd also like to acknowledge a few fellow bloggers from the thriving VMware user community who inspire me on a daily basis to help others and be the best that I can be, including Eric Sloof from ntpro.nl, Scott Lowe from blog.scottlowe.org, Duncan Epping from yellowbricks.com, Rich Brambley from vmetc.com, and my fellow bloggers at Tech Target. There are many other bloggers and members of the VMTN community who I haven't mentioned, but you know who you are and you are all an inspiration to me also. I'd also like to thank the guys and gals that I work with from Tech Target, where I got started with writing, including Hannah Drake, Colin Steele, Heather Darcy, Jo Maitland, and Rich Castagna.

Special thanks to Simon Seagrave, who signed on to contribute to this book. Simon is a joy to work with and his knowledge and skills are top-notch. I'd also like to thank my editor at Pearson, Trina McDonald, who stuck with me again on this second book. Trina is a wonderful person to work with and I enjoyed having her guide me through writing this book.

Finally, I'd like to thank my family: my mother and father, Yolanda and Edward; my siblings, Jason, Elizabeth, and Jennifer; my wife, Kimberly; my boys, Logan and Zecheriah; and my precious daughter, Sophia.

—Eric Siebert

I'm very grateful to Eric for the opportunity to contribute to this book. After reading and enjoying his *VMware® VI3 Implementation and Administration*, it is fantastic to be able to be part of the book you now hold in your hands. To work with someone of Eric's technical caliber and who shares the same passion toward virtualization has been a real privilege. Thank you very much to the VMware VI3 and vSphere Performance Guru, Scott Drummond (vpivot.com), and to VMware aficionados Ken Cline and Eric Sloof (ntpro.nl), for their time and excellent feedback. It was much appreciated.

I'd like to give a big shout-out to all my fellow virtualization, server, and storage bloggers who tirelessly keep producing brilliant content, many of whom I have had the privilege of meeting or corresponding with over the past couple of years. I would try mentioning names, but the list is far too long, though you know who you are. Keep blogging! Thanks to John Troyer for keeping the vExpert and VMware virtualization community running as well as it does. A sincere thank you to my valued TechHead (techhead.co.uk) readers who spur me on to keep writing content. I really appreciate your comments, emails, and feedback—keep it coming.

Special thanks to my other half, Sarah, whose patience and understanding know no bounds in putting up with all my IT equipment around our home and the significant amount of time I dedicate to attending IT events, working in my virtualization lab, and blogging. I am one lucky guy!

Lastly, I couldn't have my name in a book and not say... Thanks Mum!

—Simon Seagrave

ABOUT THE AUTHORS

Eric Siebert has been working with computers for more than 25 years. For the past 15 years, his main focus has been the administration of Windows server environments and supporting enterprise applications such as web, email, and database servers. Five years ago he discovered virtualization technology in the form of VMware ESX and has been hooked ever since, spending countless hours learning the product inside and out. He now spends much of his time helping others in VMware's community support forums, having achieved Guru status and become one of the forum's moderators. His own website, http://vsphere-land.com, is where he shares his tips and experiences as well as hundreds of links to technical information and top ten lists on a variety of subjects. Additionally, Eric writes tips and blogs for Tech Target on sites such as http://searchvmware.com, http://searchservervirtualization.com, and http://searchdatabackup.com. He is one of the 300 vExperts named by VMware for 2009 and 2010, author of the book *VMware® VI3 Implementation and Administration,* past VMworld speaker, and frequent Best of VMworld awards judge. Follow Eric on Twitter at http://twitter.com/ericsiebert.

Contributor **Simon Seagrave** has been working in the IT industry for the past 15 years. He is a VMware vExpert, holds various IT accreditations including a VMware VCP, and has worked for variously sized companies ranging from large corporations to small and medium-size businesses. He has been working with VMware products since the early days of VMware GSX and is passionate about virtualization and the many benefits it can provide. Along with virtualization, he particularly enjoys working with server and storage-related technologies, which are subjects that make up a large portion of the content you can find on his blog site, TechHead (http://techhead.co.uk).

INTRODUCTION TO vSPHERE

VMware released the successor to Virtual Infrastructure 3 (VI3) in May 2009 with a new name, vSphere, and a new version number, 4.0. This release introduces many new features, both small and large, which we will cover in this chapter. However, don't be intimidated by all the new features. Overall, the core product is basically the same, so many of the things you know from VI3 will also apply to vSphere.

WHAT'S NEW IN THIS RELEASE

When it came time to release the successor to its VI3 datacenter virtualization product, VMware chose to change the name of the product family from VI3 to vSphere. In addition, VMware took the opportunity to sync up the version numbers between its ESX and ESXi products with that of its vCenter Server product to be more consistent and to avoid confusion. With VI3, vCenter Server was at version 2.x and ESX and ESXi were known as version 3.x. Now with vSphere, ESX, ESXi, and vCenter Server are at version 4.x, with the initial release of vSphere being 4.0. In this section, we will cover what is new in each major area and detail each new feature and enhancement so that you can understand the benefits and how to take advantage of them.

STORAGE, BACKUP, AND DATA PROTECTION

vSphere offers many enhancements and new features related to storage, back-ups, and data protection, which is a compelling reason in and of itself to upgrade from VI3 to vSphere. From thin provisioning to Storage VMotion to the vStorage APIs, this area has greatly improved in terms of performance, usability, and vendor integration.

Thin Provisioning Enhancements

Thin provisioned disks are not new to vSphere, as they also existed in VI3; how-ever, numerous changes have made them more usable in vSphere. The changes made to thin disks in vSphere include the following.

- In VI3, thin disks could only be created manually using the vmkfstools command-line utility. In vSphere, thin disks can be created using the vSphere client at the time a virtual machine (VM) is created.
- In VI3, thick disks could only be converted to thin disks using vmkfstools and only when a VM was powered off. In vSphere, existing thick disks can be easily converted to thin disks using the Storage VMotion feature while a VM is powered on.
- In VI3, the only way to see the actual current size of a thin disk was to use the command line. In vSphere, new storage views are available in the vSphere client that use a plug-in which provides the ability to see the actual size of thin disks.
- In VI3, there are no alarms to report datastores. In vSphere, configurable alarms are built into vCenter Server that allow you to monitor datastore overallocation and space usage percentages.
- In VI3, if a thin disk could no longer grow because of insufficient datastore space, the VM would crash and possibly corrupt. In vSphere, a new safety feature automatically suspends VMs with thin disks when datastore free space is critically low to prevent corruption and OS crashes.

These new improvements make thin disks more manageable and much easier to use in vSphere compared to VI3. We will cover thin disks in more detail in Chapter 3.

iSCSI Improvements

iSCSI storage arrays have become an increasingly popular storage choice for virtual hosts due to their lower cost (compared to Fibre Channel storage area networks [FC SANs]) and decent performance. Use of iSCSI software initiators has always resulted in a slight performance penalty compared to hardware initiators with TCP offload engines, as the host CPU is utilized for TCP/IP operations. In vSphere, VMware rewrote the entire iSCSI software initiator stack to make more efficient use of CPU cycles, resulting in significant efficiency (from 7% to 52%) and throughput improvements compared to VI3.

VMware did this by enhancing the VMkernel TCP/IP stack, optimizing the cache affinity, and improving internal lock efficiency. Other improvements to iSCSI include easier provisioning and configuration, as well as support for bidirectional CHAP authentication, which provides better security by requiring both the initiator and the target to authenticate each other.

Storage VMotion Enhancements

Storage VMotion was introduced in version 3.5, but it was difficult to use because it could only be run using a command-line utility. VMware fixed this in vSphere and integrated it into the vSphere Client so that you can quickly and easily perform SVMotions. In addition to providing a GUI for SVMotion in vSphere, VMware also enhanced SVMotion to allow conversion of thick disks to thin disks and thin disks to thick disks. VMware also made some under-the-covers enhancements to SVMotion to make the migration process much more efficient. In VI3, SVMotion relied on snapshots when copying the disk to its new location, and then committing those when the operation was complete. In vSphere, SVMotion uses the new Changed Block Tracking (CBT) feature to keep track of blocks that were changed after the copy process started, and copies them after it completes. We will cover Storage VMotion in more detail in Chapter 9.

Support for Fibre Channel over Ethernet and Jumbo Frames

vSphere adds support for newer storage and networking technologies which include the following.

- **Fibre Channel over Ethernet (FCoE)**—vSphere now supports FCoE on Converged Network Adapters (CNAs) which encapsulates Fibre Channel frames over Ethernet and allows for additional storage configuration options.

- **Jumbo frames**—Conventional Ethernet frames are 1,518 bytes in length. Jumbo frames are typically 9,000 bytes in length, which can improve network throughput and CPU efficiency. VMware added support for jumbo frames in ESX 3.5 but did not officially support jumbo frames for use with storage protocols. With the vSphere release, the company officially supports the use of jumbo frames with software iSCSI and NFS storage devices, with both 1Gbit and 10Gbit NICs to help improve their efficiency.

Both of these technologies can provide great increases in performance when using network-based storage devices such as iSCSI and NFS, and can bring them closer to the level of performance that the more expensive Fibre Channel storage provides.

Ability to Hot-Extend Virtual Disks

Previously in VI3 you had to power down a VM before you could increase the size of its virtual disk. With vSphere you can increase the size of an existing virtual disk (vmdk file) while it is powered on as long as the guest operating system supports it. Once you increase the size of a virtual disk, the guest OS can then begin to use it to create new disk partitions or to extend existing ones. Supported operating systems include Windows Server 2008, Windows Server 2003 Enterprise and Datacenter editions, and certain Linux distributions.

Ability to Grow VMFS Volumes

With vSphere you can increase the size of Virtual Machine File System (VMFS) volumes without using extents and without disrupting VMs. In VI3, the only way to grow volumes was to join a separate LUN to the VMFS volume as an extent, which had some disadvantages. Now, with vSphere, you can grow the LUN of an existing VMFS volume using your SAN configuration tools and then expand the VMFS volume so that it uses the additional space.

Pluggable Storage Architecture

In vSphere, VMware has created a new modular storage architecture that allows third-party vendors to interface with certain storage functionality. The pluggable storage architecture allows vendors to create plug-ins for controlling storage I/O-specific functions such as multipathing. vSphere has built-in functionality that allows for fixed or round-robin path selection when multiple paths to a storage device are available. Vendors can expand on this and develop their own plug-in modules that allow for optimal performance through load balancing, and also provide more intelligent path selection. The PSA leverages the new capabilities provided by the vStorage APIs for multipathing to achieve this.

Paravirtualized SCSI Adapters

Paravirtualization is a technology that is available for certain Windows and Linux operating systems that utilize a special driver to communicate directly with the hypervisor. Without paravirtualization, the guest OS does not know about the virtualization layer and privileged calls are trapped by the hypervisor using binary translation. Paravirtualization allows for greater throughput and lower CPU utilization for VMs and is useful for disk I/O-intensive applications. Paravirtualized SCSI adapters are separate storage adapters that can be used for nonprimary OS partitions and can be enabled by editing a VM's settings and enabling the paravirtualization feature. This may sound similar to the VMDirectPath feature, but the key difference is that paravirtualized SCSI adapters can be shared by multiple VMs on host servers and do not require that a single adapter be dedicated to a single VM. We will cover paravirtualization in more detail in Chapter 5.

VMDirectPath for Storage I/O Devices

VMDirectPath is similar to paravirtualized SCSI adapters in which a VM can directly access host adapters and bypass the virtualization layer to achieve better throughput and reduced CPU utilization. It is different from paravirtualized SCSI adapters in that with VMDirectPath, you must dedicate an adapter to a VM and it cannot be used by any other VMs on that host. VMDirectPath is available for specific models of both network and storage adapters; however, currently only network adapters are fully supported in vSphere, and storage adapters have only experimental support (i.e., they are not ready for production use). Like pvSCSI adapters, VMDirectPath can be used for VMs that have very high storage or network I/O requirements, such as database servers. VMDirectPath enables virtualization of workloads that you previously might have kept physical. We will cover VMDirectPath in more detail in Chapter 3.

vStorage APIs

VMware introduced the vStorage APIs in vSphere, and they consist of a collection of interfaces that third-party vendors can leverage to seamlessly interact with storage in vSphere. They allow vSphere and its storage devices to come together for improved efficiency and better management. We will discuss the vStorage APIs in more detail in Chapter 5.

Storage Views and Alarms in vCenter Server

The storage view has selectable columns that will display various information, including the total amount of disk space that a VM is taking up (including snapshots, swap files, etc.), the total amount of disk space used by snapshots, the total amount of space used by virtual disks (showing the actual thin disk size), the total amount of space used by other files (logs, NVRAM, and config and suspend files), and much more. This is an invaluable view that will quickly show you how much space is being used in your environment for each component, as well as enable you to easily monitor snapshot space usage. The storage view also includes a map view so that you can see relationships among VMs, hosts, and storage components.

In VI3, alarms were very limited, and the only storage alarm in VI3 was for host or VM disk usage (in Kbps). With vSphere, VMware added hundreds of new alarms, many of them related to storage. Perhaps the most important alarm relates to percentage of datastore disk space used. This alarm will actually alert you when a datastore is close to running out of free space. This is very important when you have a double threat from both snapshots and thin disks that can grow and use up all the free space on a datastore. Also, alarms in vSphere appear in the status column in red, so they are more easily noticeable.

ESX AND ESXi

The core architecture of ESX and ESXi has not changed much in vSphere. In fact, the biggest change was moving to a 64-bit architecture for the VMkernel. When ESXi was introduced in VI3, VMware announced that it would be its future architecture and that it would be retiring ESX and its Service Console in a future release. That didn't happen with vSphere, but this is still VMware's plan and it may unfold in a future major release. ESX and ESXi do feature a few changes and improvements in vSphere, though, and they include the following.

- Both the VMkernel and the Linux-based ESX Service Console are now 64-bit; in VI3, they were both 32-bit. VMware did this to provide better performance and greater physical memory capacity for the host server. Whereas many older servers only supported 32-bit hardware, most modern servers support 64-bit hardware, so this should no longer be an issue. Additionally, the ESX Service Console was updated in vSphere to a more current version of Red Hat Linux.

- Up to 1TB of physical memory is now supported in ESX and ESXi hosts, whereas previously in VI3, only 256GB of memory was supported. In addition, vSphere now supports 64 logical CPUs and a total of 320 VMs per host, with up to 512 virtual CPUs. This greatly increases the potential density of VMs on a host server.

- In VI3, VMware introduced a feature called Distributed Power Management (DPM) which enabled workloads to be redistributed so that host servers could be shut down during periods of inactivity to save power. However, in VI3, this feature was considered experimental and was not intended for production use, as it relied on the less reliable Wake on LAN technology. In vSphere, VMware added the Intelligent Platform Management Interface (IPMI) and iLO (HP's Integrated Lights-Out) as alternative, more reliable remote power-on methods, and as a result, DPM is now fully supported in vSphere.

- vSphere supports new CPU power management technologies called Enhanced SpeedStep by Intel and Enhanced PowerNow! by AMD. These technologies enable the host to dynamically switch CPU frequencies based on workload demands, which enables the processors to draw less power and create less heat, thereby allowing the fans to spin more slowly. This technique is called Dynamic Voltage and Frequency Scaling (DVFS), and is essentially CPU throttling; for example, a 2.6GHz CPU might be reduced to 1.2GHz because that is all that is needed to meet the current load requirements on a host. The use of DVFS with DPM can result in substantial energy savings in a datacenter. We will cover this feature in detail in Chapter 2.

The new 64-bit architecture that vSphere uses means that older 32-bit server hardware will not be able to run vSphere. We will cover this in detail in Chapter 2.

VIRTUAL MACHINES

VMs received many enhancements in vSphere as the virtual hardware version went from version 4 (used in VI3) to version 7. These enhancements allow VMs to handle larger workloads than what they previously handled in VI3, and allow vSphere to handle almost any workload to help companies achieve higher virtualization percentages. The changes to VMs in vSphere include the following.

- Version 4 was the virtual hardware type used for VMs in VI3, and version 7 is the updated version that was introduced in vSphere. We'll cover virtual hardware in more detail in Chapter 3.

- In VI3, you could only assign up to four vCPUs and 64GB to a VM. In vSphere, you can assign up to eight vCPUs and 255GB of RAM to a VM.

- Many more guest operating systems are supported in vSphere compared to VI3, including more Linux distributions and Windows versions as well as new selections for Solaris, FreeBSD, and more.

- vSphere introduced a new virtual network adapter type called VMXNET3, which is the third generation of its homegrown virtual NIC (vNIC). This new adapter provides better performance and reduced I/O virtualization overhead than the previous VMXNET2 virtual network adapter.

- In VI3, only BusLogic and LSI Logic parallel SCSI storage adapter types were available. In vSphere, you have additional choices, including an LSI Logic SAS (serial attached SCSI) and a Paravirtual SCSI adapter. Additionally, you can optionally use an IDE adapter, which was not available in VI3.

- You can now add memory or additional vCPUs to a VM while it is powered on, as long as the guest operating system running on the VM supports this feature.

- In VI3, the display adapter of a VM was hidden and had no settings that could be modified. In vSphere, the display adapter is shown and has a number of settings that can be changed, including the memory size and the maximum number of displays.

- You can now add a USB controller to your VM, which allows it to access USB devices connected to the host server. However, although this option exists in vSphere, it is not supported yet, and is currently intended for hosted products such as VMware Workstation. VMware may decide to enable this support in vSphere in a future release as it is a much requested feature.

- vSphere introduced a new virtual device called Virtual Machine Communication Interface (VMCI) which enables high-speed communication between the VM and the hypervisor, as well as between VMs that reside on the same host. This is an alternative and much quicker communication method than using vNICs, and it improves the performance of applications that are integrated and running on separate VMs (i.e., web, application, and database servers).

As you can see, VMs are much more powerful and robust in vSphere. We will cover their many enhancements in detail in Chapter 3.

vCenter Server

vCenter Server has received numerous enhancements in vSphere that have made this management application for ESX and ESXi hosts much more usable and powerful. In addition to receiving a major overhaul, vCenter Server also has a simplified licensing scheme so that a separate license server is no longer required. Enhancements were made throughout the product, from alarms and performance monitoring, to configuration, reporting, and much more. Additionally, vCenter Server can scale better due to the addition of a new linked mode. The new features and enhancements to vCenter Server include the following.

- Host profiles enable centralized host configuration management using policies to specify the configuration of a host. Host profiles are almost like templates that you can apply to a host to easily change its configuration all at once, without having to manually change each setting one by one. This allows you to quickly configure a brand-new host and ensure that its settings are consistent with other hosts in the environment. You can use host profiles to configure network, storage, and security settings, and you can create many more from scratch or copy them from an existing host that is already configured. Host profiles greatly simplify host deployment and can help to ensure compliance to datacenter standards. This feature is available only in the Enterprise Plus edition of vSphere.

- vCenter Server has limitations to the number of hosts and VMs that it can manage; therefore, multiple vCenter Servers are sometimes required. The new linked mode enables multiple vCenter Servers to be linked together so that they can be managed from a single vSphere client session, which enables easier and more centralized administration. Additionally, linked mode allows roles and licenses to be shared among multiple vCenter Servers.

- vApps create a resource container for multiple VMs that work together as part of a multitier application. vApps provide methods for setting power on options, IP address allocation, and resource allocation, and provide application-level customization for all the VMs in the vApp. vApps greatly simplify the management of an application that spans multiple VMs, and ensure that the interdependencies of the application are always met. vApps can be created in vCenter Server as well as imported and exported in the OVF format.

- A new licensing model was introduced in vSphere to greatly simplify license management. In VI3, you had a license server that ran as a separate application from vCenter Server and used long text files for license management. In vSphere, licensing is integrated into vCenter Server and all product and feature licenses are encapsulated in a 25-character license key that is generated by VMware's licensing portal.

- Alarms in vSphere are much more robust, and offer more than 100 triggers. In addition, a new Condition Length field can be defined when you are setting up triggers to help eliminate false alarms.

- More granular permissions can now be set when defining roles to grant users access to specific functionality in vSphere. This gives you much greater control and protection of your environment. You have many more permissions on datastores and networks as well, so you can control such actions as vSwitch configuration and datastore browser file controls.

- Performance reporting in vCenter Server using the built-in charts and statistics has improved so that you can look at all resources at once in a single overview screen. In addition, VM-specific performance counters are integrated into the Windows Perfmon utility when VMware Tools is installed to provide more accurate VM performance analysis.

- The Guided Consolidation feature which analyzes physical servers in preparation for converting them to VMs is now a plug-in to vCenter Server. This allows you to run the feature on servers other than the vCenter Server to reduce the resource load on the vCenter Server.

vCenter Server has many enhancements in vSphere that make it much more robust and scalable, and improve the administration and management of VMs. Also, many add-ons and plug-ins are available for vCenter Server that expand and improve its functionality. We will cover vCenter Server in more detail in Chapter 4.

CLIENTS AND MANAGEMENT

There are many different ways to manage and administer a VI3 environment, and VMware continued to improve and refine them in vSphere. Whether it is through the GUI client, web browser, command-line utilities, or scripting and APIs, vSphere offers many different ways to manage your virtual environment. Enhancements to management utilities in vSphere include the following.

- The VI3 Client is now called the vSphere Client and continues to be a Windows-only client developed using Microsoft's .NET Framework. The client is essentially the same in vSphere as it was in VI3, but it adds support for some of the latest Windows operating systems. The vSphere Client is backward compatible and can also be used to manage VI3 hosts.

- The Remote Command-Line Interface (RCLI) in VI3, which was introduced to manage ESXi hosts (but which can also manage ESX hosts), is now called the vSphere CLI and features a few new commands. The vSphere CLI is backward compatible and can also manage ESX and ESXi hosts at version 3.5 Update 2 or later.

- VMware introduced a command-line management virtual appliance in VI3, called the Virtual Infrastructure Management Assistant (VIMA), as a way to centrally manage multiple hosts at once. In vSphere, it goes by the name of vSphere Management Assistant (vMA). Where the vSphere CLI is the command-line version of the vSphere Client, the vMA is essentially the command-line version of vCenter Server. Most of the functionality of the vMA in vSphere is the same as in the previous release.

- VMware renamed its PowerShell API from VI Toolkit 1.5 in VI3 to PowerCLI 4.0 in vSphere. The PowerCLI is largely unchanged from the previous version, but it does include some bug fixes plus new cmdlets to interface with the new host profiles feature in vSphere.

- The web browser access method to connect to hosts or vCenter Server to manage VMs is essentially the same in vSphere. VMware did include official support for Firefox in vSphere, and made some cosmetic changes to the web interface, but not much else.

We will cover all of these features in more detail in Chapter 10.

NETWORKING

Although networking in vSphere has not undergone substantial changes, VMware did make a few significant changes in terms of virtual switches (vSwitches). The most significant new networking features in vSphere are the introduction of the distributed vSwitch and support for third-party vSwitches. The new networking features in vSphere include the following.

- A new centrally managed vSwitch called the vNetwork Distributed Switch (vDS) was introduced in vSphere to simplify management of vSwitches across hosts. A vDS spans multiple hosts, and it needs to be configured and set up only once and then assigned to each host. Besides being a big time-saver, this can help to eliminate configuration inconsistencies that can make vMotion fail to work. Additionally, the vDS allows the network state of a VM to travel with it as it moves from host to host.

- VMware provided the means for third-party vendors to create vSwitches in vSphere. The first to be launched with vSphere is the Cisco Nexus 1000v. In VI3, the vSwitch was essentially a dumb, nonmanageable vSwitch with little integration with the physical network infrastructure. By allowing vendors such as Cisco to create vSwitches, VMware has improved the manageability of the vSwitch and helped to integrate it with traditional physical network management tools.

- Support for Private VLANs was introduced in vSphere to allow communication between VMs on the same VLAN to be controlled and restricted.

- As mentioned earlier, VMware also introduced a new third-generation vNIC, called the VMXNET3, which includes the following new features: VLAN offloading, large TX/RX ring sizes, IPv6 checksum and TSO over IPv6, receive-side scaling (supported in Windows 2008), and MSI/MSI-X support.

- Support for IP version 6 (IPv6) was enabled in vSphere; this includes the networking in the VMkernel, Service Console, and vCenter Server. Support for using IPv6 for network storage protocols is considered experimental (not recommended for production use). Mixed environments of IPv4 and IPv6 are also supported.

The networking enhancements in vSphere greatly improve networking performance and manageability, and by allowing third-party vendors to develop vSwitches, VMware can allow network vendors to continue to offer more robust and manageable alternatives to VMware's default vSwitch. We will cover the new networking features in more detail in Chapter 6.

SECURITY

Security is always a concern in any environment, and VMware made some significant enhancements to an already pretty secure platform in vSphere. The biggest new feature is the new VMsafe API that allows third-party vendors to better integrate into the hypervisor to provide better protection and less overhead. The new security features in vSphere include the following.

- VMware created the VMsafe APIs as a means for third-party vendors to integrate with the hypervisor to gain better access to the virtualization layer so that they would not have to use less-efficient traditional methods to secure the virtual environment. For example, many virtual firewalls have to sit inline between vSwitches to be able to protect the VMs running on the vSwitch. All traffic must pass through the virtual firewall to get to the VM; this is both a bottleneck and a single point of failure. Using the VMsafe APIs you no longer have to do this, as a virtual firewall can leverage the hypervisor integration to listen in right at the VM's NIC and to set rules as needed to protect the VM.

- vShield Zones is a virtual firewall that can use rules to block or allow specific ports and IP addresses. It also does monitoring and reporting and can learn the traffic patterns of a VM to provide a basic rule set. Although not as robust as some of the third-party virtual firewalls available today, it does provide a good integrated method of protecting VMs. We will discuss vShield Zones in more detail in Chapter 6.

The security enhancements in vSphere are significant and make an already safe product even more secure. Protection of the hypervisor in any virtual environment is critical, and vSphere provides the comfort you need to know that your environment is well protected.

AVAILABILITY

Availability is critical in virtual environments, and in VI3, VMware introduced some new features, such as High Availability (HA), that made recovery from host failures an easy and automated process. Many people are leery of putting a large number of VMs on a host because a failure can affect so many servers running on that host, so the HA feature was a good recovery method. However, HA is not continuous availability, and there is a period of downtime while VMs are restarted on other hosts. VMware took HA to the next level in vSphere with the new Fault Tolerance (FT) feature, which provides zero downtime for a VM in case a host fails. The new features available in vSphere include the following.

- FT provides true continuous availability for VMs that HA could not provide. FT uses a CPU technology called Lockstep that is built into certain newer models of Intel and AMD processors. It works by keeping a secondary copy of a VM running on another host server which stays in sync with the primary copy by utilizing a process called Record/Replay that was first introduced in VMware Workstation. Record/Replay works by recording the computer execution of the primary VM and saving it into a log file; it can then replay that recorded information on a secondary VM to have a replica copy that is a duplicate of the original VM. In case of a host failure, the secondary VM becomes the primary VM and a new secondary is created on another host. We will cover the FT feature in more detail in Chapter 9.

- VMware introduced another new product as part of vSphere, called VMware Data Recovery (VDR). Unlike vShield Zones, which was a product VMware acquired, VDR was developed entirely by VMware to provide a means of performing backup and recovery of VMs without requiring a third-party product. VDR creates hot backups of VMs to any virtual disk storage attached to an ESX/ESXi host or to any NFS/CIFS network storage server or device. An additional feature of VDR is its ability to provide data de-duplication to reduce storage requirements using block-based in-line destination de-duplication technology that VMware developed. VDR is built to leverage the new vStorage APIs in vSphere and is not compatible with VI3 hosts and VMs. VDR can only do backups at the VM level (VM image) and does not do file-level backups; full backups are initially performed and subsequent backups are incremental. It does have individual file-level restore (FLR) capability that is for both Windows (GUI) and Linux (CLI). We will cover VDR in more detail in Chapter 8.

- VMware made some improvements to HA in vSphere, and they include an improved admission control policy whereby you can specify the number of host failures that a cluster can tolerate, the percentage of cluster resources to reserve as failover capacity, and a specific failover host. Additionally, a new option is available to disable the host monitoring feature (heartbeat) when doing network maintenance to avoid triggering HA when hosts become isolated. We will cover HA in more detail in Chapter 9.

The FT feature is a big step forward for VMware in providing better availability for VMs. While FT is a great feature, it does have some strict limitations and requirements that restrict its use. We will cover the details in Chapter 10.

COMPATIBILITY AND EXTENSIBILITY

VMware continually expands its support for devices, operating systems, and databases, as well as its API mechanisms that allow its products to integrate better with other software and hardware. With vSphere, VMware has done this again by way of the following new compatibility and extensibility features.

- In VI3, ESX and ESXi only supported the use of internal SCSI disks. vSphere now also supports the use of internal SATA disks to provide more cost-effective storage options.
- In addition to supporting more guest operating systems, vSphere also supports the ability to customize additional guest operating systems such as Windows Server 2008, Ubuntu 8, and Debian 4.
- vCenter Server supports additional operating systems and databases including Windows Server 2008, Oracle 11g, and Microsoft SQL Server 2008.
- vSphere Client is now supported on more Windows platforms, including Windows 7 and Windows Server 2008.

- As mentioned previously, the vStorage APIs allow for much better integration with storage, backup, and data protection applications.

- A new Virtual Machine Communication Interface (VMCI) API allows application vendors to take advantage of the fast communication channel between VMs that VMCI provides.

- A new Common Information Model (CIM)/Systems Management Architecture for Server Hardware (SMASH) API allows hardware vendors to integrate directly into the vSphere Client so that hardware information can be monitored and managed without requiring that special hardware drivers be installed on the host server. In addition, a new CIM interface for storage based on the Storage Management Initiative-Specification (SMI-S) is also supported in vSphere.

As you can see, the enhancements and improvements VMware has made in vSphere are compelling reasons to upgrade to it. From better performance to new features and applications, vSphere is much improved compared to VI3 and is a worthy successor to an already great virtualization platform.

CONFIGURATION MAXIMUM DIFFERENCES FROM VI3

We already covered many of the features and enhancements in vSphere and how they differ from VI3, but there are also many maximum configuration differences that you should be aware of. VMware publishes a configuration maximum document for each version that lists the maximums for VMs, hosts, and vCenter Servers. vSphere saw a number of these maximums increase, which really made a big difference in how well it could scale and the workloads it could handle. Tables 1.1 and 1.2 display the key configuration maximum differences between VI 3.5 and vSphere.

Table 1.1   Virtual Machine Configuration Maximum Differences

Virtual Machine	VI 3.5	vSphere 4
Virtual CPUs per VM	4	8
RAM per VM	64GB	255GB
NICs per VM	4	10
Concurrent remote console sessions	10	40

Table 1.2 ESX Host and vCenter Server Configuration Maximum Differences

ESX Host and vCenter Server	VI 3.5	vSphere 4
Hosts per storage volume	32	64
Fibre Channel paths to LUN	32	16
NFS datastores	32	64
Hardware iSCSI initiators per host	2	4
Virtual CPUs per host	192	512
VMs per host	170	320
Logical processors per host	32	64
RAM per host	256GB	1TB
Standard vSwitches per host	127	248
vNICs per standard vSwitch	1,016	4,088
Resource pools per host	512	4,096
Children per resource pool	256	1,024
Resource pools per cluster	128	512

The biggest differences in vSphere are the number of VMs that you can have per host and the amount of RAM and number of CPUs that you can assign to a VM. There is an important caveat to the number of VMs per host, though: If you have a single cluster that exceeds more than eight hosts, you can have only 40 VMs per host. Be aware of this limitation when sizing your host hardware and designing your virtual environment.

UNDERSTANDING THE LICENSING CHANGES

VMware drastically changed the editions in vSphere. In VI3, only three paid editions were available: Foundation, Standard, and Enterprise. In vSphere, VMware changed Foundation, which was geared toward small to medium-size businesses, to Essentials and added an Essentials Plus edition that includes HA and VDR. The company also added an edition between Standard and Enterprise, called Advanced, which includes more features but does not include Distributed Resource Scheduler (DRS)/DPM or Storage VMotion.

Finally, VMware added a new top-tier edition called Enterprise Plus, which adds support for 12 cores per processor, eight-way vSMP, distributed vSwitches, host profiles, and third-party storage multipathing, as shown in Figure 1.1. Table 1.3 summarizes the features available in each edition of vSphere.

Table 1.3   vSphere Features by Edition

Feature	Free ESXi	Essentials	Essentials Plus	Standard	Advanced	Enterprise	Enterprise Plus
Cores per processor	6	6	6	6	12	6	12
vSMP	4-way	4-way	4-way	4-way	4-way	4-way	8-way
Max host memory	256GB	256GB	256GB	256GB	256GB	256GB	1TB
Thin provisioning	Yes	Yes	Yes	Yes	Yes	Yes	Yes
vCenter Server agent	No	Yes	Yes	Yes	Yes	Yes	Yes
Update Manager	No	Yes	Yes	Yes	Yes	Yes	Yes
High Availability	No	No	Yes	Yes	Yes	Yes	Yes
Data recovery	No	No	Yes	No	Yes	Yes	Yes
Hot-add	No	No	No	No	Yes	Yes	Yes
Fault Tolerance	No	No	No	No	Yes	Yes	Yes
vShield Zones	No	No	No	No	Yes	Yes	Yes
VMotion	No	No	No	No	Yes	Yes	Yes
Storage VMotion	No	No	No	No	No	Yes	Yes
DRS and DPM	No	No	No	No	No	Yes	Yes

Continues

Table 1.3   vSphere Features by Edition *(Continued)*

Feature	Free ESXi	Essentials	Essentials Plus	Standard	Advanced	Enterprise	Enterprise Plus
Distributed vSwitch	No	No	No	No	No	No	Yes
Host profiles	No	No	No	No	No	No	Yes
Third-party multipathing	No	No	No	No	No	No	Yes

Existing VI3 customers with active Support and Subscription (SnS) are entitled to a free upgrade to the following vSphere editions.

- VI3 Foundation or Standard customers can receive a free upgrade to vSphere Standard.
- VI3 Foundation or Standard customers with the VMotion add-on can receive a free upgrade to vSphere Enterprise.
- VI3 Foundation or Standard customers with the VMotion and DRS add-ons can receive a free upgrade to vSphere Enterprise.
- VI3 Enterprise customers can receive a free upgrade to vSphere Enterprise.

VI3 Enterprise customers are not entitled to a free upgrade to Enterprise Plus, and must pay to upgrade their licenses to use its new top-tier features. In addition, the new Cisco Nexus 1000V vSwitch required both an Enterprise Plus license and a separate license purchased from Cisco for each vSwitch. Here are some key things you should know about licensing in vSphere.

- vSphere is available in seven editions—ESXi single server, Essentials, Essentials Plus, Standard, Advanced, Enterprise, and Enterprise Plus, each with different features as shown in Table 1.3. The new Essentials editions are geared toward smaller environments and are comprehensive packages which include ESX and vCenter Server. ESXi single server remains free and includes support for thin provisioned disks. A new tier above Enterprise is called Enterprise Plus, and it includes support for host profiles and distributed vSwitches.
- All editions support up to six CPU cores per physical processor, except for Advanced and Enterprise Plus, which support up to 12 CPU cores per physical processor.

- You can upgrade your edition of vSphere if you want more features. The prices for this vary based on the edition you currently own and the edition you plan to upgrade to. Here are the upgrade path options.
  - Essentials can be upgraded to Essentials Plus.
  - Standard can be upgraded to Advanced and Enterprise Plus.
  - Advanced can be upgraded to Enterprise Plus.
  - Enterprise can be upgraded to Enterprise Plus.
- The Essentials and Essentials Plus editions include licenses for up to three physical servers (up to two 6-core processors) and a vCenter Server. Both editions are self-contained solutions and may not be decoupled or combined with other vSphere editions. vSphere Essentials includes a one-year subscription; however, support is optional and available on a per-incident basis. vSphere Essentials Plus does not include SnS; instead, it is sold separately, and a minimum of one year of SnS is required.

VMware tried to phase out the Enterprise license and highly encouraged customers with existing Enterprise licenses to upgrade to Enterprise Plus. After receiving much customer outrage over this, VMware had a change of heart and decided to keep the Enterprise license around past 2009. However, this may change in the future, and VMware may eventually try to phase it out again.

SUMMARY

When VMware released vSphere it really raised the bar and further distanced itself from the competition. The performance improvements we will cover in Chapter 7 allow applications that previously may not have been good virtualization candidates because of their intense workloads to now be virtualized. The increased scalability allows for greater density of VMs on hosts, which allows for greater cost savings. Additionally, the power management features can save datacenters a great deal of money in cooling and power expenses. However, although there are many compelling reasons to upgrade to vSphere, there are also some reasons that an upgrade may not be right for you, and we will cover them in Chapter 12.

ESX AND ESXi HOSTS

ESX and ESXi are the two versions of the hypervisor that you have to choose from in vSphere. At their core they are identical, as they both use the exact same VMkernel, but their management consoles are distinctly different. Each version has its pros and cons, and for many users it comes down to personal preference when choosing between the two. In this chapter, we will cover the differences between ESX and ESXi as well as some of the new features and enhancements that VMware added to them in vSphere.

WHAT'S NEW WITH ESX AND ESXi HOSTS IN VSPHERE

In Chapter 1, we briefly covered some of the new things pertaining to ESX and ESXi in vSphere. In this chapter, we will go over them in more detail. The improvements in ESX and ESXi in vSphere really increase the density and scalability that you can achieve, which means you can use fewer hosts than you may have needed in order to support similar workloads in VI3. Let's cover in more detail the enhancements to the ESX and ESXi hosts in vSphere.

64-BIT VMKERNEL AND ESX SERVICE CONSOLE

The VMkernel is VMware's proprietary hypervisor code that is the core component of both ESX and ESXi. The ESX Service Console is a privileged virtual machine (VM) that runs a modified version of Red Hat Linux and is used as a management application for ESX. In VI3, the ESX Service Console used version 2.4.21 of the Linux kernel. In vSphere, it uses version 2.6.18. As the Linux kernel is always improving, VMware updated the ESX Service Console to the newer 2.6.18 version to take advantage of bug fixes and improvements that were made to it. You can check the Linux version of the ESX Service Console by logging in to it and typing the command uname -a.

In VI3, both the VMkernel and the ESX Service Console were 32-bit applications/operating systems; they could run on 64-bit hardware, but they could only address memory using 32-bit addresses. In vSphere, they are 64-bit applications, which prevents vSphere from being able to run on hardware that is only 32-bit. To better understand this, a bit (binary digit) is the smallest unit of information in computing, and can have a value of 1 or 0. A 32-bit processor uses 32 bits to reference memory locations (2^{32} or 2 to the power of 32), and therefore is limited to 4,294,967,296 unique locations (hence the 4GB limit in 32-bit Windows). A 64-bit processor uses 64 bits to reference memory locations (2^{64}) and is limited to 18,446,744,073,709,551,616 unique locations, which is measured in exabytes and is much larger than the amount of memory that a server can handle. As a result, applications that are written to take advantage of 64 bits typically run faster than 32-bit applications, as they can utilize the larger 64-bit address space and wider 64-bit registers and data paths.

The VMkernel and ESX Service Console being 64-bit in vSphere means that older server hardware with 32 processors cannot run vSphere. However, most server hardware built in the past several years contains 64-bit processors from Intel and AMD, so this won't be a problem for many users. Later in this chapter we will cover this in more detail.

SUPPORT FOR MORE MEMORY, CPUs, AND VMs

Memory is almost always the first resource to be used up on virtual hosts from the many memory-hungry applications running on VMs. In VI3, only 256GB of physical host memory was supported, which limited the number of VMs that a host could support. You can always use memory overcommitment to allocate more memory to VMs, but this is only good up to a point, and must be closely monitored. Now with vSphere, a host can have up to 1TB of memory, which greatly expands the memory available to VMs. Many servers currently support up to 512GB of memory, which is still plenty of memory to assign to VMs. This new limit makes it easier to virtualize applications such as database and email servers that can use a very large amount of RAM. In addition to the increased host memory support of 1TB, the amount of RAM that can be assigned to a VM was increased from 64GB to 255GB in vSphere.

VI3 only supported 32 logical CPUs per host. In vSphere, this has increased to 64 logical CPUs. A logical CPU takes into account the number of cores and threads that a physical CPU has. The formula to compute logical CPUs is: CPU Sockets × Cores per Socket × Threads per Core. A socket simply refers to a single physical CPU. The term *socket* comes from the socket on the motherboard that a CPU is plugged into, and it started to be used once multicore processors were released to distinguish between cores and physical CPUs. Cores are the number of CPU cores that a single processor supports; a multicore processor is composed of two or more independent cores that are interconnected and share a single processor die, and perhaps cache and other interfaces. Most editions of vSphere support up to six cores per processor, except for the Advanced and Enterprise Plus editions, which support up to 12 cores per processor. Finally, threads take into account hyperthreading, which some CPUs support and which makes one physical CPU or core look like two. Hyperthreading also simulates multiple processors per socket, but unlike cores that have their own hardware, hyperthreading works by duplicating the architectural state of a processor and not the main execution resources. Hyperthreading basically simulates another processor, which allows the operating system to schedule two threads simultaneously. It takes advantage of the unused execution resources of a processor to handle the two threads at once.

Here are some examples of logical CPU counts:

- 1 socket, 4 cores per CPU with hyperthreading = 8 logical CPUs
- 2 sockets, 6 cores per CPU without hyperthreading = 12 logical CPUs
- 8 sockets, 6 cores per CPU without hyperthreading = 48 logical CPUs

The 64-logical-CPU limit is enforced regardless of how many logical CPUs a single host may have. The same is true of the current core licensing per edition: If your vSphere edition supports only six cores per processor and you have more than that, vSphere simply ignores the rest and does not use them.

Most processors these days are multicore, and the advantage to using them is that vSphere is licensed by the socket, not the core, so you can get more bang for your buck. vSphere is even licensed by single sockets now instead of in two-socket increments, so you can use a single-socket six-core server that will support many VMs at an affordable price.

The total number of VMs and the virtual CPUs that can be assigned to them has also increased in vSphere. VI3 supported up to 170 VMs with a total of up to 192 virtual CPUs per host. In vSphere, that increased to 320 VMs per host with a total of up to 512 virtual CPUs per host. Having 320 VMs on a host might seem unlikely in most cases, except for virtual desktop solutions that have lots of low-workload VMs running on them. There is a caveat to that number, though: If you have a single cluster that exceeds eight hosts, you can have only 40 VMs per host (this is a supported limit, not a hard limit). Be aware of this limitation when sizing your host hardware and designing your virtual environment.

SUPPORT FOR ENHANCED INTEL SPEEDSTEP AND ENHANCED AMD POWERNOW!

In addition to Distributed Power Management (DPM), vSphere also supports a new CPU power management technology called Enhanced SpeedStep by Intel and Enhanced PowerNow! by AMD. These technologies enable a server to dynamically switch CPU frequencies and voltages (referred to as Dynamic Voltage & Frequency Scaling or DVFS) based on workload demands, which enables the processors to draw less power and create less heat, thereby allowing the fans to spin more slowly. Earlier versions of SpeedStep and PowerNow! only supported switching between high and low frequencies. The Enhanced versions also add support for varying the voltage of the processor as well. This is accomplished by an interface that allows a system to change the performance states (P-states) of a CPU. P-states are defined by fixed operating frequencies and voltages that allow a CPU to operate at different power levels. A CPU can operate in several different P-states, depending on the processor, with the lowest level defined as P-min and the highest level defined as P-max. For example, a 3GHz processor will have a P-max of 3GHz and might have a P-min of 2GHz, along with several in-between P-states such as 2.3GHz, 2.5GHz, and 2.7GHz.

Processor P-states can be controlled by either the system ROM or an operating system. In vSphere, they are controlled by the VMkernel which optimizes each CPU's frequency to match demand in order to improve power efficiency but not affect performance. Before you can use this feature, though, you need to enable it in the server's BIOS. The tool for doing this will vary among servers, but it will typically be labeled Power Regulator, Demand Based Switching, PowerNow, or SpeedStep. For HP servers, it is labeled Power Regulator for ProLiant, and it is listed under System Options in the BIOS. Using an HP ProLiant DL385 G6 as an example, you will see there are four modes listed in the BIOS for Power Regulator for ProLiant, as described by HP.

- **HP Dynamic Power Savings Mode**—This uses a ROM-based algorithm developed by HP to monitor processor activity. It adjusts processor power use to match performance levels to the application load.

- **HP Static Low Power Mode**—The system's processors operate continuously at the lowest power state (P-min). In this mode, Power Regulator programs the processors to run continuously in the low-power state to allow the server to run at a guaranteed lower maximum power level.

- **HP Static High Performance Mode**—The system's processors operate continuously at the highest power and performance state (P-max). In this mode, neither the system's firmware nor the operating system will ever program the processors to run in a lower power or performance state.

- **OS Control Mode**—Dynamic power management for the system is managed by the operating system through its policy mechanism. For this mode, system administrators must configure the operating system to activate the OS-based power management feature.

The option you want to use for vSphere to enable your hosts to take advantage of the power management feature is the OS Control Mode. This allows the VMkernel to change P-states on the CPUs in a host to conserve power whenever possible. In vSphere, you configure this feature on each host by selecting the host in the vSphere Client, and then choosing Configuration tab→Hardware→Processors. If you disable the feature in the BIOS or set it to Static, the processor configuration in the vSphere Client will show that Power Management Technology is not available. Once the power management feature in the server's BIOS is set to OS Control mode, you will see this change to reflect whichever technology is being used (PowerNow! or SpeedStep), as shown in Figure 2.1.

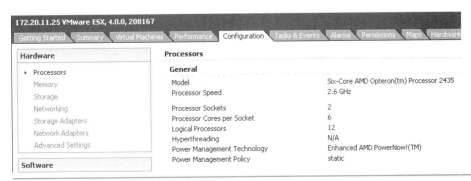

Figure 2.1   Power Management Technology enabled when OS Control Mode is selected

vSphere will default to Static mode, though, and to take advantage of this feature you need to change it to Dynamic. To do this, select the Configuration tab in the vSphere Client, and then in the Software panel select Advanced Settings. Next, select Power in the left pane, and in the right pane change the Power.CpuPolicy from Static to Dynamic; then click OK. The Static and Dynamic settings for Power.CpuPolicy are defined as follows.

- **Static**—The default. The VMkernel can detect power management features available on the host, but does not actively use them unless requested by the BIOS for power capping or thermal events.
- **Dynamic**—The VMkernel optimizes each CPU's frequency to match demand in order to improve power efficiency but not affect performance. When CPU demand increases, this policy setting ensures that CPU frequencies also increase.

There is no way to monitor the operation of this feature in vSphere once it is enabled, but some server management tools will show you P-state and power consumption. For example, on an HP server using the Integrated Lights-Out (iLO) management board, you can see this information as shown in Figure 2.2, which shows the change in P-states from 0 (highest or P-max) to 4 (lowest or P-min) after this feature is enabled.

You can see the reduction in power usage when this feature is enabled in Figure 2.3.

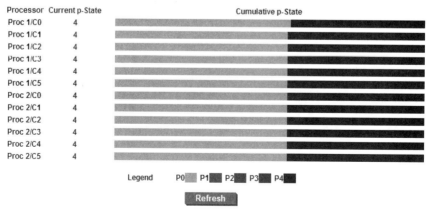

P0 is the highest processor state and provides maximum performance.
P4 is the lowest processor state and provides the highest efficiency.

Figure 2.2   P-states changing from P0 to P4 on all processors after power management is enabled due to low activity

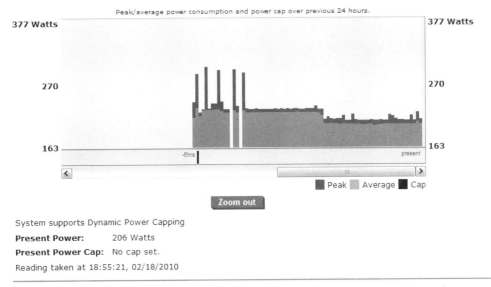

Figure 2.3   Power usage dropping processors after power management is enabled due to low activity

Using this feature along with DPM can amount to some significant energy savings, especially in larger datacenters that have regular periods of low workloads. Using these features is a must in virtual desktop environments where almost two-thirds of the day and weekends typically see very little activity.

IMPROVED HOST SERVER HARDWARE INTEGRATION AND REPORTING IN THE vSPHERE CLIENT

In VI3, to monitor the hardware health of an ESX host you needed to install vendor-specific agents inside the Service Console. To support ESXi, which has a limited management console, VMware integrated a set of tools and APIs into the VI Client so that you could read this information without requiring agents. In vSphere, this was enhanced even further to provide more hardware health status data, asset information, and alarm reporting. VMware has established close relationships with its hardware vendors so that enhanced information can be reported, as well as providing plug-ins to vCenter Server for managing vSphere, server hardware, and storage.

The vCenter Server can retrieve hardware information by using an industry-standard Common Information Model (CIM) interface. CIM defines how managed hardware elements are represented as a common set of objects, and is extensible for vendor-specific extensions to the common objects. Another standard, called Systems Management Architecture for Server Hardware (SMASH), is also used to organize this information into logical groups, called profiles. The advanced monitoring of hardware natively in vSphere using CIM/SMASH is a big improvement, as installing agents inside the ESX Service Console can cause problems and is more difficult to manage.

SELECTING PHYSICAL HOST HARDWARE TO USE WITH vSPHERE

Most x86 processors are either 32-bit or 64-bit; however, almost all enterprise servers manufactured today have 64-bit CPUs, but many older server models support only 32 bits. Sixty-four-bit CPUs are capable of running both 32-bit and 64-bit operating systems and applications. Many applications and operating systems have both 64-bit and 32-bit versions that can be installed based on the server hardware that is being used. Unlike operating systems and applications that have different versions for 32-bit and 64-bit CPUs, ESX 3.x supports both by default, and there is no need to install a special version. vSphere, however, only supports 64-bit CPUs, and if you try to install it on a server that has 32-bit CPUs, you will get an error message that states "Your CPU does not support long mode. Use a 32-bit distribution." In this case, 32-bit distribution refers to ESX 3.5.x, which supports 32-bit CPUs.

64-BIT CPUS AND LONG MODE

Sixty-four-bit CPUs can operate in two modes: legacy mode and long mode. When operating in legacy mode the CPU runs 32-bit code exclusively and none of the 64-bit extensions is utilized. When operating in long mode the CPU can run native 64-bit applications but can also run 32-bit applications in a special compatibility mode. ESX 3.x could run in legacy mode or long mode depending on the type of CPU that was used in the server; however, vSphere has been rewritten to support only long mode, thereby requiring a CPU that has 64-bit CPUs. VMware chose to do this for increased scalability and performance.

Not all 64-bit CPUs are created equal, though. Just because your server may be 64-bit doesn't necessarily mean you can run 64-bit VMs on it. The x86 64-bit architecture was designed to use an improved memory model which consists of a flat 64-bit address space, and the segmented memory model used in the 32-bit architecture was removed. Consequently, this caused issues when running 64-bit VMs on virtual host servers, as they did not have an efficient mechanism for isolating the VM monitor from 64-bit guest OSs. To deal with this, both Intel and AMD added features to their CPUs to support memory segmentation when running in long mode, but early models of their 64-bit CPUs did not have this feature. Early AMD64 CPUs (Revision C and earlier) were missing memory segmentation support when running in long mode, and Revision D or later CPUs are required; for the AMD Opteron family CPUs, Revision E or later is required.

AMD AND INTEL VIRTUALIZATION EXTENSIONS

Additionally, many AMD servers have a BIOS feature called AMD-V (AMD's virtualization extensions) that must be enabled for 64-bit VMs to be supported. Intel CPUs require both EM64T and VT support in the CPU and the BIOS of the server; EM64T is Intel's 64-bit technology and VT is Intel's virtualization technology. Intel EM64T CPUs also do not have memory segmentation support in long mode, but the VT feature allows ESX to work around this, so you can run 64-bit VMs on Intel 64-bit CPUs.

Both the Intel VT and AMD-V features may be disabled in a server's BIOS by default, so you should check your BIOS to see if this is the case. Depending on the server manufacturer, this option may be located in different areas in your BIOS setup, but it is typically located under Advanced or Security Options. In some cases, you may not see the option to enable these features in your server's BIOS. This could be because the server does not support it, which is common among older servers, or it could be that you have an older BIOS version you may need to upgrade. You should check with your server manufacturer to see if a newer BIOS version is available that will let you enable these features. For example, to enable AMD-V on an HP server the option is located under Advanced Options→Processor Options→AMD Virtualization.

CHECKING YOUR SERVER HARDWARE

So, now that you know what 64-bit processors are, how can you tell if your servers have them? There are a few utilities that you can use to check your servers to see if they have 64-bit CPUs and if they can run 64-bit VMs. The first is a CPU Identification Utility that is a small ISO file which VMware provides on its website; it will identify the CPU in your host and let you know if it supports 64-bit long mode and the ability to run 64-bit VMs. You can burn the ISO file to a CD or mount it using a remote management board so that you can shut down and boot your host from it. The utility is meant to be run directly on a host, which requires shutting it down, but I've also mounted the ISO file to a VM's virtual CD-ROM and booted from it, and I have received the same results.

I believe this is because although much of a VM's hardware is generic virtual hardware, the CPU is always seen as the actual brand and model of whatever is in the host server. Once the utility runs, it will display output showing CPU information along with what CPU features are supported. Figure 2.4 shows an example of an HP DL385 G1 server with AMD Opteron CPUs.

You can see that this server supports both 64-bit long mode and 64-bit VMware, so you can install vSphere on it and run both 32-bit and 64-bit VMs on it.

Another utility that VMware developed specifically to check servers to see if they were compatible with the new Fault Tolerance (FT) feature in vSphere, which has strict requirements (see Chapter 9), is called SiteSurvey. It is available as either a Windows or a Linux download, and once you install and run it you will be prompted to connect to a vCenter Server. Once you are connected to the vCenter Server, you can choose from your available clusters to generate a SiteSurvey report that shows whether your hosts support FT and if the hosts and VMs meet the individual prerequisites to use the feature. You can also click on links in the report that will give you detailed information about all the prerequisites along with compatible CPU charts. These links go to VMware's website and display the help document for the SiteSurvey utility which is full of great information about the prerequisites for FT. The SiteSurvey utility, though, will not tell you specifically if a host's CPU is 64-bit, but if the host is reported

```
Random_Init: Using random seed: 2051388443 (0x7a45b41b)
Reporting CPUID for 1 logical CPU...

        Family: 0f Model: 21 Stepping: 2

        ID1ECX      ID1EDX      ID81ECX      ID81EDX
        0x00000001 0x078bbbff 0000000000 0xe3d3fbff

Vendor                       : AMD
Processor Cores              : 2
Brand String                 : "AMD Opteron(tm) Processor 285"
SSE Support                  : SSE1, SSE2, SSE3
Supports NX / XD             : Yes
Supports CMPXCHG16B          : No
Supports RDTSCP              : No
Supports 3DNow! Prefetch     : Yes
Supports FFXSR               : Yes
Supports Extended Migration  : Yes
Supports 64-bit Longmode     : Yes
Supports 64-bit VMware       : Yes
Supported EVC modes          : None

PASS: Test 56983: CPUID
Press any key to reboot.
```

Figure 2.4 Output from CPU Identification Utility showing a CPU capable of running vSphere and 64-bit VMs

as compatible with FT, it has to be a 64-bit host. Both utilities are available for download at https://www.vmware.com/download/shared_utilities.html.

Another method to check your host's CPUs is to use a utility called VMware CPU Host Info (www.run-virtual.com/?page_id=155). You can run this utility on any workstation, and you can connect a vCenter Server to it (it won't work on individual ESX hosts) and report on each host's CPU capabilities. One limitation of this utility is that it will only show if the host is VT-capable, meaning that it can run 64-bit VMs. It will not show if the host only supports 64-bit long mode, like the other utility will. The CPU Identification Utility works by using the VI SDK to query vCenter Server to gather system information from each host and then presents it in a spreadsheet format. As an added bonus, this utility will show if the host will work with the FT utility in vSphere, which works with only the latest CPU types. Once you download and run this utility on your workstation, you specify a vCenter Server to connect to and it will display all the hosts managed by that vCenter Server and their CPU information, as well as whether the CPUs support FT and are VT-capable and whether VT is enabled. If a host shows up as being VT-capable but not VT-enabled, you probably need to modify its BIOS setting to enable the VT feature.

So, now that you know how to check your hosts to see if they have 64-bit CPUs, you can check to see if you can use them with vSphere. Knowing this information will help you plan your upgrade, allowing you to budget for new server hardware if necessary.

DIFFERENCES BETWEEN ESX AND ESXi

VMware ESX was the company's bare-metal hypervisor until it released ESX 3i in December 2007. One little-known fact about ESX is that it stands for Electric Sky X, which was the codename for it when it was in development. ESX 3i eventually became just ESXi as VMware dropped the version number from the name. At their core, ESX and ESXi are the same: They are both bare-metal hypervisors using the exact same VMkernel code. The major difference between the two concerns their management components: Both ESX and ESXi utilize a privileged VM running on each host as a management console to the VMkernel. The management console is what you connect to with one of the management tools, such as the vSphere Client, SSH, a web interface, PowerShell, and more. vCenter Server also connects to the management console of each host it manages.

ESX SERVICE CONSOLE

The management console in ESX is called the Service Console, and inside it resides a full Red Hat Linux operating system that has been modified and optimized for ESX. VMware has added a number of drivers, services, processes, and utilities to it to enable VMkernel management. This includes all the ESX-specific commands, such as `esxcfg-vnics` and `vmware-cmd`. Because of the full Linux operating system, the Service Console is about 8GB when using the default partition sizes. VMware also modified some of the existing Linux filesystem-related commands to support VMFS volumes. You can log in to the Service Console using an SSH client and run commands, view logs, run scripts, and install drivers and applications (not recommended). You can do a lot with the Service Console, and it's often handy when troubleshooting host problems, but if you are not careful you can cause problems as well. Because of the power of the Service Console, it is often seen as a security risk if it is not properly secured. If someone were to gain root access to the Service Console he could easily compromise all the VMs running on that host.

The most useful features of the Service Console are the following.

- **Executing scripts**—Many administrators like to write scripts to automate tasks and host configuration. One common script method is to configure new hosts once they are built.

- **Viewing logs**—You can view many log files for different components of ESX, such as the VMkernel log and the VM log files. Using the `tail` command, you can also view the output to these files in real time.

- **Troubleshooting**—Many command-line utilities are available to make it easier to troubleshoot problems, such as the `esxtop` and `vscsistats` commands. One common task is to use the `ps` command to forcibly terminate a VM that will not power off using conventional methods. Being able to run commands, view logs, and change settings all in one console session can make troubleshooting much easier.

- **Configuration**—All configuration of an ESX host can be done via the command line if you desire. Sometimes this is necessary if you are having network problems and cannot connect to the host using the vSphere Client.

- **Administration**—Just like configuration, an ESX host can also be administered using the command line. Most of the functionality of the vSphere Client is available in the command line using special ESX commands.

- **Backups**—Many backup applications need to install an agent inside the Service Console to back up VMs. The need for this has decreased, though, with the new vStorage APIs in vSphere.

In addition to the many ESX-specific commands that you can run in the Service Console, you can also run most Linux commands, such as `find`, `ps`, `cat`, `ls`, `tail`, and `ping`. You can also edit text files using either the nano editor or the vi editor. For a full list of ESX-specific commands and their usage, see the Appendixes of the ESX Configuration Guide, which is part of the vSphere documentation.

ESXi Management Console

ESXi's management console is simply referred to as the management console. Instead of using a full operating system, it uses a small POSIX environment called BusyBox that provides a very limited remote interface. Because of this, VMware was able to reduce the footprint of ESXi to 32MB and also deliver it as a preconfigured image file instead of requiring a full installation, like ESX does. To decrease the size of ESXi, VMware removed all the commands from it and instead relied on remote management tools that connect to ESXi using APIs through the management console. The tools used to manage ESXi include the vSphere CLI (formerly known as the Remote Command Line Interface or RCLI), which also works with ESX. The vSphere CLI (vCLI) installs on a PC and is a remote scripting environment (Perl) that interacts with ESXi hosts to enable host configuration through scripts or specific commands. It replicates nearly all the equivalent Service Console commands for configuring ESX.

ESXi has a very limited user interface, called the Direct Console User Interface (DCUI), on its management console that allows you to do such things as set up basic networking, restart the management agent, view logs, and perform other basic configuration tasks. However, a hidden command-line interface is available for use if you need to troubleshoot problems. This CLI is referred to as Tech Support Mode, and VMware does not encourage people to use it unless VMware support instructs them to. To enable this mode, you can follow the steps in VMware's Knowledge Base article 1003677 (http://kb.vmware.com/kb/1003677). By default, you cannot use SSH to remotely access an ESXi management console, and the RCLI is meant to be the main management tool for ESXi. However, the following unsupported method will enable SSH support on an ESXi host.

1. Enter Tech Support Mode.
2. Once you are logged in, type `vi /etc/inetd.conf`.
3. Scroll down to find the line that begins with #SSH and remove the # character (press x when on the character).

4. Save the file by typing :wq!.

5. Restart the service by typing /sbin/services.sh restart.

This is generally not recommended, though, as it can open up another attack vector to your ESXi host.

As the vSphere CLI is meant to manage ESXi hosts, you should install it and read through the documentation (available at www.vmware.com/pdf/vsphere4/r40 /vsp_40_vcli.pdf) so that you are familiar with how to use it and the syntax for the commands.

Functionality Differences between ESX and ESXi

Both ESX and ESXi can be licensed for any of the many editions of vSphere by simply adding a license key to unlock the additional features. However, VMware does offer a free edition of ESXi that is fully functional but does not contain any of the advanced features, such as VMotion, High Availability (HA), and the Distributed Resource Scheduler (DRS). Table 2.1 compares some of the differences between ESX and ESXi.

Table 2.1　ESX and ESXi Comparison

	ESX	ESXi
Command-line interface	ESX has a local CLI (Service Console) that you can connect to using an SSH client. It also supports the vCLI and the vSphere Management Assistant (vMA).	ESXi has a limited local console (DCUI) and an unsupported local CLI (Tech Support Mode). It supports the vCLI and the vMA. vCLI is limited to read-only access for the free version of VMware ESXi. To enable full functionality of vCLI on a VMware ESXi host, the host must be a licensed paid edition.
Web client access	This is supported for VM management by connecting to an ESX host or vCenter Server.	This is not supported.
Management console	The ESX Service Console is based on a Red Hat Linux installation. Default access is through the root user and provides a method for accessing the filesystem, running scripts, and executing standard Linux commands.	The traditional ESX Service Console is removed; instead, ESXi uses a management interface based on the very small BusyBox shell that combines multiple utilities into a single executable. VMware has provisioned the vCLI to allow the execution of scripts.

Table 2.1   ESX and ESXi Comparison *(Continued)*

	ESX	ESXi
Scriptable installations	ESX supports scriptable installations through utilities such as kickstart.	ESXi Installable currently does not support scriptable installations, like ESX does. ESXi does provide support for post-installation configuration scripts using vCLI-based configuration scripts, as well as taking advantage of the PowerCLI.
Patching and updates	ESX software patches and updates behave like traditional Linux-based patches and updates. The installation of a software patch or update may require multiple system boots as the patch or update may have dependencies on previous patches or updates.	ESXi patches and updates behave like firmware patches and updates. Any given patch or update is all-inclusive of previous patches and updates. Because ESXi is smaller and does not have a Service Console, it also requires fewer patches than ESX.
Built-in firewall	The built-in firewall protects the Service Console and is more complex, with more than a dozen inbound and outbound connection types allowed by default.	The built-in firewall is much simpler because there is no Service Console to protect. Only two connection types are allowed by default.
Hardware monitoring	Vendor-specific agents are installed on the Service Console agents to provide hardware statistics and status. Currently, these agents do not integrate into vCenter Server and must be viewed and configured through the vendor's interface. With vSphere, CIM providers can also be used with ESX, so agents may not always be necessary.	ESXi provides hardware instrumentation through CIM providers. Standards-based CIM providers are distributed with all versions of ESXi. Server hardware health monitoring is built into vCenter Server.
Boot from storage area network (SAN)	ESX supports boot from SAN. Booting from SAN requires one dedicated LUN per server.	ESXi does not yet support boot from SAN, but does support booting from iSCSI using iBFT in version 4.1.
Active Directory Integrations	ESX supports Active Directory integration through third-party agents installed on the Service Console. Beginning in version 4.1 this is can be configured in the vSphere Client.	ESXi does support Active Directory authentication beginning in version 4.1.
Boot from SAN	ESX supports boot from SAN. Booting from SAN requires one dedicated LUN per server.	ESXi does not yet support boot from SAN but does support booting from iSCSI using iBFT in version 4.1.

Both ESX and ESXi have advantages and disadvantages, and many shops tend to favor ESX over ESXi. Here are some reasons you might choose ESXi over ESX.

- The base version of ESXi is available for free.
- It's OEM-installed on many server models from vendors such as HP, IBM, and Dell.
- The lack of the Linux-based Service Console makes it more secure and requires less patching than ESX.
- It boots up faster than ESX because of its reduced footprint.
- Hardware management agents are preinstalled with ESXi and the data is displayed directly in the VI Client, so there is no need to install them separately and use a separate management console to display hardware information. These agents can also integrate with third-party tools such as HP's Systems Insight Manager.
- It can boot from a USB flash drive without requiring a local hard disk.

The Service Console can increase administration and require additional training because it's based on Linux. Windows administrators may not have experience working with Linux.

Here are some reasons you might choose ESX over ESXi.

- The Service Console can be very useful for performing command-line operations and running scripts.
- Additional components (i.e., backup agents) can be installed inside the Service Console. This is not recommended, but it is sometimes necessary.
- Currently, ESXi supports only a limited range of hardware vendors/models for its CIM extensions which monitor the host's hardware. This support is expected to increase and expand in the future.
- Both ESX and vCenter Server support integration with Active Directory. The free, stand-alone version of ESXi does not support this.
- ESX supports booting from a SAN, and ESXi currently does not.
- ESX has centralized management through vCenter Server. The entry-level ESXi cannot be managed by vCenter Server, as it does not include a VC agent and does not include a web interface for VM management.

VMware continually states that the ESXi architecture is the future and that at some point in a future release ESX and its Service Console will no longer exist. For the short term, the Service Console is here to stay, but in the next major release of vSphere, it may finally be retired. As a result, it is best to plan to use ESXi if you are not already doing so, so you are prepared when VMware eventually pulls the plug on ESX.

USING HOST PROFILES

VMware introduced host profiles in vSphere as a way to easily configure new hosts and ensure compliance with configuration standards. If you're familiar with Microsoft Active Directory, think of host profiles as Group Policy for VMware ESX and ESXi hosts. When a new ESX or ESXi host is built it typically requires a lot of configuration for things such as network adapters and vSwitches, datastores, storage, time, security settings, and much more. Having to do this manually can be time-consuming and can lead to misconfigurations due to mistakes when making changes. In VI3, scripts were commonly used to change configuration settings on hosts, but you typically had to have scripting knowledge to do that. Host profiles are useful in environments of any size, but they are especially useful in larger environments with many hosts.

CREATING AND CONFIGURING HOST PROFILES

Host profiles are available only in the vSphere Enterprise Plus edition and are available on the Management section of the vSphere Client home page when you are connected to a vCenter Server. To create a host profile you typically clone the configuration of an existing host to use as your template for the profile. Optionally, you can import a profile using a special Virtual Profile Format file format (.vpf). The process for using host profiles is as follows.

1. Configure a template using an existing host's settings (reference host) as you want it to apply to all hosts that use the profile.
2. Create a host profile from your reference host which copies all of its applicable settings into the newly created host profile.
3. Attach a host or cluster to the newly created host profile.

Once you have a host configured and are ready to create a host profile from it, follow these steps.

1. Go to the Host Profiles view in the vSphere Client and click the Create Profile button.
2. Select "Create Profile from existing host" and click Next.

3. Select an existing host to use as your source reference host and click Next.

4. Give the profile a unique name and optionally a description and click Next.

5. Review the Summary information and click Finish.

Once the profile is created, it will appear in the Host Profile folder in the left pane. New profiles are not attached by default, and you can edit the profile to go over it and make any adjustments to it before attaching it. To edit a profile select it and click the Edit Profile button. Once you edit a profile, you will see all the profiles/policies contained within it and can add/remove or edit them. A profile is grouped into several subprofiles that relate to different host configuration areas, as shown in Figure 2.5.

You can expand the different sections and edit the existing policies or right-click on some of the objects and add or remove them. Once you have your profile set up as you want it, you can attach it to hosts or clusters. To do this you click the Attach Host/Cluster button, and then select the hosts and clusters you want to attach to and click the Attach button.

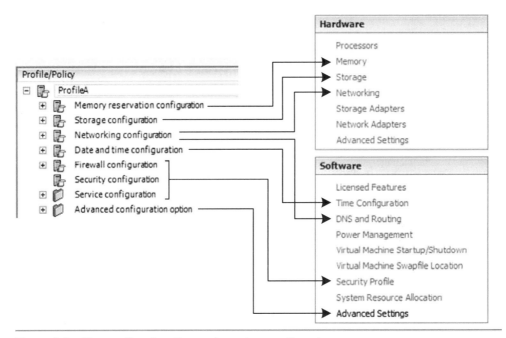

Figure 2.5   Host profile subprofile mapping to host configuration areas

APPLYING HOST PROFILES

When you attach a host to a profile it is not automatically applied to the host. Before you apply it, you can check to see the state of compliance of the host so that you will know what changes will be made to it to apply it. To do this select the host and click the Check Compliance link (or right-click on the host and select the option). A list of any noncompliant hosts will appear in the bottom pane, as shown in Figure 2.6.

Before you can apply the profile to the host, you must put it into maintenance mode. Doing this moves all VMs that are on shared storage to other hosts using VMotion; VMs on local disks must be manually powered off, though. You can right-click on the host and select the Enter Maintenance Mode option to do this. Once the host is in maintenance mode, you can select the Apply Profile option, and once it completes you can right-click on the host again and select Exit Maintenance Mode. You can then move your VMs back to the host, or if you have DRS configured you can allow it to automatically move them. After the profile is applied, the host will display as Compliant on the Hosts and Clusters

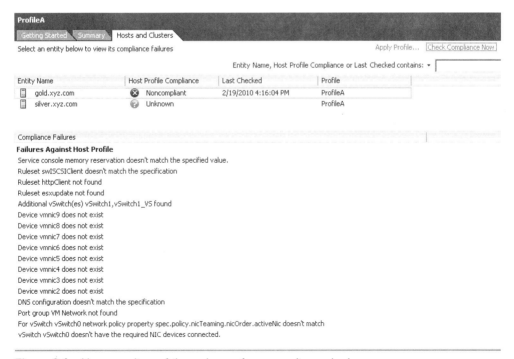

Figure 2.6   Host compliance failures shown after a compliance check

tab. There are some additional options that you can use with host profiles once they have been created. If you right-click on a profile in the left pane you will see these options. Besides the Edit, Delete, and Attach options, you can change the reference host that is used as the template for that profile. You can also update the profile from the selected reference host if changes have been made to it. Finally, you can export the profile to a .vpf profile so that you can use it in other environments or save it as a backup. The resultant file that is created is just an XML-based text file. It is recommended that you always make a backup before making changes to a host profile so that you can quickly roll back if something goes wrong. Once a profile is attached to a host, if it is out of compliance you will see a message whenever you select the host and click on the Summary tab. For additional monitoring and administration of host profiles, you can select a cluster in the right pane and then select the Profile Compliance tab.

Host profiles are a great way to maintain standard configurations between your hosts and also to satisfy the many compliance regulations that exist today. They reduce the need for post-installation scripting and can make ESX and ESXi hosts become stateless, as generic installations can be performed and profiles can be used to bring them into the required state. They are also very useful for spotting any configuration deviations between hosts in a cluster which may cause problems such as when using VMotion.

SUMMARY

ESX and ESXi have seen many significant enhancements in vSphere that allow them to scale much higher than they could in VI3. In addition to increased VM capacity, they are also more efficient and can reduce operational costs thanks to advanced power-saving features. Although the switch to 64-bit-only server hardware in vSphere may cause some incompatibilities with older hardware, it does provide better overall performance. Host profiles can help save administration time by allowing hosts to be quickly and consistently configured once they are built. They are also a great way to help secure your hosts and ensure that they meet your compliance standards. Compared to VI3, the improvements to ESX and ESXi in vSphere are significant and increase performance, scalability, and manageability while making vSphere more cost-effective to operate.

VIRTUAL 3 MACHINES

Virtual machines (VMs) benefited from some big changes in vSphere, especially to their virtual hardware. The CPU and memory capacity was increased, which allows bigger workloads to be virtualized in vSphere compared to in VI3, and new virtual NICs (vNICs), storage adapters, virtual disks, and other enhancements allow VMs to perform better and more efficiently in vSphere than they did in VI3. Furthermore, vSphere offers additional support for more VM guest operating systems. In this chapter, we will cover in detail some of the new VM features in vSphere, and I will provide some in-depth technical information regarding VMs.

WHAT'S NEW WITH VIRTUAL MACHINES IN VSPHERE

In Chapter 1, we briefly covered some of the new features and enhancements to VMs in vSphere. In this chapter, we will discuss them in more detail, and cover the new types of virtual adapters and the increased support that VMs have in vSphere.

VIRTUAL MACHINE HARDWARE VERSION

Version 4 was the hardware type used for VMs in VI3, and version 7 was introduced in vSphere. You might be wondering what the version means. Since VMs have no physical hardware, the version is simply used by the VM configuration file (.vmx) to determine what settings and features can be used with the VM. If you open a VM's .vmx file with a text editor, you will see a line that says "virtualHW.version" and a value of either 4 or 7, which will determine whether the VM is using the new vSphere hardware format (7) or the VI3 format (4). If the VM is in a mixed environment comprising vSphere and VI3 hosts, and it may be migrated to a VI3 host due to a High Availability (HA), Distributed Resource Scheduler (DRS), or VMotion event, you should use version 4; otherwise, stick with version 7, as it is required for some of the features in vSphere to work.

You can always upgrade the VM hardware version from 4 to 7 at any time by selecting the VM while it is powered off using the vSphere Client, and then choosing Inventory→Virtual Machine→Upgrade Virtual Machine Hardware. Some of the benefits of using version 7 include Fault Tolerance (FT) capability, use of the Changed Block Tracking (CBT) feature of the vStorage API, and CPU and memory hot-add capability. You can check to see what version a VM is currently at by selecting it using the vSphere Client and then choosing the Summary tab. In the General pane, the VM version will be displayed. You have the option of choosing which version to use when creating a VM by choosing the Custom configuration type in the New Virtual Machine Wizard. If you choose Typical, you will not have the option to choose version 4, as all new VMs default to version 7 in vSphere.

SUPPORT FOR EIGHT vCPUs AND 255GB OF RAM

When it comes to choosing CPU and memory for your VM you have more options in vSphere. VI3 only allowed for up to four vCPUs and 64GB to be assigned to a VM; in vSphere, you can assign up to eight vCPUs and 255GB of RAM to a VM. However, to support more than four vCPUs your host must have an Enterprise Plus license, your host CPUs/cores must total more than four, and the guest OS must be able to support four vCPUs. Also new with vSphere is the ability to assign an odd number of vCPUs to a VM. In VI3, you could only assign one, two, or four vCPUs to a VM, whereas in vSphere you can assign any number of vCPUs, up to a maximum of eight, as long as the guest OS supports an odd number of vCPUs. In terms of memory, you can assign more to a VM (up to 255GB) than the host physically has available, thanks to memory over-commitment.

Remember, though, that just because you can assign up to eight vCPUs and 255GB of memory to a VM doesn't mean you should do that. Assigning too many vCPUs to a VM and using memory overcommitment can drastically reduce the performance of your VMs under certain circumstances.

SUPPORT FOR ADDITIONAL GUEST OPERATING SYSTEMS

You have more supported guest OS choices in vSphere when creating a VM than you did in VI3. VI3 supported 392 operating system releases; this includes different versions of the same operating system. In vSphere, that number increases to 486 supported operating system releases, as support for many more Linux distributions was added. Table 3.1 shows the breakdown of supported operating system releases in each version.

Table 3.1   Number of Supported Guest Operating System Types in VI3 and vSphere

Operating System	VI3 (3.5 Update 5)	vSphere (4.0 Update 1)
Asianux	0	3
Canonical (Ubuntu)	45	40
CentOS	6	18
Debian	0	20
FreeBSD	0	10
IBM (OS/2)	0	2
Microsoft	115	130
Novell (NetWare and SUSE Linux)	45	46
Oracle (Linux)	6	18
Red Hat	157	157
SCO	0	4
Serenity Systems	0	1
Sun Microsystems (Solaris)	18	34

VMXNET3 VIRTUAL NETWORK ADAPTER

In vSphere, VMware has introduced a new virtual network adapter type called VMXNET3 which is the third generation of its homegrown vNIC. You might wonder why VMware developed its own vNICs instead of emulating existing physical NIC (pNIC) types; the reason is that the company needed a vNIC that was virtualization-aware to help minimize I/O virtualization overhead. VMXNET3 offers better performance than VMXNET2, which was introduced in VI3. It also offers some new features, such as Receive Side Scaling (RSS), TCP Segmentation Offloading (TSO) over IPv6, and large TX/RX ring sizes that can help increase host scalability for VMs with high network loads. We will cover the VMXNET3 virtual network adapter in more detail in Chapter 6, along with all the other adapter types.

PARAVIRTUAL SCSI ADAPTER AND IDE ADAPTER

When it comes to virtual storage adapters for your VM you now have several new types from which to choose. In VI3, only two storage adapter types were available: either a BusLogic or an LSI Logic parallel SCSI adapter. In vSphere, you have additional choices, including an LSI Logic SAS (serial attached SCSI) and a Paravirtual SCSI adapter. Additionally, you can use an IDE adapter, an option which was not available in VI3. The new LSI Logic SAS adapter is only intended to be used with Windows Server 2008 in clusters with shared disks.

Paravirtualization technology is available for certain operating systems that utilize a special driver to communicate directly with the hypervisor. Paravirtualization allows for greater throughput and lower CPU utilization for VMs and is useful for disk I/O-intensive applications. We will cover the new storage adapters in more detail in Chapter 5, along with all the other adapter types.

MEMORY HOT ADD AND CPU HOT PLUG FEATURES

The new Memory Hot Add and CPU Hot Plug features in vSphere enable you to add additional memory and CPUs while a VM is powered on. These features are available only in the Advanced, Enterprise, and Enterprise Plus editions, and will appear only if you select a guest operating system in the VM's general settings that supports these features. Depending on the OS you select, you may be able to use either one or both of these features. Although you can add memory to a VM, removing memory still requires that the VM be powered off. vSphere supports hot removal of CPUs, but many guest operating systems do not.

To enable Memory Hot Add and CPU Hot Plug you need to first enable the features in the VM's settings. As mentioned, though, you will see the option for this only if you select a guest operating system version in the VM's settings that supports the features. The guest OS version is set when you create a VM, but you can change it by editing a VM's settings and selecting the Options tab and

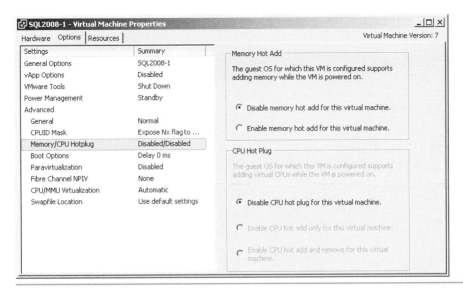

Figure 3.1   Memory/CPU Hotplug options for a Red Hat Enterprise Linux 5 64-bit VM

then the General Options setting. If you do select a supported guest OS, a new option will appear on the Options tab under the Advanced section, called Memory/CPU Hotplug, as shown in Figure 3.1

You can also see in Figure 3.1 that Memory Hot Add can be enabled but CPU Hot Plug is grayed out and cannot be enabled. This is because the guest OS chosen for this VM (Red Hat Enterprise Linux 5, 64-bit) supports Memory Hot Add but not CPU Hot Plug. You can determine whether a guest OS supports CPU Hot Plug by changing the VM's settings to whatever guest OS you want to check, and then saving the VM's settings and editing the settings again to see if the option appears. Table 3.2 shows some popular operating systems and their support for Memory Hot Add and CPU Hot Plug.

Table 3.2   Guest Operating System Support for Memory Hot Add and CPU Hot Plug

Operating System	Memory Hot Add Support	CPU Hot Plug Support
Windows Server 2003 Standard 32-bit and 64-bit	No	No
Windows Server 2003 Enterprise 32-bit and 64-bit	Yes	No
Windows Server 2003 Datacenter 32-bit and 64-bit	Yes	No

Continues

Table 3.2   Guest Operating System Support for Memory Hot Add and CPU Hot Plug *(Continued)*

Operating System	Memory Hot Add Support	CPU Hot Plug Support
Windows Server 2008 Standard 32-bit	Yes	No
Windows Server 2008 Standard 64-bit	Yes	Yes
Windows Server 2008 Enterprise 32-bit	Yes	No
Windows Server 2008 Enterprise 64-bit	Yes	Yes
Windows Server 2003 Datacenter 32-bit	Yes	No
Windows Server 2003 Datacenter 64-bit	Yes	Yes
Debian GNU/Linux 5 32-bit and 64-bit	Yes	Yes
Red Hat Linux Enterprise 5 32-bit	No	No
Red Hat Linux Enterprise 5 64-bit	Yes	No
SUSE Linux Enterprise 11 32-bit and 64-bit	Yes	Yes
Ubuntu Linux 32-bit	Yes	No
Ubuntu Linux 64-bit	Yes	Yes
Sun Solaris 10 32-bit and 64-bit	No	No

To enable these features the VM must be powered off, so it's best to enable them when you create a VM. Once you have enabled the features, you can edit the VM's settings while it is powered on and add more memory or more CPUs to it. In some cases, depending on the operating system, your VM may see the additional memory/CPU after you add it but will not be able to use it until it has been restarted. Consult your guest operating system documentation to find out if this is the case in your situation. Memory Hot Add and CPU Hot Plug are great features that can help to ensure that your VMs are highly available while being expandable when needed and without interruption.

DISPLAY ADAPTER SETTINGS

In VI3, a VM's display adapter was hidden and had no settings that you could modify. In vSphere, the display adapter is shown and has a number of settings that you can change, including the memory size and the maximum number of displays, as shown in Figure 3.2.

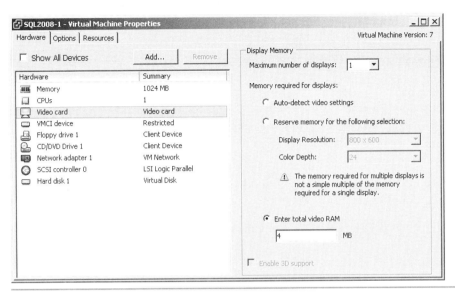

Figure 3.2   Display adapter settings for a VM

In most server applications you will not want to adjust these settings; they are intended more for virtual desktops running on ESX. You will also see an option to enable 3D support that is grayed out, as this feature is not yet supported in ESX, but rather is intended for hosted products, such as vSphere Workstation, that share the same type of virtual hardware format as ESX.

SUPPORT FOR USB CONTROLLERS

You can now add a USB controller to your VM which allows the VM to access USB devices connected to the host server. Although this option exists in vSphere, it is not actually supported yet and is currently intended for hosted products such as vSphere Workstation. VMware may decide to enable this support in vSphere in a future release, as it is a much requested feature.

VIRTUAL MACHINE COMMUNICATION INTERFACE

VMware introduced a new interface in vSphere that allows two VMs on the same host to communicate with each other via a high-speed interface without going through the network stack that is typically between them. Additionally, it allows for high-speed communication between a VM and its host server. Since the Virtual Machine Communication Interface (VMCI) operates independently of the guest networking stack, the communication rate is close to that of the host server's memory bus. To get an example of the speed difference compared to traditional 1GB/s networking, you can use the following formula to calculate memory bandwidth and throughput:

Base DRAM frequency in MHz (millions of DRAM clock cycles per second) ×
Memory interface (or bus) width (DDR, DDR2, and DDR3 are 64 bytes) ×
Number of interfaces (single-, dual-, or triple-channel) ×
Number of bits per clock cycle per line (two for DDR, DDR2, and DDR3)

Using an HP DL385 G6 that uses PC2-6400 DDR2 DIMMs at 800MHz the memory bandwidth would be:

800 megahertz × 64 bits × 2 interfaces × 2 bits = 23.84GB/s

This is almost 24 times as fast as a 1GB/s network connection, and it is not subject to the typical latency that is inherent in most networks. This type of speed is very beneficial in multitier applications that have different components running on different servers, such as a web/application/database servers. But note that this will work only with applications that are designed to communicate via VMCI instead of the network.

VMware does provide a special VMCI Sockets API that allows developers to adapt their applications to use the VMCI interface, though. The drivers for VMCI are provided inside VMware Tools for both Windows and Linux VMs, and are installed by default with a typical installation. Once the drivers are installed, you need to enable VMCI by editing the VM's settings, as VMCI is disabled by default. When a VM is created with virtual hardware version 7 a few lines will be added to the VM's configuration files (.vmx) automatically for VMCI, as shown in the following code snippet:

```
vmci0.present = "TRUE"
vmci0.pciSlotNumber = "33"
vmci0.id = "-1848525795"
```

The VMCI adapter is essentially a special NIC and is assigned a PCI slot number as well as a unique ID which is equivalent to a MAC address. This ID is automatically generated and must be unique among the other VMs on a host. To enable VMCI you edit a VM's settings, and on the Hardware tab you will see a VMCI device that is automatically created when a VM is created. This device cannot be removed and can only be enabled or disabled. Once you check the box to enable it, the status will change from restricted to unrestricted, which allows it to be used.

As mentioned previously, you must have applications that specifically support this new feature to take advantage of it. At the time of this writing, there does not seem to be much vendor support for this feature, despite its clear advantages. VMCI is a great feature that will greatly speed up multitier applications once they are modified to use it.

VMDIRECTPATH FEATURE

VMDirectPath is similar to paravirtualized SCSI adapters in that a VM can directly access host adapters and bypass the virtualization layer to achieve better throughput and reduced CPU utilization. It is different in that with VMDirectPath you must dedicate an adapter to a VM and it cannot be used by any other VMs on that host.

VMDirectPath is available for specific models of both network and storage adapters; however, currently only network adapters are fully supported in vSphere, and storage adapters have only experimental support (they are not ready for production use). Like pvSCSI adapters, VMDirectPath can be used for VMs that have very high storage or network I/O requirements, such as database servers. VMDirectPath enables virtualization of workloads that you previously might have kept physical. A downside to using VMDirectPath is that you cannot use features such as VMotion and DRS.

VMDirectPath relies on a relatively new chipset technology from Intel and AMD and is available on only certain model servers. Intel uses a technology called Virtualization Technology for Directed I/O (VT-d) and AMD uses a technology called I/O Memory Management Unit (IOMMU). These technologies allow a VM to directly access server hardware when it normally cannot do this because it does not know the physical addresses of the host memory that is being accessed. Usually if a VM tries to access physical hardware using direct memory access (DMA) it will corrupt the memory because the hardware is unaware of the mapping between the virtual memory addresses and physical memory addresses used by the guest OS running inside the VM. The VMkernel avoids this corruption by trapping the I/O operation and applying the necessary translations to it. Doing this does cause a tiny delay in the I/O operation, which you can avoid by using VMDirectPath, which allows for the remapping of I/O DMA transfers and device-generated interrupts.

VMDirectPath uses a special pass-through driver that intercepts all communication between the guest VM device and the hardware device. The pass-through driver performs the translation between the guest virtual address spaces and the actual physical address spaces. It does this by setting up I/O page tables that map the hardware physical addresses to the guest physical addresses. It then sets up a protection domain for the guest OS which is unaware of the underlying translations and proceeds as it normally would. These pass-through drivers are specific to each vendor's hardware devices (i.e., NIC, storage controller), as the command format is often unique and must be decoded to perform the necessary translations. Figure 3.3 shows a visual representation of how this technology works.

Figure 3.3 illustrates the normal method used in virtualization and the method VMDirectPath uses. In the normal method, the VMkernel controls all the I/O between VMs and hardware devices. I/O goes from the VM through the VMkernel to the hardware device, and from the hardware device through the VMkernel back to the VM. With VMDirectPath, the VM uses the regular device driver and not the VMware-specific one, and directly controls the hardware device. For data received from the hardware device, the DMA remapping hardware converts the guest physical address to the host physical address, which goes directly to the buffers of the guest OS without going through the VMkernel.

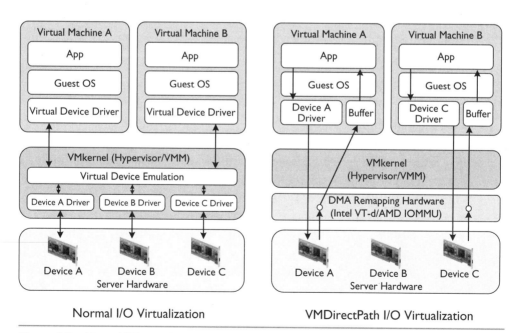

Figure 3.3   Normal I/O virtualization compared to VMDirectPath I/O virtualization

If you plan to use VMDirectPath, be aware of the following limitations.

- Only two host devices can be assigned to a VM.
- The host devices assigned to a VM cannot be used by any other VMs or the host itself.
- The following features do not support VMDirectPath:
  - FT
  - VMotion
  - Storage VMotion
  - DRS
  - HA
  - Snapshots
  - Memory Hot Add, Virtual Disk Hot Add, and CPU Hot Plug
  - VM suspension
- VMDirectPath is fully supported on Intel systems with VT-d with Xeon 5500 processors; vSphere 4.0, Update 1 only had experimental support for AMD systems with IOMMU. In vSphere 4.1 and 4.0, Update 2, VMware fully supports AMD systems with IOMMU for use with VMDirectPath. The first standard AMD server with IOMMU supported by ESX is a Magny Cours processor with an SR56x0 chipset.
- Many servers do not support this feature. If you do not see an option to enable this feature in your server BIOS, your server may not support it. Currently, more servers with Intel CPUs support this feature than servers with AMD CPUs.
- Although VMDirectPath will work with most I/O devices, VMware supports its use with only a handful of devices, which currently includes the Intel 82598 10 Gigabit Ethernet controller and Broadcom 57710 and 57711 10 Gigabit Ethernet controllers. VMDirectPath is experimentally supported for storage I/O devices with QLogic QLA25xx 8Gb Fibre Channel, Emulex LPe12000 8Gb Fibre Channel, and LSI 3442e-R and 3801e (1068 chip-based) 3Gb SAS adapters. Check VMware's online Hardware Compatibility Guide for the most current supported device information.

Once you are ready to enable VMDirectPath follow these steps.

1. Make sure either Intel VT-d or AMD IOMMU is enabled in your server BIOS.

2. In the vSphere Client, select the host on which you want to enable VMDirectPath in the left pane, and then select the Configuration tab in the right pane. In the Hardware section, select Advanced Settings.

3. If your server does not support VMDirectPath or if the feature is disabled, you will see a message that says "Host does not support passthrough configuration." Otherwise, you will see a message that says "No devices currently enabled for passthrough." Click the Configure Passthrough link to configure a pass-through device.

4. Select a device to use with pass-through from the list of presented devices, which will include NICs, storage controllers, and USB controllers; then click OK.

5. Once the Update Host Configuration task completes, reboot the host so that you can assign the device to a VM.

6. Once the host has been rebooted, power off and edit the settings for the VM to which you want to assign the device, and on the Hardware tab click the Add button.

7. In the Add Hardware Wizard, select PCI Device and click Next. On the Select PCI/PCIe Device tab, select the device that you want to assign to the VM.

8. Power the VM back on and the operating system should discover the new device and load the appropriate driver for it; you may be prompted for the location of the driver.

Your device is now ready to use. Note that some additional advanced configuration settings may need to be set in the VM's .vmx file; see the VMware white paper at www.vmware.com/pdf/vsp_4_vmdirectpath_host.pdf for more information on this.

VMDirectPath has some very specific use cases, and its use is not recommended unless your applications will definitely benefit from it because of the many limitations that occur when using it.

ANATOMY OF A VIRTUAL MACHINE

Although you may know what a VM is, do you really know all the details regarding its components? In this section, we will cover the various virtual hardware components and files that comprise a VM. A VM is defined as the representation of a physical machine by software that has its own set of virtual hardware upon which an operating system and applications can be loaded. All VMs use the same type of virtual hardware, regardless of the physical hardware the host is running on.

VIRTUAL MACHINE HARDWARE

When you create a VM and assign virtual hardware components to it, such as CD/DVD drives and SCSI adapters, the operating system will see these components as specific hardware components. The exception to this is virtual CPUs, which the VM sees as whatever brand and type is running on the host (this is why you cannot VMotion between hosts with different physical CPU families and brands). A VM sees the following standard virtual hardware in vSphere.

- **System manufacturer**—The system manufacturer will always be VMware.
- **BIOS**—The BIOS will always be Phoenix 6.0.
- **Motherboard**—The motherboard will always be Intel 440BX.
- **CPU**—This will vary based on whatever CPU brand and model is in the host servers. VMs running on AMD hosts will see whatever AMD processor is in the host, and VMs running on Intel hosts will see whatever Intel processor is in the host. VMs will only see the number of vCPUs that are assigned to it and not the actual physical number that the host has. All CPUs presented to VMs are seen as single-core CPUs regardless of whether the host has multicore CPUs.
- **Memory**—VI3 had only four virtual memory slots for VMs that are configured with virtual DIMMs automatically based on the amount of memory assigned to the VM. In vSphere, this was increased to 32 virtual memory slots to accommodate the increase in memory that can be assigned to a VM (255GB). The maximum memory module size that you can use is 32GB, but ESX will present different sized modules based on the amount of memory assigned to a VM. For example, a VM with 32GB of memory assigned to it will see two 16GB virtual memory modules; a VM with 8GB of memory assigned to it will see a single 8GB virtual memory module.
- **Video controller**—VMware Standard VGA Graphics Adapter with 4MB of video memory is the default. If you adjust the amount of memory allocated to the video card in the VM's settings, the OS will see that amount of video memory.
- **CD/DVD-ROM drive**—This will always be NEC VMware IDE CDR10.

- **Network controller**—You can choose from multiple types of virtual network adapters for your VM, as listed here and discussed in more detail in Chapter 6:
  - **Vmxnet3**—Displays as "Vmxnet3 Ethernet Adapter"
  - **Vmxnet2**—Displays as "VMware PCI Ethernet Adapter"
  - **E1000**—Displays as "Intel PRO/1000 MT Network Connection"
  - **Flexible**—Displays as "VMware Accelerated AMD PCNet Adapter"
- **IDE controller**—This will always be the Intel 82371 AB/EB/MB PCI Bus Master EIDE Controller.
- **SCSI controller**—You can choose from multiple types of storage adapters for your SCSI virtual disks:
  - **LSI Logic Parallel**—Displays as "LSI Logic PCI-X Ultra320 SCSI Host Adapter"
  - **BusLogic Parallel**—Displays as "BusLogic BA80c30 PCI-SCSI MultiMaster"
  - **LSI Logic SAS (serial)**—Displays as "LSI Adapter, SAS 3000 series, 8-port with 1068"
  - **VMware Paravirtual**—Displays as "VMware PVSCSI Controller"

We will discuss all of these virtual storage adapters in more detail in Chapter 5.

VMware has changed the number of supported devices for VMs in vSphere as compared to VI3 (see Table 3.3). The most dramatic change concerns the number of NICs that can be assigned to a VM.

Table 3.3   Maximum Supported Devices in a VM for VI3 and vSphere

	VI3	vSphere
SCSI controllers per VM	4	4
SCSI targets per controller	15	15
IDE controllers per VM	1	1
IDE devices per VM	4	4
NICs per VM	4	10
USB controllers per VM	0	1
Floppy drives per VM	2	2

Table 3.3   Maximum Supported Devices in a VM for VI3 and vSphere *(Continued)*

	VI3	vSphere
Serial ports per VM	4	4
Parallel ports per VM	3	3
VMDirectPath PCI/PCIe devices per VM	0	2
VMDirectPath SCSI targets per VM	0	60

Here are some additional notes on VM device support in vSphere.

- The IDE controller supports two channels (primary and secondary), each with a master and slave device.
- The four IDE devices can be split between CD/DVD drives and IDE virtual hard disks.
- VI3 supported only six PCI devices in a VM that was split between the video card, SCSI controllers, and NICs. Therefore, if you had two SCSI controllers you were limited to only three NICs. In vSphere, this limit has been raised, so you can have the full number of supported SCSI controllers (four) and NICs (ten) assigned to a VM.
- Audio devices (sound cards) are not supported on ESX hosts.
- You cannot add a SCSI controller to a VM; controllers are automatically added or removed when you add hard disks and assign them a virtual device node ID.

Now you know what virtual hardware devices make up a VM and are presented to the guest operating system. Virtual hardware is emulated and then translated to the host's actual hardware devices by the VMkernel. Having consistent virtual hardware regardless of the physical host hardware used makes VMs easily transferable to other hosts, no matter what hardware they are running.

VIRTUAL MACHINE FILES

Virtual hardware is just one part of a VM. A VM also consists of many different files which are stored in its home directory on the host server's datastore. Each file type has a different purpose, such as the VM's BIOS, virtual disk, configuration, and so forth. The names of most of these files will match the name of the VM, but will have different extensions based on file type. Depending on the state of your VM, you may not see certain files unless the state changes. For example, the .vswp file is present only when a VM is powered on, and the

.vmss file is present only when a VM is suspended. Here are the various file types that comprise a VM.

- **.nvram**—This small binary format file (less than 10k) contains the Phoenix BIOS that is used as part of the VM boot process. This is the same type of BIOS that is used in a physical server that lets you set hardware configuration options. You can access the BIOS by pressing the F2 key at the black splash screen that is displayed when a VM boots up. Any changes made to the VM hardware configuration are saved in the .nvram file. If this file is deleted or missing from a VM's directory, it is automatically re-created when the VM is powered on.

- **.vmx**—This small text file contains all of the VM's configuration information and hardware settings. The data in this file is written when you make changes to the VM's configuration using the vSphere Client. You can also edit this file directly when a VM is powered off, but you should be careful and make a backup copy beforehand. This file contains such data as the specific hardware configuration (i.e., RAM size, NIC and hard drive configurations), resource settings, VMware tools, and power management options.

- **.vswp**—This is the memory swap file that is created when a VM is powered on; it is used if a host is overcommitted and uses all of its physical memory, or when a memory limit is placed on a VM. You can also assign more virtual memory to a VM than a host physically has, and this file will make up for the physical memory that the host does not have. This file is equal in size to the amount of memory assigned to a VM, minus any memory reservations (the default is 0) that a VM may have set on it (e.g., a 4GB VM with a 1GB reservation will have a 3GB .vswp file created). Although these files are always created for VMs when they are powered on, they are used only if a host exhausts all of its physical memory. These types of files can take up a large amount of disk space on your VMFS volumes, so you should ensure that you have adequate space available for them as a VM will not power on if there is not enough free space available to create this file. These files are deleted when a VM is powered off or suspended.

- **.vmss**—This file is used when VMs are suspended and to preserve the memory contents of the VM so that it can start up again where it left off. This file will be approximately the same size as the amount of memory that is assigned to a VM, as even empty memory contents are written to it. When a VM is brought out of a suspended state the contents of this file are written back into the physical memory of a host server. After this file is created, it is not automatically deleted until the VM is powered off (not rebooted). If a previous suspend file exists when a VM is suspended again, this file is reused instead of deleted and re-created. If this file is deleted while the VM is suspended, the VM will start normally and not from a suspended state.

- **.vmsd**—This text file is used with snapshots to store metadata and other information about each snapshot that is active on a VM. It is initially 0 bytes in size and is updated with information as snapshots are created or deleted. Only one of these files will be present regardless of the number of snapshots running, as they all update this single file. The information in this file consists of the names of the .vmdk and .vmsn files used by each snapshot, the display name, a description, and the UID of each snapshot. When you delete snapshots this file still retains old snapshot information but increments the snapshot UID to be used with future snapshots. It also renames the first snapshot to "Consolidate Helper" which is used if you ever use Consolidated Backup which relies on snapshots.

- **.vmsn**—This file is similar to the .vmss file and is used with snapshots to store the state of a VM when a snapshot is taken. One of these files will be created for every snapshot that is created for a VM, and they are automatically deleted when the snapshot is deleted. This file will vary in size depending on whether you choose to include the memory state of the VM with the snapshot. If you choose to store the memory state, this file will be slightly larger than the amount of memory assigned to the VM, as the entire memory contents, including empty memory, is copied to this file. If you do not choose to store the memory state of the snapshot, this file will be fairly small (less than 32KB).

- **.vmxf**—This file is a supplemental configuration file that is not used with ESX but is retained for compatibility purposes with vSphere Workstation. It is in text format and is used by vSphere Workstation for VM teaming whereby multiple VMs can be assigned to a team so that they can be powered on/off or suspended and resumed as a single object.

- **.vmdk**—These are the virtual hard disk files. Two different types of these files make up a single virtual disk. The first type is a large data file that is equal in size to the virtual disk and contains its raw data. The second type is a small (less than 2k) text disk descriptor file which describes the size and geometry of the virtual disk file and contains a pointer to the large data file as well as information on the virtual disk's drive sectors, heads, cylinders, and disk adapter type. In most cases, these files will have the same name as the data file that they are associated with (e.g., orangevm.vmdk and orangevm-flat.vmdk). You can tell which descriptor file is tied to which data file by checking the Extent Description field in this file to see which –flat, –rdm, or –delta file is linked to it. Four different types of virtual disk data files can be used with VMs.

- **–flat.vmdk**—This is the default large virtual disk data file that is created when you add a virtual hard drive to your VM that is not a Raw Device Mapping (RDM). When using thick disks this file will be approximately the same size as what you specify when you create your virtual hard drive. One of these files is created for each virtual hard drive that a VM has configured.

- **–delta.vmdk**—This virtual disk data file is used only when VM snapshots are created. When a snapshot is created all writes to the original –flat.vmdk file are halted and the file becomes read-only; changes to the virtual disk are then written to these delta files instead. The initial size of these files is 16MB, and they grow in 16MB increments as changes are made to the VM's virtual hard disk. Because these files are a bitmap of the changes made to a virtual disk, a single –delta.vmdk file cannot exceed the size of the original –flat.vmdk file. A delta file will be created for each snapshot that you create for a VM and their filenames will be incremented numerically (e.g., orangevm-000001-delta.vmdk, orangevm-000002-delta.vmdk). These files are automatically deleted when the snapshot is deleted after they are merged back into the original –flat.vmdk file.

- **–rdm.vmdk**—This is the mapping file for an RDM that contains information for the mapping to a storage area network (SAN) LUN. The mapping file is presented to the ESX host as an ordinary disk file and is available for the usual filesystem operations. However, to the VM the storage virtualization layer presents the mapped device as a virtual SCSI device. The metadata in the mapping file includes the mapped device's location (name resolution) and its locking state. If you do a directory listing you will see that these files will appear to be taking up the same amount of disk space on the VMFS volume as the actual size of the LUN that they are mapped to, but in reality they just appear that way and their size is very small. One of these files is created for each RDM that is created for a VM.

- **–ctk.vmdk**—This is the file where the new CBT feature stores the information about changed blocks for a virtual disk. These files are created in a VM's home directory for every virtual disk on which the CBT feature is enabled. The size of this file is fixed based on the size of the virtual disk (a virtual disk is approximately .5MB per 10GB of virtual disk size). Inside this file, the state of each block is stored for tracking purposes using sequence numbers that can tell applications if a block has changed or not. One of these files will exist for each virtual disk on which CBT is enabled.

- **.log**—These are the files that are created to log various types of information about the VM. A number of these files will be present in a VM's directory. The current log file is always named vmware.log; up to six older log files will also be retained with a number at the end of their name (e.g., vmware-2.log). A new log file is created either when a VM is powered off and back on, or if the log file reaches the maximum defined size limit. The number of log files that are retained and the maximum size limits are both defined as VM advanced configuration parameters (log.rotateSize and log.keepOld).

Together, all of these files make up a VM and reside in a VM's home directory by default. It is possible to alter the locations of some of these files so that they reside on other datastores. For example, you might want to put your VM swap files on another datastore to help save space on datastores that use more expensive disks. Virtual disks can be created on any available datastore, and swap files can be moved to other directories by changing the cluster or host swap file location settings. If a host is in a cluster, the cluster setting overrides the host settings. You can change the cluster setting by editing the cluster settings and selecting the Swapfile Location option; you can edit the host setting by selecting a host, and on the Configuration tab, under Software, selecting the Virtual Machine Swapfile Location option. Just remember that if you move a VM's files to another location and that location becomes unavailable, it may crash the VM.

VIRTUAL MACHINE DISKS

In the previous section, we covered the different types of .vmdk files that can be present in your VM's directory. Now we will cover the different virtual disk formats. A virtual disk can be one of three general format types: raw, thick, or thin. This section describes the differences between each format type.

Raw Disks

Raw disks are known as RDMs and enable a VM to have a virtual disk that is mapped directly to a LUN on a SAN. As mentioned previously, RDMs have a small mapping file on a VMFS volume in the VM's home directory that contains mapping data to the SAN LUN. When you create an RDM for a VM you can choose one of two modes in which it can operate: Virtual compatibility mode virtualizes the mapped device and is mostly transparent to the guest operating system; physical compatibility mode provides minimal SCSI virtualization of the mapped device. In this case, the VMkernel passes most SCSI commands directly to the device, which allows for closer integration between the VM and the LUN.

Thick Disks

When you create a thick disk all space on a volume is allocated at the time the disk is created, so the resultant .vmdk file will take up as much room on the volume as the size of the disk that you create. There are several types of thick disks, with the main difference among them being how disk blocks are zeroed before they are written to.

- **Thick disks**—Referred to as monotholitic preallocated zeroed_out_never. All space is allocated at creation time and may contain stale data on the physical media. Disk blocks are not zeroed before being written to the first time, which makes these types of disks less secure because any previously written data has not been cleared from the disk blocks.

- **Lazy-Zeroed thick disks**—Referred to as monotholitic preallocated zeroed_out_later. All space is allocated at creation time and is wiped clean of any previous data on the physical media. Disk blocks are zeroed out on demand as they are written, but only for the first write to a disk block. This type of disk is the default used when creating virtual disks on VMFS volumes using the vSphere Client. These disks have slightly less I/O performance on the first write to a disk block because the disks must be zeroed before they are written to. Subsequent writes to a disk block have the same optimal performance as the other disk types.

- **Eager-Zeroed thick disks**—Referred to as monotholitic preallocated zeroed_out_now. All space is allocated at creation time and is wiped clean of any previous data on the physical media. All disk blocks are zeroed out when the disk is created, which increases the time it takes to create these disks compared to the other types. These types of disks are the most secure and offer slightly better performance on the first write to a disk block because the disk has already been zeroed. Subsequent writes to a disk block have the same optimal performance as the other disk types. You must have this type of disk to use the FT feature.

Thin Disks

Thin provisioned disks (monotholitic growable) are virtual disks that start small and grow as data is written to them. Unlike thick disks, in which all space is allocated when the disk is created, when a thin disk is created its initial size is 1MB (or up to 8MB depending on the default block size), and it then grows up to the maximum size that was defined when it was created as the guest OS writes data to it. Thin disks have a slight performance penalty both as they grow and space is allocated on demand, and when the first write to a disk block is zeroed on demand. Once the disk has grown and its blocks have been zeroed, its performance is the same as the other disk types. Thin disks are good for conserving disk space on a VMFS volume, but they can cause problems if you do not monitor their growth to make sure you do not run out of disk space on your VMFS volume. Thin disks are often used by default on Network File System (NFS) protocol datastores based on the allocation policy of the NFS server and not the ESX server.

You can view the current actual size of a thin disk using the vSphere Client. On the Virtual Machines tab there are columns for Provisioned Space (maximum size of the disk) and Used Space (actual size of the disk). The Datastore Browser that is built into the vSphere Client will also show you the actual size of a thin disk and not the provisioned size. You can also see this information on the Summary tab of the VM and in the Storage View when connected to a vCenter Server. If you use the Service Console command-line `ls -ltr` command, it will show the maximum size of the disk and not the actual size. You can instead use the `du -a -h` command to see the actual size of a thin disk.

If left unmonitored and unmanaged, thin disks can cause big problems in your environment. Thin disks allow you to overcommit disk space in the same way that you can with memory in ESX. When you do this, though, you risk depleting the space on your VMFS datastores as your thin disks grow over time. If this happens, it can cause big problems in your environment. In VI3, if a datastore ran out of space it could crash and corrupt your VMs. In vSphere, a safety mechanism was added that will suspend VMs if a datastore becomes critically low on free space. To prevent this from happening there are a few things you should know and do if you plan to use thin disks.

- Monitor your datastore free space carefully. There is a new alarm in vSphere for monitoring datastore free space, called Datastore Usage on Disk, that will alert you when your datastore disk space usage grows to a defined percentage. Additionally, there is another alarm that you can set, called

Datastore Disk Overallocation %, which will trigger when your disk space overallocation reaches a defined limit (e.g., 300%).

- Be aware of snapshots in your environment which can affect the amount of free disk space on your datastores. Having two types of disk files that can grow on your datastores is a double threat. You can now set alarms for snapshot size, so it's a good idea to set them so that you know when any snapshots grow too large and must be deleted.

- The new Storage View is your friend; it shows detailed VM file information all in one view, including snapshot sizes, true thin disk sizes, and .vswp and other file sizes. Use this view so that you can see all your VM file sizes at once. You can also click on column headings to sort on them.

- Avoid using thin disks with servers that will have disks that will not grow that much and will be near their capacity right away. There's not much benefit to using thin disks if a VM is going to be using most of its disk space right away. It's better to size your VM's virtual disks to what they will need and not give them space that they will never use. The greatest benefit of thin disks comes from servers whose disk space usage will start small and grow over time, such as file and database servers. If you have mostly static servers such as application and web servers, just give them the disk they need and don't go overboard. You can always grow the disks later if you find you are running out of space.

- Avoid doing operating system disk defragmentation on VMs with thin disks. This will cause the VM disk file to grow quickly and dramatically, which may fill up your datastore before you can react to any alarms that may trigger.

- One common question about thin disks is whether you should use them in VMware if your storage array supports them (referred to as thin-on-thin). Use thin provisioning at both the array level and in vSphere if you can; just make sure you carefully monitor your overallocation of both the array and VMware to ensure that you have adequate space available.

- Be aware that thin disks grow or inflate as data is written to previously unwritten disk blocks, but they do not automatically shrink or deflate when data is deleted. If you have a VM with a thin disk that had a lot of data on its virtual disk that was later deleted, you can manually recover this space by doing a Storage VMotion and specifying a thin disk type again. This will create a new disk file that will be slightly larger than the amount of data that is in use on the disk.

A concern with thin disks is the performance impact of the operation that occurs when they grow, as well as the increased fragmentation that may occur. VMware has conducted performance studies that show that this is very negligible and should not discourage anyone from using thin disks. By being aware of these things and staying vigilant, you can enjoy the disk savings that thin disks provide without causing problems or disruptions in your environment.

2GB Sparse Disks

A sparse disk is a special-format disk that cannot be used with a running VM on an ESX/ESXi host, and is instead often used to import/export virtual disks to and from ESX hosts. This format divides a virtual disk into multiple 2GB pieces, which is handy when you need to copy a virtual disk to another host or when it needs to fit on physical media such as DVD-ROMs. The 2GB file sizes are used because some older filesystems do not support file sizes larger than 2GB. Other VMware products, such as vSphere Workstation and Server, can use this format for running VMs, but for the ESX host you must first import these types of disks into a thick or thin format using the vmkfstools utility.

Changing Disk Formats

In most cases, you will want to use the default Lazy-Zeroed thick disks, as administration is simpler. In the following situations, though, you may want to use the other disk formats.

- If you are concerned about security and want slightly better performance on initial disk writes, you might want to use Eager-Zeroed thick disks.
- If you have limited disk space on your VMFS volumes, you might want to use thin disks.

Whatever format you use, just remember that the disk performance is equal on all the formats once the initial write to a previously unwritten disk block is made. One exception to this is with thin disks which can become fragmented as the disk file is not allocated all at once. If this happens, you can experience slightly reduced performance. Lazy-Zeroed thick disks are the default format using the vSphere Client, and if you wish to use the other formats there are several ways in which to do so.

- To create a thin disk choose the option to "Allocate and commit space on demand (Thin Provisioning)" when creating the disk, as shown in Figure 3.4.

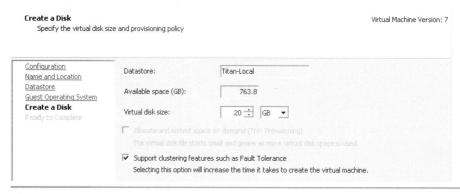

Create a Disk   Virtual Machine Version: 7
Specify the virtual disk size and provisioning policy

Configuration		
Name and Location	Datastore:	Titan-Local
Datastore		
Guest Operating System	Available space (GB):	763.8
Create a Disk		
Ready to Complete	Virtual disk size:	20 ⬍ GB ▾

☑ Allocate and commit space on demand (Thin Provisioning)
   The virtual disk file starts small and grows as more virtual disk space is used.

☐ Support clustering features such as Fault Tolerance
   Selecting this option will increase the time it takes to create the virtual machine.

Figure 3.4   Choosing the option to create a thin disk when creating a new virtual disk

- To create an Eager-Zeroed thick disk, choose the option to "Support clustering features such as Fault Tolerance" when creating the disk, as shown in Figure 3.5.

Create a Disk   Virtual Machine Version: 7
Specify the virtual disk size and provisioning policy

Configuration		
Name and Location	Datastore:	Titan-Local
Datastore		
Guest Operating System	Available space (GB):	763.8
Create a Disk		
Ready to Complete	Virtual disk size:	20 ⬍ GB ▾

☐ Allocate and commit space on demand (Thin Provisioning)
   The virtual disk file starts small and grows as more virtual disk space is used.

☑ Support clustering features such as Fault Tolerance
   Selecting this option will increase the time it takes to create the virtual machine.

Figure 3.5   Choosing the option to create an Eager-Zeroed thick disk when creating a new virtual disk

- To change a thin disk to a thick disk or a thick disk to a thin disk at any time, you can use Storage vMotion. Just select a VM and choose Migrate. Then select the Change datastore type, select the same datastore that the VM is on, and choose the new format (thick/thin).

- To change a thin disk to a thick disk you can also use the Datastore Browser in the vSphere Client by selecting the VM's folder, and right-clicking on the disk and choosing Inflate.

- To change a Lazy-Zeroed thick disk to an Eager-Zeroed thick disk at any time you must use the Service Console vmkfstools utility. Type `vmkfstools`

-k /vmfs/volumes/<volume name>/<vm name>/<virtual disk file name> to convert the disk, as shown in Figure 3.6. Depending on the size of the virtual disk, this operation can take a long time to complete. (Note that the -k option of vmkfstools is not supported with the vSphere CLI version of vmkfstools.)

```
[root@titan WebSphere7-1]# vmkfstools -k WebSphere7-1.vmdk
Eagerly zeroing: 5% done.
```

Figure 3.6   Converting a Lazy-Zeroed thick disk to an Eager-Zeroed thick disk using the vmkfstools command

There is no way to tell if a thick disk is Lazy-Zeroed or Eager-Zeroed using the vSphere Client. You can use the Service Console vmkfstools command to find out, though; if you type vmkfstools -t0 /vmfs/volumes/<volume name>/<vm name>/<virtual disk file name> you will see output similar to that shown in Figure 3.7. Looks for [VMFS in the output of each line; if there is a Z- after it that means the disk is Lazy-Zeroed, as the Z indicates blocks that have not been written to yet.

```
[root@titan WebSphere7-1]# vmkfstools -t0 WebSphere7-1.vmdk
Mapping for file WebSphere7-1.vmdk (19327352832 bytes in size):
[          0:    1048576] --> [VMFS -- LVID:4b7d3c82-d96a5252-c41d-18a9054f1a8
a/4b7d3c82-d16f9d61-0d0c-18a9054f1a8a/1:( 585131667968 -->   585132716544)]
[    1048576:   837812224] --> [VMFS Z- LVID:4b7d3c82-d96a5252-c41d-18a9054f1a8
a/4b7d3c82-d16f9d61-0d0c-18a9054f1a8a/1:( 585132716544 -->   585970528768)]
[  838860800:   155189248] --> [VMFS Z- LVID:4b7d3c82-d96a5252-c41d-18a9054f1a8
a/4b7d3c82-d16f9d61-0d0c-18a9054f1a8a/1:( 586025054720 -->   586180243968)]
[  994050048:    53477376] --> [VMFS Z- LVID:4b7d3c82-d96a5252-c41d-18a9054f1a8
a/4b7d3c82-d16f9d61-0d0c-18a9054f1a8a/1:( 585970528768 -->   586024006144)]
[ 1047527424: 18279825408] --> [VMFS Z- LVID:4b7d3c82-d96a5252-c41d-18a9054f1a8
a/4b7d3c82-d16f9d61-0d0c-18a9054f1a8a/1:( 586180243968 -->   604460069376)]
```

Figure 3.7   Output from a Lazy-Zeroed disk

If a disk is Eager-Zeroed, you will see output similar to that shown in Figure 3.8. If you see -- and no Z's after [VMFS that means the blocks have all been written to.

```
[root@titan WebSphere7-1]# vmkfstools -t0 WebSphere7-1.vmdk
Mapping for file WebSphere7-1.vmdk (19327352832 bytes in size):
[          0:   838860800] --> [VMFS -- LVID:4b7d3c82-d96a5252-c41d-18a9054f1a8
a/4b7d3c82-d16f9d61-0d0c-18a9054f1a8a/1:( 585131667968 -->   585970528768)]
[  838860800:   155189248] --> [VMFS -- LVID:4b7d3c82-d96a5252-c41d-18a9054f1a8
a/4b7d3c82-d16f9d61-0d0c-18a9054f1a8a/1:( 586025054720 -->   586180243968)]
[  994050048:    53477376] --> [VMFS -- LVID:4b7d3c82-d96a5252-c41d-18a9054f1a8
a/4b7d3c82-d16f9d61-0d0c-18a9054f1a8a/1:( 585970528768 -->   586024006144)]
[ 1047527424: 18279825408] --> [VMFS -- LVID:4b7d3c82-d96a5252-c41d-18a9054f1a8
a/4b7d3c82-d16f9d61-0d0c-18a9054f1a8a/1:( 586180243968 -->   604460069376)]
```

Figure 3.8   Output from an Eager-Zeroed disk

Note that the -t option of vmkfstools is not supported with the vSphere CLI version of vmkfstools.

The vmkfstools command that is part of the Service Console and vSphere CLI is a Swiss army knife of virtual disk administration, and it is good to be familiar with how to use it. You can read more about how to use the vmkfstools command in Appendix C of VMware's ESX Configuration Guide in the documentation section of the company's website. You can also read how to use it with the vSphere CLI in Chapter 3 of the vSphere Command-Line Interface Installation and Reference Guide, also available on VMware's website. Note that there are some differences in the supported options of vmkfstools between the Service Console and the vSphere CLI. VMware offers a Knowledge Base article at http://kb.vmware.com/kb/1008194 that details the differences.

SUMMARY

VMs are complicated and you can add a variety of virtual hardware to them. Since VMs are the vessels for all of the servers you host on ESX and ESXi, it's important to understand how they work and how you can optimize them for the workloads they support. This will make troubleshooting and configuring VMs easier and will ensure that they run smoothly.

VCENTER SERVER

vCenter Server provides centralized management of hosts by allowing the vSphere Client to connect to vCenter Server instead of to individual hosts. In addition, vCenter Server is necessary if you want to use many of the advanced features in vSphere, such as VMotion, High Availability (HA), and the Distributed Resource Scheduler (DRS). Because of its centralized management capability, vCenter Server is a must-have in large environments where you have many hosts. vCenter Server is not included with vSphere and must be purchased separately. VMware does offer some bundles aimed at the small-business market, which makes vCenter Server more affordable by including it in a package with some host licenses.

WHAT'S NEW WITH vCENTER SERVER IN vSPHERE

In Chapter, 1 we briefly covered some of the new features in vCenter Server. In this chapter, we will discuss them in more detail.

vCENTER SERVER LINKED MODE

VMware introduced a new feature called vCenter Server Linked Mode that benefits large environments housing more than one vCenter Server. vCenter Server has some limitations regarding the number of hosts and virtual machines (VMs) that it can support, so larger environments require more than one vCenter Server. Additionally, sometimes you may need more than one vCenter Server—for instance, when you want to segregate environments, or if your company operates in different geographical locations.

vCenter Server Linked Mode allows you to centrally manage multiple vCenter Server installations using the vSphere Client without having to connect to each one individually. It does this by joining multiple vCenter Servers together into a Linked Mode group, either during a new vCenter Server installation or on already installed vCenter Servers. Linked Mode allows roles and licenses to be shared among multiple vCenter Servers. To use vCenter Server Linked Mode, you must meet the following prerequisites.

- All vCenter Servers must be members of an Active Directory (AD) domain; if they are not, you will receive an error message when you try to install Linked Mode. The vCenter Servers do not have to be part of the same AD domain, but a two-way trust relationship must be established between them. Likewise, if you have more than two vCenter Servers/domains, all of the domains for each vCenter Server must have a two-way trust relationship among them.

- Accurate time is critical, and all vCenter Servers must be within five minutes of each other; VMware recommends that you sync all of them from the same NTP time source. The installer checks this and will not let you proceed until the clocks are corrected.

- DNS is important for linked mode; make sure all your vCenter Servers have DNS host records as IP addresses cannot be used.

- When installing Linked Mode you must use an AD domain user account that must be an Administrator of all vCenter Servers.

Once you have met these prerequisites, you can set up Linked Mode on existing vCenter Servers or when installing a new vCenter Server. Linked Mode is available in all editions of vSphere. For new installations, once you launch the vCenter Server Installation Wizard you will have the option to join a vCenter Server Linked Mode group. You will then be prompted for an existing vCenter Server instance (it must be a host name) to connect to. The vCenter Server installation will then proceed as usual, and once it completes the new vCenter Server will be joined to the Linked Mode group.

For existing vCenter Servers, you can launch a special setup program that is located in the VMware folder of the Start menu, called vCenter Server Linked Mode Configuration. Once that application launches, you will be presented with a Modify Linked Mode Configuration option. You can then select to join the vCenter Server instance to an existing Linked Mode group. Finally, you select an existing vCenter Server to connect to.

Once you have multiple vCenter Servers in a Linked Mode group, you can connect to any one of them to see the inventories of all the vCenter Servers, as shown in Figure 4.1.

Figure 4.1   Two vCenter Servers in a Linked Mode group

If you want to remove a vCenter Server from a Linked Mode group you simply run the vCenter Server Linked Mode Configuration application on the vCenter Server, choose the Modify Linked Mode Configuration option, and then choose the "Isolate this vCenter Server from the Linked Mode group" option.

vCenter Servers that are in Linked Mode groups replicate with each other, so all the inventory, tasks, and other data is up-to-date between them. This is done using a special service that is installed on each vCenter Server that is in a Linked Mode group, called VMwareVCMSDS.

Even though the servers are linked, they are still isolated environments, so you cannot do things such as VMotion a VM from one vCenter Server to another. Here are some additional considerations for using Linked Mode.

- Roles are replicated among vCenter Servers, so if you create a role on one vCenter Server it will be applicable on all of them.
- Users will only see objects that they have permission to see. This is true across all vCenter Servers.
- vCenter Server uses Microsoft Active Directory Application Mode (ADAM) to enable Linked Mode, which uses the Windows RPC port mapper to open RPC ports for replication. ADAM is a lightweight version of AD which can run as a service on a Windows server. The vCenter Server uses ADAM to

store the replicated data for Linked Mode. It then uses replication with LDAP to update data between vCenter Servers. Essentially, the vCenter Servers in Linked Mode act like domain controllers for vCenter Server. When you install vCenter Server in Linked Mode, the firewall configuration on the local machine must be modified. Linked Mode uses dynamic RPC ports, so you'll need to open a range as specified in the Microsoft Knowledge Base article at http://support.microsoft.com/kb/908472/en-us.

- If two vCenter Server systems have roles with the same name, the roles are combined into a single role if they contain the same privileges on each vCenter Server system. If two vCenter Server systems have roles with the same name but containing different privileges, you must resolve this conflict by renaming at least one of the roles. You can choose to resolve the conflicting roles either automatically or manually.

vCenter Server Linked Mode can make administration much easier when you have multiple vCenter Servers. Having to go back and forth between multiple instances of the vSphere Client is cumbersome and uses more resources on a workstation. In addition to easier management, Linked Mode can provide consistent access permissions across all your vCenter Servers for better security.

vApps

A vApp is basically a resource container for multiple VMs that work together as part of a multitier application. An example of a multitier application is a typical web-based application in which you might have three tiers—web, application, and database—which are often run on three separate servers. For example, you may have Microsoft IIS running on one server (tier 1), IBM WebSphere running on another server (tier 2), and Microsoft SQL Server running on a third server (tier 3). The three applications on each server all work together and are mostly dependent on each other for the application to function properly. If one of the tiers becomes unavailable, the application will typically quit working.

Virtualization can introduce some challenges with multitier applications. For example, if one tier is performing poorly due to resource constraints on a host, the whole application will suffer as a result. Another challenge comes when powering on a host server, as oftentimes one tier relies on another tier to be started first or the application will fail. VMware introduced vApps as a method to deal with these problems by providing ways to set power on options, IP address allocation, and resource allocation, as well as provide application-level customization for all the VMs in the vApp. When you configure a vApp in vSphere you specify properties for it, including CPU and memory resources, IP allocation, application information, and start order. To use vApps you must have a DRS-enabled cluster; all of the metadata information for a vApp is stored in the vCenter Server database. To create a vApp follow these steps.

1. Select a cluster or resource pool, right-click on it, and select New vApp.

2. Enter a name and inventory location for the vApp.

3. Use the Resource Allocation screen to adjust CPU/Memory shares/limits/reservations, or accept the defaults (unlimited). With the resource controls you can guarantee a certain amount of resources for all of the VMs in your vApp.

4. At the Ready To Complete screen, click Finish.

Once your vApp container is created, it will appear in the left pane view. You can add VMs to it by dragging them using the vSphere client; you can also create resource pools inside them and nest vApps inside vApps. In addition, you can edit the settings of a vApp to set its properties. The Resources section lets you set resource controls for the vApp and the Properties section is for entering custom properties that are set on the Advanced tab. The IP Allocation Policy is where you can control how IP addresses are assigned to the VMs in the vApp. The default is Fixed, in which VMs use whatever IP addresses are assigned in their guest OS. You can change this to Transient, which uses IP addresses assigned from an IP Pool configured in vCenter Server. You can also specify that an external DHCP server is used. IP Pools are configured by selecting a Datacenter object in vCenter Server and clicking the IP Pools tab.

IP Pools are pools of IP addresses that you can associate with virtual switch (vSwitch) port groups, and they essentially act as DHCP servers to assign IP addresses from the pool to a VM; in this way, the vCenter Server is basically acting as a DHCP server. When you configure an IP Pool you specify a range of either IPv4 or IPv6 addresses, as well as DNS and proxy settings, and then you select which vSwitch port groups the pool will be available to. You must configure an IP address range in the following format (starting IP address, pound sign, number of IP addresses):

```
172.20.20.155#10, 172.20.20.175#5
```

The preceding range would make the following IP addresses available in the IP Pool:

```
172.20.20.155 - 172.20.20.164 and 172.20.20.175 - 172.20.20.179
```

Once you have an IP Pool configured, you can assign it to a vApp by editing its properties and changing the IP Allocation Policy from Fixed to Transient.

The next section in the vApp settings is the Advanced section. Here you can set information about the vApp itself, such as URLs, versions, custom properties for the OVF file, and an advanced IP allocation scheme. The other tab in the vApp settings, the Start Order tab, lets you set startup and shutdown orders for the VMs in the vApp. In multitier applications, there are usually dependencies between the systems—for instance, the database must be up and running before the application server. Here you can set the startup order to delay the start of certain VMs so that the other VMs on which they depend start first. Additionally, you can specify shutdown actions as well.

In addition to the settings you can specify in a vApp that affect all VMs, you can also specify settings on individual VMs. To edit a VM's settings, select the Options tab and enable the vApp Options. You can then set some additional parameters for that VM. Once you have created a vApp, you can easily export it in OVF format as well as deploy new vApps from it. vApps make managing an application that spans multiple VMs much easier and ensures that the interdependencies of the application are always met.

LICENSING

Licensing in VI3 was difficult, as it relied on an independent licensing server that used FLEXlm and large text-based license files that had to be maintained whenever any licenses were added or modified. In vSphere, the licensing server is gone and licensing has been integrated into vCenter Server. In addition, license text files have been replaced with 25-character license keys that you can obtain from VMware's licensing portal. By going to VMware's website and accessing the licensing portal, you can view your license purchases and combine or divide them into multiple keys to use for single host installations or multiple vCenter Servers.

To manage license keys in vCenter Server, select the Home page and then, under Administration, choose Licenses. You will see all evaluation licenses as well as paid license keys. To enter new license keys assign them to hosts/vCenter Servers, and to remove license keys click the Manage vSphere Licenses link. A new window will open, and on the first screen you can add new license keys (one per line) and click the Add button to add them to vCenter Server. On the next screen, you can assign licenses to ESX/ESXi hosts and vCenter Servers; the default is to show unlicensed assets, but you can change this to show licensed assets or to show all assets.

The final screen allows you to remove license keys, but they first need to be unassigned from existing assets in the previous screen. An additional option is available that allows you to export license keys to a CSV format file so that you have them available for safekeeping. Licensing in vSphere is much simpler and, as a result, easier to manage than in VI3, and makes administration much less complicated.

ALARMS AND EVENTS

Being alerted about problems in your virtual environment was one of the biggest shortcomings in VI3. In vSphere, this was vastly improved, and many more alarm options are available to alert you about problems in many areas. Dozens of alarms are configured by default. However, be aware that although alarms are preconfigured with triggers, no actions are assigned to them by default. You will still see the alerts from alarms that trigger in the Alarms view in vCenter Server, but no action will be taken for them. As a result, you will need to edit the alarms and add an appropriate action to them, such as send an alert email, power off a VM, or place a host in maintenance mode.

Alarms are a feature of vCenter Server and are not available when connected directly to ESX and ESXi hosts. Before you edit and manage alarms, you should be aware of how they are assigned to objects in vCenter Server. Alarms can be set at different levels in the vCenter Server hierarchy, and they apply to all objects farther down the chain. Here is an example of this hierarchy:

vCenter Server → Datacenter → Cluster → Host → Virtual Machine

In the preceding example, if an alarm was set at the Cluster level it would apply to all hosts and VMs in that cluster, but not to those in other clusters or datacenters. The default alarms are set at the vCenter Server level, which is at the top of the hierarchy, so they apply to all objects managed by that vCenter Server. You can choose to use the alarms at the vCenter Server level or set them on other objects below that.

To create an alarm you select the object on which you want to set the alarm (i.e., cluster or host) in the left pane of the vSphere Client, and then select the Alarms tab in the right pane. By default, alarms that have triggered are displayed, but you can switch to the Alarm Definitions view by clicking the button at the top of the pane. Here you can edit or view alarms that are already defined, or create new ones. If an alarm is defined at a higher level, which will be evident by the Defined In column, you will only be able to view the settings for the alarm. To edit the alarm you will have to select the level at which it is defined. To create a new alarm, just right-click in the right pane and select New Alarm. Then follow these steps.

1. On the General tab, enter a name for your alarm and optionally a description. In the Alarm Type section, you can select the type of object to which the alarm will apply. The options you see here will vary based on the object you initially chose when you created the alarm. For example, if you selected a Host object the only alarm type you will be able to choose is Host. If you selected a Cluster object, the alarm types you will see are Cluster, Hosts, and Virtual Machines. If you create an alarm at the top vCenter Server object you will see the following objects:
   - Virtual Machines
   - Hosts
   - Clusters
   - Datacenters
   - Datastores
   - Networks
   - Distributed Virtual Switches
   - Distributed Virtual Port Groups
   - vCenter Server

2. After you choose an alarm type, select whether you want to monitor either conditions/states or events. Depending on the alarm types, you may only be able to choose one option; for example, Clusters and Datacenters only have events and not conditions/states. Whichever option you choose here will determine what triggers are available on the Triggers tab. You can also enable or disable an alarm on the General tab.

3. On the Triggers tab, add or remove the triggers that will cause the alarm to generate an alert. The options shown here will vary based on the alarm type you chose on the General tab. You will see multiple condition fields if you chose a condition/state alarm type; for event alarm types you will see a status field and an optional Advanced field where you set more complex triggers. The Condition Length field is new to vSphere and was desperately needed to reduce false alarms. In VI3, if you set an alarm so that VMs with

more than 90% CPU usage would send an alert, the alarm would trigger if that threshold was reached for only a few seconds. In most cases, you will not care if a VM has brief high CPU usage, but you'll want to know if that level of usage is sustained over a period of time. The new Condition Length field allows you to specify this so that the alarm condition will have to exist for a defined period of time before you are alerted. You can specify multiple triggers for an alarm, and specify if either any or all of the conditions must be satisfied before performing whatever actions are defined for the alarm.

4. On the Reporting tab, set a tolerance range and trigger frequency for the alarm. The tolerance range specifies a percentage above or below the configured threshold point, after which the alarm triggers or clears. A nonzero value triggers and clears the alarm only after the triggering condition falls above or below the tolerance range. The default value of 0 triggers and clears the alarm at the threshold point that is configured. The following calculation is used to trigger an alarm:

Condition threshold + Tolerance Range = Trigger alarm

For example, if you specified a trigger of 80% for host CPU usage and a tolerance range of 10%, the alarm would trigger at 90% and go back to normal at 70%, as shown in Figure 4.2.

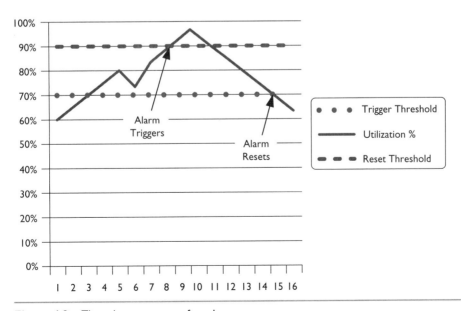

Figure 4.2   The tolerance range of an alarm

This is done to ensure that you do not transition alarm states based on false changes in a condition. The trigger frequency protects against repeated reporting of insignificant alarm transitions. If an alarm triggers, it will not trigger again based on the number of minutes set here. For example, if a VM with high CPU usage triggers at 1:00 p.m. and you had a ten-minute trigger frequency set, it would not trigger again until 1:10 p.m. if the conditions to satisfy the trigger still existed. Both of these settings are designed to protect against needless and false alarms.

5. On the Actions tab, define the actions that will occur once an alarm triggers. The available actions that are displayed will vary based on the object type that you chose on the General tab. For example, if you chose a Virtual Machine object, you will see actions related to VMs, such as Reboot, Power Off, and Migrate. The Configuration column is where you can enter text for actions that require configuration, such as an email address for the Send a Notification Email action or a command to run for the Run a Command action. The columns with the alert symbols represent the possible changes in alarm conditions (i.e., from warning to alert or warning to normal), and here you can set whether an action should occur once or repeatedly. For example, you may want to send emails or SNMP notifications every five minutes when a condition goes from warning to alert. If you do select the repeat option for an action, you can specify in the Frequency section how many minutes later the action should repeat.

vSphere has more than a hundred triggers that you can use, and alarms in vSphere are much more robust and powerful than what was available in VI3. You should spend some time exploring the different trigger options so that you can be alerted to events and conditions that occur in your environment. The new datastore disk usage alarm is especially valuable when you are using snapshots and thin disks, as you can be alerted when disk space is low.

PERMISSIONS AND ROLES

More granular permissions can now be set when defining roles to grant users access to specific functionality in vSphere. This allows much greater control and protection of your environment. You have many more permissions on datastores and networks now, so you can control such actions as vSwitch configuration and datastore browser file controls.

Permissions and Privileges

Permissions allow you to assign privileges to AD or local users or groups to perform certain actions and make changes to objects inside vCenter Server. vCenter Server permissions only affect users who log in to vCenter Server and do not apply when logging in to an ESX host directly. Permissions can be very granular, and dozens of them can be assigned to control specific access to the various objects inside vCenter Server. Permissions can be set on many different levels, from the very top datacenter level down to an individual VM. You can also control whether permissions propagate down from the level they are set to other objects below in the hierarchy. In addition, you can set multiple permissions for a user or group to control different access levels for different levels of objects inside VC. For example, you could grant a user read access at the top datacenter level so that the user can read all of the objects in the datacenter, but set higher access to specific objects such as ESX hosts or VMs.

Permissions work with roles, which allow you to create a set of privileges as a role to assign to a user and group. You cannot assign privileges directly to a user or group, and instead must assign privileges to a role and then assign a user to that role. Users can be assigned multiple roles with different privileges on different objects in vCenter Server. However, if a user has different levels of permissions on the same object, the most restrictive permissions apply. For example, if a user has read-only permission on a host and full administrator permission, the user would only have read-only permission.

Privileges are grouped into categories which are further broken down into subcategories and then down to the individual privilege. You can select privileges at any level of the category hierarchy, and the privileges below it are included with whatever you select. For example, selecting the Virtual Machine category selects all the subcategories and privileges under it. If you want to be more granular, you can uncheck the items under the category that you selected to achieve the desired privileges for the user or group.

You'll notice that a lot of privileges can be assigned, especially on a host and VM. Some actions in vCenter Server require multiple privileges to be assigned for the action to be completed. Many of the privileges are self-explanatory, but trying to figure out which ones are needed for certain actions can be confusing. Try creating a test user account and assign/remove privileges to it; then log in as that user and see if you can complete the action. If you can't, go back and add a privilege and try again. It is helpful sometimes to select a whole category of privileges and then remove them one by one until you achieve the desired permission level. Permissions can be set on many different types of objects in vCenter Server. You can view the permissions on a particular object in vCenter Server by clicking on the object and selecting the Permissions tab.

To assign permissions to users or groups, follow these steps.

1. Select an object in vCenter Server (e.g., Virtual Machine) in the left pane.
2. In the right pane, select the Permissions tab.
3. Right-click in the right pane and select the Add Permission option.
4. In the Users and Groups section, click the Add button.
5. In the Select Users window, select an Active Directory domain (or server) to use local users and groups. Once you select a domain, it will list the users and groups from which you can select. You can choose an individual user/group or multiple users/groups by holding the Ctrl and Shift keys when selecting. As you select users and groups, they will appear in the Users and Groups fields separated by a semicolon. A drop-down selection offers the option to display users or groups first, and to display everything in alphabetical order. You can also search for users/groups by entering text in the Input box and clicking the Search button. Once you have selected the users/groups, click the Add button to add them.
6. Select a role from the Assign Roles section and choose whether you want to propagate the permissions to child objects. Once you have selected the users/groups and role, click OK to save the permissions.

Roles

A role is a set of privileges that can be assigned to a user or group. Roles can be customized to include or exclude any of the many privileges that exist in vCenter Server. Privileges provide the right to perform a specific action; roles are a collection of privileges, and permissions are the application of a role to a user or group for an object. If a user is assigned to a role which is granted privileges on an object (e.g., ESX host), the user is able to see all information on that object, but will be able to perform only those actions for which he has been granted privileges, and nothing more. Many of the actions that will show for a full administrator will be masked or grayed out if the user does not have permissions for that action on that object. Additionally, if you apply permissions at a low level of a hierarchy (e.g., VM), users will not see the other objects (VMs) that they do not have permissions to see unless those permissions are specifically applied at a higher level. For example, if you assign a user the permission to manage a specific VM when the user logs in to vCenter Server, the user will see only the datacenter object and the VM. He will not see any other VMs, the ESX host that the VM is on, clusters, resource pools, and so on.

vCenter Server comes with some preconfigured roles that you can use, or you can create your own custom roles. These roles fall into two categories: system roles that are permanent and cannot be deleted or changed, and sample roles that are configured for certain types of access and can be modified and deleted. To access roles click the Administration button in vCenter Server and then select Roles. Once you select the Roles tab, you will see a list of configured roles. If you click on a role, you will see the users associated with that role, along with their assigned level of access.

You can add, rename, remove, and edit roles, as well as clone them when creating new roles so that you can make a copy of an existing role and modify it rather than starting from scratch. To create a role, follow these steps.

1. In vCenter Server, select the Administration button and then the Roles tab.

2. Click the Add Role button (or optionally select an existing role and click the Clone Role button).

3. Provide a name for the role and then select the privileges to assign to that role. If you select a category, everything under that category is automatically selected. You can deselect privileges if you do not want to include them.

4. Once you have selected all of the privileges that you want to grant to that role, select OK to save it.

5. To assign users to the role, click on the Permission tab for an object and add a permission and assign a user to the role.

Roles are a great way to assign access inside vCenter Server and should definitely be utilized to ensure that more access than is needed is not assigned to vCenter Server users. Toward that end, here are some best practices for using roles.

- Never assign more privileges than a user needs. Instead, create roles that are customized to a user's specific requirements. For example, to create a role for an operations team that is responsible for monitoring VMs, create a role that allows VM interactions only (i.e., power on, power off, reset, and console interaction). That way, the team can look at the console of a VM to see what is happening and power-cycle a VM if needed.

- Never assign more permissions than a user needs. Instead, assign permissions at the required level and avoid assigning them at the highest level, if possible. For example, if a network group needs access to only one or two VMs on a host, only assign permissions at the specific VM level to which the group needs access.

- Certain privileges can be very harmful to your hosts and should be assigned to users only if absolutely required. This includes any privilege that allows a user to delete, rename, remove, or create anything that can cause data loss, or that can cause datastores to be filled (e.g., snapshot creation), which can cause a denial of service attack on your VMs.

NEW HOME PAGE

In vSphere, VMware introduced a Home page concept for vCenter Server that provides better organization of inventory, administration, and management. VMware also reorganized things and added some new items, such as a Search function and a vCenter Server Status page. The Home page duplicates the functionality of the View menu but provides an easier visual reference for the many different areas that you can access in vCenter Server. It is grouped into the following four categories.

- **Inventory**—Contains views for the various inventory items, such as Hosts and Clusters, Datastores, and Networking. Also contains the Search function that allows you to search through the inventory for specific things.

- **Administration**—Contains views for the configuration of different settings specific to vCenter Server, including Roles, Licensing, and Settings. Also allows you to display the status of the various components that comprise vCenter Server.

- **Management**—Contains views for the items that are used to manage ESX and ESXi hosts, including Scheduled Tasks, Events, Host Profiles, and Maps.

- **Solutions and Applications**—Contains views for the add-on components that can be plugged into vCenter Server via plug-ins, such as Guided Consolidation and Update Manager, as well as other third-party plug-ins. Initially, this area is empty until plug-ins are installed.

All the items on the Home page can also be accessed by selecting View from the top menu and then choosing a category from the drop-down list. The Home page simply makes navigation a bit easier than continually having to select things from drop-down menus.

vCENTER SERVER SETTINGS

The vCenter Server Settings area is where you can configure settings that are specific to the operation of vCenter Server and have nothing to do with hosts and VMs. You can leave many of the settings at their defaults, but sometimes you may want to change them if you are experiencing problems, are troubleshooting, or have a large environment. You can access the settings from the Home page under Administration. Here is a description of the various settings.

- **Licensing**—This section only pertains to the licensing for the vCenter Server. Here you can choose which license key is used by vCenter Server, and assign a new key to use. You can also set this under Administration→Licensing. The other option in this section is to specify a VI3 licensing server to be used with VI3 hosts that are managed by the vCenter Server. This is used to preserve compatibility with the VI3 servers that require the old licensing server type. Once you no longer have any VI3 servers, you do not need this option.

- **Statistics**—This section is for specifying the collection interval for statistics from hosts and VMs. You can specify the collection interval (interval duration), retention period (save for), and amount of information collected (statistics level). The defaults are relatively conservative; if you adjust these settings, be aware that your database can grow quite large. For this reason, a database size estimator is also provided in this section. Also, be aware that if you change these settings, the existing data that was collected for the interval that you changed will be purged. The intervals are rolled up automatically into the next level via SQL stored procedures, so the database will grow to only a certain size and will not continue growing as older statistics are purged.

- **Runtime Settings**—This section is for changing information that is unique to the identity of the vCenter Server; this includes the vCenter Server's unique ID, managed IP address, and name. The unique ID is a number from 0 to 63 that uniquely identifies each vCenter Server system running in a common environment, and is generated randomly. You will normally not have to modify these settings unless you have multiple vCenter Servers operating in a Linked Mode group.

- **Active Directory**—This section is for specifying AD-related settings. You can increase the Timeout setting if your AD servers are on wide area networks. You can increase the Query Limit if you have a large AD domain with many group/user objects. The Validation section is used to validate that users and groups are still valid in AD. By default, vCenter Server will validate all the users and groups that are used in permissions on vCenter Server objects once per day. This means it will look at all the users and groups and make sure they still exist in AD; if they do not, the permissions are automatically deleted. vCenter Server does not use system identifiers (SIDs), which are long strings of letters and numbers that Windows uses to uniquely identify users. If an account is deleted in AD and re-created with the same name, it will have a different SID in Windows and will not have access to any of the Windows permissions it previously had. However, to vCenter Server it will look like the same account and will have the same permissions, because vCenter Server only uses the domain and username of the user and not the SID. You can disable this feature entirely and change the interval from the default of 1,440 minutes (one day). If you are concerned about security in your environment, you should lower the validation period (e.g., 120 minutes). VMware recommends that you do not disable this feature, as it protects the VC by automatically removing permissions that are no longer valid.

- **Mail**—This section is where you set the IP address of the SMTP server that will be used to send email from any alarm actions that are configured to send emails when triggered. The account is simply the email address that will be used in the From portion of the email.

- **SNMP**—This section is where you set the SNMP receivers that will be used to receive SNMP alerts from any alarm actions that are configured to send SNMP alerts when triggered. You can enter the receiver URL/IP address, port number, and community string that is required to send alerts to the external monitoring system that will be receiving them.

- **Ports**—This section is used to configure the ports that will be used by the Tomcat web server that is installed as part of vCenter Server for web access. You will not need to change these unless you have another web server (e.g., IIS) running on the vCenter Server that is using those ports.

- **Timeout Settings**—This section is used to specify the timeout intervals for vCenter Server operations. These intervals specify the amount of time after which the vSphere Client times out. You can increase these if you have problems with client timeouts during operations. Do not set these to 0.

- **Logging Options**—This section specifies the details of the logging information that is written to vCenter Server's log file, which is typically located in C:\Documents and Settings\All Users\Application Data\VMware\VMware VirtualCenter\Logs. You can specify more or less logging from the default

Informational setting. This can be useful when troubleshooting problems. Changes to this setting take effect immediately without requiring that you restart vCenter Server.

- **Database**—This section specifies the maximum number of database connections that vCenter Server will open to its SQL database that is used to store configuration and performance information. The default of 10 is usually sufficient in most cases, but you might want to increase this number if your vCenter Server system frequently performs many operations and performance is critical. You might want to decrease this number if the database is shared and connections to the database are costly.

- **Database Retention Policy**—This section specifies when old tasks and events should be purged from the vCenter Server database. The default is to keep them forever and to never purge them, which can make your database quite large over time. In VI3, there was no way to purge these without running manual and complicated SQL scripts. These settings were added to vSphere to make this operation easier, and VMware recommends that you use them to keep your database size down, which can help to increase the performance of vCenter Server.

- **SSL Settings**—This section is where you can configure vCenter Server to check the SSL certificates of hosts to which it connects. If you select this option, vCenter Server, the vSphere Client, and Web Access clients check for valid SSL certificates before connecting to a host for such operations as adding a host or making a remote console connection to a VM.

- **Advanced Settings**—This section is where you can specify advanced configuration parameters for vCenter Server. Many of these settings are populated automatically from the settings that are set via the vCenter Server Settings GUI. It is not recommended that you add/change/remove these settings unless you are sure what the results will be or are instructed to do so by VMware support.

SEARCHING

The new searching feature can be very useful for running custom queries against your hosts and VMs in your vCenter Server environment. Using search, you can build queries using the information that is provided in the vCenter Server inventory columns. The drop-down field allows you to select the object to search on; you can then type a search phrase, such as "Windows Server 2003" to show all the VMs running that operating system. If you click the Show Options link, you can build queries by selecting inventory fields. You can use the drop-down field to select a property and then add search criteria for that property. For example, if you wanted to display all your VMs that had VMware Tools not installed, you could select that property and run the search to get the results. You can also build complex queries using multiple properties by using the Add button. Search results cannot be exported or printed, but they can still be useful for quickly finding information without having to search multiple areas for it.

PLUG-INS

Plug-ins are additional modules that VMware and third-party vendors have developed to seamlessly integrate with vCenter Server. The benefit of plug-ins is that they add additional functionality and management to vCenter Server and allow for a single console to be used for everything. They can also leverage the authentication in vCenter Server so that users do not have to log in multiple times. Some plug-ins install on the vCenter Server itself, and others also have a client piece that installs on workstations in the vSphere Client. vSphere Client plug-ins must be installed into each instance of the vSphere Client as that is where they are executed and launched. The following plug-ins are installed by default with vCenter Server.

- **vCenter Storage Monitoring**—This plug-in supports a special storage view that shows as a tab when selecting objects such as hosts, VMs, and clusters. It is enabled by default. Once you select an object in the left pane, you can select the Storage View tab in the right pane. The Storage View is a very handy view that shows detailed storage information. Only a few columns show by default, but you can add more by right-clicking on the column headings and selecting them, as shown in Figure 4.3.

  One particularly valuable column is labeled "Snapshot Space"; in this column you can sort and quickly see the size of all snapshots in your environment. Additionally, you can see the actual sizes of thin disks and the amount of space taken up by VM swap files and other files.

- **vCenter Service Status**—This plug-in is used to display the status of the various vCenter Server services. It is enabled by default, and you can see the information that it monitors on the Administration→vCenter Service Status page.

- **vCenter Hardware Status**—This plug-in is used to gather the hardware status of hosts using Common Information Model (CIM) monitoring. It is

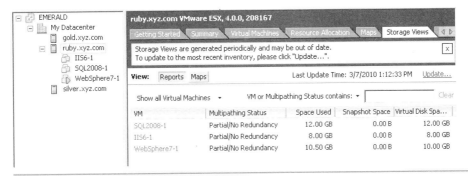

Figure 4.3   The Storage View plug-in

enabled by default, and it displays the information on the Hardware Status tab in the right pane when a host is selected in the left pane.

You can manage plug-ins by selecting the Plug-ins option from the top menu when connected to a vCenter Server, and then selecting Manage Plug-ins. A new window will appear that will display both installed and available plug-ins. You will not see any available plug-ins until you install them first on the vCenter Server. Once they are installed there, you can install them on individual vSphere Clients. There are some additional plug-ins that VMware provides, as well as many third-party plug-ins, that we will cover next.

GUIDED CONSOLIDATION

Guided Consolidation uses a built-in wizard to discover physical servers, analyze them to see if they are good candidates for conversion into VMs, and convert them into VMs using the Converter application. This feature is based on the Capacity Planner tool that VMware business partners use to analyze customer environments; however, Guided Consolidation only works with servers running Microsoft Windows. This plug-in is not installed by default, and must be installed either on the vCenter Server or on a separate server so that it does not impact the vCenter Server. The installation media for this plug-in is on the vCenter Server install media. If you execute autorun, you will see a menu where you can choose to install Guided Consolidation.

When you install the plug-in you will be prompted for a user account to use for the collector service; this must be a local administrator on the server on which you are installing on the plug-in. You will also be prompted for ports to use as well as a vCenter Server and credentials to connect to it. As part of the installation, the plug-in will install a special collector server to gather perform-ance statistics from physical servers that will be used to analyze them as part of sizing an appropriate VM for them. Once the plug-in is installed, you can launch it from the vSphere Client by selecting the Guided Consolidation icon located under the Solutions and Applications section of the Home page.

You should first configure Guided Consolidation by specifying default creden-tials to use to log in to physical servers so that they can be analyzed. This can be a local administrator account, but it is often easier to use a domain administra-tor account that has privileges on all servers. You can also specify AD domains that contain physical servers that you wish to analyze. Once you have that con-figured, you can specify physical servers to begin analyzing by name, IP address, or domain. You should analyze servers for long enough (30 days is recommend-ed) that you get a good idea of their resource usage over a period of time and through multiple business process cycles. Once you analyze the servers and want to convert them into VMs, you use the Converter plug-in, which we will cover next.

CONVERTER

Converter is used to convert physical servers into VMs, but it can also be used for VM-to-VM conversions. It comes in two editions. The free Standalone edi-tion is a stand-alone application that can install on any Windows system to con-vert it to a VM. The Enterprise edition has two components: a service that is installed on the vCenter Server or another server, and a vSphere Client plug-in component that is installed on any workstations that are running the vSphere Client and want to use Converter. The Enterprise edition is integrated into both the vCenter Server and the vSphere Client and provides easy Physical-to-Virtual and Virtual-to-Virtual (P2V and V2V) conversions with just a few simple steps.

This plug-in is not installed by default, and must be installed either on the vCenter Server or on a separate server so that it does not impact the vCenter Server. The installation media for this plug-in is on the vCenter Server install media. If you execute autorun, you will see a menu where you can choose to install vCenter Converter.

When you install the plug-in you will be prompted for a vCenter Server to con-nect to; once the plug-in is installed, you have to install a client component into the vSphere Client. If you connect to the vCenter Server and launch the Plug-in Manager, you will see vCenter Converter listed under Available Plug-ins. You can click the Download and Install link to add the plug-in to the vSphere Client; this must be done for every separate instance of the vSphere Client. Once the plug-in is installed on your vSphere Client, an Import Machine option will appear in the menu when you right-click on a host or cluster. When you select this option it will launch the Converter Wizard where you can specify a source physical server or VM and a host destination.

The plug-in allows you to do hot cloning of powered-on servers; a separate cold clone option enables you to boot from a live CD so that the source server operating system is not running. The cold clone method ensures that no files are in use on the server that you are cloning, and is the most reliable and safest cloning method. The live CD contains a slim Windows PE operating system which loads the same Converter application that is used in the Standalone edition. The cold clone ISO is available for download from the vCenter Server download page. To ensure successful conversions, there are some best practices that you should follow, available at http://vsphere-land.com/tips-tricks/converter-tips. Following these best practices will help to ensure that your conversions are successful. For more information on Converter, see the Converter Administration Guide on VMware's website (www.vmware.com/pdf/vsp_vcc_41_admin_guide.pdf).

VMWARE DATA RECOVERY

The VMware Data Recovery plug-in is installed by a separate download file that is available as an ISO file from VMware's website. VMware Data Recovery is VMware's disk-to-disk backup application for VMs. You will be able to install and use this plug-in only if your edition of vSphere supports it. We will cover this plug-in in more detail in Chapter 8.

UPDATE MANAGER

Update Manager is a plug-in for vCenter Server that adds additional patching capabilities to vSphere. You can use it to patch both ESX and ESXi hosts as well as VMs running Windows or Linux. Update Manager automates patching and works by using a baseline and then installing patches and updates on hosts and VMs that need them. Update Manager can scan and remediate VMs and templates in any power state (on/off/suspended), as well as any host that is powered on. Snapshots are taken of VMs prior to upgrading them so that they can be reverted back in case there is a problem with the patches that have been applied. You can run Update Manager on Windows workstations. It consists of the plug-in component to the vSphere Client, a Windows service that can run on the vCenter Server, and a database that is used to store patch metadata and other information. This database is different from the one vCenter Server uses, and you can use any of the formats that are also supported by vCenter Server. You can use SQL 2005 Express, which can be installed with Update Manager, but it is recommended that you use one of the other databases for larger production environments.

This plug-in is not installed by default, and must be installed either on vCenter Server or on a separate server so that it does not impact vCenter Server. The installation media for this plug-in is on the vCenter Server install media. If you execute autorun, you will see a menu where you can choose to install vCenter Update Manager.

When you install the plug-in you will be prompted for a vCenter Server to connect to, and you will then be prompted to either create a new database using SQL 2005 Express or use an existing database. If you have a large environment, it is recommended that you install Update Manager on a separate server and to not use SQL 2005 Express. For smaller environments where vCenter Server uses SQL 2005 Express, you can use that existing instance when installing Update Manager on vCenter Server. You will also be prompted for ports to use; normally, the defaults are fine—a directory location to install Update Manager to and a directory location to store downloaded patches. It is recommended that the location for downloaded patches have at least 20GB of free disk space, as many patches are downloaded.

Once Update Manager is installed, you can install the plug-in into the vSphere Client by going to the Plug-in Manager. Windows Services for Update Manager will be installed on either the vCenter Server or the server that you specified during installation. Once the plug-in is installed, you can launch it from the vSphere Client by selecting the Update Manager icon located under the Solutions and Applications section of the Home page. Four main tabs or pages are used with Update Manager. The Getting Started tab is optional, and you can close it if you do not want to see it. The Baselines tab is where you create and manage your host and VM baselines. The Configuration tab is where you set options for guest and host settings, how frequently updates are downloaded, and Internet connection and port settings. The Events tab shows you all the events that have taken place that are associated with Update Manager. The Patch Repository tab shows you all of the host and VM updates that have been downloaded and can be applied.

To use Update Manager you must first download any patches for it. The settings and schedule for this are located on the Configuration tab. Next you create baselines, which can be either upgraded or patch baselines and which contain a collection of one or more patches, service packs and bug fixes, or upgrades. Baseline groups are made from existing baselines and might contain one upgrade baseline per type and one or more patch baselines, or a combination of multiple patch baselines. Once you have baselines configured, you scan hosts and VMs to evaluate them against baselines and baseline groups to determine their level of compliance. Ones that are missing patches are considered not in compliance with the baseline, so the final step is to remediate them. Remediation installs the missing patches and upgrades to your hosts and VMs. For ESXi hosts, updates are all-inclusive because ESXi consists of a single image file, so the most recent update contains the patches from all previous releases. For ESX hosts, if a patch is dependent on another patch, Update Manager will install it together with the prerequisite patch. Patches that conflict with each other are automatically not installed or are uninstalled if another patch supersedes the conflicting patch.

Update Manager greatly simplifies the patching process of your virtual hosts. An added benefit is that it can patch many of your guest operating systems and applications that run on them. For more information on using Update Manager check out the Update Manager Administration Guide at www.vmware.com/pdf/vsp_vum_40_admin_guide.pdf.

THIRD-PARTY PLUG-INS

Many third-party vendor plug-ins are available to integrate the management of third-party software and hardware with vCenter Server. These plug-ins range from simple web UIs that integrate as a tab in the vSphere Client, to applications that are fully integrated into the vSphere Client. Plug-ins allow for the centralized management of various vCenter Server subcomponents, such as storage and backup applications. An example of this is a plug-in from NetApp, called the Virtual Storage Console, which allows you to manage the network storage devices that you use with vSphere directly from within vCenter Server without having to use a separate management application. Third-party plug-ins are a great way to integrate all aspects of your vSphere environment into one console, and more and more vendors are developing them for use with vSphere.

SUMMARY

vCenter Server has many enhancements in vSphere that make it much more robust and scalable, as well as improve the administration and management of VMs. If you are using vCenter Server to manage your hosts, you should ensure that you always connect to it instead of the individual hosts with the vSphere client to do all your administration. vCenter Server's database is critical to its proper operation, so ensure that you maintain it properly and do not allow it to grow too large. As vCenter Server is your centralized management component for all your hosts, ensuring that it stays healthy and problem-free will make administration much easier.

STORAGE IN vSPHERE

You have a lot of options when it comes to choosing what storage to use with vSphere. You also have many choices to make when configuring whatever storage you are using. Storage is the most critical resource in vSphere, and making the wrong decisions when choosing or configuring it can be costly in both dollars and performance. Therefore, you should take your time and make sure you understand your requirements and all the options available when making your storage decisions.

WHAT'S NEW WITH STORAGE IN vSPHERE

In Chapter 1, we briefly covered some of the new storage features in vSphere, and in Chapter 3 we covered two of them—thin disks and VMDirectPath—in detail. In this chapter, we will discuss some additional storage features in detail. (We will not cover Storage VMotion in this chapter, and instead will do so in Chapter 9.)

vSTORAGE APIs

The vStorage APIs were introduced in vSphere and were developed to allow tight integration of advanced storage capabilities between vSphere and third-party storage applications and devices. The vStorage APIs allow vSphere and its storage devices to come together for improved efficiency and better management. The vStorage APIs consist of a collection of interfaces that third-party vendors can leverage to seamlessly interact with storage in vSphere. "vStorage APIs" is a marketing term used to describe the various ways in which the APIs integrate into different storage areas. The following four categories of vStorage APIs are available.

- **vStorage APIs for Array Integration**—The framework exists in vSphere, but the specific APIs are not currently available and are being co-developed with specific storage vendors (Dell, NetApp, and EMC) to enable storage array-based capabilities directly from within vSphere. These capabilities include array-based snapshots, copy offload, write same offload, atomic test and set, integration between VMware and array-level thin provisioning, storage provisioning, and replication. These capabilities will enable vSphere to act more efficiently for certain storage-related operations by allowing the storage array to perform certain operations. Here are additional details regarding three of these capabilities.

  - **Copy offload**—Virtual machine (VM) cloning or template-based deployment can be hardware-accelerated by array offloads rather than file-level copy operations at the ESX server. This technology could also be applied to Storage VMotion.

  - **Write same offload**—When provisioning an Eager-Zeroed VMDK the formatting process sends gigabytes' worth of zeros from the ESX/ESXi host to the array. With offload the array could format the Eager-Zeroed thick VMDK.

  - **Enhanced file locking**—VMware may upgrade its traditional "File locking" and "SCSI reservation" mechanism by implementing a more efficient mechanism which is atomic (i.e., handled in a single operation). This enhancement should allow for an increase in the number of ESX/ESXi hosts deployed in a cluster with VMFS datastores. Note that with Network File System (NFS) datastores, locking and reservations are handled by the array.

  As the vStorage APIs mature, expect to see more API integration in the areas of NFS enhancements, snapshot offload, and array management.

- **vStorage APIs for Multipathing**—These APIs are specifically designed for third-party storage vendors to leverage array multipathing functionality through plug-ins that they can develop. The Pluggable Storage Architecture (PSA) uses these APIs so that vendors can more intelligently utilize multipathing to achieve better storage I/O throughput and storage path failover for their specific storage array. Each storage vendor must certify its Multipathing Extensions Modules with VMware for use with ESX(i). Currently, the multipathing plug-ins only exist for iSCSI and Fibre Channel (FC) storage; support for NFS may be added in the future.

- **vStorage APIs for Site Recovery Manager (SRM)**—These APIs are part of VMware's Site Recovery Manager product and are used to integrate SRM with array-based replication for block and network attached storage (NAS) storage models. This allows SRM to seamlessly handle both VM and host failover as well as storage replication failover, and also enables SRM to control the underlying array-based replication that it relies on. Storage vendors that want to provide support for SRM must develop a Site Recovery Adapter (SRA) for their storage subsystem. The SRA, once certified by the vendor and accepted by VMware, allows the storage subsystem to be used by SRM to protect sites against disasters.

- **vStorage APIs for Data Protection**—These APIs are the successor to the VMware Consolidated Backup (VCB) Framework that was introduced in VI3. The vStorage APIs make up for many of the shortcomings of VCB. However, unlike VCB, they are not a separate stand-alone framework; instead, they are built directly into vSphere and require no additional software installation, like VCB did. Although the vStorage APIs for Data Protection include the functionality that was available in VCB, they also add new functionality such as Changed Block Tracking (CBT) and the ability to directly interact with the contents of virtual disks via the VMware Virtual Disk Development Kit (VDDK). These APIs are specifically targeted at third-party backup and data protection applications to provide better integration and greater flexibility.

CBT is a significant new storage feature that is especially important to backup, replication, and data protection applications. In vSphere, the VMkernel now has the ability to track which disk blocks of a VM have changed from a particular time, and using the vStorage APIs for Data Protection applications third-party backup and replication applications can simply query the VMkernel to obtain this information rather than try to figure it out on its own. CBT has a big impact in several areas. The first is when replicating VM disk files to other locations for disaster recovery purposes. Because of CBT, near-real-time continuous data protection can be achieved. Another impact concerns incremental backups, which are much faster using CBT as the backup application can simply query the VMkernel and instantly know which blocks to back up since the last backup. Finally, CBT makes restoring data much easier as the backup application knows exactly what blocks need to be put back to the virtual disk for the select-ed restore point.

CBT is disabled by default because there is a slight performance overhead asso-ciated with using the feature. It can be enabled on only certain VMs that require it by adding a configuration parameter to the VM. Backup applications that support CBT can also enable it on VMs. Once enabled, CBT stores information about changed blocks in a special –ctk.vmdk file that is created in each VM's home directory. To do this, CBT utilizes changeIDs, which are unique identifiers for the state of a virtual disk at a particular point in time. New changeIDs are created anytime a snapshot of a VM is created, which all backup applications do before backing up a VM. With that changeID, the next time a backup applica-tion goes to back up a VM, it will know the time of the last backup and all the blocks that have changed since then. CBT is only supported on VMs that have VM hardware version 7, which is new to vSphere, so any VMs with an older VM hardware version will need to have their virtual hardware upgraded before you can begin using CBT with them.

The vStorage APIs are actually a combination of various SDKs that VMware has made available with vSphere as well as with its VDDK. The vStorage APIs lever-age these technologies to integrate directly with vSphere and perform certain operations. For example, whereas VM snapshots can be managed using the SDK functionality, other operations such as mounting virtual disks are handled through the VDDK. Some of the vStorage APIs are publicly available (e.g., Data Protection), while others are only available to specific vendors because they require significant co-development work with VMware (e.g., Array Integration). The vStorage APIs enable third-party vendors and developers to bring signifi-cant enhancements to the VMware product line. I view these APIs as one of the most significant improvements to the vSphere platform.

PARAVIRTUALIZATION

Paravirtualization is a technology that is available for certain operating systems that utilize a special driver to communicate directly with the hypervisor, as shown in Figure 5.1.

Unlike the normal binary translation method, paravirtualization allows for greater throughput and lower CPU utilization for VMs, and is useful for disk I/O-intensive applications. Paravirtualized SCSI (PVSCSI) adapters are sepa-rate storage adapters that you can enable by editing a VM's settings and

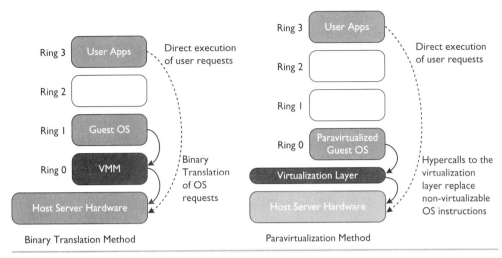

Figure 5.1   Binary translation compared to paravirtualization

enabling the paravirtualization feature. Unlike VMDirectPath, where you must dedicate adapters to a VM, PVSCSI adapters can be shared by multiple VMs on host servers.

PVSCSI adapters are only supported on Windows 2003, Windows 2008, and Red Hat Enterprise Linux 5 VMs. You can use PVSCSI adapters with any type of storage, including FC, hardware and software iSCSI, and NFS. You can also use them with Direct Attached Storage (DAS), but VMware does not recommend this because there is not much benefit to it. When VMware released vSphere 4.0, PVSCSI adapters were only supported for use with nonboot operating system disks. So, you had to use a regular LSI Logic or BusLogic virtual SCSI adapter for the boot disk of a VM and add an additional disk using the PVSCSI adapter for your applications. Beginning with vSphere 4.0, Update 1, this changed, and you can now use PVSCSI adapters for boot disks, but only on Windows 2003 and 2008 VMs; Red Hat Enterprise Linux 5 still does not support use of PVSC-SI adapters for boot disks. PVSCSI adapters can provide increased I/O perform-ance for applications that may need it, but they do have some limitations.

- The Fault Tolerance (FT) feature cannot be used with VMs that have PVSC-SI adapters.
- Disk hot add or remove requires a bus rescan from within the guest.
- Disks with snapshots might not experience performance gains when used on PVSCSI adapters or if memory on the ESX host is overcommitted.

- If you upgrade from Red Hat Enterprise Linux 5 to an unsupported kernel, you might not be able to access data on the VM's PVSCSI disks. You can run vmware-config-tools.pl with the `kernel-version` parameter to regain access.

- Because the default type of newly hot-added SCSI adapters depends on the type of primary (boot) SCSI controller, hot-adding a PVSCSI adapter is not supported.

You can add a PVSCSI adapter to a new VM or to an existing VM. To add a PVSCSI adapter when you create a new VM you must choose the Custom wizard type, and then choose VM hardware version 7. If you are using a PVSCSI adapter for your boot disk on Windows 2003 and 2008, be aware that these operating systems do not include the special OS driver needed to use the adapter, and consequently you will not see the disk when you try to install the OS. As a result, you will need to tell Windows to use a special driver disk during installation. Fortunately, VMware has made this easy; beginning with version 4.0, Update 1, the company has included the drivers on a floppy image located in the vmimages folder that is installed by default on all hosts. To install the PVSCSI driver for Windows follow these steps.

1. During the Windows installation, press F6 when prompted to use a third-party SCSI driver.

2. Edit the settings of the VM. Select the floppy drive and choose the "Use existing floppy image in datastore" option for the device type.

3. Click the Browse button and select the vmimages folder in the Browse Datastores list.

4. Select the floppies folder and then select the appropriate (Win2003 or Win2008) PVSCSI floppy image.

5. Select the "Connected in the device status" checkbox and click OK.

6. In Windows, when the appropriate screen appears, press S to specify an additional device driver, and then press Enter when prompted to insert a floppy disk containing the driver.

7. The VMware PVSCSI controller will be displayed and highlighted. Press Enter to select it and then press Enter again to continue the Windows installation.

If you are adding a PVSCSI controller to a VM after the OS has been installed, the driver for it is included as part of the VMware Tools installation. You can also choose an LSI Logic controller when you first create a VM, and install the OS and then change the adapter to a PVSCSI adapter type afterward.

It is recommended that you use PVSCSI adapters only for applications that have high disk I/O requirements. In testing PVSCSI adapters against the standard LSI Logic adapter, VMware has seen improvements in both disk throughput and CPU efficiency. In particular, PVSCSI adapters provide the most benefit for CPU efficiency no matter what type of storage is used. The degree of CPU efficiency is greatest for smaller I/O sizes and tapers off above 32KB. So, you might be wondering whether you should use PVSCSI all the time. VMware has conducted tests on this and has found that for low I/O workloads the LSI Logic adapter is so efficient that there is no need to use PVSCSI to improve efficiency. The CPU efficiency difference between the two at low I/O-per-second (IOPS) levels is so small that it is insignificant. However, where there are very high IOPS levels (10,000–15,000 IOPS) the CPU efficiency is much greater.

In its tests, VMware has found that PVSCSI is better than LSI Logic, except when the VM is performing at less than 2,000 IOPS and is issuing more than four outstanding I/Os. You can read more details on when to use PVSCSI in Knowledge Base article 1017652 (http://kb.vmware.com/kb/1017652), and you can read more about the performance benefits of PVSCSI in VMware's white paper, "PVSCSI Storage Performance" (www.vmware.com/pdf/vsp_4_pvscsi_perf.pdf).

GROWING VMFS VOLUMES

The ability to grow a VMFS volume without using extents is new to vSphere. In VI3, it was possible to increase the size of an existing VMFS volume by appending an additional LUN to it so that the VMFS volume extended across multiple LUNs. Although this works, it is generally not a recommended practice because a LUN failure at the root extent can take down the whole VMFS volume. Also, VMs can end up spanning LUNs when using extents, which can cause performance problems. In vSphere, you can grow a VMFS volume up to the 2TB LUN size limit without using extents, simply by increasing the LUN size on your storage array. Extents can still be used if you wish to grow a VMFS volume larger than the 2TB limit of a single LUN. VMFS volumes have a maximum size of 64TB minus 16KB. You can grow a VMFS volume without any downtime to the VMs that are on that datastore. To grow a VMFS volume follow these steps.

1. First you must increase the size of the LUN on your storage array. In this example, a 1,024GB LUN with an existing 1,024GB VMFS volume will be expanded to 1,536GB, as shown in Figure 5.2.

Figure 5.2   Expanding a LUN on an HP Modular Smart Array (MSA) storage array

2. Once you have increased the LUN size, in the vSphere Client, select a host to which the VMFS volume is visible, and on the Configuration tab, choose Storage. Select the storage volume that you want to expand, and click the Properties link.

3. The storage volume properties will be displayed similar to Figure 5.3. As you can see, the existing volume is 953GB and the device is showing as 1.4TB. Click the Increase button to expand it.

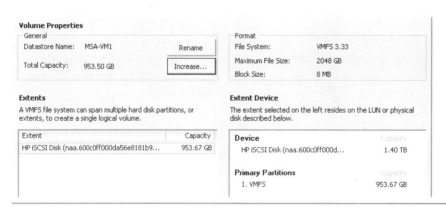

Figure 5.3   VMFS storage volume

4. The Increase Datastore Capacity Wizard will launch and display the LUNs connected to that host, similar to Figure 5.4. You can add LUNs to the

datastore as extents, or if the LUN has grown it will show "Yes" in the Expandable column. Select the Expandable LUN and click Next.

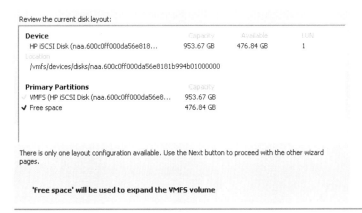

Extent Device
Select a LUN to create a datastore or expand the current one

Name	Path ID	LUN	Capacity	Expandable
HITACHI Fibre Channel Disk (t10.HI...	vmhba0:C0:T0:L9	9	600.00 GB	No
HITACHI Fibre Channel Disk (t10.HI...	vmhba0:C0:T0:L11	11	600.00 GB	No
HP iSCSI Disk (naa.600c0ff000da56...	iqn.1986-03.com....	1	953.67 GB	Yes
HITACHI Fibre Channel Disk (t10.HI...	vmhba0:C0:T0:L13	13	600.00 GB	No

Figure 5.4 Layout showing the LUNs attached to a host, and whether they are expandable

5. On the Current Disk Layout screen, you can see the device and the free space that will be used to expand the datastore, similar to Figure 5.5. Click Next to continue.

Review the current disk layout:

Device	Capacity	Available	LUN
HP iSCSI Disk (naa.600c0ff000da56e818...	953.67 GB	476.84 GB	1

Location
/vmfs/devices/disks/naa.600c0ff000da56e8181b994b01000000

Primary Partitions	Capacity
VMFS (HP iSCSI Disk (naa.600c0ff000da56e8...	953.67 GB
✔ Free space	476.84 GB

There is only one layout configuration available. Use the Next button to proceed with the other wizard pages.

'Free space' will be used to expand the VMFS volume

Figure 5.5 Disk layout showing current size of the storage volume and available space

6. On the Extent Size screen, you can specify the size by which to increase the datastore. The default is Maximize Capacity, which uses all the free space on the LUN. Select the size and click Next.

7. On the Ready to Complete screen, click Finish to begin expanding the datastore, or go back and change your settings. Once the operation completes, you will see that the datastore is now 1.4TB, as shown in Figure 5.6.

Figure 5.6   VMFS storage volume, grown to 1.4TB

The ability to increase VMFS datastore size can be very useful, as most virtual environments grow over time and more space is needed. In particular, it can be extremely useful if you are running large snapshots that you need to delete, but you do not have the necessary room on your datastore. Some vendors provide vCenter plug-ins which will automate the process of expanding VMFS volumes. One example is the Virtual Storage Console for NetApp NAS and SAN, and another is the Celerra plug-in for NAS from EMC. This type of integration may be standard from all vendors in the future.

CHOOSING A STORAGE TYPE

Storage is probably the most important hardware choice you will make when selecting hardware for your vSphere environment. Because most storage relies on a mechanical device (except for solid-state drives), it is often the first resource bottleneck that is encountered in a virtual infrastructure. Consequently, choosing a proper storage solution is critical to ensuring a successful virtualization project. Many variables will come into play when choosing a storage option for your virtual environment. What you can afford will play a large part in determining which option you choose; likewise, the disk I/O requirements for the applications you plan to run will also be a major factor. So, analyze the storage choices carefully and make sure you understand the differences between the various choices available to you.

LOCAL STORAGE

Local storage is typically cheap and reliable and is good to have on ESX hosts, even if you plan to run all your VMs on shared storage.

Advantages of using local storage include the following.

- It is cheap and reliable.
- It is a good choice for running development and test VMs so that you can save your shared storage for production servers.

- It is good for backing up VMs that are on shared storage. You can run scripts that periodically snapshot a VM and then copy the VM's disk files from shared storage to local storage as an additional backup option.

- The Storage VMotion feature allows you to move running VMs from one ESX host to another by first copying the VM to shared storage and then copying it back to local storage on another ESX host.

- It could be a great low-cost option for hosting stateless VDI VMs that do not require advanced feature support, such as High Availability (HA), Distributed Resource Scheduler (DRS), and VMotion.

Disadvantages of using local storage include the following.

- It cannot use advanced features (e.g., HA, DRS, VMotion) that require shared storage.

- It is not available for other hosts to use. Only the local host can access it.

- It adds additional expense to the physical host server cost.

Unless you are using the boot from SAN feature, you should consider getting at least two local disks that are using RAID on your ESX host, and more if you can afford it. Another option for local storage is to turn it into shared storage that other ESX hosts can use. This is considered a virtual storage area network (SAN) that can be accessed over the network using either the iSCSI or NFS protocol. Several free and paid products can do this, including OpenFiler, StarWind iSCSI SAN, and LeftHand's Virtual Storage Appliance. These applications provide a lower-cost alternative to using one of the traditional shared storage solutions.

DIRECT ATTACHED STORAGE

DAS is similar to local storage, but instead of being internal to a server it is external and connected to the server using a SCSI controller (typically Serial Attached SCSI or SAS) and cable. Unlike local internal storage, though, DAS can be shared among several servers as DAS units have multiple SCSI ports on them. As a result, you can use it with vSphere as shared storage among several hosts. Because DAS connects directly to servers via SCSI cables, no expensive switches are needed between the storage unit and the server, as is the case with other types of shared storage. DAS runs at the speed of the SCSI controller, which is either 3GB/s or 6GB/s, and offers great performance at an affordable price. DAS is best for smaller environments, as it does not support as many connections as other shared storage solutions due to its limited connection ports. The HP StorageWorks 2000sa G2 MSA is one example of a DAS array.

Advantages of using DAS include the following.

- It is an affordable shared storage option, as no expensive switches are needed.
- It provides good speed and performance due to the direct connection to the host.
- It has some of the same features (e.g., management, snapshots) that SAN storage devices have.
- Its block-level storage can be used with VMFS volumes.
- It is a form of secure and isolated storage that is not directly exposed to the network.

There is one disadvantage to using DAS.

- It has a limited number of host connections.

FIBRE CHANNEL STORAGE

FC traditionally uses fiber-optic cables to connect FC host bus adapters (HBAs) to SAN storage devices (arrays) through special FC switches. Speeds can vary from 1GB/s to 8GB/s with 4GB/s being the most popular speed today. All components in an FC network must support whichever speed you use. This includes the FC HBA, the FC switch, and the FC controller on the storage device. If the devices have different speeds, the speed of the slowest component will determine the speed for that path. Each FC HBA has a unique World Wide Name (WWN) which is similar to a network MAC address. FC networks typically have multiple redundant paths from the host servers to the arrays that include multiple HBAs, switches, and controllers.

vSphere supports a technology called N_Port ID Virtualization (NPIV) which enables a single FC HBA port to register several unique WWNs with the SAN fabric, each of which can be assigned to an individual VM. This is similar to assigning multiple IP addresses to a single network adapter and allows you to monitor and route storage access on a per-VM basis. Without NPIV, VMs access storage LUNs with the WWNs of their host's physical HBAs.

FC storage is generally the most popular storage choice for ESX in larger environments. This is because of its speed (4GB/s FC has been around for years, and 8GB/s is now supported) and reliability (FC networks are isolated and more secure than Ethernet network storage devices).

Advantages of using FC storage include the following.

- It is a commonly deployed enterprise storage architecture.
- It typically is the best performing and most secure storage access technology.
- ESX is able to boot from FC storage.
- It features block-level storage that can be used with VMFS volumes.

Disadvantages of using FC storage include the following.

- It is typically the most expensive storage option to implement from scratch.
- It can be complex to implement and manage, and it typically requires dedicated storage administrators.

If you already have an FC SAN solution in your environment, using it with ESX just makes sense. Expanding an existing SAN is much easier and cheaper than implementing a new SAN from scratch. Also, designing a SAN architecture and administering it usually requires specialized training which can further add to the expense of implementing it. Many larger environments that use SANs have dedicated storage administrators to do this.

If you plan to have many high disk I/O VMs running on your ESX hosts, you should seriously consider using SAN storage to achieve maximum performance. Ultimately, cost is usually the factor that determines whether you will use SAN storage or choose a less expensive alternative.

iSCSI Storage

iSCSI is a relatively new type of network storage that was supported beginning with ESX 3.0. It works by using a client called an initiator to send SCSI commands over a local area network to SCSI devices (called targets) located on a remote storage device. An iSCSI target is not the same thing as a SCSI target. An iSCSI target is the server that communicates with the iSCSI initiator to facilitate the exchange of SCSI commands between the client and the server. A SCSI target is the number used to identify which device on the SCSI bus you're talking to; for example, the boot device is typically target 0 (0:0 = bus 0 : target 0). iSCSI utilizes traditional networking components and TCP/IP and does not require special cables and switches, like FC storage does. iSCSI is considered a type of SAN storage device because it writes using a block-level method rather than a file-level method, which NFS uses.

iSCSI initiators can be either software-based or hardware-based. An initiator is the client that replaces the traditional SCSI adapter that servers typically use to access traditional SCSI storage. Software initiators utilize device drivers that are built into the VMkernel to use Ethernet network adapters and protocols to write to a remote iSCSI target. The use of a software initiator can cause additional CPU and network overhead on the host server. Some characteristics of software initiators include the following.

- They use Ethernet NICs and the native VMkernel iSCSI stack.
- They are a good choice for blade servers and servers with limited expansion slots.
- They are a cheaper solution than using hardware initiators.
- They can be CPU-intensive due to the additional overhead of protocol processing.
- The ESX server is unable to boot from a software-based initiator. ESXi can do so by using iBFT (see the Boot from SAN section later in this chapter).

Hardware initiators use a dedicated iSCSI HBA which combines a network adapter, a TCP/IP offload engine, and a SCSI adapter into one device to help improve host server performance. Some characteristics of hardware initiators include the following.

- They use dedicated iSCSI HBAs.
- They offer moderately better I/O performance than software initiators.
- They use fewer ESX server host resources, especially CPU resources.
- The ESX server is able to boot from a hardware initiator.

Advantages of using iSCSI storage (either hardware- or software-based) include the following.

- It can cost less to implement iSCSI storage than FC storage.
- Software or hardware initiators can be used.
- It features block-level storage that can be used with VMFS volumes.
- Speed and performance are increased with 10Gbps Ethernet.

Disadvantages of using iSCSI storage (either hardware- or software-based) include the following.

- As iSCSI is most commonly deployed as a software protocol, it has additional CPU overhead compared to hardware-based storage initiators.
- It cannot store Microsoft Cluster Server shared LUNs (unless you use an iSCSI initiator inside the guest operating system).

iSCSI is a great alternative to using FC storage as it may be cheaper to implement and provides very good performance. vSphere supports the use of 10Gbps Ethernet which provides a big performance boost over 1Gbps Ethernet. Previously in VI3, it only supported up to 1Gbps Ethernet, which made FC and its 4Gbps (now 8Gbps) data transfer rate a better option. The biggest risks to using iSCSI are the additional CPU overhead when using software initiators, which you can mitigate by using hardware initiators, and the more fragile and volatile network infrastructure that it relies on, which you can mitigate by completely isolating iSCSI traffic from other network traffic.

NAS/NFS Storage

NAS utilizes the NFS protocol to allow hosts to mount files on a remote filesystem and access them as though they were local disks. NAS storage has performance characteristics similar to software iSCSI; however, the performance is heavily dependent on the speed and health of the network connection between the host and the remote storage, as well as the type of NAS device you are connecting to. Using an enterprise class NAS appliance will provide much better performance than using a Linux or Windows server that is running NFS services.

Advantages of using NAS/NFS storage include the following.

- There is no substantial performance difference compared to iSCSI.
- It can be a lower-cost shared storage option.
- It is possible to use existing infrastructure components.
- There is no single disk I/O queue. Performance strictly depends upon the size of the network connection and the capabilities of the disk array.
- File locking and queuing are handled by the NFS device, which can result in better performance as compared to iSCSI/FC, where locking and queuing are handled by the ESX/ESXi host.
- It offers the smallest storage footprint because most NFS devices use thin provisioned disks by default.

Disadvantages of using NAS/NFS storage include the following.

- You cannot boot ESX or ESXi from it.
- It does not support VMFS volumes or Raw Device Mappings (RDMs).
- It cannot store Microsoft Cluster Server shared LUNs.
- As NFS is a software protocol, it has additional CPU overhead compared to hardware-based storage initiators.
- Some vendors do not recommend NFS storage for certain applications (e.g., Exchange, Domino) due to latency that can occur.

Table 5.1 provides a summary of the features that each storage option supports.

Table 5.1   Storage Option Characteristics

	Boot from SAN	Supports RDMs	Supports VMFS	Supports MSCS	Speed	Type
Local storage	N/A	N/A	Yes	Yes	3Gbps, 6Gbps	Block-level
Direct Attach Storage	Yes	Yes	Yes	Yes	3Gbps, 6Gbps	Block-level
Fibre Channel	Yes	Yes	Yes	Yes	4Gbps, 8Gbps	Block-level
iSCSI—Software	ESXi only w/ iBFT	Yes	Yes	No	1Gbps, 10Gbps	Block-level
iSCSI—Hardware	ESX only	Yes	Yes	Yes	1Gbps, 10Gbps	Block-level
NFS	No	No	No	No	1Gbps, 10Gbps	File-level

MIXING STORAGE TYPES

With so many storage types to choose from, it's common to mix them on your ESX hosts by configuring separate datastores for each type. You cannot mix storage types on a single datastore, however. You may have one datastore that is configured to use local disk storage on your ESX host, another datastore that uses shared storage on an FC SAN, and one more that uses storage on an NFS device. You can then choose the placement of your VMs based on the characteristics of each storage type.

Most likely you will want your most critical and disk I/O-intensive VMs on your best-performing shared storage. Local disk storage is good for nonessential VMs, and NFS datastores can be set up relatively easily on Windows servers that can be used to store ISO files and templates. You can also easily move VMs from one storage type to another as needed by cold-migrating them while they are powered off or while they are running by using the Storage VMotion feature. The important thing to know when using multiple storage options in your environment is to recognize the performance and feature differences between each option, as shown in Table 5.1, and to use each one appropriately.

ADDITIONAL STORAGE CONSIDERATIONS

Choosing a storage type is just one of the considerations you will have to make when architecting storage for your virtual environment. There are also a number of additional choices you will need to make. Some of them may seem like small decisions, but they can have a big impact and are also difficult to change later on, so it's best to know what they are and make the right decisions up front.

LUN SIZE CONSIDERATIONS

This is always a common question among those who are new to VMware: "How big should I make my LUNs to use with my hosts?" vSphere supports use of up to 2TB LUNs without using extents, but there is no magic number when it comes to selecting an optimal LUN size; generally, it is recommended that you keep your LUNs between 500GB and 600GB in size. Many, smaller LUNs are more difficult to manage and also limit the size of your VMFS volumes. It is recommended that you have only one VMFS volume per LUN, and that you not create multiple VMFS volumes on a single LUN. It is possible to put multiple LUNs together to make one VMFS volume using extents, as mentioned earlier, but it is generally best to avoid this if you can. However, if you want to create VMFS volumes greater than 2TB in length, extents are your only option.

A more important question than LUN size is: "How many VMs should I have per LUN?" This will help determine the size of your LUNs. There has been a lot of debate on this subject, with many recommending about 14 to 16 VMs per LUN. Having too many VMs on a single LUN can cause problems with metadata locking issues (SCSI reservations). However, this number can vary greatly depending on the I/O requirements of the applications running on the VMs.

VMware's Configuration Maximums document states that 256 VMs per volume is the limit, but this is not a hard limit, and in reality it can scale much higher.

For VMs that have very light I/O workloads, such as application servers, you could easily fit 100 VMs per LUN. You should consider fewer VMs per LUN (eight to ten) if you will have very disk I/O-intensive applications running on them, and you should consider more VMs per LUN (20–22) if you have low to medium disk I/O-intensive applications running on them. For very low disk I/O applications, you can scale much higher. In some cases, you might put more VMs on a LUN, such as VDI implementations where you have many low disk I/O virtual desktops running on your host servers. But one thing to be careful about with virtual desktops is that although they typically have lighter workloads, they sometimes have high peaks in their I/O during certain times of the day. In addition, operations such as powering a VM on or off can cause SCSI reservations, and when multiple people turn on their VMs in the morning at around the same time, you could run into performance problems. As a result, you should factor in both your average and peak I/O workloads when deciding on the number of VMs to put on a LUN.

You should also factor in IOPS measurements, which play a key role in sizing your LUNs properly. To do this you will first need to determine the number of IOPS required by your application workloads using a performance monitor. Once you know your IOPS requirements, you can then compare them to the number of IOPS provided by the storage subsystem backing the LUN. Performance benchmarking tools are available, such as Iometer (www.iometer.org/), that can measure the IOPS of your host storage when run inside a VM with a virtual disk on that storage device. For more information on using Iometer with vSphere, see the document at http://communities.vmware.com/docs/DOC-3961.

Once you figure out how many VMs you will have per LUN, you should look at your disk storage requirements per VM and allow for additional storage for things such as .vswp, log, and snapshot files that will also be created in your VM's working directory. How much extra storage you will need for your VMs will be heavily influenced by how much you plan to use snapshots with your VMs. A general rule of thumb is to allow for about 20% additional disk space in addition to the size of the VM's virtual disks. For example, if you have a VM with a 20GB disk you should allow for at least 4GB of additional space. Here are some things to consider about the extra files that your VMs will have.

- A .vswp file will be created equal in size to the amount of memory assigned to a VM minus any memory reservations. So, a VM with 4GB of RAM and no memory reservation will have a 4GB .vswp file created on your VMFS volume.

- Snapshots will vary in size based on the number of changes made to a VM's disk after the snapshot is created. They are initially small (16MB) and can grow to the total size of the original VM disk (but cannot exceed it). How much and how fast they change depends on your applications. Static servers such as web and app servers will grow slowly; dynamic servers such as database and email servers will grow more quickly. So, how much space you should allow for snapshots will depend on how many snapshots you plan to take and how long you need to keep them. You should also allow for additional disk space so that you can delete multilevel snapshots which require extra disk space to commit. If you plan to use a lot of snapshots, you should allow for plenty of extra disk space on your VMFS volumes. Additionally, if you plan to save memory state with your snapshots (.vmsn files), this will require extra disk space equal to the amount of memory a VM has configured.

- VM log files do not take up that much room, and generally total fewer than 50MB of disk space per VM.

- If you suspend a VM, a .vmss file is created that holds the contents of the VM's memory and is equal in size to the amount of memory a VM has. You typically don't have to allow for extra space for these, as the .vswp file is deleted when the .vmss file is created, so they balance each other out.

Once you add up the amount of disk space your VMs will need based on these considerations, you can calculate the size of the LUNs that will work best for you. You can then create your VMFS volumes to be equal in size to that of your LUNs. If you do have a need for VMs with very large virtual disks (greater than 1TB), you should consider using RDMs instead of VMFS volumes, which we will talk about in a moment. If you plan to use thin provisioned disks with your VMs, you may also factor that in as your virtual disks will utilize less disk space. However, don't cut yourself too short when overallocating disks, because as your thin disks grow you will need free space on your VMFS volumes to accommodate their growth.

One final note on the 2TB VMFS datastore limit when using a single LUN: The actual maximum size of a LUN in vSphere is 2TB minus 512 bytes, or 1.9999999995343387GB. If you try to create a 2TB datastore you will get an error message that says "Failed to get disk partition information." This is because the extra 512 bytes are needed by ESX for the configuration overhead information that is written to the LUN. So, if you want to create a 2TB LUN you should specify it as 1.99TB instead. This behavior is new to vSphere. In VI3, you could create 2TB LUNs, but the 512 bytes were still needed for configuration overhead. Because the LUN was provisioned as the full 2TB, it could cause an out-of-space condition if the LUN was completely filled up, which could corrupt the LUN. As a result, the safeguards were put into vSphere to allow for that additional necessary 512 bytes to not be overwritten by data on the LUN.

The 2TB limit is not actually a VMFS limit, and is actually a limitation of the underlying SCSI-2 standard that vSphere uses, which can only address 2TB of disk space. The Logical Volume Manager (LVM) that vSphere uses concatenates multiple LUNs as extents into a VMFS volume up to 64TB in size when using the maximum 32 extents that are 2TB in size. If you do present a LUN larger than 2TB to vSphere, only the space above 2TB is used for the VMFS datastore. That means that if you presented a 2.5TB LUN, the VMFS datastore would only be 500GB and you would be wasting 2TB of space, so make sure you keep your LUNs below 2TB in size.

CHOOSING A BLOCK SIZE

Another consideration you should make when you create your VMFS volumes is the maximum size of the virtual disks that you will be assigning to your VMs. By default, VMFS volumes are created with a 1MB block size which allows for a single virtual disk (.vmdk) to be created up to 256GB. If you try to create a virtual disk that is larger than 256GB when using a 1MB block size, you will not be allowed to. Once you set a block size on a VMFS volume, you cannot change it later. Instead, you need to move all the VMs from the volume, delete it, and re-create it with a new block size. Therefore, you should make sure you choose a block size that works for you based on your current and future needs. The block size choices and related maximum virtual disk sizes are as follows:

- **1MB block size**—256GB maximum virtual disk file size (default)
- **2MB block size**—512GB maximum virtual disk file size
- **4MB block size**—1,024GB maximum virtual disk file size
- **8MB block size**—2,048GB maximum virtual disk file size

Choosing a larger block size will not impact disk performance and will only affect the minimum amount of disk space that files will take up on your VMFS volumes. Block size is the amount of space that a single block of data takes up on the disk; subsequently, the amount of disk space a file takes up will be based on a multiple of the block size. However, VMFS does employ sub-block allocation, so small files do not take up an entire block. Sub-blocks are always 64KB in size, regardless of the block size chosen. As a result, there is some wasted disk space, but this is negligible as VMFS volumes do not have a large number of files on them and most of the files are very large and are not affected that much by having a larger block size.

Block size also affects the growth rate for thin disks as they grow in the increment of the block size as data is written to them. However, there is no performance benefit to using different block sizes with thin disks. In most cases, it's probably best to use an 8MB block size when creating a VMFS volume, even if you are using volume sizes smaller than 300GB, as you may decide to grow them later on. If you do choose a 1MB block size, and later you need larger virtual disks, you will have to delete your volume and re-create it, which can be difficult and disruptive. So, if you think you may use larger virtual disks, by all means, go ahead and use a larger block size.

VMFS VERSUS RAW DEVICE MAPPINGS

When you add a virtual disk to a VM you have the option of using a traditional virtual disk on a VMFS volume or using an RDM instead. An RDM is a mapping from a VM directly to a raw LUN on a SAN, and the VM's virtual disk does not reside on a VMFS volume as the VM is given raw access to the underlying storage subsystem (LUN). Instead, a small .vmdk disk descriptor file is created for the virtual disk in the VM's working directory on the VMFS volume. Providing a VM with direct access to a LUN gives it some additional benefits over using virtual disks on VMFS volumes.

The performance characteristics between an RDM and a VMFS volume are very similar, and there is only a slight difference between them in certain situations. For random workloads, they both produce similar I/O throughput. For sequential workloads with small I/O block sizes, RDMs provide a small increase in throughput compared to VMFS. For all workloads, RDMs have slightly better CPU costs because of the filename metadata that VMFS maintains. Both VMFS and RDM provide many of the same features, such as file locking and VMotion.

RDMs can be configured in two different modes: virtual compatibility mode and physical compatibility mode. Virtual compatibility mode virtualizes the mapped device and is mostly transparent to the guest operating system. This mode also provides some advantages of VMFS volumes, such as the ability to create snapshots. Physical compatibility mode provides minimal SCSI virtualization of the mapped device and the VMkernel passes almost all SCSI commands directly to the device, thereby allowing closer integration between the VM and the LUN.

Here are some reasons and situations where you might choose to use an RDM instead of a VMFS volume.

- RDMs can easily be grown in place to increase their size via SAN utilities. Growing a VMDK file on a VMFS volume is a bit more difficult and requires more steps.

- RDMs are useful for advanced SAN functions and when running a SAN-aware application inside a VM.

- If you plan to use Microsoft Cluster Services on your VMs, you will need to use an RDM if the cluster nodes are going to be on separate hosts.

- If you need to create a virtual disk for a VM that is greater than 1TB, you should consider using an RDM (this is just a best practice, not a limitation).

- RDMs are formatted by the guest operating system and use whatever filesystem the guest chooses (e.g., NTFS, ext3, reiserfs, etc.).

- RDMs can be easily disconnected from a VM and connected to another VM or physical server.

Here are some reasons and situations where you might not choose to use an RDM over a VMFS volume.

- RDMs can be a bit more difficult to manage than VMFS volumes. RDMs cannot be seen in the VI Client datastore list.

- Physical mode RDMs cannot use snapshots, which can cause problems for backup applications (VCB) that snapshot a VM before backing it up. In some cases, this can be advantageous, though, if you want to snapshot a VM with multiple disks and do not want the RDMs to be included in the snapshot.

- If you cold-migrate a VM and change the disk location of the VM, any RDMs that are configured on the VM will be converted to VMFS volumes as part of the migration. To prevent this, you need to temporarily remove the RDMs before you cold-migrate and add them back after the VM has been migrated.

- You must assign a whole LUN to be used as an RDM for a virtual disk. You cannot use part of a LUN for this.

In general, it is recommended that you use VMFS volumes for your VM's virtual disks, unless you are using MSCS (Microsoft Cluster Server), you plan to use disks greater than 1TB, or you need to use SAN functionality from within a VM. If you do choose to use an RDM on a VM, it's a good idea to create a small virtual disk file on a VMFS volume for the VM's operating system and then add one or more RDMs to the VM as additional virtual disks.

10K VERSUS 15K RPM HARD DRIVES

Most SCSI hard drives are available in two speeds: 10,000 rpm (10K) and 15,000 rpm (15K). This speed is how fast the hard drive's platters spin and is otherwise known as rotational speed. When the drive platter spins faster it means data can be read and written faster and overall latency is reduced. However, even though the drive platter is spinning faster, the head actuator that moves across the drive to access the data does not move any faster. This means that even though the drive is spinning 50% faster the overall drive performance isn't increased by 50%. Typical performance increases for 15K drives over 10K drives are about 30%, which results in higher IOPS and decreased average access times.

There are generally two deciding factors when it comes to choosing between 10K rpm and 15K rpm drives. The first is whether you will be using applications that will have heavy disk utilization and could benefit from the extra speed that 15K rpm drives provide. The second is whether you can afford the more expensive drives. If you can afford them, it is generally best to get them. If you are planning to run disk I/O-intensive applications on your VMs, you should definitely consider them.

RAID LEVELS

The more drive spindles you have in your RAID groups, the more IOPS you can typically handle. This is because the storage controller has more drives to choose from when reading and writing data. Selecting RAID levels is a trade-off between redundancy and performance/available disk space. Since RAID is a data protection technology, it has an I/O cost penalty when using it. That penalty is only on disk writes and will vary based on the RAID level you choose to use. For RAID 1 the penalty is two I/Os for every write; this is because the data must be written to two different drives for redundancy. For RAID 5 the penalty is four I/Os, because as old data and parity are read off separate disks, the new parity is calculated and the new data and parity are written to separate disks.

And finally, for RAID 6 the penalty is six I/Os, as double parity data is written to three separate disks.

As a result, you should create your RAID groups based on your storage I/O and data protection requirements. If you need maximum performance, you should consider RAID 1, but as this is the most inefficient use of disk space, this can be more expensive. RAID 6 offers a good combination of protection (two drives can fail), performance, and usable disk space. RAID 5 offers the most usable disk space and the least amount of protection (only one drive can fail), but better performance than RAID 6. One additional nonstandard RAID level that NetApp developed is called RAID-DP, which offers the same protection as RAID 6 but with the same I/O penalty as RAID 1. By caching and aggregating disk writes, the I/O penalty for RAID-DP is about the same as RAID 1. If you are using a NetApp storage system RAID-DP is your only choice, as RAID 4 was supported but is now deprecated. Table 5.2 shows the various RAID level choices that you have.

Table 5.2   Raid Levels Shown with Associated I/O Penalties and Tolerated Drive Failures

RAID Level	I/O Penalty	Drive Failures Tolerated
0	0	0
1	2	1 per 2 drives
5	4	1
6	6	2
DP	2	2

As you can see, there are trade-offs between cost, performance, and protection that you must choose from when using RAID. Just remember that no matter what RAID level you choose, having more drive spindles available offers the best performance.

JUMBO FRAMES

Conventional Ethernet frames are 1,518 bytes in length. Jumbo frames are typically 9,000 bytes in length, which can improve network throughput and CPU efficiency. With the vSphere release, jumbo frames are supported for use with iSCSI and NFS storage devices using both 1Gbit and 10Gbit NICs to help improve their efficiency. Jumbo frames must be supported by the NIC within the host, the connected physical switch, and the storage subsystem to which you are connecting. You cannot enable jumbo frames in the vSphere Client, and they must instead be enabled using command-line utilities. To enable jumbo frames for NFS and software iSCSI, you must enable them in the virtual switch (vSwitch) that is used for your storage NICs.

- If you are using the vSphere CLI for ESXi or ESX, run the `vicfg-vswitch -m <mtu size> <vSwitch name>` command which sets the MTU for all uplinks on that vSwitch; for example, `vicfg-vswitch -m 9000 vSwitch1`. You can use the `vicfg-vswitch -l` command to display the vSwitch information and configuration.

- If you are using the ESX Service Console, run the `esxcfg-vswitch -m <mtu size> <vSwitch name>` command. You can use the `esxcfg-vswitch -l` command to display the vSwitch information and configuration.

Hardware initiators do not use vSwitches as they are considered storage adapters. To enable jumbo frames on hardware initiators, you must first ensure that jumbo frame support is enabled in the BIOS of the hardware initiator. This is typically done by pressing the appropriate key to enter the adapter BIOS when prompted during the initial boot of the server. You must then run one of the following commands based on your storage NICs.

- If you are using the vSphere CLI for ESXi or ESX, run the `vicfg-iscsi -p -M <mtu_size> <adapter_name>` command which sets the MTU for the specified storage adapter; for example, `vicfg-iscsi -p -M 9000 vmhba4`. You can use the `vicfg-iscsi -p -l <adapter_name>` command to display the storage adapter information and configuration.

- If you are using the ESX Service Console, run the `esxcfg-hwiscsi -j [enable¦disable] <adapter name>` command. `enable` sets the MTU to 9000 and `disable` sets it to 1500; for example, `esxcfg-hwiscsi -j enable vmhba4`. You can use the `esxcfg-hwiscsi -l` command to display the storage adapter information and configuration.

Boot from SAN

The boot from SAN option allows ESX hosts (currently this is not supported on ESXi hosts) to be configured without any internal disk, and instead to boot directly from an FC SAN or hardware iSCSI device. This can be particularly advantageous when using blade servers that have very limited internal storage. When you use boot from SAN the ESX Service Console is installed on a LUN that is located on the SAN storage. Then when the ESX host starts up, it boots directly from the LUN on the SAN. When you enable boot from SAN you configure your HBA to boot from the specific LUN for that ESX host; each host must have its own separate LUN on the SAN and the boot LUN must be configured as the lowest-numbered LUN visible to the HBA. Booting from SAN has advantages and disadvantages.

Advantages of booting from SAN include the following.

- It entails a lower server hardware cost because local disks are not needed.
- It is easier to replace the server hardware. You can replace old servers with new ones and simply point to the old boot location on the SAN.
- It is very useful for disaster recovery. By having the boot images of the ESX hosts stored on the SAN array, you can easily replicate them to remote sites where standby ESX hosts can quickly boot up in case of a disaster.
- SAN-level snapshots can be used to create point-in-time backups of the Service Console when patching ESX hosts.
- You can deploy ESX hosts more quickly by cloning existing boot images.

Disadvantages of booting from SAN include the following.

- A SAN disk can be expensive, and having the local disk on your ESX hosts available for VMs can be a low-cost alternative to storing all your VMs on a SAN disk.
- If something happens to the SAN or the connection to the SAN, the whole ESX host and all of its VMs will go down. Having a local disk enables VMs that are not on the SAN to continue running when the SAN is unavailable.
- It adds more load on the SAN because of the additional load from the disk I/O from the Service Console partitions.
- It can be more complex to configure and to troubleshoot.
- It requires a separate LUN for each ESX, which can be complicated to manage and more expensive if your SAN is licensed by zones.

As stated, there are definitely certain situations when booting from SAN makes sense and should be considered. Booting from local disk is used in most cases because many people prefer to have local disk storage and do not want to waste the SAN disk for the Service Console.

A new feature in vSphere 4.1, called iSCSI Boot Firmware Table (iBFT), allows you to boot from an iSCSI target using software initiators. Previously, only hardware initiators on ESX supported this feature. This feature has some restrictions, though; it will only work with ESXi (not ESX), and the only currently supported network card is the Broadcom 57711 10GBe NIC.

When booting from software iSCSI the boot firmware on the network adapter logs in to an iSCSI target. The firmware then saves the network and iSCSI boot parameters in the iBFT which is stored in the host's memory. Before you can use iBFT, you need to configure the boot order in your server's BIOS so that the iBFT NIC is first before all other devices. You then need to configure the iSCSI configuration and CHAP authentication in the BIOS of the NIC before you can use it to boot ESXi.

The ESXi installation media has special iSCSI initialization scripts that use iBFT to connect to the iSCSI target and present it to the BIOS. Once you select the iSCSI target as your boot device, the installer copies the boot image to it. Once the media is removed and the host is rebooted, the iSCSI target is used to boot and the initialization script runs in first boot mode, which permanently configures the iBFT networking information for the iSCSI target.

DRIVES AND STORAGE ADAPTERS

You can use different types of storage adapters in your ESX hosts: local storage adapters (SCSI/SAS/SATA), FC HBAs, and iSCSI HBAs. It's very important to make sure that whatever adapters you end up using are listed in the vSphere Hardware Compatibility Guide which is available on VMware's website. When you are choosing storage adapters for your ESX host keep the following in mind.

- For local storage adapters, it is best to get adapters that have the largest read/write caches on them, especially if you plan to exclusively use the local disk on your ESX hosts. Additionally, having a Battery Backed Write Cache (BBWC) on your array controller significantly improves performance and reliability. BBWCs add some additional memory that is used to cache disk writes, and they also have a battery backup to protect data that has not yet been written to disk in case of a power failure. This combination of features enables write caching, which is where the performance boost comes from.
- For FC adapters, you will typically want two of them for maximum reliability: The default FC drivers that are included with ESX and ESXi support the

QLogic and Emulex FC adapters, which are usually rebranded by server manufacturers (e.g., HP, IBM, etc.).

- If you plan to use iSCSI hardware initiators, you will again want two of them for maximum reliability. The default iSCSI drivers that are included with ESX and ESXi support only the QLogic adapters, which are usually rebranded by server manufacturers (e.g., HP, IBM, etc.). If you use a non-QLogic storage adapter, it will usually be seen as a standard Ethernet network adapter instead.

- If you plan to use NFS or software iSCSI storage, your network adapter becomes your storage adapter and it is best to use dedicated NICs that are not used for any other purpose. You should also check to see if your NIC supports jumbo frames which can give an extra boost in throughput. For high I/O workloads, you may consider 10Gb Ethernet, which adds considerable speed over the more commonly used 1Gb Ethernet. This technology is new, though, and purchasing all of the infrastructure to support it can be very expensive.

- Both SAS and SATA adapters are supported in vSphere, but SAS is recommended due to better speed and performance. SATA should only be used on hosts that have low I/O requirements.

Solid State Drives (SSDs) can be used, but they are a relatively new technology that has not fully matured yet. Although they offer great performance due to their lack of mechanical parts that cause limitations in traditional hard drives, they are currently very expensive. As of March 2010, an HP 1.5Gbps SATA 32GB SSD drive costs $700, an HP 3Gbps SATA 60GB drive costs $1,459, and a larger HP 3Gb SATA 120GB SSD drive costs $2,799. Be aware that there are two types of SSD drives: multi-level cell (MLC) and single-level cell (SLC). MLC drives are denser as they write more than a single bit of information to a cell. As a result, they are slower and tend to be less reliable. SLC drives are typically used in enterprise storage devices. One disadvantage of SSDs is that they have limited lifetimes, as they wear out after too many write cycles. MLC drives often wear out after 1 million to 2 million write cycles (1,000 to 10,000 per cell), and SLC drives often wear out after 5 million write cycles (100,000 per cell). To help prolong the life of an SSD drive, some filesystems use a technique called "wear leveling" that arranges data so that rewrites are distributed evenly across the SSD drive. Doing this helps to ensure that no single block fails prematurely due to a high concentration of writes. Currently, only a few filesystems support wear leveling (e.g., TrueFFS and ExtremeFFS), but as SSDs gain in popularity wear leveling may also be supported in the VMware VMFS filesystem. Storage vendors can also implement wear leveling at the array level which is more efficient than doing it at the filesystem level.

Table 5.3 provides a drive comparison based on HP's line of hard drives. Currently, 3Gb/s SAS drives are the most popular choice in medium to large businesses; 6Gb/s drives are fairly new and provide even greater transfer rates for high I/O workloads.

Table 5.3   HP Hard Drive Comparison

	Usage	RPM	Transfer Rate	Connectivity
SSD	Extreme operating environments: local storage/boot	N/A	1.5Gb/s	Single-port
SSD G2	Midline drive environments where data is highly random, with heavy reads where low latency and high I/O performance are more important than capacity	N/A	3.0Gb/s	Single-port
SATA Entry	Low I/O non-mission-critical: boot	5.4K 7.2K	1.5Gb/s 3Gb/s	Single-port
SATA Midline	High-capacity storage: backup, archive	7.2K	3Gb/s	Single-port
SAS Midline	Midline: high-capacity, high-availability storage: backup, archiving, and reference	7.2K	3Gb/s 6Gb/s	Dual-port
SAS Enterprise	Enterprise: mission-critical, high I/O: email, ERP, CRM	10K 15K	3Gb/s 6Gb/s	Dual-port
SCSI Ultra320	Mission-critical, high I/O: email, ERP, CRM	15K	320 MB/s	Single-port

As you can see, there are many other considerations when choosing storage for your virtual environment. As disk storage is the slowest resource, you should make sure you understand your I/O requirements before choosing and configuring your storage. And don't just consider the needs of applications and servers individually; you need to consider them as a whole, as all your VMs will be competing for your storage resources.

STORAGE CONFIGURATION

Storage is one of the configuration tasks that you want to make sure you get right the first time. It can be difficult and time-consuming to change storage configurations later. If you make the wrong choices when configuring storage it can affect the performance of your hosts and VMs. As a result, it's best to take some time to understand your needs and requirements and ensure that you thoroughly understand your options before configuring storage on your hosts.

LOCAL STORAGE

In most cases, you will have local storage on your host servers (unless you are using boot from SAN), which you can use to create nonshared VMFS volumes on your hosts. Even if you only plan to use shared storage for your VMs, you should still configure local VMFS volumes as they can be useful in many situations, such as storing VM backups and moving VMs to local datastores during maintenance periods on your shared storage. It also sometimes pays to have a few infrastructure-type (DNS/DHCP/Active Directory) VMs on local storage so that those services are still available in case of a problem with your shared storage.

DIRECT ATTACH STORAGE

Although DAS is a form of local storage, it is usually configured and managed much differently than traditional internal storage. DAS is often configured using a management interface whereby you configure storage volumes and LUNs to use with the hosts that are connected to it. Many DAS units have the option for dual controllers which provides redundancy in case of a component failure and also to avoid downtime when upgrading controller firmware. The SAS cables used to configure DAS have a maximum length of 12 feet, so make sure you keep your hosts and DAS near each other. DAS is much simpler to manage than other types of shared storage, as it does not have the additional configuration and extra components that the others have.

FIBRE CHANNEL STORAGE

Configuring FC storage can be complicated and usually involves working with your SAN administrator to get everything set up for your host servers. Proper preparation is the key for proper configuration, and you should work closely with your SAN administrator to ensure that she understands your needs and configures the LUNs that you will use properly. VMware has created two very detailed white papers dedicated to SAN configuration, and I recommend that both you and your SAN administrator read them before proceeding. The first white paper, "Fibre Channel SAN Configuration Guide," is available in the vSphere documentation section on VMware's website, at http://vmware.com/pdf/vsphere4/r40_u1/vsp_40_u1_san_cfg.pdf. The second white paper, "SAN System Design and Deployment Guide," is available at www.vmware.com/pdf/vi3_san_design_deploy.pdf. Here are some additional considerations when using FC storage.

- Design and create your SAN LUNs. When you present SAN LUNs to hosts you should ensure that you present each LUN as the same LUN ID to every host. This is essential, as every host needs to see each LUN as being the same for it to work properly, and to ensure that features such as DRS, HA, and VMotion work. Many SAN administrators may be resistant to setting up the LUNs this way, as they may think that if multiple hosts see the same LUNs it could cause data corruption. This is not the case with vSphere, though. By design, the VMFS filesystem is made to work this way and prevents multiple hosts from writing to the same file at the same time with its unique file locking technique. It is helpful if you explain that from a storage perspective, you can consider a vSphere cluster to be a single host with multiple HBAs. This will often help storage administrators understand how to configure things correctly.

- If for some reason you wish to hide certain LUNs from specific hosts, you can do this in one of two ways. The first way is to mask the LUN at the SAN switch level so that the host cannot see it. The second way is to change a setting in vSphere. To access the setting, select your host in the vSphere Client, choose the Configuration tab, and then choose the Advanced Settings link. Next, choose Disk in the left-hand pane of the Settings window. In the right-hand pane find the Disk.MaskLUNs setting and enter the LUN numbers that you wish to hide from that host server, in the following format: <HBA adapter#>:<target #>:<LUN #>, using commas to separate multiple entries. For example, if you wish to mask IDs 10–20 plus 28 and 30, enter the following: vmhba1:1:10-20,28,30.

- Check your multipathing by selecting your host server in the vSphere Client and going to the Configuration tab and then selecting Storage. Next, choose a storage volume and select the Properties link. In the bottom-right window, you will see your paths displayed; the currently active path will show as a solid green diamond. You can manage your paths by clicking the Manage Paths button, where you can select a path policy. If your host sees the storage as Active-Passive the default path policy is Most Recently Used, where the same path that was most recently used continues to be used until a failure occurs. If it sees it as Active-Active, Fixed is used. Besides Most Recently Used and Fixed, there is also a round-robin option which was considered experimental in ESX 3.5 and is now fully supported in vSphere. For more information on round-robin load-balancing see VMware's tech note at www.vmware.com/pdf/vi3_35_25_roundrobin.pdf.

- By default, Active/Passive storage arrays use the Most Recently Used path policy. Do not use the Fixed path policy for Active/Passive storage arrays to avoid LUN thrashing. By default, Active/Active storage arrays use the Fixed path policy. When using this policy you can maximize the utilization of your bandwidth to the storage array by designating preferred paths to each LUN through different storage controllers.

- Create separate LUNs for development, test, and production VMs. This prevents development and test VMs from negatively impacting the performance of production VMs.

- Consider separating VM disks onto different LUNs (e.g., system disks on one LUN, data disks on another LUN). This can make management more complex, but is useful in some situations to maximize performance.

- The default ESX SCSI command queue depth is 32. Consider raising this to 64 using the `esxcfg-module` service console command (see VMware's Fibre Channel Configuration Guide for instructions). Also change the Disk.SchedNumReqOutstanding setting in the vSphere Client to 64 under Advanced Settings→Disk.

iSCSI STORAGE

You can configure iSCSI storage with your ESX hosts using either a software or a hardware initiator. If you are using hardware initiators you will be using an iSCSI HBA installed in your host server to offload all the iSCSI processing and management from the host server's CPU and NICs. Software initiators are already part of the VMkernel, and they let you use your existing NICs to connect to iSCSI storage targets. Be sure to read through the iSCSI SAN Configuration Guide located in the vSphere documentation section of VMware's website (http://vmware.com/pdf/vsphere4/r40_u1/vsp_40_u1_iscsi_san_cfg.pdf). Another good guide to read is VMware's iSCSI Design Considerations and

Deployment Guide (www.vmware.com/files/pdf/iSCSI_design_deploy.pdf).
Here are some additional considerations when using iSCSI storage.

- The performance of iSCSI storage is highly dependent on network health and utilization. For best results, always isolate on a dedicated network.
- You can configure only one software initiator on an ESX Server host. When configuring a vSwitch that will provide iSCSI connectivity use multiple physical NICs (pNICs) to provide redundancy.
- Ensure that the NICs that are used in your iSCSI vSwitch connect to separate network switches to eliminate any single points of failure.
- It is not recommended that you extend a VMFS volume using extents to another iSCSI target. A failure of any one of your extents will bring down the whole VMFS volume.
- Use jumbo frames if your NICs, switches, and iSCSI targets support them.
- Always use at least gigabit NICs; 100MBps NICs are not supported for iSCSI use. Use 10GB Ethernet if you can afford to.
- Always use static IP addresses for initiators. ESX Server does not support DHCP for iSCSI connections.

NFS STORAGE

ESX has a built-in NFS client to connect to NAS devices that are running the NFS version 3 protocol. NFS storage is different as it is a file-level protocol and you do not create VMFS volumes on your NFS storage devices. Additionally, many NFS storage devices use thin provisioned virtual disks by default; unlike VMFS volumes that use thick provisioned virtual disks. Thin provisioned disks do not allocate all the space assigned to a VM's virtual disk at once, as thick provisioned disks do. They will be created at a smaller size and will then grow in increments as needed, up to the maximum size of the assigned disk. NFS storage volumes will appear in the VI client as VMFS volumes do, and you can use them to store your VMs on them the same way you would a VMFS volume. Be sure to read through the Best Practices white paper on VMware's website, at http://vmware.com/files/pdf/VMware_NFS_BestPractices_WP_EN.pdf. Here are some additional considerations when using NFS storage.

- When a host accesses a VM disk file on an NFS-based datastore, a special .lck-XXX lock file is generated in the same directory where the disk file resides to prevent other hosts from accessing this virtual disk file. Do not remove the .lck-XXX lock file, because without it, the running VM cannot access its virtual disk file.

- Just like iSCSI, the performance of NFS storage is highly dependent on network health and utilization. For best performance and security, isolate on a dedicated network.

- Mount your datastores in exactly the same way on all hosts to prevent the datastore UUID from changing if your host name is not consistent (e.g., if you are using nfs1.xyz.com on one host, don't use just nfs1 or the IP address on the others).

- Use jumbo frames if your NICs, switches, and NFS server support them.

- Always use at least gigabit NICs; 100MBps NICs are not supported for NFS use. Use 10Gbe if you can afford to.

- Ensure that the NICs that are used in your VMkernel vSwitch connect to separate network switches to eliminate any single points of failure.

- Change the following ESX advanced settings for NFS from their defaults.
  - Change NFS.MaxVolumes from 8 to 64.
  - Change Net.TcpipHeapSize from 16 to 30.
  - Change NFS.HeartbeatMaxFailures from 3 to 10.
  - Change NFS.HeartbeatFrequency from 9 to 12.

SUMMARY

Storage is the most important consideration in virtualization, and therefore you need to make sure you understand it so that you can choose a storage solution that meets your needs. With so many decisions, it can quickly get confusing, and mistakes can easily be made. Most storage vendors are heavily involved in virtualization and know how to design solutions specifically for virtual environments which have much different requirements than traditional physical environments. Therefore, when choosing a storage solution you should consult with the various storage vendors that can provide you with the expertise and knowledge to help you make the right choices.

There is a lot to learn about storage, and fortunately a lot of real-world knowledge and experience is shared on a daily basis on the Internet. To find out even more about storage, check out the following websites:

- **Virtual Storage Guy (Vaughn Stewart, NetApp)**—
  http://blogs.netapp.com/virtualstorageguy/

- **Virtual Geek (Chad Sakac, EMC)**—
  http://virtualgeek.typepad.com/virtual_geek/

- **Around the Storage Block (Calvin Zito, HP)**—
  www.communities.hp.com/online/blogs/datastorage/default.aspx

- **SearchStorage.com (Various, Tech Target)**—
  http://searchstorage.techtarget.com/

NETWORKING IN vSPHERE

6

Networking is one area that often does not receive much attention when planning or architecting a virtual environment. There is much more to networking in vSphere than simply plugging your host's physical NICs into physical switches and then configuring vSwitches. Networking in VI3 was pretty simple, as you only had a standard vSwitch to choose from. In vSphere you have more choices with the new Distributed vSwitch and support for third-party vSwitches. As a result, you have more decisions to make when planning your vSphere environment, as the additional vSwitch options make virtual network administration easier as well as add better management and more features. This chapter covers what you will need to know about networking in vSphere to help you make the right decisions.

WHAT'S NEW WITH NETWORKING IN vSPHERE

Although there are not as many new networking features in vSphere as there are in other areas of the product, an important new networking feature is the introduction of the new Distributed vSwitch and third-party vSwitches. Other, smaller features include support for private VLANs and support for IP version 6.

DISTRIBUTED AND THIRD-PARTY vSWITCHES

The new Distributed vSwitch delivers centralized management to vSwitches across multiple hosts, but does not add any intelligence or management capabilities to the vSwitch. The support for third-party vSwitches enables vendors to develop more powerful and manageable vSwitches for vSphere. Cisco was the first vendor to create a third-party vSwitch, called the Nexus 1000V, which was released at the same time vSphere was released. This added better manageability to the vSwitch and enabled physical switch management to extend into virtual hosts. We will cover the different vSwitch types in detail later in this chapter.

PRIVATE VLANS

vSphere also added support for private VLANs that allows communication between virtual machines (VMs) on a vSwitch to be controlled and restricted. This feature, which is normally available on physical switches, was only added to the Distributed vSwitch and not to the standard vSwitch. Usually, traffic on the same port group on a vSwitch has no restrictions and any VM in that port group can see the traffic from other VMs. Private VLANs allow you to restrict this, and in essence, are sort of a firewall within the VLAN. In order to use a private VLAN, you must first configure it on the physical switch ports of the uplink NICs on the vNetwork Distributed Switch (vDS). Then, click the Private VLANs tab and edit the settings on the screen that appears. The concept and configuration of private VLANs can be difficult to understand; for more information on them visit Cisco's website, www.cisco.com/en/US/products/hw/switches/ps700/products_tech_note09186a008013565f.shtml.

IP VERSION 6

Another new feature in vSphere is support for IP version 6 (IPv6), which is the successor to the traditional IPv4 IP addresses that are commonly used today. IPv6 was created to deal with the exhaustion of the number of IP addresses that IPv4 supported. IPv4 uses 32-bit IP addresses which yields a maximum number of around 4 billion unique IP addresses. IPv6 uses 128-bit IP addresses which results in an insanely high number of unique IP addresses (340 undecillion, or 3.4×10 to the power of 38). Besides more IP , IPv6 also has many enhanced features over IPv4, including stateless host auto-configuration to obtain IP addresses, mandatory IPsec for security, and mandatory multicast. IPv4 addresses are all numeric, and an IPv4 address is 4 bytes and is made up of four 8-bit numbers called octets (4 bytes of 8 bits = 32 bits). An example of an IPv4 address is 192.168.1.125 (or 11000000 10101000 00000001 11111101 in binary). Each byte contains eight bits, which results in possible values of 0 through 255, or a total of 4,294,967,296 possible IP addresses.

IPv6 addresses are 16 bytes (128 bits) and are represented in hexadecimal. A typical IPv6 address is in the following form: hhhh:hhhh:hhhh:hhhh:hhhh:hhhh:hhhh:hhhh. IPv6 addresses have both a full and a shorthand notation. The full notation displays the whole address of eight sections (e.g., E3D7:0000:0000:0000:51F4:9BC8:C0A8:7625). The shorthand notation drops the extra zeros which are common in IPv6 addresses (e.g., E3D7::51F4:9BC8:C0A8:7625). The double colon denotes the zero sections that were dropped. Support for IPv6 was enabled in vSphere for the networking in the VMkernel, Service Console, and vCenter Server. Support for using IPv6 for network storage protocols is currently considered experimental and not recommended for production use. Mixed environments of IPv4 and IPv6 are also supported.

To enable IPv6 on a host you simply select the host, and choose the Configuration tab and then Networking. If you click the Properties link (not the vSwitch Properties), you will see a checkmark to enable IPv6 for that host. Once it is enabled, you must restart the host for the changes to take effect. At that point, you will see both an IPv4 and an IPv6 address in the VMkernel, Service Console (ESX), or Management Network (ESXi) properties of the vSwitch, as shown in Figure 6.1.

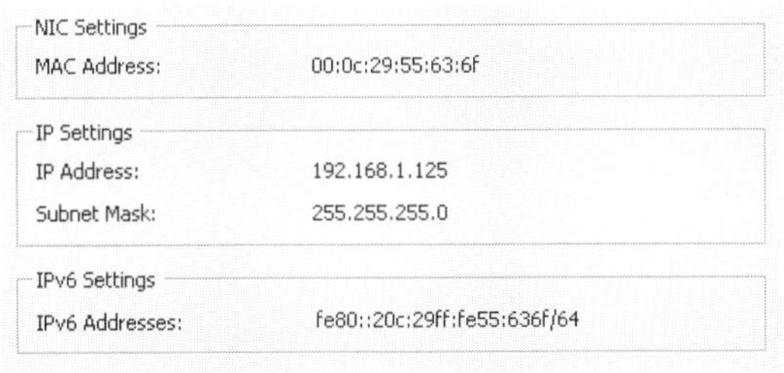

```
┌─ NIC Settings ─────────────────────────────────────────
│  MAC Address:          00:0c:29:55:63:6f
│
├─ IP Settings ──────────────────────────────────────────
│  IP Address:           192.168.1.125
│  Subnet Mask:          255.255.255.0
│
├─ IPv6 Settings ────────────────────────────────────────
│  IPv6 Addresses:       fe80::20c:29ff:fe55:636f/64
```

Figure 6.1   Service Console networking showing both IPv4 and IPv6 addresses

You can edit the IPv6 settings and specify that you want to obtain IPv6 addresses automatically through DHCP or through router advertisements, as well as set a static address. Although IPv6 is more robust than IPv4, it has not seen widespread adoption, and in order to use it your network environment, including DNS/DHCP servers, switches, and routers, needs to support it. In many cases, IPv6 is tunneled through IPv4 networks, so both can coexist on the same network.

PHYSICAL NICS

Physical NICs (pNICs) are not configured using traditional methods in ESX and ESXi hosts. You do not assign an IP address to each pNIC as you would in a standard operating system. Instead, pNICs serve as uplink ports that provide a connection between the virtual switches (vSwitches) and physical networks. When it comes to the VM networks, however, the IP addresses are assigned to them through their operating systems as usual. VMs have virtual NICs (vNICs) which connect to a port group on a vSwitch. If VM traffic needs to egress the vSwitch to a pSwitch, it will traverse one of the uplink pNICs associated with the vSwitch to access the external pSwitch. Even the ESX Service Console management interface (vswif) which you configure when you install ESX does not have an IP address directly assigned to a pNIC; because the Service Console runs as a privileged VM it too connects through a vSwitch just like other VMs.

When it comes to pNICs in your hosts, you will typically want at least two, preferably four, and sometimes more depending on your storage choice, if you plan to use VMotion. It also depends on how you plan to configure your virtual networking. Also, additional pNICs provide you with the ability to isolate sensitive traffic for the Service Console and VMkernel as well as provide fault tolerance in your vSwitch configurations. When planning the number of pNICs for your host you should follow these considerations.

- It's not necessary, but it's a best practice, to isolate the Service Console traffic for security reasons. Therefore, you should isolate the Service Console on its own vSwitch with its own pNIC. For maximum reliability, it is recommended that you add a second pNIC in case of a failure. The second pNIC should be plugged into a separate physical switch so that a single switch failure cannot affect both pNICs assigned to the Service Console vSwitch. Optionally, you can add a second Service Console interface (vswif) to another vSwitch to provide redundancy; however, it is a best practice to provide the redundancy at the vSwitch layer rather than adding the complexity of a second interface to the Service Console. The Service Console network is critical for a large portion of the ESX host functionality, and it is important to ensure that it does not lose network connectivity. For example, the High Availability (HA) feature relies on a heartbeat that is broadcast over the Service Console network; without redundancy, if a pNIC on it failed, it would trigger an HA event which could shut down the VMs and move them to other hosts. Additionally, if the Service Console network loses connectivity, vCenter Server will be unable to communicate with the host and you won't be able to manage or monitor it.

- If you plan to use VMotion, you will need to configure a VMkernel network on a vSwitch. The best practice is to also isolate this traffic such that only the VMotion interfaces of the ESX(i) hosts are connected to the VMotion network. As with the Service Console, you will want to add a second pNIC to this vSwitch that is connected to a separate physical switch.

- The number of pNICs that you need for your VM networks will depend on how many VLANs your VMs will need to connect to, and whether you plan to use 802.1Q VLAN tagging. If you plan to use only one VLAN or use tagging, you need only one pNIC in your vSwitch. However, you should add a second pNIC for redundancy purposes in case of load balancing and failover. If you plan to plug many VMs into the vSwitch and expect heavy network I/O, you should add additional pNICs to the vSwitch as needed. You may also consider creating additional vSwitches for your VM traffic to isolate the traffic onto separate pNICs. Another reason you may want to do this is to isolate internet DMZ traffic from your internal network traffic. It's best to isolate your DMZ traffic on a separate vSwitch with separate pNICs for maximum security.

- If you plan to use network storage such as software iSCSI or Network File System (NFS) storage, you should isolate this traffic onto its own vSwitch with redundant pNICs as well.

- If you plan to use Fault Tolerance (FT), you will need at least one NIC dedicated for FT logging, and preferably two for redundancy.

You need to take all these factors into account when trying to determine how many pNICs you need for each host. It's better to have too many pNICs in your hosts instead of too few. You can purchase pNIC cards that contain up to four pNICs on a single card. Having six pNICs in your host servers will give you a lot of flexibility and redundancy when configuring your vSwitches. ESX and ESXi do support up to 32 pNICs in a single host, so it's best to get as many as you think you will need up front. If you do find yourself running into a network bottleneck later on, or if you need to add additional capacity to your host, you can always add additional pNICs. Table 6.1 lists the recommended number and speed of NICs to use for the non-VM networks on an ESX/ESXi host.

Table 6.1 Recommended Number and Speed of NICs to Use for non-VM Networks

Function	Minimum NICs/speed	Recommended NICs/speed
Management (ESX Service Console, ESXi Management Network)	1 @ 1Gbps	2 @ 1Gbps
VMotion	1 @ 1Gbps	2 @ 1Gbps or faster
Fault Tolerance	1 @ 1Gbps	2 @ 1Gbps or faster
IP Storage	1 @ 1Gbps	2 @ 1Gbps or faster

If you have smaller hosts and do not plan to use features such as VMotion or network-based storage, you should plan to have at least two NICs, but preferably four. Additionally, if you plan to physically segment your virtual networks for cases such as setting up a DMZ environment, you should consider additional NICs so that you can set up separate vSwitches for them as well as provide network redundancy on all vSwitches.

VIRTUAL NICs

A vNIC is what you assign to a VM and it's connected to a port group on the ESX host server. You can assign up to ten vNICs to a single VM. A vNIC that is assigned to VMs does not use the MAC address of the pNIC; instead, it uses a MAC address that is generated by the ESX host and is within the 00-50-56 range that has been assigned to VMware.

In most cases, you will assign only a single vNIC to a VM, unless you need to connect the VM to multiple vSwitches to access separate network VLANs. Assigning multiple vNICs to a VM to try to team them at the operating system layer can be problematic in a virtual environment.

There are multiple types of vNICs to choose from when configuring a VM. The types that you have to choose from will vary based on the host version and the operating system type that you select when setting up a new VM. In vSphere, VMware added a new vNIC called the VMXNET3 which is an improved version of the VMXNET2 vNIC that was used in VI3. The VMXNET vNICs were developed by VMware and are virtualization–aware; as a result, they are optimized for VMs to minimize I/O overhead. I discuss the various types in the following subsections. They are also described in VMware's Knowledge Base article 1001805 (http://kb.vmware.com/kb/1001805).

VLANCE

Vlance is an emulated version of the AMD 79C970 PCnet32 LANCE NIC, an older 10 Mbps NIC with drivers available in most 32-bit guest operating systems except for Windows Vista and later. This vNIC has been deprecated in vSphere and is not available for use.

VMXNET

VMXNET is the first generation of the VMXNET virtual network adapter which has no physical counterpart. VMXNET is highly optimized for performance in a VM. Because there is no physical version of the VMXNET vNIC, operating system vendors do not provide built-in drivers for this card. This vNIC has been deprecated in vSphere and is not available for use.

FLEXIBLE

The Flexible network adapter identifies itself as a Vlance adapter when a VM boots, but initializes itself and functions as either a Vlance or a VMXNET adapter, depending on which driver initializes it. With VMware Tools installed, the VMXNET driver changes the Vlance adapter to the higher-performance VMXNET adapter.

E1000

E1000 is an emulated version of the Intel 82545EM Gigabit Ethernet NIC, with drivers available in most newer guest operating systems, including Windows XP and later and Linux versions 2.4.19 and later. Performance of the E1000 is intermediate between Vlance and VMXNET.

VMXNET2

Introduced in VI 3.5, the VMXNET2 adapter is based on the original VMXNET adapter but provides some high-performance features commonly used on modern networks, such as jumbo frames. This virtual network adapter provides better performance than the VMXNET adapter, but it is available only for some guest operating systems.

VMXNET3

Introduced in vSphere, the VMXNET3 is the successor to VMXNET2 and is a new third-generation vNIC which includes support for the following advanced new features.

- **Receive Side Scaling (RSS)**—This feature is supported for Windows Server 2008 and is a network driver technology that enables the efficient distribution of network receive data processing across multiple CPUs on a vSMP VM. Without RSS, all of the processing is performed by a single CPU, resulting in inefficient system cache utilization. RSS is designed to increase network performance by reducing processing delays by distributing receive processing from a NIC across multiple CPUs. RSS must be explicitly enabled within Server 2008 to work.

- **Large TX/RX ring sizes**—A ring serves as a staging area for packets in line to be transmitted or received. The ring buffer size can be tuned to ensure enough queuing at the device level to handle the peak loads generated by the system and the network. With a larger ring size, a network device can handle higher peak loads without dropping any packets. The default receive (RX) ring size is 150 for enhanced VMXNET2 (120 in VI3) and 256 for VMXNET3. You can increase the default for VMXNET2 to 512 and for VMXNET3 to 4,096. To increase the default for VMXNET2, you add a parameter to the VM config file (Ethernet<x>.numRecvBuffers=<value>); the only way to increase the default for VMXNET3 is inside the guest operating system. Currently, only Linux guests support this capability (ethtool -G eth<x> rx <value>), as there is no mechanism to set this within Windows.

- **MSI/MSI-X support**—Message-Signaled Interrupts (MSI) and Extended Message-Signaled Interrupts (MSI-X) are an alternative and more efficient way for a device to interrupt a CPU. An interrupt is a hardware signal from a device to a CPU informing it that the device needs attention and signaling that the CPU should stop current processing and respond to the device. Older systems used a special line-based interrupt pin for this which was limited to four lines and shared by multiple devices. With MSI and MSI-X, data is written to a special address in memory which the chipset delivers as a message to the CPU. MSI only supports passing interrupts to a single processor core and supports up to 32 messages; MSI-X is the successor to MSI, and allows multiple interrupts to be handled simultaneously and load-balanced across multiple cores, as well as up to 2,048 messages. VMXNET3 supports three interrupt modes: MSI, MSI-X, and INTx (line-based). VMXNET3 will attempt to use the interrupt modes in that order, if the server hardware and guest OS kernel support them. Almost all hardware today supports MSI and MSI-X; for Windows servers MSI and MSI-X are only supported on Windows 2008, Vista, and Windows 7, and line-based interrupts are used on Windows 2000, XP, and 2003.

- **IPv6 checksum and TSO over IPv6**—Checksums are used with both IPv4 and IPv6 for error checking of TCP packets. For IPv6, the method used to compute the checksum has changed, and the VMXNET3 driver supports this new method. Both VMXNET2 and VMXNET3 support the offload of computing the checksum to a network adapter for reduced CPU overhead. TCP Segmentation Offloading (TSO; also known as large send offload) is designed to offload portions of outbound TCP processing to a NIC, thereby reducing system CPU utilization and enhancing performance. Instead of processing many small MTU-sized frames during transmit, the system can send fewer, larger virtual MTU-sized frames and let the NIC break them into smaller frames. In order to use TSO, it must be supported the physical NIC and enabled in the guest operating system (usually a registry setting for Windows servers).

In order to use VMXNET3, your VMs must be using virtual hardware version 7. VMware has compared the performance of VMXNET2 against VMXNET3 and found that the performance of VMXNET3 is better than or equal to VMXNET2 in both Windows and Linux guests (see www.vmware.com/pdf/vsp_4_vmxnet3 _perf.pdf). Additionally, the advanced features that VMXNET3 support can further increase the performance of certain workloads. In most cases, it is recommended that you use the VMXNET3 over the older VMXNET2 adapter. If you plan to use the FT feature, note that it currently does not support the VMXNET3 adapter.

When you create a VM the VM Setup Wizard automatically hides vNIC types based on your operating system choice and will only display the types that are appropriate for your VM operating system, as listed in Table 6.2.

Table 6.2   Available vNIC Types Based on Operating System

	Flexible	E1000	VMXNET2	VMXNET3
Windows 2008 32/64-bit Windows 2008 R2 64-bit Windows 2003 Standard/Enterprise 64-bit Windows 2003 Datacenter 32/64-bit Windows XP 64-bit		X	X	X

Continues

Table 6.2   Available vNIC Types Based on Operating System *(Continued)*

	Flexible	E1000	VMXNET2	VMXNET3
Windows 7 32/64-bit Windows Vista 32/64-bit		X		X
Windows 2003 Standard/Enterprise 32-bit Windows XP 32-bit	X	X	X	X
Windows 2000 Server Windows 2000 Professional Windows NT 4 Windows 95/98	X	X		
SUSE Linux 8/9 32-bit	X	X		
SUSE Linux 8/9 64-bit		X	X	
SUSE Linux 10 32-bit	X	X	X	X
SUSE Linux 10 64-bit SUSE Linux 11 32/64-bit		X	X	X
Red Hat Linux 4 32-bit	X	X		
Red Hat Linux 4 64-bit		X	X	
Red Hat Linux 5 32-bit	X	X	X	X
Red Hat Linux 5 64-bit		X	X	X
Red Hat Linux 6 32/64-bit		X		X

You can no longer change the adapter type after adding a NIC to a VM. Instead, you must remove it and add a new one with a different type. One thing to note is that the NIC speed shown within a guest operating system is not always a true reflection of the pNIC speed that is in the vSwitch. For example, the new VMXNET3 adapter will show connected as 10Gbps in the Windows system tray regardless of the pNIC speed. Despite showing a different speed, the vNIC runs at the speed of the pNIC. So, with so many adapter types to choose from in some cases, which one should you choose? For older 32-bit operating systems that do not support VMXNET2 or VMXNET3, the Flexible adapter is a good choice. For older 64-bit operating systems, the E1000 adapter is a good choice. For newer operating systems, use VMXNET3 if the system supports it; otherwise, use VMXNET2.

STANDARD vSWITCHES

vSwitches are the core networking component on an ESX and ESXi host. A vSwitch is built and contained in the RAM of a host and connects the pNICs in the host server to the vNICs in VMs. vSwitches emulate many of the traits of traditional Ethernet switches and can perform many of the same functions, such as forwarding frames at the data link layer and VLAN segmentation.

As of this writing, each host may have up to 248 vSwitches configured on it with up to 512 port groups per vSwitch and a maximum of 4,088 total vSwitch ports per host. Depending on the pNIC type that you use, you may use up to 32 pNICs in a single host which you can then assign to your vSwitches. You can assign up to 32 pNICs to a vSwitch to team them for load balancing and failover purposes, but a pNIC can be assigned to only one vSwitch at any one time.

vSwitches support 802.1Q VLAN tagging, which allows for multiple VLANs to be used on a single physical switch port. This capability can greatly reduce the number of pNICs needed in a host. Instead of needing a separate pNIC for each VLAN that you need to connect to on a host, you can use a single NIC to connect to multiple VLANs. The way tagging works is that tags are applied to all network frames to identify them as belonging to a particular VLAN. There are several methods for doing this in vSphere, with the main difference between the modes being where the tags are applied. VGT mode does this at the guest operating system layer, whereas EST mode does this on the external physical switch and VST mode does this inside the VMkernel. The differences between the VLAN tagging modes are as follows.

- **Virtual Machine Guest Tagging (VGT)**—With this mode the 802.1Q VLAN trunking driver is installed inside the VM. Tags are preserved between the VM networking stack and external switch when frames are passed to and from vSwitches. To enable VGT mode, configure your port group with VLAN ID 4095.

- **External Switch Tagging (EST)**—With this mode you use external switches for VLAN tagging. This is similar to a physical network, and VLAN configuration is normally transparent to each individual physical server. The tag is appended when a packet arrives at a switch port and stripped away when a packet leaves a switch port toward the server. With EST, a vSwitch can process traffic on only one VLAN, and the vSwitch will not see the VLAN tag since it is stripped at the pSwitch port.

- **Virtual Switch Tagging (VST)**—With this mode you configure port groups on a vSwitch for each VLAN and connect the vNIC of the VM to the port group. The vSwitch port group tags all outbound frames and removes tags for all inbound frames. It also ensures that frames on one VLAN do not leak into a different VLAN.

VST mode is the mode that is most commonly used with ESX because it's easier to configure and manage. Additionally, it eliminates the need to install a specific VLAN driver inside a VM, and there is almost no performance impact by doing the tagging inside the vSwitches.

When you create a vSwitch the first thing you do is assign one or more physical network adapters to it. If you assign more than one, the additional NICs can be configured as a team to support load balancing and failover. It is also possible to not assign a pNIC to a vSwitch, thereby creating an internal-only or private vSwitch that is isolated from the rest of the network. This is useful for testing purposes or when building a new VM to prepare it before joining it to the rest of the network. After you have assigned pNICs to a vSwitch, you can create port groups for individual VLANs. You can also create vSwitches without pNICs to use as a private vSwitch.

Port groups are a networking feature that is unique to VMware vSwitches. Even though port groups can be assigned VLAN IDs, they should not be considered VLANs. They are more like configuration templates for the vNIC ports on the vSwitch. It is possible to have different port groups using the same VLAN ID on the same vSwitch. In addition to the VLAN ID, port groups also allow you to set different networking characteristics, such as traffic shaping (Quality of Service or QoS) and security settings such as Promiscuous mode, as well as allowing MAC address changes.

DISTRIBUTED VSWITCHES

vNetwork Distributed vSwitches (known as vDS or vNDS) are a new feature that VMware introduced in vSphere to address a pain point that existed in previous releases when it came to creating vSwitches for host servers. The problem has always been that vSwitches with identical configurations must be created on each host for features such as VMotion to work properly. When a VM moves from one host to another it must find the network name and configuration that it is using on one host to be the same on the other host so that it can connect to it and use it. For this reason, most hosts have very similar vSwitch configurations. Configuring vSwitches individually on each host can be a tedious process, as all configurations must be identical on each host to avoid VMotion compatibility issues. VMware's answer to this problem was the Distributed vSwitch, which allows a single vSwitch to be used across multiple hosts.

Distributed vSwitches are very similar to standard vSwitches. But whereas standard vSwitches are configured individually on each host, vDSs are configured centrally using vCenter Server. You can have up to 16 vDSs per vCenter Server and up to 64 hosts may connect to each vDS. Distributed vSwitches are created and maintained using vCenter Server, but they do not depend on vCenter Server for their operation. This is important, because if the vCenter Server becomes unavailable, you don't want the hosts that are using the vDSs to lose their vDS configurations. To avoid this, when a vDS is created in vCenter Server a hidden vSwitch is created on each host that is connected to the vDS in a folder named .dvsData on a local VMFS volume. Distributed vSwitches provide more than just centralized management of vSwitches. They also provide the following features that are not available with standard vSwitches.

- They support private VLANs to provide segmentation between VMs.
- The network port state of a VM is maintained when VMotioned from one host to another, which enables uninterrupted statistic monitoring and facilitates security monitoring. This is known as Network Policy VMotion.
- They support bidirectional traffic shaping, which supports both TX and RX rate limiting; the standard vSwitch supports only TX rate limiting.
- They enable support for third-party distributed vSwitches such as the Cisco Nexus 1000V.
- New in vSphere 4.1, Network I/O control allows for flexible partitioning of pNIC bandwidth between different traffic types. It does this using network resource pools that can be used to control the priority for FT traffic, iSCSI traffic, VMotion traffic, management traffic, NFS traffic, and VM traffic. You can configure network resource pools by selecting a vDS and choosing the new Resource Allocation tab.

DEPLOYMENT CONSIDERATIONS

The requirements for using a vDS are simple. All hosts that will use the vDS must have an Enterprise Plus license, and your hosts must be managed by vCenter Server. You can use standard vSwitches in combination with distributed vSwitches as long as they do not use the same pNICs. It is a common practice to use standard vSwitches for VMkernel, ESX Service Console, and ESXi Management networking and to use Distributed vSwitches for VM networking. This is considered a hybrid mode, as shown in Figure 6.2.

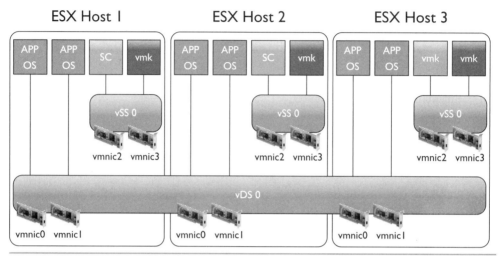

Figure 6.2   Hybrid environment with both standard vSwitches and distributed vSwitches

This prevents any changes made to vDSs from impacting the critical networking of a host server. Use of vDSs for that traffic is fully supported, but many prefer to keep it separate, as once it is set up and configured per host it typically does not change. You can also use multiple vDSs per host, as shown in Figure 6.3. This is commonly done to segregate traffic types; for example, running the VMkernel, ESX Service Console, and ESXi Management networking on one vDS and VM networking on another. Another example is for a DMZ configuration to isolate all of the DMZ networking on a separate vDS with separate pNICs.

If you are setting up a new virtual environment, configuring vDSs is fairly straightforward, since you do not have to worry about disrupting any VMs. If you are migrating existing hosts using standard vSwitches, you have several options. You can migrate the entire host networking at once to a vDS; doing so will cause a brief disruption in the networking to the host and VMs, however. You can also migrate existing hosts in a phased manner, moving one NIC at a time from the old standard vSwitches to the new vDSs so that your VMs have

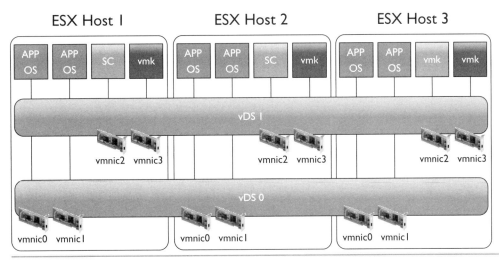

Figure 6.3   Multiple distributed vSwitches used to segregate traffic

continuous network connectivity. To do this you create your new vDS and configure the port groups, and then move your redundant NICs over to the newly
created vDS from the old vSwitch. Once both vSwitches have connectivity, you
can edit their vNIC settings and move them to the new vDS. After all the VMs
have been moved to the new vDS, you can then move the remaining NICs from
the old vSwitch to the new vDS. You can also leverage the Host Profile feature to
migrate multiple hosts to a vDS. To do so requires that the host be placed in
maintenance mode first, so all VMs must be shut down or moved to other hosts.

VMware has published a white paper titled "VMware vNetwork Distributed
Switch: Migration and Configuration" that covers the migration options in
detail (www.vmware.com/files/pdf/vsphere-vnetwork-ds-migration-configura-
tion-wp.pdf).

vDS CONFIGURATION

Distributed vSwitches are not configured in the same manner as standard
vSwitches. Instead of selecting a host and then choosing Configuration→
Networking, you must go to the Inventory view and select Networking. This is
because vDSs are not specific to a host and are considered a vCenter Server
object. vDSs are created at the datacenter level, so they can be used by all hosts.
You first create a vDS and configure it, and then assign it to your hosts. To create a vDS follow these steps.

1. Select your datacenter object, right-click on it, and select New vNetwork Distributed Switch. This will launch the vDS Creation Wizard.

2. In version 4.1, you will receive a prompt to choose a vDS version (either 4.0 or 4.1). If your hosts are all at version 4.1, you can choose the 4.1 version, which enables additional features such as network I/O control and dynamic load balancing.

3. At the General Properties screen, select a unique name for your vDS and the number of uplink ports; these are for host pNICs that will be connected to the vDS and is the total for all hosts combined. You will need one uplink port for each pNIC from every host connected to the vDS. You can always increase this number later if needed.

4. At the Add Hosts and Physical Adapters screen, choose to either add hosts and pNICs to the vDS now, or add them later. To add them now, select each host and choose unused adapters to use with the vDS. If you are unsure of the VLAN configuration for each pNIC, click the View Details link to see the pNIC brand/model and other information, such as the observed IP networks, which will show which VLANs the pNICs see traffic on.

5. At the Ready to Complete screen, you can choose to have a default port group created or you can configure them later. Click Finish and your vDS will be created.

Once the vDS is created, you will have an uplinks group (and a ports group if you chose to create a default one). The uplinks group will show all the uplink port connections. You can edit its properties to change default settings and policies. The ports group will show all the ports that VMs connect to; by default, 128 ports are created. You can edit the ports group by either decreasing or increasing that number based on your needs. You can also edit the settings for the ports group that will override the default settings of the vDS. Here you can set the VLAN ID for the ports group, set the security, traffic, and load-balancing policies, and set the port binding type.

Port bindings specify how ports are assigned to VMs, and you can choose from Static, Dynamic, and Ephemeral. Static bindings assign ports to VMs when they are configured; once all the ports that the port group has been configured with have been assigned to VMs, no more can be added unless the port group number is increased. Dynamic bindings only assign ports to a VM when it is powered on; once it is powered off the port is unassigned. Ephemeral bindings set the number of ports in the port group to zero, and ports are assigned statically up to the maximum limit that is supported on the distributed vSwitch.

If you select a vDS in the left pane of the vSphere Client you have several tabs to choose from in the right pane that display vDS information and allow you to configure various options. The Configuration tab shows a visual representation of the uplinks and port groups and the hosts and VMs connected to them. Here you can also add hosts, edit the vDS, and add new port groups. If you edit the settings of a vDS, you can configure the number of uplink ports, maximum MTU (for jumbo frames), Cisco Discovery Protocol, and Private VLANs. You will see a number of port settings that are not editable on the Properties tab in the General section. This number is computed from the number of ports configured in each port group and the uplink ports on a vDS. For example, if you had two port groups with 128 ports and four uplink ports, the total number of ports would show as 260 ($2 \times 128 + 4$).

One other configuration component of the vDS is the virtual adapters, which are simply the VMkernel and Service Console interfaces that are added to standard vSwitches. You will need to configure these if you choose to have your VMkernel and Service Console on a vDS. You cannot do this in the Inventory Networking view where you configure the other vDS settings. You need to go to Inventory→Hosts and Clusters, select a host, and choose the Configuration tab and then Networking. You will see your vDSs there, as well as Manage Virtual Adapters and Manage Physical Adapters links. The Manage Physical Adapters link simply allows you to change uplink adapters for the vDS. If you click the Manage Virtual Adapters link, a new window will open that lets you add, edit, or remove a virtual adapter as well as migrate an existing one back to a standard vSwitch. Adding a new one launches a wizard that will let you either add a new virtual adapter or migrate an existing one from a standard vSwitch. Once you select an option and a virtual adapter type, you will be able to assign existing vDS port groups to the virtual adapter as well as set IP address information for it.

Distributed vSwitches can be a bit more confusing than standard vSwitches, as they are configured and managed differently. If you choose to use them, spend some time getting used to administering them before you begin using them in a production environment. It's better to make any configuration mistakes early on when there will be less of an impact to the hosts using your vDSs.

CISCO NEXUS 1000V

When VMware created support for third-party vSwitches in vSphere, it collaborated with Cisco to develop a vSwitch that went above and beyond what

VMware offered and provided more advanced network features that are commonly found in physical network switches. The result was the Nexus 1000V (N1KV), which was released at the same time as vSphere. The N1KV is a distributed vSwitch that adds more intelligence and features to the standard vSwitch to better manage and protect VM traffic.

ADVANCED FUNCTIONALITY FOR vSWITCHES

The Nexus 1000V, as shown in Figure 6.4, is a distributed vSwitch developed by Cisco that uses Cisco's NX-OS networking operating system, which is based on the company's SAN-OS software that is standard in many of its physical switches.

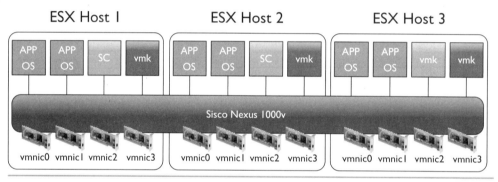

Figure 6.4   A single Cisco Nexus 1000V spanning multiple hosts

The N1KV consists of two components: a Virtual Supervisor Module (VSM) and a Virtual Ethernet Module (VEM). The VSM manages one or more VEMs as one logical switch and supports up to 64 VEMs. All VEM configuration is accomplished using the VSM with the NX-OS command-line interface, which is pushed to all the VEMs. The VSM uses port profiles, which are configured in the VSM for each VEM and then appear as port groups in vCenter Server. Although VEMs can operate without a VSM, you can have multiple VSMs to ensure redundancy in case of a VSM failure. The VSM is integrated with the vCenter Server, so all network configuration involving the VEMs is synchronized between them. The VSM is packaged as a virtual appliance and is deployed to an ESX or ESXi host using the vSphere Client. Once deployed and powered on, it is managed using a command-line interface.

The VEM is installed onto each ESX and ESXi host, and only one VEM can exist on a single host. It is packaged as a .VIB module and can be downloaded from the VSM web interface page. Once downloaded, it is deployed to a host as a patch update using standard patching tools, such as Update Manager, esxupdate, or vihostupdate. The VEM executes as part of the VMkernel and utilizes the vDS API to interface with vCenter Server and VMs. The VEM gets all of its configuration information from the VSMs, and if it loses connectivity to the VSM, it will continue to switch traffic based on the last known configuration.

It's important to note that although the Nexus 1000V is a Cisco product, it can be used with any physical switch regardless of the manufacturer. This allows people who use non-Cisco physical network gear to take advantage of the 1000V in their virtual environments. Although it may not be managed in the same way as non-Cisco switches, it does provide advanced functionality to vSwitches regardless.

In March 2010, Cisco announced a new VSM called the Nexus 1010V, which is a physical version of the VSM virtual appliance. The 1010V is a more powerful version of the 1000V VSM and can contain four VSMs to manage up to 256 VEMs. The 1010V is an alternative for those who are not comfortable having their VSMs running as virtual appliances on ESX and ESXi hosts. In addition, it helps offload the resource requirements of the VSM from the host to a physical device.

Benefits of Using Nexus 1000V

Before server virtualization, the network was usually all physical and stopped at the NIC of a server. With virtualization, it extends further into the server to vSwitches and vNICs that are all managed by the host server. Virtual hosts are typically managed by server administrators who also became network administrators because of the networking inside their hosts. This causes tension in many cases between server administrators and network administrators because part of the network is now managed by server administrators. In addition, because some of the virtual networking traffic does not leave the host and go over the physical network, the network administrators are unable to monitor and manage it.

The Nexus 1000V shifts that network management inside a virtual host back to the network administrators and helps to make peace between server and network administers. In addition to solving the political problem of administration, it also adds many advanced features and better security to the virtual networking inside a host. The Nexus 1000V provides the following benefits.

- The Cisco Nexus 1000V includes the Cisco Integrated Security Features that are found on Cisco physical switches to prevent a variety of attack scenarios; this includes Port Security, IP Source Guard, Dynamic ARP inspection, and DHCP Snooping.

- The Cisco Nexus 1000V allows virtualization administrators to continue using VMware's vCenter GUI to provision VMs. At the same time, network administrators can provision and operate the VM network the same way they do the physical network using Cisco CLI and SNMP along with tools such as Encapsulated Remote SPAN (ERSPAN) and NetFlow.

- Standard and distributed vSwitches only operate at Layers 2 and 3 of the network; the Cisco Nexus 1000V enables Layer 4 through Layer 7 services for VMs to be specified as part of the VM network policy.

- To complement the ease of creating and provisioning VMs, the Cisco Nexus 1000V includes a Port Profile feature to address the dynamic nature of server virtualization from the network's perspective. Port Profiles enable you to define VM network policies for different types or classes of VMs from the Cisco Nexus 1000V VSM, and then apply the profiles to individual VM vNICs through VMware's vCenter GUI for transparent provisioning of network resources. Port Profiles are a scalable mechanism for configuring networks with large numbers of VMs.

- The Cisco Nexus 1000V Series enables true packet capture and analysis by supporting features such as Switched Port Analyzer (SPAN) and ERSPAN, which allow traffic to be copied to a local or remote destination, enabling thorough network troubleshooting and reducing time to resolution for virtual network problems.

- Advanced Cisco IOS features that are often used on physical servers can be used with VMs. This includes features such as access control lists, QoS, NetFlow, advanced load balancing algorithms, rate limits, SPAN, and port channels.

The Nexus 1000V offers a huge improvement over the standard vSwitches that are available in vSphere and you should seriously consider it for larger environments or where security is a concern.

INSTALLING AND CONFIGURING NEXUS 1000V

The basics of installing and configuring the Nexus 1000V are to first deploy the VSM as a virtual appliance on a host and then to install VEMs on each ESX and ESXi host. Afterward, you configure the VSM and then use both the VSM and vCenter Server to configure your VEMs and VM networking. Although those are the basics, the actual installation process can be a bit complicated, so it is recommended that you follow Cisco's detailed documentation on installing and configuring the Nexus 1000V that is available on the company's website. Because much of the configuration involves using the NX-OS, which you may not be familiar with, it's best to hand that piece over to your network administrators. Be sure to check out the Additional Resources section at the end of this chapter for more information on the Nexus 1000V.

CHOOSING A vSWITCH TYPE

With multiple vSwitch choices available, you might be wondering how you should decide which one to use. If you do not have an Enterprise Plus license the answer is simple: Standard vSwitches are your only choice. If you do have an Enterprise Plus license distributed vSwitches become an option, as well as the Cisco Nexus 1000V. However, whereas the vDS is included with vSphere, the 1000V costs an additional $795 per host. Here are some things to consider when choosing a vSwitch type.

- Standard vSwitches are easy to use, and if you have a smaller environment they might be the best choice. However, they lack the advanced networking features that are present in the vDS, and even more so in the 1000V.
- Distributed vSwitches add centralized administration and some advanced features that are not present in the standard vSwitch. However, vDSs can be a bit more difficult to manage, and although centralized administration makes things easier, one wrong change will impact all of your hosts. Change management is critical when using vDS in a production environment.
- The Cisco Nexus 1000V adds advanced features and intelligence to the vSwitch and makes it manageable by your physical network admins. However, it costs more and is much more complicated to manage than the built-in vSwitches.

Table 6.3 shows a feature comparison for the different kinds of vSwitches.

Table 6.3   Feature Comparison between Different vSwitch Types

	Standard vSwitch	Distributed vSwitch	Cisco Nexus 1000V
802.1Q VLAN tagging	X	X	X
EtherChannel	X	X	X

Continues

Table 6.3 Feature Comparison between Different vSwitch Types *(Continued)*

	Standard vSwitch	Distributed vSwitch	Cisco Nexus 1000V
Multicast support	X	X	X
Layer 2 forwarding	X	X	X
iSCSI multipathing	X	X	X
Cisco Discovery Protocol v1/v2	X	X	X
IPv6 for management	X	X	X
Network Policy Groups	X	X	X
Transmit rate limiting (from VM)	X	X	X
Receive rate limiting (to VM)		X	X
Network VMotion		X	X
Private VLANs		X	X
Link Aggregation Control Protocol (LACP)			X
Access control lists			X
IGMPv3 snooping			X
Virtual port channels			X
QoS marking			X
DHCP snooping			X
IP Source Guard			X
Dynamic ARP inspection			X
SPAN			X
ERSPAN			X
NetFlow v9			X
Packet capture and analysis			X
RADIUS and TACACS+			X

Although it is common to mix standard and distributed vSwitches in a virtual environment, if you choose to implement the Nexus 1000V it is best to not use other vSwitch types with it. If you have the Nexus 1000V you should use it for everything; it's far superior to the other vSwitch types. In addition, your network administrators will probably not appreciate being able to manage only part of the virtual network and will want to manage it all.

vShield Zones

With the release of vSphere, VMware also released a new product called vShield Zones that is essentially a virtual firewall integrated with vCenter Server and designed to protect VMs and analyze virtual network traffic. vShield Zones is built on the technology acquired by VMware when it purchased Blue Lane Technologies in 2008. The current 1.0 version of vShield Zones is not yet integrated with VMware's new VMsafe technology, but VMware plans to use the VMsafe APIs in vSphere in a future release of vShield Zones. vShield Zones is available as a free download with the Advanced, Enterprise, and Enterprise Plus editions of ESX and ESXi.

VMware developed vShield Zones to provide some basic capabilities to protect virtual networks in it core product. vShield Zones provides the same basic protection and analysis as some of the similar third-party products, such as Reflex Systems Virtualization Management Center, Altor Networks Virtual Firewall, and Catbird V-Security, but vShield Zones is not as complex or feature-rich as those products. The plus side of this is that VMware administrators should find vShield Zones easier to use and should not require them to become security experts to better secure their virtual environment. vShield Zones adds the following features to your virtual network.

- **Firewall protection**—Provides firewall protection across vSwitches using rules to allow and block specific ports, protocols, and traffic direction. The firewall function is termed "VM Wall" and provides a centralized, hierarchical access control list at the datacenter and cluster levels. Two types of rules are configurable: Layer 4 rules and Layer 2/3 rules. These are the data link, network, and transport layers of the OSI networking protocol model.
- **Traffic analysis**—All traffic that passes through the vShield appliances are inspected, and information on source, destination, direction, and service is gathered and aggregated into the vShield Manager. The traffic analysis data is termed "VM Flow" and can be used for network troubleshooting or investigating suspicious traffic, as well as to create access rules.
- **Virtual Machine Discovery**—The vShield agents utilize a discovery process when analyzing traffic which notes the operating system, application, and

ports in use. Once this information is collected and analyzed, it can be used for firewall rule configuration.

vShield Zones consists of two components: the vShield Manager and vShield agents, both of which are deployed as virtual appliances from the included OVF files. The vShield Manager is the centralized management device that is used to manage the vShield agents and configure rules and monitor network traffic. A single vShield Manager can manage vShield agents on multiple ESX/ESXi hosts and is accessed using a web-based interface. The vShield Manager can manage up to 50 vShield agents and a single vShield Zones agent can protect up to 500 VMs. Once you select a vSwitch to protect with vShield Zones, the vShield Manager will deploy the vShield agent onto the host on which the vSwitch is located. The vShield agent provides the firewall protection, performs the network traffic analysis, and utilizes zones of trust which separate traffic into protected and unprotected zones. Network traffic enters from the unprotected zone and goes through the vShield agent to get to the protected zone where the VMs reside.

The basic requirements for vShield Zones are that you need to have ESX/ESXi 4.0 hosts and a vCenter Server 4.0. Beyond that, you need to have permission to add and power on VMs, and you'll need static IP addresses for each vShield agent that you deploy as well as the vShield Manager. There is also an additional memory requirement. The vShield Manager VM is created with 2GB of memory and also has a preset memory reservation of 2GB. The vShield agents are created with 1GB or memory and have 1GB preset memory reservations. Because of these reservations, you must ensure that you have enough available free physical host memory to satisfy the reservations when the Manager and agents are powered on. Although it is possible to edit the VM settings and remove the reservations, this is not recommended because this can affect the performance of the appliances and their ability to function properly. Do not increase the amount of memory assigned to the vShield Manager and agents, as this will not increase their performance. Additionally, there are some port requirements for the few ports that vShield uses, which include the following.

- **Port 22**—SSH (TCP): Used for all communication between the vShield Manager and agents.

- **Port 123**—NTP (UDP): Used for time synchronization of the vShield Manager and agents.

- **Port 443**—HTTPS (TCP): Used for PCs to access to the web UI for administration of the vShield Manager.

- **Port 1162**—SNMP (UDP): Used to send SNMP trap messages from vShield agents to the vShield Manager. All other statistics, including memory and CPU, use port 22.

Both the vShield Manager and agents do use host resources, and although the memory and disk usage is static, the CPU usage will vary based on the amount of network traffic passing through the agent. Additionally, there is some very slight network latency for the traffic passing through the agent due to the additional hops the traffic is taking to pass through the agent en route to the destination VMs. By design, each vShield agent allows up to 40,000 concurrent sessions and there are no throughput limitations as it uses the hardware on which it runs and the resources that are assigned to the agent. Table 6.4 lists the resource usage and overhead for both the vShield Manager and the agents.

Table 6.4 vShield Zones Resource Requirements and Network Overhead

Resource	vShield Manager	vShield Agents
Disk space usage	8GB	5GB
Memory usage	2GB (reserved)	1GB (reserved)
CPU usage	3%–7%	3%–10%
Network latency	N/A	500 microseconds

Here are some additional notes and tips on vShield Zones that you should be aware of.

- The vShield Manager and agent VMs will show in the vSphere Client that VMware Tools is not installed. Do not attempt to install VMware Tools on those VMs, as it is not required and the performance optimization that VMware Tools provides is already built into the vShield Zones VMs.

- The agents are not true privileged VMs like the Service Console is, but they should be treated as such, and although they do have reservations for memory by default, they do not for the CPU. Consider using shares or reservations to guarantee CPU resources for the agents.

- vShield Zones was built to protect VMs, and not the VMkernel or Service Console. Do not install an agent on a Service Console or VMkernel vSwitch.

- Do not remove the preinstalled NICs from either the vShield Manager or the agent VMs. If you do remove and then add NICs on a vShield agent you must uninstall the vShield Zones agent and reinstall it. If you remove the NICs from a vShield Manager you may have to reinstall your entire vShield Zones deployment to ensure communication between vShield agents and the vShield Manager. Do not reconfigure the hardware or decrease the allotted resources of a vShield Zones Manager or agent VM as they have already been optimized for vCenter Server.

- VMotion is supported for VMs that are protected by vShield, but you must first make sure you have an agent on the host that you are VMotioning to and that your port groups are set up the same. By default, you cannot VMotion a VM connected to a internal-only (no NICs) vSwitch, so you must configure vCenter Server to allow this by editing the vpxd.cfg file and adding a VMOnVirtualIntranet parameter. Details on how to do this are in the appendix of the vShield Zones Administration Guide.

- VMotion is not supported for vShield agents, but it is supported for the vShield Manager. You do not want the vShield agents to move to other hosts, so be sure to disable the Distributed Resource Scheduler (DRS) and HA on the individual vShield agent VMs. Additionally, Distributed Power Management (DPM) is not supported on hosts that are running vShield agents; see the release notes for more information on this.

- The vShield Manager and agent VMs can be installed to local disk or shared disk storage. It's best to install the Manager to shared disk storage if possible so that you can leverage VMotion and HA. Since the agents cannot be moved from the host, it's best to install them to local disk storage if you can.

- When deploying vShield agents your VMs will not be disrupted as they are moved from one vSwitch to another. In testing, only one missed response was seen while doing a continuous ping on a VM during the agent deployment operation.

- If the vShield Manager is powered off, it will not affect vShield agent operation and the VMs that are protected. In the event the vShield Manager is unavailable for some time, each vShield agent can queue data and send it to the vShield Manager once it is available. But if a vShield agent is powered off, all VMs in the protected zone will lose network connectivity. It is a good idea to limit access to who can access and control the agent VM in vCenter Server, and also set the VM for automatic startup when the host is rebooted or powered on.

- vShield Zones supports both standard vSwitches and distributed vSwitches. The agent install will automatically configure standard vSwitches, but you have to manually configure distributed vSwitches; see the vShield Administration Guide for instructions on how to do this.

vShield Zones shows a lot of promise, and future versions will offer better integration and usability as well as more features and functionality to better protect your virtual environment. If you're looking to improve the security of your virtual environment, you should definitely give vShield Zones a try. Not only will it help to protect your virtual environment, but it will also provide you with some insight into what is occurring on your virtual networks.

ADDITIONAL RESOURCES

Here are some additional resources for networking in vSphere:

- VMware's Technical Resources for Virtual Networking (www.vmware.com/technical-resources/virtual-networking/resources.html)
- "The Great vSwitch Debate," an eight-part epic miniseries on vSwitch configuration options by Ken Cline, a very experienced virtualization veteran (http://kensvirtualreality.files.wordpress.com/2009/12/the-great-vswitch-debate-combined.pdf)
- "VMware vNetwork Distributed Switch: Migration and Configuration" (www.vmware.com/files/pdf/vsphere-vnetwork-ds-migration-configuration-wp.pdf)
- "DMZ Virtualization Using VMware vSphere 4 and the Cisco Nexus 1000V Virtual Switch" (www.cisco.com/en/US/prod/collateral/switches/ps9441/ps9902/dmz_virtualization_vsphere4_nexus1000V.pdf)
- "Best Practices in Deploying Cisco Nexus 1000V Series Switches on Cisco UCS Systems" (www.ciscosystems.ch/en/US/prod/collateral/switches/ps9441/ps9902/white_paper_c11-558242.html)
- "Virtual Networking Features of the VMware vNetwork Distributed Switch and Cisco Nexus 1000V Switches" (www.vmware.com/files/pdf/technology/cisco_vmware_virtualizing_the_datacenter.pdf)
- "Guidelines for Implementing VMware vSphere 4 with the Cisco Nexus 1000V Virtual Switch" (www.vmware.com/files/pdf/partners/cisco/Cisco-vSphere-vNetwork-Implementation-Guidelines-V5.1.pdf)

SUMMARY

We've barely scratched the surface on networking in vSphere in this chapter; a whole book could be devoted to this subject alone. There is more to networking than simply plugging cables into NICs, and you should really make sure you understand it well enough so that you can configure and secure it properly. The Nexus 1000V helps in that area, as it takes much of the burden off the virtualization administrator. Even if you don't use the 1000V, be sure to work closely with your network administrators who can help you understand some of the network concepts. On the other hand, it helps if you make them understand the virtualization concepts which are foreign to many network administrators. Having a good relationship with them and sharing information will benefit both groups and will make the management and configuration of your virtual network much easier.

PERFORMANCE IN vSPHERE

VMware has invested considerable resources in the area of performance with the release of vSphere. In fact, the company claims that vSphere has seen the largest performance increase of any of its releases to date, a statement which VMware has backed up with an impressive array of published benchmark results. Performance monitoring and diagnosis is usually an area of confusion and misinterpretation among many administrators, and although getting your vSphere environment up and running out of the box is a straightforward process, fine-tuning and ensuring that your vSphere environment is running optimally is more complex. Even if you are familiar with the basics of vSphere administration, it is well worth it to take the time to familiarize yourself with the subject of performance in vSphere, particularly troubleshooting performance issues.

Understanding the processes of monitoring, alerting, and troubleshooting performance issues in vSphere is key to being a successful vSphere administrator. This chapter will discuss the new performance-related improvements and features in vSphere and will provide some basic recommendations regarding how to use vSphere's tools and utilities to monitor and troubleshoot performance-related issues. There are many levels of complexity to vSphere performance which could easily warrant a book unto itself; the purpose of this chapter is to provide you with a basic foundation from which you can build and expand your vSphere performance knowledge further.

WHAT'S NEW WITH PERFORMANCE IN VSPHERE

vSphere has seen enhancements in the areas of CPU, memory, storage, and networking performance. Let's take a high-level look at the new performance-related features found in each of these areas.

CPU ENHANCEMENTS

vSphere now benefits from the following new CPU-related features and enhancements.

- vSphere has an improved awareness of multicore CPUs and CPUs with the more recent implementation of hyperthreading, as found in Intel Nehalem CPUs, delivering performance gains of up to 24%. It also has a heightened awareness of the CPU topology (i.e., number and placement of CPU sockets and cores), which means it can deliver more predictable performance via the ESX/ESXi Resource Scheduler. vSphere also now supports Extended Page Tables (EPT), which is a hardware-based virtualization feature found in Intel Nehalem CPUs. EPT is similar in function to Rapid Virtualization Indexing (RVI) which AMD has been running for a while, and both of these technologies can provide noticeable performance benefits.

- The esxtop/resxtop utility has been updated to include a number of new performance counters, with a particular emphasis on the visibility of multicore CPU systems.

- vSphere now also provides the ability to hot-add or remove CPU and memory resources to a virtual machine (VM) while it is powered on, guest OS permitting.

- vSphere offers better host and VM performance when using Intel (Intel VT) or AMD (AMD-V) CPU hardware assist, and improved Large Page Support over that found in VI3.

- Finally, improvements to the virtual CPU (vCPU) core scheduler have led to an increase in utilization efficiency on available physical CPUs (pCPU) in the host.

MEMORY ENHANCEMENTS

Memory compression is an exciting new feature in vSphere version 4.1 that can obviate the need for a VM to swap some of its memory pages down to slow-performing disk at times of memory pressure due to high levels of memory oversubscription. Via this new mechanism, performance gains are achieved because the memory is being compressed and moved to an allocated area in the host's memory, rather than being swapped out to slower-performing disk-based storage.

STORAGE ENHANCEMENTS

VMware made the follow new storage-related features and enhancements in vSphere.

- vSphere boasts an overall reduction in CPU overhead when performing storage I/O, and it features improved I/O concurrency of the storage stack. It achieves the latter by allowing the VMkernel of the host to process any physical I/O requests from a guest VM while the vCPU of the guest is free to process other tasks.

- Paravirtualized SCSI (PVSCSI) is the new, more efficient storage driver in vSphere. This driver is presented to VMs as a virtual storage adapter and is suited to VMs with a high level of storage requirements—for example, large databases performing disk-intensive overnight processing jobs. Note, however, that this current version of the PVSCSI driver is not suited to low I/O workloads and only delivers performance benefits over the older LSI Logic virtual storage adapter when used on VMs with high storage I/O requirements connected to fast storage (i.e., >2,000 I/O per second or IOPS). Users can actually experience a slight increase in latency if they are running a VM with the PVSCSI storage adapter against low I/O workloads or with low I/O performing storage, though any degradation in performance for the VM is minimal.

- vSphere 4.1 introduces a Quality of Service (QoS) feature for host storage I/O. Through the use of I/O shares and limits, you can ensure that particular VMs connecting to a datastore have a required level of I/O resources at times of heavy storage I/O utilization.

- vSphere has improved iSCSI efficiency, especially when using the software-based iSCSI adapter. This performance is considerably better in vSphere 4.0 when compared to its predecessor, VI 3.5. With vSphere 4.1, you can now use a hardware-based iSCSI 10Gb offload adapter (the Broadcom 57711). At the time of this writing, a limited selection of 10Gb iSCSI offload adapters are available for use with ESX/ESXi, though this list of officially supported adapters will no doubt increase as 10GbE becomes more mainstream in enterprise IT environments.

- A significant feature found in vSphere 4.1 is support for 8Gb Fibre Channel (FC) connectivity. With the majority of modern storage area networks (SAN) offering 8Gb FC, this is a welcome addition.

- vSphere v4.1 sees the introduction of improved visibility via the vCenter Server performance charts and esxtop/resxtop of the storage throughput and latency of hosts and VMs, which also includes NFS-based storage. All of this comes in very handy when troubleshooting performance-related issues.

NETWORKING ENHANCEMENTS

vSphere now offers the following new features and enhancements in relation to networking.

- vSphere introduces a new network adapter, VMXNET3, which comes with Receive Side Scaling (RSS), which improves Windows vSMP VM scaling. It also features a new version of NetQueue (v2), which allows for multiple send and receive queues, similar to the asynchronous I/O described in the Storage Enhancements section. In addition, the TCP/IP stack in vSphere's VMkernel received a complete overhaul, leading to greater performance and efficiency, particularly with iSCSI, NFS, and VMotion network traffic.
- Load-based teaming found in vSphere 4.1 provides the ability to dynamically adjust the teaming algorithm which will balance the network load across a team of physical adapters connected to a vNetwork Distributed Switch (vDS). The VMotion algorithm was rewritten to provide improved VMotion performance and the ability to move more VMs simultaneously.

MONITORING vSPHERE PERFORMANCE

Traditionally in a nonvirtualized server environment, you would monitor and troubleshoot any performance-related issues from within the operating system itself. This is straightforward enough, as the operating system is installed straight onto the physical hardware, and as such, it has full awareness of the physical resources it has access to and, importantly, doesn't even need to consider the possibility of local resource contention from another operating system.

Things change, however, when you are dealing with virtualized server environments, as the operating system now uses virtual devices which, along with other resources, are scheduled and presented by the virtualization hypervisor. The operating system is not aware that it is no longer running on dedicated physical server hardware. When using a popular Windows performance utility such as Perfmon in the guest OS of a VM, the operating system can produce inaccurate results on some of the performance counters, as it is not aware of any resource limitations or contention from other VMs that are also sharing the underlying physical resources, although with the introduction of vSphere, "VM Memory" and "VM Processor" specific counters are incorporated into Perfmon that provide accurate usage for both of these resource areas. There is a requirement for VMware Tools to be installed on the guest OS before these performance objects are available within Perfmon. Despite the memory and processor performance objects being present within Perfmon, I recommend that any performance management or troubleshooting be conducted within vCenter or esxtop/resxtop, both of which provide access to performance metrics at the hypervisor level, and therefore are actually aware of what underlying physical resources are currently allocated and what is available.

With all the exciting performance enhancements found in vSphere, you may be wondering how you monitor your host to determine whether it is running to its full potential and to ensure that you are alerted in the event of any performance-related issues. The good news is that host performance monitoring in your vSphere environment is made easy through the use of performance charts accessed via the vSphere Client, along with the esxtop/resxtop commands which we will cover later in the chapter. vSphere features an increase in the number and granularity of performance-related counters and alarms, which is particularly useful for taking a proactive and responsive approach to managing your vSphere environment.

RESOURCE VIEWS

As noted earlier, the performance charts provide a more detailed look at what is going on "under the hood" with your ESX/ESXi hosts. The "Resources" section provides an easy-to-read summary of the assigned and consumed resources. You can find these resource views on the Summary tab of the vSphere Client for either the host or the individual VM. This is a useful interface for quickly viewing and detecting any obvious resource issues that may be occurring, such as high CPU utilization on a particular host.

As you can see in Figure 7.1, the resource summary information that is displayed varies depending on whether you have selected a host or a VM. However, both views give an easy-to-read, basic summary of the four core resource groups: CPU, memory, disk/storage, and networking.

One other area in the vSphere Client where you can view a summary of resources, in this case for VMs, is the Virtual Machines tab. From here you can view multiple VMs at once, which can also be useful in quickly identifying VMs

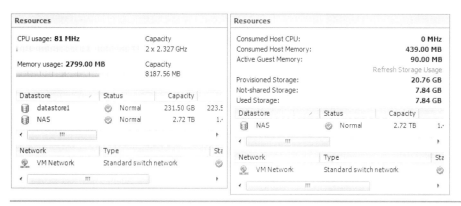

Figure 7.1 Host (left) and VM (right) Resources summary from the vSphere Client

experiencing high resource utilization issues. This list of VMs can be at a host, datacenter, or vCenter Server level, each of which will determine the VMs you will see in that particular view. For example, when you select the Virtual Machines tab after selecting an individual host, you will only see the VMs on that host; a datacenter view will display all VMs running on hosts in that datacenter logical group.

Although these views are useful for quickly gaining insight into the overall resource status of your hosts and VMs, to really find out the more detailed information which you can use to troubleshoot issues, you will need to look at the performance charts. In the next two sections, we will discuss performance charts, the objects and counters to look out for, and alarms. This will help you gain a better understanding of how to use these features to respond to performance problems more effectively, and to be more proactive in heading off any potential performance issues.

PERFORMANCE CHARTS

One of the easiest ways to check the performance of a host or VM is to view the performance charts provided in vSphere. VMware made a number of performance chart enhancements in vSphere that can help you review real-time and historical performance metrics from which you can identify performance baselines and bottlenecks. One of the exciting new features in vSphere 4.1 is the extra storage performance and NFS statistics that you can access via the performance charts and esxtop. These metrics provide useful information regarding storage throughput and any host or VM latency.

Performance Charts via a Direct vSphere Client Connection

It is important to note that there are some differences when accessing the performance charts directly from the host as opposed to via vCenter Server. As you'd expect, when accessed directly via the vSphere Client the performance charts are more limited in the detail they present and the amount of historical performance data they keep.

When connecting to a host or a VM directly via the vSphere Client, you can access the resource types shown in Table 7.1 from the performance charts drop-down listbox near the top right-hand side of the screen. The ESX and ESXi performance objects are almost identical; the only difference is that ESX also has a Management Agent object, which is for the Service Console (which is present in ESX, but not in ESXi).

Table 7.1   Host and VM Performance Objects

ESX/ESXi Host Performance Objects	VM Performance Objects
CPU	CPU
Datastore*	Datastore*
Disk	Memory
Management Agent (ESX only)	Network
Memory	Power*
Network	System
Power *	Virtual Disk
Storage Adapter*	
Storage Path*	
System	

* Indicates it is new to vSphere 4.1.

Fewer performance objects are associated with a VM compared to an ESX/ESXi host. The extra objects associated with the ESX/ESXi host are based on the area of storage and the Management Agent, as previously mentioned. The amount of performance data held between an ESX and ESXi host varies, with an ESXi host capturing only the last 60 minutes of data as opposed to the full 24 hours' worth of performance data retained by ESX. When troubleshooting a performance-related issue it is useful to be able to view at least the last 24 hours' worth of performance data so that trends or causes of degraded performance stand a better chance of being identified.

The Chart Options link in the performance chart view lets you choose your chart type—choices are "Line graph," "Stacked graph," and "Stacked graph (Per VM)"—as well as select between the resource objects and their associated counters. This level of detail and length of performance data collection may be sufficient for some vSphere environments, though the real value of the performance charts can be found when you access them via VMware vCenter Server.

Performance Charts via vCenter Server

Since the vCenter Server has a backend database, it can store a large amount of historical performance-related data which can then be used in the various performance chart views found in vCenter Server. However, note that the new resource objects found in vSphere 4.1, which include Datastore, Power, Storage Adapter, and Storage Path, only display real-time data.

You can view the performance charts within the Hosts and Clusters, VMs and Templates, and Datastores inventory views in vCenter Server, and then from a datacenter, ESX/ESXi host, cluster, resource pool, or VM level. Viewing the performance charts from each of these objects will provide you with some variation on the available performance objects and counters. The performance charts in vSphere feature a number of improvements which further enhance the ease with which performance information can be viewed. Here is a list of the main performance chart enhancements found in vSphere.

Single view—There is now a single-screen overview of all the various performance metrics (i.e., CPU, memory, disk, and network), providing a convenient, quick view of the performance of these ESX/ESXi host or VM resources.

Thumbnail views—These views provide a convenient method from which to navigate to individual views of hosts, clusters, resource pools, and datastores.

Aggregated charts—The performance charts now provide a useful high-level summary of the resource distribution, meaning that the top consumers of resources can be easily identified.

Drill-down views—As the name suggests, these views allow you to quickly drill down into the performance chart views to get to the information you're looking for.

Datastore-level views—These views show the level of utilization by either file type or unused capacity, which could prove useful in troubleshooting storage consumption issues.

Both Overview and Advanced performance chart layouts display one or more types of graph, from among four different types.

Line chart—This is used to display the metrics of a single inventory object. Performance data from each object counter is displayed on a separate line on the chart. For example, disk read latency and disk write latency each appear on their own line.

Stacked chart—This chart displays the metrics of a parent object's children with those having the highest statistical values being shown. This is a useful for when you wish to compare metrics such as CPU utilization across multiple hosts or VMs.

Bar chart—This is used to display datastore metrics for a selected datacenter. The bars, each of which represents a single datastore, are displayed showing metrics which are based on particular file types such as virtual disks, snapshots, swap files, and other miscellaneous files.

Pie chart—This chart type is used for displaying the storage metrics of an individual datastore or VM.

Overview Layout   There are two types of performance chart views in vCenter Server. In the top left-hand corner of the performance chart screens you will notice two buttons: Overview and Advanced. By default, Overview is selected, which provides you with an overview of what VMware considers to be the key performance objects in that particular view. Just below the Overview button are two drop-down listboxes, labeled View and Time Range. The View drop down allows you to change the current view to another predefined view, and the Time Range drop down lets you adjust the displayed period of performance data in the charts. Table 7.2 outlines the available views for each object type when viewing the performance charts in the Overview layout.

Table 7.2   Overview Page Performance Views Available for Different Object Types

Performance Tab—Object	Available Views
Datacenter	Clusters, Storage
Cluster	Home, Resource Pools and Virtual Machines, Hosts

Continues

Table 7.2   Overview Page Performance Views Available for Different Object Types *(Continued)*

Performance Tab—Object	Available Views
ESX/ESXi Host	Home, Virtual Machines
Resource Pools	Home, Resource Pools, and Virtual Machines
Virtual Machine (VM)	Home, Storage, Fault Tolerance

The Overview layout, as shown in Figure 7.2, contains a wealth of performance information via different resource graphs. In fact, these Overview layouts

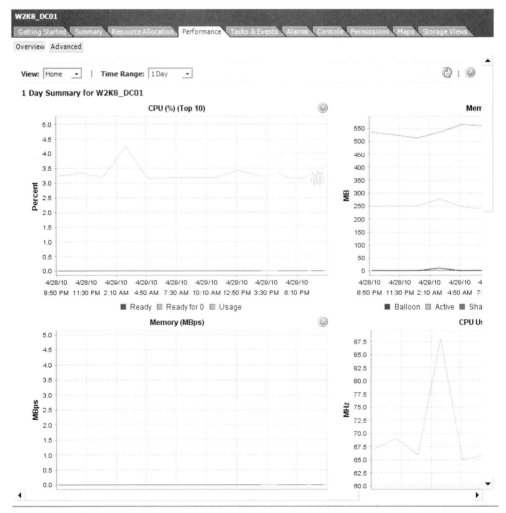

Figure 7.2   The default Overview layout contains a wealth of resource performance information. You will have to use the scroll bars to view the additional charts.

often display so much information that you will need to use the scroll bars to view it all.

You'll find the Overview layout very useful in many situations, though if you want some extra flexibility in determining what performance objects and associated counters are to be displayed, you will want to take a look at the performance chart's Advanced mode. To enter this mode, simply click on the Advanced button next to the Overview button on the Performance tab.

Advanced Layout   Although the Advanced layout, with its single chart, is much simpler in appearance than the Overview layout, it does allow you to be more granular with the performance objects and counters you select. Figure 7.3

Figure 7.3   With the Advanced layout you can be more precise with the objects and counters that are displayed.

displays the resource types along with some of their objects and counters from the Chart Options. As you can see, there is plenty of scope for creating a customized performance chart.

As with the Overview mode, the object type you select from the vSphere Client—for example, the datacenter, the host, or an individual VM—will determine which views will be presented in the Switch To drop-down listbox. Table 7.3 outlines the differences in available views between the object types.

Table 7.3   Advanced Page Performance Views Available for Different Object Types

Performance Tab—Object	Available Views
Datacenter	Default, Virtual Machine Operations
Cluster	Default, CPU, Memory, Virtual Machine Operations
ESX/ESXi Host	Default, CPU, Datastore, Disk, Management Agent (ESX only), Memory, Network, Power, Storage Adapter, Storage Path, System
Resource Pools	CPU, Memory
Virtual Machine (VM)	CPU, Datastore, Memory, Network, Power, System, Virtual Disk

When viewing a performance chart in Advanced mode you can print or save the chart in a handful of popular image formats, including PNG and JPG, or as an Excel spreadsheet. This can be useful if you want to send the performance graphs or data to others. In addition, you can adjust the time range for both the Overview and the Advanced layouts from the default of "Real-time" to "1 Day," "1 Week," "1 Month," "1 Year," or "Custom." You can configure vCenter Server to retain up to a massive five years' worth of performance data, though as you can probably imagine the size of the database holding this data would be quite large.

You can view and adjust the amount and level of statistical performance data that vCenter Server collects by going into the vCenter Server Settings. Click on the Administration drop-down menu on the vCenter Server's main menu bar, select vCenter Server Settings, and then click on the Statistics menu option. At this point, you can see the various defined statistics retention levels and interval duration.

The number of monitored hosts and VMs, combined with the level at which statistics are captured and the length of the retention period, will strongly influence the size of the vCenter Server's database. On the Statistics setting screen, you can see that there is a built-in database size estimator (Database Size) which can help you to estimate how much disk space to allocate to the vCenter Server database. Note that this estimator is exactly that, an estimator, and the values given shouldn't be taken as being exact.

The default statistics level for all of the defined interval durations (i.e., 5 minutes, 30 minutes, 2 hours, 1 day) is 1, which is the most basic of statistical logging levels. There are four levels: Level 4 offers the most comprehensive level of statistical logging, and level 1 (the default) offers the most basic. The statistics level for a collection interval cannot be greater than the statistics level set for the preceding collection interval. For example, if the Month interval is set to collection level 3, the Year interval can be set to collection level 1, 2, or 3, but not to collection level 4. Setting these levels higher can dramatically increase the size of the vCenter Server database and decrease the performance of the vCenter Server. Therefore, take care when changing these levels and increase them only as needed, such as when troubleshooting performance problems. If you do increase these levels, make sure you remember to decrease them when you are done; otherwise, you might end up filling your database server.

Existing statistics data is reset (lost) when you change the interval configuration. However, only the data for that specific interval is reset. For example, if you change only the weekly time interval, the daily and monthly data is retained.

UNDERSTANDING HOST SERVER PERFORMANCE METRICS

Gaining a good working knowledge of how to access and customize the various performance views in vSphere is essential, but it's only half of the equation. You can now view some interesting-looking graphs, but what do they mean and what performance objects and counters should you be looking at to determine if there are any performance-related issues?

Following are some basic host and VM-level performance counters to look for in each of the four main resource groups: CPU, memory, disk, and network. While reading through these, be mindful that although the counter names are similar between those used by the host and the VMs, there are often some subtle differences.

Following are host performance counters.

- **CPU: Usage (average)**—A basic measurement of CPU usage, and is the total amount of CPU usage by all the VMs on a host (including the Service Console, but excluding the VMkernel).

- **CPU: Usage in MHz (average)**—Another basic measurement of CPU usage, but is displayed in megahertz rather than as a percentage.

- **Memory: Usage (average)**—A basic measurement of what percentage of the host's total memory is in use by all of the VMs, including the Service Console and VMkernel memory usage.

- **Memory: Active (average)**—The amount of memory that is actively being used by all of the VMs on a host. This is just the total amount that has been recently used and is not the total amount being consumed by all of the VMs on a host, including the Service Console and VMkernel memory usage.

- **Memory: Consumed (average)**—The amount of actual host memory that is in use by all the VMs on a host, plus the overhead memory and memory used by the Service Console. This is the memory usage total that is displayed on the Summary tab of a host.

- **Memory: Granted (average)**—The amount of memory that was granted to all VMs on a host. Memory is not granted by the host until it is touched one time by a VM, and granted memory may be swapped out or ballooned away if the VMkernel needs the memory.

- **Memory: Swap Used (average)**—The amount of swap memory (VSWP files) that is in use by all the VMs on a host. A high number can indicate that the host is running low on physical memory or that VMs with memory limits set below their allocated memory are exceeding their limits and are using swap memory instead of physical host memory.

- **Memory: Overhead (average)**—The amount of additional host memory used by the VMkernel to maintain and execute the VM. This memory is separate from the memory that is assigned to a VM for its use.

- **Memory: Balloon (average)**—The amount of memory ballooning that is occurring on all the VMs on a host. A value greater than zero indicates that the host is starting to take memory from less-needful VMs to allocate to those with large amounts of active memory that the VMkernel cannot satisfy with the current free memory available.

- **Memory: Shared (average)**—The amount of memory pages shared by all VMs on a host as a result of the transparent page sharing (TPS) feature. A high number here is good, as it results in physical memory savings on the host.

- **Disk: Usage (average)**—A basic measurement of the total size of data read and written for all disk instances of the host.

- **Disk: Command Aborts**—The number of disk command aborts which is a result of the disk subsystem having not responded in an acceptable amount of time. If a host is waiting too long to access a disk because of contention with other hosts, this can indicate a disk I/O bottleneck or a poorly configured disk (e.g., too many hosts accessing a LUN).

- **Disk: Read Latency**—Average time taken for a read by a guest OS, or the sum of kernel read latency and physical device read latency. High latency times can indicate a disk I/O bottleneck or a poorly configured disk (e.g., too many VMs per LUN).

- **Disk: Write Latency**—Average time taken for a write by a guest OS, or the sum of kernel write latency and physical device write latency. High latency times can indicate a disk I/O bottleneck or a poorly configured disk (e.g., too many VMs per LUN).

- **Disk: Command Latency**—Average time taken for disk commands by a guest OS, or the sum of kernel command latency and physical device command latency.

- **Network: Usage (average)**—A basic measurement of the amount of network bandwidth being used by all the VMs on a host, and is measured in kilobytes per second. This includes all NICs in a host as well as VMotion and Service Console traffic.

Following are VM performance counters.

- **CPU: Usage (average)**—A basic measurement of CPU usage, and is a percentage of the amount of CPU a VM is using compared to the total percentage of megahertz from all CPUs that are available on a host, which is 100%.

- **CPU: Usage in MHz (average)**—Another basic measurement of CPU usage, but displayed in megahertz rather than as a percentage.

- **CPU: Ready**—The amount of time that is spent waiting for a CPU to become available. High ready times (> 10%) can indicate a CPU bottleneck or too many vSMP VMs on a host.

- **CPU: Used**—The amount of CPU time that is used, in milliseconds. A high value can indicate that a VM is saturating its CPU and may benefit from an additional vCPU, especially if this value is high and CPU Ready is low.

- **Memory: Usage (average)**—A basic measurement of the percentage of memory allocated to the VM that is actually being used.

- **Memory: Active (average)**—The amount of "true" memory used by the VM in the past small window of time. Any unused memory may be swapped out or ballooned with no impact to the guest's performance.

- **Memory: Swap In (average)**—The rate at which memory is being swapped in from a VM's virtual disk swap file. A large number here represents a problem with lack of memory and is a clear indication that performance is suffering as a result.

- **Memory: Swap Out (average)**—The rate at which memory is being swapped out to a VM's virtual disk swap file. A large number here represents a problem with lack of memory and is a clear indication that performance is suffering as a result.

- **Memory: Consumed (average)**—The amount of actual host memory that is in use by the VM, which does not include any shared memory that a VM may be using. If a VM has 2GB of RAM assigned to it and is using only 512MB of consumed memory, this can be an indication that you can reduce the amount of memory assigned to the VM.

- **Memory: Balloon (average)**—The amount of memory that is in use by the balloon driver inside the VM's guest OS. A value greater than zero indicates that the host is starting to take memory from less-needful VMs for those with large amounts of active memory.

- **Virtual Disk: Read Rate**—A basic measurement of disk usage by a VM, and is displayed as a kilobytes per second (KBps) measurement for the rate of disk reads by the VM.

- **Virtual Disk: Write Rate**—A measurement of disk usage by a VM, and is displayed as a kilobytes per second (KBps) measurement for the rate of disk writes by the VM.

- **Virtual Disk: Read Latency**—Another basic measurement that shows the average time in milliseconds (ms) that it takes to read from the virtual disk. Any high prolonged periods of read latency will almost certainly indicate a level of contention or substandard performance with the virtual disks, and likely the storage LUNs on which they reside.

- **Virtual Disk: Write Latency**—Shows the average time in milliseconds (ms) that it takes for a write to occur down to the virtual disk. High prolonged periods of write latency can be caused by the reasons given earlier in this list.

- **Network: Usage (average)**—A basic measurement of the amount of network bandwidth a VM is using measured in kilobytes per second.

PERFORMANCE ALARMS

vSphere performance charts are great for when you have the time to proactively monitor them or during times of performance troubleshooting, but what about the rest of the time when you are away from the vSphere Client, or after hours? This is where the vCenter Server alarm feature can be very useful. As the name suggests, an alarm can be raised and an action taken when a particular threshold or criterion relating to a particular resource object is breached. The number of objects and types of alarms have increased significantly with vSphere. Some default alarms come preconfigured with vSphere, and these cover many of the basic areas within vSphere about which an administrator would want to be notified. Here is a list of the default alarms that are particularly relevant to vSphere performance:

- Host CPU usage
- Host memory usage
- Host service console swap rates
- Datastore usage on disk
- Network uplink redundancy degraded
- VM CPU usage
- VM memory usage
- VM total disk latency

These default alarms only have a notification trap associated with them, which means that only a triggered alarm notification to vCenter Server will be presented. Unless you are constantly sitting in front of the vCenter Server, this won't be sufficient for you to respond in a timely manner to any issues triggered by an alarm. It is therefore recommended that you modify the action of any alarms, either default or manually created, to also include a notification being sent to a monitored email account or similar. Other action types can be taken which may be better suited to the alarm type and to your IT management or monitoring environment.

The default performance-related alarms won't be sufficient for most vSphere environments, so new performance alarms should be created with appropriate trigger types, warnings, and alert conditions set. Here is an example list of VM and host-related trigger types that can be used in creating your new performance alarms:

- Host CPU Usage (%)
- Host Disk Usage (KBps)
- Host Memory Usage (%)
- Host Network Usage (KBps)
- Host Swap Pages Write (KBps)
- VM CPU Usage (%)
- VM CPU Ready Time (ms)
- VM Disk Usage (KBps)
- VM Fault Tolerance Latency (if applicable)
- VM Memory Usage (%)
- VM Network Usage (KBps)
- VM Total Disk Latency (ms)

If you haven't already done so, take the time to read the Alarms and Events section in Chapter 4, as it provides more detail on vSphere alarms and how to configure them.

TROUBLESHOOTING VSPHERE PERFORMANCE ISSUES

Whether you are the administrator of an existing vSphere environment or are looking at architecting or implementing a new vSphere installation, you have a number of performance-related configuration issues to consider. Knowing what to look for and how to configure even the most basic of settings can deliver significant vSphere performance gains.

For the remainder of this chapter, we will look at how to troubleshoot basic performance problems in each of the four main resource areas found in a host or VM: CPU, memory, disk/storage, and networking. You should use these basic troubleshooting tips as a starting point for expanding your knowledge on vSphere performance troubleshooting, though as so many different variables are at play on a host, even the most basic performance issue can be caused by something more complicated and difficult to locate. At the end of each section on troubleshooting a particular resource, you will find some configuration hints and tips. So, let's start by taking a look at how to troubleshoot basic performance issues on a host using the *esxtop/resxtop* command.

ESXTOP AND RESXTOP

For many vSphere administrators, the most useful method of accessing the real-time performance information of a single host is via a Service Console command called esxtop, which also provides the ability to capture data on all system resources for further offline review. Using esxtop allows you to view the real nuts and bolts of the host, including some advanced performance statistics not available via the vSphere Client. The command fetches system resource counter information from the VMkernel and displays it in an easy-to-read format. In addition to the counters provided by the VMkernel, esxtop adds a few counters of its own which it obtains by calculating the counter information provided by the VMkernel.

From esxtop, you can gain insight into the resource utilization of both your host and its running VMs, covering the four main resource areas mentioned previously. If you are not familiar with esxtop, think of it as the dashboard of your car, providing real-time information on the various statistics of the vehicle, for example: speed, rpm, oil pressure, and fuel.

Remote esxtop (resxtop) and the vSphere Management Assistant (vMA)

As mentioned earlier, esxtop is an ESX Service Console command, so how do you use it with ESXi hosts which, as you probably know, don't come with a Service Console? For this, ESXi hosts are accommodated through the use of the remote esxtop (resxtop) command, which is included with the vSphere Management Assistant (vMA), which we'll cover in Chapter 10. You can connect to the Service Console remotely or to the vMA via an SSH connection with a tool such as Putty. Once a connection has been established to the vMA, you can use resxtop to connect to a remote ESX/ESXi host by entering the following command:

```
resxtop --server <name/IP of the ESX/ESXi host>
```

You can also connect to a vCenter Server using this command:

```
resxtop --server <name/IP of the vCenter Server> --vihost
<name/IP of the ESX/ESXi>
```

Once connected, you will be prompted to enter a username and a password. If you're connecting directly to a host, this should be the root username and password; when connecting to a vCenter Server, this can be an Active Directory (AD) user account with permissions to log on to the vCenter Server.

esxtop and resxtop Basics

When you establish an SSH connection to esxtop or you are using resxtop, widen the display window as there are often fields to the right-hand side of the screen that are not displayed.

At first, the sheer amount of data you receive from esxtop/resxtop can be a little overwhelming. However, it is well worth investing the time to understand and recognize the key performance fields and processes to look for and to understand what each of their acceptable thresholds should be. It is recommended that you filter your view when in esxtop to only display the counters you are interested in; this way, you will not be distracted by the noise presented by the other counters. We will cover how to apply an esxtop/resxtop filter later in this section.

The default refresh interval between samples for the counter statistics is five seconds. This is relevant, as many of the metrics in esxtop get their values by working out the average between two samples over the sample interval. By adjusting this time interval, you can determine the level of granularity you can expect to receive from the statistics. The larger the refresh interval, the greater the time over which the statistics will be averaged, thereby not displaying any temporary spikes in utilization which may occur. However, if you increase the sample period, you will receive a better appreciation of longer-term trends in the performance statistics of the counter you are viewing. esxtop/resxtop also displays some counters that are actually running averages from metrics stored in the VMkernel—for example, the CPU load average.

A key point to remember when using either esxtop or resxtop is that they are effectively being run from a Linux-based interface, so unlike the Windows command line, these commands and any related interaction with them are case-sensitive. Forgetting about the case sensitivity is a common pitfall for many people using ESX's Service Console or the vMA.

esxtop and resxtop Terminology

esxtop/resxtop use a couple of terms that you may not be familiar with, such as "worlds" and "entities". Knowing what these terms mean and how they relate in esxtop/resxtop will make it easier to read the interface. It will also help you when reading any of VMware's excellent white papers on vSphere performance. Here is some basic esxtop/resxtop terminology.

- **World**—A VMkernel schedulable entity found in ESX/ESXi. Those of you from a Microsoft Windows background would best relate to a world as being similar to a process. Note that not all worlds have to be related to a VM.
- **Field**—A column of statistical data displayed in esxtop/resxtop.
- **Entities**—The rows displayed within esxtop/resxtop; these can be VM or non-VM-related. The displayed entities can contain multiple worlds which are indicated by the NWLD field.
- **Group**—A grouping of related entities.
- **Group ID (GID)**—A unique numeric identifier given to a group of entities.

The running worlds presented at the top of each esxtop/resxtop screen are a mixture of both VM and VMkernel-related worlds, as shown in Figure 7.4.

For example, in Figure 7.4, we can see that the W2K8R2 (Entity) VM is identified with an entity ID of 57, which matches its group identifier (GID) of 57. In

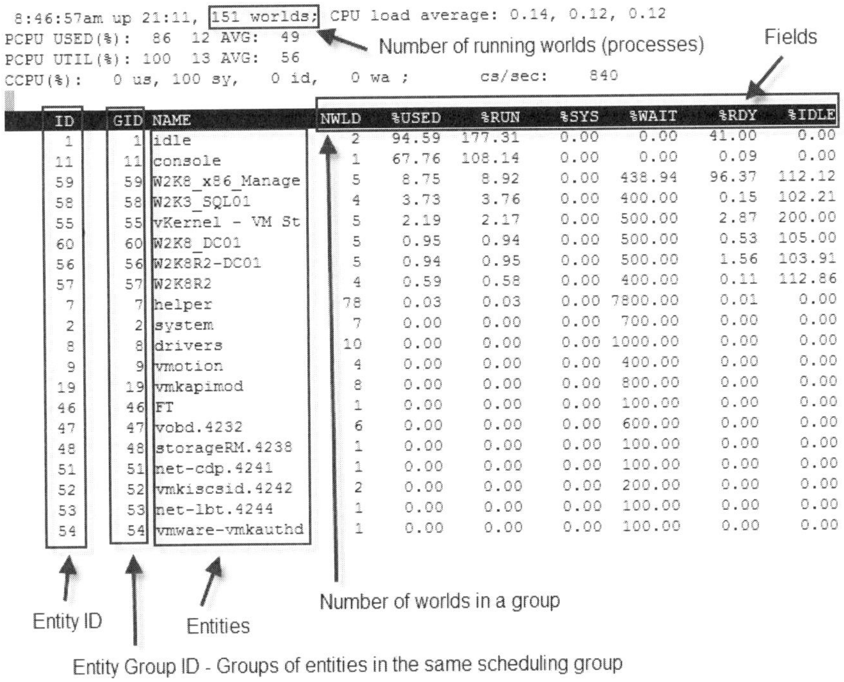

```
8:46:57am up 21:11, 151 worlds; CPU load average: 0.14, 0.12, 0.12
PCPU USED(%):  86  12 AVG:  49
PCPU UTIL(%): 100  13 AVG:  56
CCPU(%):    0 us, 100 sy,    0 id,    0 wa ;        cs/sec:    840
```

ID	GID	NAME	NWLD	%USED	%RUN	%SYS	%WAIT	%RDY	%IDLE
1	1	idle	2	94.59	177.31	0.00	0.00	41.00	0.00
11	11	console	1	67.76	108.14	0.00	0.00	0.09	0.00
59	59	W2K8_x86_Manage	5	8.75	8.92	0.00	438.94	96.37	112.12
58	58	W2K3_SQL01	4	3.73	3.76	0.00	400.00	0.15	102.21
55	55	vKernel - VM St	5	2.19	2.17	0.00	500.00	2.87	200.00
60	60	W2K8_DC01	5	0.95	0.94	0.00	500.00	0.53	105.00
56	56	W2K8R2-DC01	5	0.94	0.95	0.00	500.00	1.56	103.91
57	57	W2K8R2	4	0.59	0.58	0.00	400.00	0.11	112.86
7	7	helper	78	0.03	0.03	0.00	7800.00	0.01	0.00
2	2	system	7	0.00	0.00	0.00	700.00	0.00	0.00
8	8	drivers	10	0.00	0.00	0.00	1000.00	0.00	0.00
9	9	vmotion	4	0.00	0.00	0.00	400.00	0.00	0.00
19	19	vmkapimod	8	0.00	0.00	0.00	800.00	0.00	0.00
46	46	FT	1	0.00	0.00	0.00	100.00	0.00	0.00
47	47	vobd.4232	6	0.00	0.00	0.00	600.00	0.00	0.00
48	48	storageRM.4238	1	0.00	0.00	0.00	100.00	0.00	0.00
51	51	net-cdp.4241	1	0.00	0.00	0.00	100.00	0.00	0.00
52	52	vmkiscsid.4242	2	0.00	0.00	0.00	200.00	0.00	0.00
53	53	net-lbt.4244	1	0.00	0.00	0.00	100.00	0.00	0.00
54	54	vmware-vmkauthd	1	0.00	0.00	0.00	100.00	0.00	0.00

Figure 7.4 The esxtop/resxtop user interface

this VM's group, it has four worlds (the "4" in the NWLD column). Each VM will comprise of at least the following basic worlds.

- **vCPU-#**—This world assists the VM with its vCPU. One vCPU world is allocated for each vCPU assigned to the VM. For example, a dual vCPU VM would have two VMX worlds, vcpu-0 and vcpu-1.
- **VMware-VMX**—The VMX world assists the vCPU world outlined in the preceding bullet point.
- **MKS**—This world assists in mouse, keyboard, and screen virtualization.
- **VMAssistant**—This is a new world that handles memory scanning for TPS.

Modes of Operation

There are three modes of operation in esxtop/resxtop: interactive, batch, and replay. When you first start esxtop/resxtop you are in the default interactive mode, where you can use predefined keys to view and adjust the metrics that are displayed on the screen. Batch mode is a noninteractive mode that exports data from the default fields in esxtop/resxtop to a file in CSV format. You can then open this performance data in Excel or in Windows Perfmon for further analysis. There is also a useful free tool called ESXplot which lets you view and explore the data collected by esxtop/resxtop in batch mode; for more details, visit www.durganetworks.com/esxplot/. Replay mode will prove very useful when troubleshooting, as it captures the data in esxtop/resxtop and then allows you to play it back in real time, enabling you to view the events leading up to and after an issue you may be having with your ESX/ESXi host. This chapter will only be focusing on the default interactive mode, as this is the most useful for real-time monitoring and troubleshooting. For more information on the other modes, take a look at the following article: www.techhead.co.uk/esxtop-modes.

In the next few sections, we will discuss a number of possible views and commands within esxtop/resxtop, all of which you can obtain via different keystrokes. Don't be daunted by the number of commands; you may not end up using all of them, at least not initially. Table 7.4 highlights the main esxtop/resxtop commands; by pressing the h or ? key on your keyboard you will be provided with a comprehensive list pertaining to the resource utilization panel you are viewing at the time.

Table 7.4 Most Commonly Used esxtop/resxtop Commands

Key	Command
c	CPU resource utilization view
i	Interrupt (new in vSphere; displays the interrupts on the ESX/ESXi host) resource utilization view
m	Memory resource utilization view
n	Network resource utilization view
d	Storage adapter (e.g., RAID adapters, host bus adapters [HBAs]) resource utilization view
u	Storage device (e.g., the view from a LUN level) resource utilization view
v	VM storage (e.g., the view from a VM level) resource utilization view
p	Power management (new in vSphere) resource utilization view
h or ?	Help: lists the available commands at the current utilization view
s	Changes the delay between the updates
\<Spacebar\>	Updates the current view
V	Displays only the VM worlds
e	Expands or rolls up the world view after also entering the Group ID (GID)
F or f	Allows you to select the fields to display
O or o	Changes the order of the displayed fields in the view
2	Selects and highlights a row: up
8	Selects and highlights a row: down
4	Removes the highlighted row from the current view
W	Saves your esxtop configuration including any view changes you may have made to a file
q	Quit

By default, not all of the available fields are displayed in the various resource utilization views. You can toggle fields on or off via a screen that you access by pressing either the F or f key. You can also adjust the order in which fields are displayed in the various resource utilization views by using the O or o key to open a field order option which allows you to move fields left or right on the screen. After customizing your esxtop/resxtop views, you can save your configuration for future use by pressing the W key, at which point you will be prompted for a name for the configuration file. By default, esxtop/resxtop will save it to ~/.esxtop4xrc, though you can specify an alternative filename and location. To reload a user-defined configuration file, specify its name and location using the -c option when starting esxtop/resxtop; for example, esxtop -c <config file location & name>. This can save valuable time each time you start esxtop/resxtop. Take the time to try each of these commands to become familiar with what they do and how you'd use them.

CPU PERFORMANCE TROUBLESHOOTING

CPU performance problems can occur for a number of reasons, with the most common and obvious being a high demand for the limited CPU resources on a host by the VMs running on it. Any such CPU utilization could be due to a single CPU-intensive VM running a heavy application workload, or high overall CPU utilization by multiple VMs on the host. As this section of the chapter is focused on basic performance troubleshooting, we will look at the fundamental areas of high CPU utilization only.

CPU LOAD AVERAGE

To determine whether the host or any of the VMs running on it are experiencing high CPU utilization, or even saturation, there are a couple of metrics within esxtop/resxtop that you should check. The first metric is the physical CPU load average, which you can view in the CPU resource utilization panel. After starting esxtop/resxtop against the host you want to monitor, press the c key to ensure that you are on the CPU resource utilization screen. The "CPU load average" section of the screen shows three values, as shown in Figure 7.5, which are the average CPU loads over the past one, five, and 15 minutes, respectively.

This is a useful metric for quickly gauging how the physical CPUs in your ESX/ESXi host are bearing up. A value of 1.0 in any of these three fields indicates that the physical CPU is fully utilized, and a value greater than 1.0 indicates that the host requires more physical CPU capacity than is available. For example, a value of 2.0 means the host potentially needs twice the amount of physical CPU resources that were available at the indicated time.

```
1:03:24pm up 3 days  7:12, 154 worlds; CPU load average: 0.39, 0.42, 0.40
PCPU USED(%):  37  39 AVG:  38
PCPU UTIL(%):  38  40 AVG:  39
CCPU(%):   2 us,  11 sy,  15 id,  73 wa ;       cs/sec:    320
```

ID	NAME	GID	NWLD	%USED	%RUN	%SYS	%WAIT	%RDY
60	W2K8R2	60	4	53.76	54.25	0.01	300.89	46.22
62	W2K8_x86_Manage	62	5	11.98	12.67	0.02	483.30	5.75
64	vSphere Managem	64	4	2.12	2.18	0.01	398.06	1.07
59	W2K3_SQL01	59	4	1.12	1.17	0.00	399.22	0.95
57	W2K8_DC01	57	5	0.75	0.81	0.00	499.59	1.17
58	W2K8R2-DC01	58	5	0.62	0.69	0.00	500.00	0.61
61	W2K8_Test01	61	4	0.51	0.53	0.00	400.00	0.53

Figure 7.5   CPU load average can help identify whether the host's physical CPUs are overutilized.

PHYSICAL CPU UTILIZATION (PCPU USED (%))

The PCPU USED (%) metric provides a real-time view of the host's physical CPU utilization. It provides a reading for each physical CPU core, along with an average CPU utilization figure, as shown in Figure 7.6. If these figures are consistently showing between 90% and 100% for prolonged periods of time, this indicates that the CPUs on the host are probably oversubscribed. Even regular spikes in CPU utilization of over 90% can indicate a similar CPU oversubscription issue. One important point of note with this metric is that the values shown can be a little misleading when the physical server on which ESX/ESXi is running has hyperthreading enabled on its CPU. With hyperthreading enabled, the PCPU USED (%) value can appear lower when two threads are being run, as the figure is calculated against the utilization of the physical core. This means that a single thread which is not sharing the core can show a value of up to 100 (%), depending on its utilization. However, when two threads are being used, this value won't go above 50 (%) for each thread, unless turbo mode on the CPU is also being used, which means each thread could show a value slightly over 50 (%).

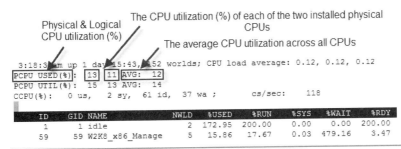

Figure 7.6   The PCPU USED (%) metric provides real-time physical CPU core utilization figures.

PHYSICAL CPU UTILIZATION BY A WORLD (%USED)

The %USED field is another useful metric which you can use to determine if there is an excessive load on a VM's vCPU. The %USED value can be greater than 100%, as it is cumulative and is made up of the %USED values of the worlds contained within that VM's entity group. You can tell from the NWLD field how many worlds an entity has, and you can multiply this figure by 100% to determine the maximum %USED value. For example, an entity with five worlds in its entity group could theoretically reach a maximum of 500%, though this would be extremely unlikely, even with the heaviest of CPU loads.

To better explain how the %USED field can help you determine if a VM (entity) is experiencing high vCPU utilization, let's take a look at an example using the values shown in Figure 7.7. From this figure, we can see that the W2K8R2 VM has a high %USED value (94.12), especially compared to the other entities/VMs on the host. The W2K8R2 VM has an entity ID and entity group ID of 60, and we can tell that it has four worlds within its entity group by looking at the NWLD field.

```
 9:56:49am up 3 days  4:06, 154 worlds; CPU load average: 0.67, 0.41, 0.25
PCPU USED(%):  55  66 AVG:  60
PCPU UTIL(%):  55  66 AVG:  61
CCPU(%):   1 us,  12 sy,  88 id,   0 wa ;       cs/sec:    174
```

ID NAME	GID	NWLD	%USED	%RUN	%SYS	%WAIT	%RDY
60 W2K8R2	60	4	94.12	94.53	0.06	298.31	7.78
1 idle	1	2	77.95	136.12	0.00	0.00	64.11
62 W2K8_x86_Manage	62	5	11.22	11.25	0.00	482.65	6.88
11 console	11	1	10.72	10.74	0.07	86.74	2.68
64 vSphere Managem	64	4	2.21	2.22	0.00	396.51	1.88
59 W2K3 SOI01	59	4	0.95	0.92	0.02	398.05	1.64

Figure 7.7   A high %USED value should be investigated further by looking at the worlds which are part of that entity's group.

This doesn't really show enough detail, so you should now take a look at the worlds contained within the VM's entity group, which you can do by pressing the e key and then entering the VM's group ID (GID). Figure 7.8 shows the four worlds which make up the entity group, and as such, the VM. Notice that each world has its own unique ID. It is obvious now that an individual world is creating the high %USED utilization: vcpu-0:W2K8R2. This indicates that the VM is experiencing high CPU utilization on vCPU 0, at which point further investigation should take place within the guest OS on the VM to determine the application or process that is creating the high CPU utilization.

```
10:28:02am up 3 days  4:37, 154 worlds; CPU load average: 0.66, 0.67, 0.67
PCPU USED(%):  57  65 AVG:  61
PCPU UTIL(%):  57  65 AVG:  61
CCPU(%):   1 us,  10 sy,  61 id,  28 wa ;       cs/sec:    257
```

ID NAME	GID	NWLD	%USED	%RUN	%SYS	%WAIT	%RDY
4282 vmware-vmx	60	1	0.04	0.04	0.00	99.33	0.06
4285 vmassistant.428	60	1	0.02	0.02	0.00	99.41	0.00
4290 mks:W2K8R2	60	1	0.22	0.22	0.00	97.20	2.01
4291 vcpu-0:W2K8R2	60	1	92.99	93.47	0.02	0.00	5.96
1 idle	1	2	77.39	136.64	0.00	0.00	63.26
62 W2K8_x86_Manage	62	5	10.71	10.65	0.03	474.69	11.69

Figure 7.8 Expanding an entity's group to display the running worlds within it can help narrow down a CPU performance issue.

WORLD PHYSICAL CPU WAIT (%RDY)

The Ready Time (%RDY) field is an important metric to view when diagnosing CPU performance issues, as this metric can help you determine if there is a problem with any of the VMs or host processes getting sufficient time to run commands on the physical CPU due to scheduling contention. The value in the %RDY field, as shown in Figure 7.9, indicates the percentage of time a VM or host process has been ready to execute a command on the CPU, but instead has spent time waiting to be scheduled.

```
11:52:30am up 3 days  6:02, 155 worlds; CPU load average: 0.67, 0.68, 0.67
PCPU USED(%):  65  76 AVG:  70
PCPU UTIL(%):  65  76 AVG:  71
CCPU(%):   1 us,  10 sy,  88 id,   0 wa ;       cs/sec:    146
```

ID NAME	GID	NWLD	%USED	%RUN	%SYS	%WAIT	%RDY
60 W2K8R2	60	4	80.67	81.14	0.01	296.26	21.92
1 idle	1	2	58.21	104.55	0.00	0.00	95.50
62 W2K8_x86_Manage	62	5	42.84	43.04	0.01	434.29	21.74
11 console	11	1	10.24	10.23	0.04	86.89	2.83
64 vSphere Managem	64	4	2.24	2.24	0.01	393.07	3.97
57 W2K8_DC01	57	5	1.61	1.61	0.00	494.09	3.50
58 W2K8R2-DC01	58	5	1.14	1.13	0.00	493.49	4.56
59 W2K3_SQL01	59	4	0.94	0.92	0.02	395.70	2.74
61 W2K8_Test01	61	4	0.63	0.63	0.01	395.03	3.65

Figure 7.9 A high ready time could indicate insufficient physical CPU resources on the host.

Don't pay any attention to the large %RDY figure associated with the "idle" entity, as it is normal for this to be high. High ready times—for example, 10+—can indicate a number of underlying resource issues, though the most typical causes are the physical CPUs of the host being too oversubscribed, meaning that there are often insufficient CPU cycles to meet the demands of the VMs or host processes. A CPU resource limit that has been set on the VM can also delay the CPU scheduling of its cycles to meet the configured CPU limit. For example, a

VM's vCPU which is running on a 3.4GHz physical processor may have a CPU scheduling delay set so that it doesn't exceed the equivalent of 2.0GHz. You can further confirm if there are any CPU scheduling resource issues for a particular VM which you have already confirmed as having a high ready time by looking at the max limited (%MLMTD) field.

MAX LIMITED (%MLMTD)

The %MLMTD field displays the percentage of time that an entity (e.g., a VM) and its worlds were made to wait before having time scheduled on the CPU due to a predefined limit placed on its vCPU. To demonstrate this, I have applied a CPU limit of 1GHz to the VM named W2K8R2. The underlying physical CPU in the ESX/ESXi host runs at a 2.3GHz clock speed. As you can see in Figure 7.10 from the %MLMTD field for this VM, it has spent 55.95% of its time, due to the 1GHz CPU limit, waiting to have its commands scheduled on the CPU.

If both the %RDY and %MLMTD values for a VM are high, subtract %MLMTD from %RDY (i.e., %RDY – %MLMTD), which will provide a figure from which you can gauge the level of contention. Although there are no hard and fast thresholds to indicate CPU contention from the figure gained from the subtraction of the aforementioned values, a good starting point is a value of 20 (%). The higher this value is, the stronger the probability that CPU contention is occurring.

```
12:39:53pm up 3 days  6:49,  155 worlds; CPU load average: 0.40, 0.29, 0.51
PCPU USED(%):   41   30 AVG:   36
PCPU UTIL(%):   42   32 AVG:   37
CCPU(%):    1 us,   10 sy,  87 id,   2 wa ;       cs/sec:    265
```

ID	NAME	GID	NWLD	%USED	%WAIT	%RDY	%IDLE	%OVRLP	%MLMTD	%SWPWT
1	idle	1	2	125.78	0.00	200.00	0.00	0.55	0.00	0.00
60	W2K8R2	60	4	46.54	293.37	59.05	0.00	0.17	55.95	0.00
11	console	11	1	10.55	86.21	2.79	86.21	0.03	0.00	0.00
62	W2K8_x86_Manage	62	5	10.23	481.59	6.43	182.16	0.06	0.00	0.00
64	vSphere Managem	64	4	2.15	396.75	0.24	97.38	0.01	0.00	0.00
59	W2K3_SQL01	59	4	1.13	397.92	0.13	98.52	0.01	0.00	0.00
58	W2K8R2-DC01	58	5	0.78	497.19	1.08	98.00	0.01	0.00	0.00
57	W2K8_DC01	57	5	0.72	497.63	0.80	98.31	0.01	0.00	0.00

Figure 7.10   The %MLMTD field indicates the percentage of time an entity and its worlds have to wait to be scheduled on the physical CPU due to defined CPU resource restrictions placed on a VM.

WORLD VMKERNEL MEMORY SWAP WAIT TIME (%SWPWT)

This field is a new addition found in vSphere which indicates the percentage of time that a world is waiting for the host's VMkernel to swap memory. A high figure in this field indicates that the VM's aggregate active memory is exceeding the available physical memory.

vCPU Co-deschedule Wait Time (%CSTP)

If you are running multiple vCPUs on a VM, this is a useful figure to take a look at, as it shows the percentage of time that a world has spent in ready, co-deschedule state. The host's CPU scheduler puts a vCPU into the co-deschedule state if it advances too far in front of a VM's other vCPUs. So, a high figure here indicates that the VM's workload is not being effectively balanced across its multiple vCPUs, with the vCPU showing a high %CSTP doing the most work. If this is the case, look at reducing the number of vCPUs assigned to the VM.

CPU Configuration Tips

A number of different configuration parameters, both within and outside of vSphere, can influence the performance of an ESX/ESXi host. It is possible to install vSphere out of the box and expect to obtain decent performance, though to accommodate high volume or high resource utilization scenarios it is good to ensure that your vSphere environment is as performance-optimized as possible. You can achieve this by adjusting a number of configuration parameters. We will cover some of these in the following sections, though bear in mind that not all of them are necessarily applicable to every environment due to differences in hardware and vSphere requirements.

Single vCPU versus Multiple vCPUs

Take a cautious approach to allocating multiple vCPUs to a VM, as you can create extra overhead by scheduling two or more vCPUs in a VM, which as you would expect can be detrimental to performance, particularly when the VM is under heavy vCPU load. VMs with four or more allocated vCPUs can prove to be more susceptible to this scheduling overhead than those with two vCPUs; in fact, the overhead created by allocating two vCPUs is minimal in the vast majority of cases. Also, VMs running single-threaded or non-multiprocessor-aware applications won't be getting the benefit from the additional vCPUs. It is worth taking the time to review the VMs of servers which have been converted from a physical server environment, as often, many of these won't require the equivalent number of virtual processors that they had in the physical world. For more information on determining whether a VM's performance is impacted by running too many vCPUs, take a look at the informative VMware Knowledge Base article located at http://kb.vmware.com/kb/1005362. Also ensure that a

VM's guest OS is using the correct hardware abstraction layer (HAL). For example, a guest OS with a single vCPU should only be using a uniprocessor and not an SMP HAL. This is quite a common oversight after performing a physical to virtual (P2V) conversion from a physical multiprocessor server and then reducing the number of vCPUs allocated to the VM to a single vCPU.

vSphere Power Management Policy

The Power Management Policy feature found in vSphere 4.0 has been further enhanced in version 4.1 to include a handful of different power policies, which can potentially reduce power consumption, though at the expense of performance. The Power Management Policy setting integrates the host with power efficiency features found in modern AMD and Intel processors. The power policy allows the host to dynamically adjust CPU frequencies based on the current workload placed on the host by the VMs. See Chapter 2 for more information on configuring this.

Server BIOS Settings

A number of settings in the server BIOS can impact performance when running a hypervisor such as is found in vSphere. With the widespread adoption of virtualization, many of the virtualization-related enhancements, such as Intel VT and AMD-V, are now enabled in servers by default, though there are still some settings which are disabled and, depending on the configuration of your server, could provide some level of performance enhancement. In servers that are one to two years old, it is recommended that you check the BIOS settings, because they may not have all of the latest CPU virtualization performance enhancements, though they will almost certainly have some of them.

Many modern enterprise-level servers provide the ability to specify a "power profile" in the BIOS which can enable or disable a number of fully or semi-automated power-saving features. For example, on an HP ProLiant G6 server, you can choose from balanced, power saving, maximum performance, and custom power profiles. How this is set can have a bearing on the performance you can expect from the server, and as such, this setting, or similar settings with other manufacturers, should ideally be set to maximum performance to reduce the risk of any degraded performance while the server changes power states.

To maximize virtualization performance offered by modern CPUs from both Intel and AMD, ensure that Intel VT or AMD-V is enabled in the BIOS. Until relatively recently, this setting was always turned off in the BIOS by default, though this is now changing, as in newer models of servers it is turned on by default. Once again, this does vary between server manufacturers, and it is usually located under Advanced or Processor options. With older CPUs which have first-generation Intel VT or AMD-V functionality on the die, running this form of hardware-based virtualization assistance doesn't always guarantee better performance over that of software-assisted binary translation. As a result, ESX/ESXi will use either hardware (Intel VT or AMD-V) or software (binary translation) based virtualization technologies to ensure the best operating mode for a particular workload running on the host.

MEMORY PERFORMANCE TROUBLESHOOTING

VMware's vSphere can achieve high levels of VM consolidation through the use, in part, of some highly effective memory sharing and resource allocation mechanisms, such as TPS and ballooning. Both of these memory management techniques enable an administrator to oversubscribe the amount of physical memory found in a host, while at the same time providing VMs with access to the required physical memory when necessary. The amount of memory in a physical server is a finite resource which must be shared between the host and its VMs. During times of heavy VM memory utilization, the host can use the two mentioned memory resource management techniques to reallocate physical memory to the requesting VMs.

- **Memory ballooning**—This physical memory reclaiming technique is made possible by a driver (vmemctl) that is installed with VMware Tools on the guest OS. When the host detects that it is running out of memory it asks the vmemctl driver to allocate RAM from the guest OS (it inflates an imaginary "balloon") which starts the guest OS paging up to 65% (default) of its memory out to disk (page swapping). This frees up available physical memory for the host to reallocate elsewhere. This balloon expands and contracts as needed and reacts to what is happening in physical memory on the host.

- **ESX/ESXi page swapping**—Page swapping helps to reduce the memory footprint of a VM and only occurs when the host has exhausted the amount of physical memory it is able to free up through the use of memory ballooning. At this point, the host will start to swap out parts of the VM's memory without taking into account what parts of the VM's memory it is seizing and writing out to disk. This is less than desirable, as it can seriously impact the performance of a VM, so as such, ESX/ESXi page swapping is seen as a last resort.

TRANSPARENT PAGE SHARING (TPS)

Before we move on to discussing memory troubleshooting in esxtop/resxtop, I want to mention one of vSphere's most useful features, transparent page sharing (TPS). This memory-saving mechanism is enabled by default on the host and allows for the sharing of identical guest memory pages between VMs, which offers significant savings in overall memory page usage, particularly between VMs running the same version of the guest OS. Note that TPS does not work with large memory pages, though when the host comes under memory pressure the VMkernel's memory scheduler breaks up the large pages used by the VM into small 4K pages transparently, and TPS is then applied, thereby freeing up needed physical memory. To view the extent of the benefit your host is receiving from TPS, start esxtop/resxtop and press the m key, which will bring you to the memory resource utilization view where you can see the PSHARE /MB statistic, as shown in Figure 7.11.

```
 7:08:58am up 4 days  4:18,  156 worlds; MEM overcommit avg: 1.16, 1.16, 1.16
PMEM  /MB:  8190  total:   300  cos,    555 vmk,   4899 other,   2434 free
VMKMEM/MB:  7739 managed:  464 minfree,  2195 rsvd,   5544 ursvd,  high state
COSMEM/MB:    24   free:   596  swap t,   585 swap f:  0.00 r/s,   0.00 w/s
PSHARE/MB: 11938 shared,   288  common: 11650 saving
SWAP  /MB:     2   curr,     0 rclmtgt:               0.00 r/s,   0.00 w/s
ZIP   /MB:     6 zipped,     3  saved
MEMCTL/MB:   344   curr,   343  target,  8142 max

 GID NAME              MEMSZ    GRANT    SZTGT     TCHD   TCHD W   SWCUR
  58 W2K8R2-DC01     4096.00  4013.97   729.30   122.88   122.88   0.00
  60 W2K8R2          4096.00  4012.24   688.02    40.96    40.96   0.00
  61 W2K8_Test01     4096.00  4013.73   620.07    40.96     0.00   0.00
  62 W2K8_x86_Manage 2048.00  2047.74  1556.50   389.12    81.92   0.00
  57 W2K8_DC01       1024.00  1013.29   547.75    92.16    61.44   2.25
  59 W2K3_SQL01       768.00   422.79   433.02    93.08    55.00   0.00
  64 vSphere Managem  512.00   497.98   544.55    15.36     5.12   0.00
```

Figure 7.11 The PSHARE /MB row displays the TPS benefits the ESX/ESXi is receiving.

The TPS or PSHARE /MB row provides you with the following information:

- **Shared**—The total amount of physical memory which is being shared

- **Common**—The amount of VM-related memory which is common across all VMs on that host

- **Saving**—The total amount of VM memory which has been saved across all VMs due to TPS

In Figure 7.11, you can see that my VMs have 288MB of "common" memory between them, combined with 11.6GB of memory savings thanks to shared

memory pages. Now that you are familiar with these memory reclaiming techniques, let's take a look at some of the memory metrics on this front screen.
Many of these metrics can be used to determine if the host has to swap memory
due to memory pressure from the VMs, which will almost certainly cause poor
performance.

PHYSICAL MEMORY (PMEM /MB)

The physical memory (PMEM /MB) row offers a good overall summary of the
host's physical memory (PMEM) allocation, in megabytes, across the following
areas, as shown in Figure 7.12:

- **total**—The total physical memory installed in the host.

- **cos**—The total amount of physical memory which has been allocated to the
  ESX Service Console (excludes ESXi).

- **vmk**—The total amount of physical memory being use by the VMkernel.

- **other**—The total amount of remaining memory used by "other" items, such
  as the VMs. This figure excludes the memory consumed by the Service
  Console and the VMkernel.

- **free**—The amount of memory that is free and able to be allocated by the
  VMkernel.

From these PMEM /MB metrics, you can easily determine how much physical
memory a host has and how much of this has already been allocated and consumed. The amount of physical free memory will be a good basic "first-glance"
indication as to whether any host-level memory swapping is occurring. The
example in Figure 7.12 shows a host with just over 8GB of physical memory,
300MB of which is taken by the COS, 555MB by the VMkernel, and 5.3GB by
things other than the COS or VMkernel, which will almost certainly be the
VMs. There is 1.9GB of free physical memory, so this indicates that there is
unlikely to be a memory issue at the host level.

```
   2:58:26am up 4 days 7 min, 154 worlds; MEM overcommit avg: 1.16, 1.16, 1.16
PMEM  /MB:   8190   total:    300     cos,    555 vmk,   5362 other,   1971 free
VMKMEM/MB:   7739 managed:    464  minfree,  2190 rsvd,   5548 ursvd,   high state
COSMEM/MB:     24    free:    596   swap_t,   585 swap_f:  0.00 r/s,   0.00 w/s
PSHARE/MB: 11488  shared,    300  common: 11188 saving
SWAP  /MB:      2    curr,      0  rclmtgt:                0.00 r/s,   0.00 w/s
ZIP   /MB:      6  zipped,      3    saved
MEMCTL/MB:    348    curr,    349   target,  8142 max
```

Figure 7.12   A wide range of useful host-level memory metrics are available in the top part of the
memory resource utilization screen.

MEMORY OVERCOMMITMENT AVERAGE

Similar to the CPU resource utilization view, the "MEM overcommit avg" metric, as shown in the top right-hand corner of Figure 7.13, provides an average view over a one-, five-, and 15-minute window. In this case, it indicates the level of memory overcommitment on the host. If the value is greater than 0, this indicates that the amount of memory the VMs requested is greater than the physical memory in the host. This doesn't necessarily mean there is a memory performance issue, however, as ESX/ESXi is likely using TPS, which will be providing the needed spare physical memory.

```
  2:58:26am up 4 days 7 min, 154 worlds; MEM overcommit avg: 1.16, 1.16, 1.16
PMEM  /MB:  8190   total:    300   cos,    555 vmk,    5362 other,   1971 free
VMKMEM/MB:  7739 managed:    464 minfree,  2190 rsvd,  5548 ursvd,  high state
COSMEM/MB:    24   free:    596 swap_t,    585 swap_f:  0.00 r/s,   0.00 w/s
PSHARE/MB: 11488 shared,    300 common: 11188 saving
SWAP  /MB:     2   curr,      0 rclmtgt:                 0.00 r/s,   0.00 w/s
ZIP   /MB:     6 zipped,      3  saved
MEMCTL/MB:   348   curr,    349 target,  8142 max
```

Figure 7.13   The memory overcommitment average gives a basic view as to the extent of any memory overcommitment on the ESX/ESXi host.

ESX SERVICE CONSOLE MEMORY (COSMEM /MB)

COSMEM /MB is the amount of memory consumed by the ESX Service Console (COS). As you might expect, this value is not present in ESXi, as ESXi doesn't have a Service Console. The metrics on this row include "free," which indicates the amount of idle physical memory allocated to the COS; "swap t," which is the amount of configured swap memory configured; and "swap f," which is the amount of free swap memory. In Figure 7.14, you can see that the COS has only 24MB of memory free and has already swapped 11MB (swap_t – swap_f), so in this instance this would be one area to watch for any performance issues.

```
  2:58:26am up 4 days 7 min, 154 worlds; MEM overcommit avg: 1.16, 1.16, 1.16
PMEM  /MB:  8190   total:    300   cos,    555 vmk,    5362 other,   1971 free
VMKMEM/MB:  7739 managed:    464 minfree,  2190 rsvd,  5548 ursvd,  high state
COSMEM/MB:    24   free:    596 swap_t,    585 swap_f:  0.00 r/s,   0.00 w/s
PSHARE/MB: 11488 shared,    300 common: 11188 saving
SWAP  /MB:     2   curr,      0 rclmtgt:                 0.00 r/s,   0.00 w/s
ZIP   /MB:     6 zipped,      3  saved
MEMCTL/MB:   348   curr,    349 target,  8142 max
```

Figure 7.14   The COSMEM /MB metrics can indicate whether the Service Console has insufficient memory and is swapping to disk.

The final two metrics in the COS memory row indicate any current read ("r/s") or write ("w/s") memory swapping that may be occurring. Read/write activity here can indicate that the amount of COS memory may be insufficient, the result of which may be slow COS or management agent responsiveness.

VMKERNEL MEMORY (VMKMEM /MB)

VMKMEM /MB is the amount of memory managed by the VMkernel. This figure will always be less than the PMEM /MB figure, as it does not include the memory consumed by the Service Console and any PCI devices installed in your physical host. Even with an ESXi host, which doesn't have a Service Console, this figure is still less than the PMEM /MB figure due to the memory consumed by the PCI devices. Toward the right-hand side of Figure 7.15, you will see the VMkernel state, which can be at one of four settings: high, soft, hard, or low. This value indicates the free memory state for the VMkernel and is a good indicator for determining whether the host's memory is under any pressure, as well as what mechanism it will use to reclaim any memory, if required.

```
 2:58:26am up 4 days 7 min, 154 worlds; MEM overcommit avg: 1.16, 1.16, 1.16
PMEM  /MB:  8190   total:   300    cos,    555 vmk,    5362 other,   1971 free
VMKMEM/MB:  7739 managed:   464 minfree,  2190 rsvd,   5548 ursvd,   high state
COSMEM/MB:    24    free:   596 swap_t,    585 swap_f:  0.00 r/s,    0.00 w/s
PSHARE/MB: 11488 shared,   300 common: 11188 saving
SWAP  /MB:     2    curr,     0 rclmtgt:               0.00 r/s,    0.00 w/s
ZIP   /MB:     6  zipped,     3  saved
MEMCTL/MB:   348    curr,   349 target,  8142 max
```

Figure 7.15 Although not used as much as PMEM /MB and COSMEM /MB in basic memory performance troubleshooting, the VMKMEM /MB metrics should still be considered.

Table 7.5 summarizes the different states, their associated thresholds, and the preferred method of reclaiming memory, if necessary.

Table 7.5 VMkernel States with Memory Thresholds and Memory Reclamation Mechanism

VMkernel State	Amount of Memory Available (Total Memory—VMkernel Memory)	Preferred Memory Reclamation Mechanism
High	6%	Memory ballooning
Soft	4%	Memory ballooning
Hard	2%	Swapping
Low	1%	Swapping

You want this value to ideally be indicating a "high" state, which means there is sufficient free memory for use by the VMkernel. Note, however, that guest OS swapping can still occur even when this value is in a "high" state, as this relates to the VMkernel's available memory and not the available memory at the guest OS level.

Swap (SWAP /MB)

The swap usage statistics row, shown in Figure 7.16, is probably one of the most important when determining whether a host is experiencing memory pressure and has to swap memory out to disk. When the VMkernel swaps out to disk it usually indicates that ballooning wasn't being widely used—for example, perhaps VMware Tools wasn't installed on all of the VMs, or if ballooning was working, maybe it wasn't aggressive enough, or maybe there isn't enough physical memory in the ESX/ESXi host to meet the memory demand. The SWAP /MB row contains four metrics.

- **curr**—The current VMkernel swap usage in megabytes.

- **rclmtgt**—The amount of swap file usage that the VMkernel thinks there should be. You can reclaim this amount of swap memory by either swapping or using compression.

- **r/s and w/s**—The rate at which memory is swapped from or to the disk by the VMkernel.

```
   2:58:10pm up 1 day  5:49, 151 worlds; MEM overcommit avg: 3.50, 3.32, 2.29
PMEM   /MB:  4086    total:    300     cos,    518 vmk,    2923 other,     344 free
VMKMEM/MB:  3677 managed:    220 minfree,   1622 rsvd,   2054 ursvd,  high state
COSMEM/MB:     4    free:    596  swap_t,    596 swap_f:    0.00 r/s,    0.00 w/s
PSHARE/MB:  8311  shared,     21  common:   8290 saving
SWAP   /MB:   938    curr,   1432 rclmtgt:                 1.33 r/s,    1.22 w/s
ZIP    /MB:   813  zipped,    533   saved
MEMCTL/MB:  3965    curr,   4096 target,   8142 max
```

Figure 7.16 The VMkernel's swap (SWAP /MB) row will clearly show whether memory pages are being swapped out to disk.

In Figure 7.16, a large amount of VMkernel memory page swapping is occurring. From the metrics shown, we can see that the VMkernel has currently swapped 938MB of memory pages to disk, with both active swap read and writes also happening. This is a good example of a host whose physical memory is far too overcommitted.

MEMORY COMPRESSION (ZIP /MB)

Memory compression, or ZIP /MB, as the row title is called, is a new feature found with vSphere 4.1. The purpose of memory compression, which is enabled by default, is to provide a faster mechanism for swapping memory rather than transferring it to slower disk. Any memory pages that are smaller than 2KB and are to be swapped are first compressed, if possible, and stored in a memory cache. Figure 7.17 highlights the ZIP /MB row.

```
 2:58:10pm up 1 day  5:49, 151 worlds; MEM overcommit avg: 3.50, 3.32, 2.29
PMEM  /MB:  4086    total:    300     cos,    518 vmk,    2923 other,    344 free
VMKMEM/MB:  3677 managed:    220 minfree,   1622 rsvd,    2054 ursvd,  high state
COSMEM/MB:     4    free:    596  swap_t,    596 swap_f:   0.00 r/s,   0.00 w/s
PSHARE/MB:  8311   shared,     21  common:   8290 saving
SWAP  /MB:   938     curr,   1432 rclmtgt:             1.33 r/s,   1.22 w/s
ZIP   /MB:   813   zipped,    533    saved
MEMCTL/MB:  3965     curr,   4096 target,   8142 max
```

Figure 7.17 Memory compression can offer a faster method of swapping memory pages compared to writing to disk.

You can see in Figure 7.17 that 813MB of physical memory have been compressed, which has resulted in a savings of 533MB of memory. This will almost certainly be quicker than writing this much memory down to swap on a disk.

MEMORY BALLOON STATISTICS (MEMCTL /MB)

You can view the extent of memory ballooning initiated by the VMkernel in the MEMCTL /MB row, shown in Figure 7.18. This row has three metrics:

- **curr**—The total amount of physical memory that has been reclaimed via the balloon driver (vmmemctl) running on the guest OSs
- **target**—The total amount of physical memory that the host will attempt to reclaim using the balloon driver
- **max**—The total amount of physical memory that the host can reclaim using the balloon driver

Figure 7.18 shows that the balloon driver has reclaimed 3.9GB of memory, though it could reclaim a maximum of 8.1GB of physical memory among all the VMs.

```
 2:58:10pm up 1 day  5:49, 151 worlds; MEM overcommit avg: 3.50, 3.32, 2.29
PMEM   /MB:  4086   total:    300    cos,    518 vmk,    2923 other,    344 free
VMKMEM/MB:  3677 managed:    220 minfree,  1622 rsvd,   2054 ursvd,  high state
COSMEM/MB:     4    free:    596 swap_t,    596 swap_f:  0.00 r/s,   0.00 w/s
PSHARE/MB:  8311  shared,     21  common:  8290 saving
SWAP   /MB:   938    curr,   1432 rclmtgt:                1.33 r/s,   1.22 w/s
ZIP    /MB:   813  zipped,    533    saved
MEMCTL/MB:  3965    curr,   4096  target,  8142 max
```

Figure 7.18 Memory ballooning can be the first indication of insufficient physical memory in the ESX/ESXi host.

MEMORY PERFORMANCE TROUBLESHOOTING A VIRTUAL MACHINE (VM)

You have seen how to detect whether a host is running short on physical memory and must use either the ballooning or page swapping technique to reclaim memory. Let's now look at how to determine whether a VM is experiencing memory issues. First, press the V key to filter the view so that it is only showing the VMs running on the host, and none of the other entities, and then press the f key to bring up all the fields that you will want to view. Now enable the following fields:

- A: ID = Id
- D: NAME = Name
- E: NWLD = Num Members
- H: SIZE = MEM Size (MB)
- I: ACTV = MEM Active (MB)
- J: MCTL = MEM Ctl (MB)
- K: SWAP STATS = Swap Statistics (MB)

To enable all of these fields you will need to expand your window horizontally as much as possible and use the scroll bar if necessary to view all of the fields. As you can see in Figure 7.19, there are quite a few fields.

The following fields can provide valuable information to help you determine whether there are any performance-related issues at the VM level, due to insufficient memory, memory ballooning, or page swapping.

- **MEMSZ (MB)**—This is a good basic metric to start with, as it indicates the amount of physical memory which has been allocated to a VM.
- **GRANT (MB)**—This is a new field introduced in esxtop in vSphere. It displays the amount of memory that has been allocated to the VM at the request of the guest OS. You will notice that the granted memory for these

```
 3:42:53am up 15:44, 155 worlds; MEM overcommit avg: 1.15, 1.15, 1.13
PMEM  /MB:  8190   total:    300   cos,    555 vmk,   4641 other,   2693 free
VMKMEM/MB:  7739 managed:    464 minfree,  2143 rsvd,   5595 ursvd,  high state
COSMEM/MB:     8    free:    596  swap_t,   596 swap_f:   0.00 r/s,    0.00 w/s
PSHARE/MB: 11170  shared,    125 common: 11045 saving
SWAP  /MB:   568    curr,    417 rclmtgt:                0.00 r/s,    0.00 w/s
ZIP   /MB:     0  zipped,      0  saved
MEMCTL/MB:   322    curr,    322 target,  8142 max
```

ID	NAME	NWLD	MEMSZ	GRANT	SZTGT	TCHD	TCHD W	%ACTV	%ACTVS	%ACTVF	%A
57	W2K8_Test01	4	4096.00	3829.32	425.21	0.00	0.00	0	0	0	
58	W2K8R2-DC01	5	4096.00	3781.61	558.67	40.96	0.00	0	0	0	
65	W2K8R2	4	4096.00	3930.74	687.41	81.92	40.96	3	1	2	
75	W2K8_x86_Manage	5	2048.00	2047.73	2028.54	491.52	204.80	3	7	4	
66	W2K8_DC01	5	1024.00	1004.16	439.20	92.16	30.72	2	3	3	
64	W2K3_SQL01	4	768.00	406.10	428.27	71.25	31.17	10	8	10	
73	vSphere Managem	4	512.00	223.98	276.21	15.36	0.00	4	1	3	

Figure 7.19 Expand your view of esxtop/resxtop as much as possible, or use the scroll bar to ensure that you are not missing any useful fields.

Windows-based VMs is pretty close to their allocated memory. This is because upon start-up, Windows (and especially Windows Server 2008) touches most of its memory pages, unlike other operating systems, such as Linux. Much of this memory, however, is reclaimed via memory page sharing and memory ballooning.

- **MCTL? (Y/N)**—This is a useful field, as it shows whether a VM has the balloon driver installed, which usually indicates whether the VM is running VMware Tools. If the value is "N," investigate further; also, if the guest OS is capable of running VMware Tools it is highly recommended that it be installed and run.

- **MCTLSZ (MB)**—This field is important when determining if and how much memory in megabytes the host has reclaimed from a VM's guest OS via the memory ballooning driver. If this value is greater than 0, it could indicate that the host's memory is too overcommitted. In this case, more investigation at the host level should be undertaken to confirm this.

- **SWCUR (MB)**—If the host has had to swap memory pages out to disk for this VM, this amount in megabytes is indicated here. You ideally don't want to see any figure other than 0 here; otherwise, it could indicate that the host's memory is too overcommitted.

- **SWR/s and SWW/s (MB)**—These values show the rate at which the host is actively swapping read or write memory pages. As outlined in the entry for the SWCUR field, any value greater than 0 indicates that the host doesn't have enough physical memory to go around, and after attempting to use the balloon driver, it is swapping out pages to disk as a last resort.

%SWAP WAIT TIME (SWPWT)

The last esxtop/resxtop metric that we will look at in this section on memory is located on the CPU's memory resource utilization view. So, once again, let's return to this view by pressing the c button. By default, the swap wait time (%SWPWT) field is found on the far right-hand side of the screen and is a useful field to first check when a VM is experiencing slow or unresponsive performance. This field, newly introduced with vSphere, indicates how long a VM spends waiting for the VMkernel to swap required memory pages from disk.

In extreme cases, as seen in Figure 7.20, high %SWPWT figures are a sure indication of a physical memory oversubscription issue, as the VMs are spending large lengths of time waiting on the VMkernel to retrieve memory pages that have been written down to disk.

```
1:28:59pm up  2:09, 155 worlds; CPU load average: 0.66, 0.50, 0.20
PCPU USED(%):  28  23 AVG:  26
PCPU UTIL(%):  30  25 AVG:  27
CCPU(%):    5 us,   7 sy,  80 id,   8 wa ;       cs/sec:   1421
```

ID	GID	NAME	NWLD	%USED	%RUN	%SYS	%WAIT	%RDY	%IDLE	%OVRLP	%CSTP	%MLMTD	%SWPWT
65	65	W2K8R2-DC01	5	22.85	24.11	0.75	462.36	6.39	0.00	0.54	0.00	0.00	65.66
62	62	W2K8_x86_Manage	5	8.49	9.14	0.56	472.38	16.66	170.60	0.84	0.54	0.00	0.00
56	56	W2K8_Test01	4	3.24	3.39	0.30	392.27	3.36	0.00	0.39	0.00	0.00	95.85
64	64	W2K8_R2	5	1.78	1.98	0.18	495.45	1.29	52.10	0.20	0.00	0.00	39.37
59	59	W2K8_DC01	5	0.82	0.87	0.07	496.59	1.29	0.00	0.04	0.00	0.00	98.86
58	58	W2K3_SQL01	4	0.76	0.78	0.06	397.59	0.64	0.00	0.04	0.00	0.00	96.46
63	63	vSphere Managem	4	0.41	0.44	0.04	397.08	1.47	0.00	0.02	0.00	0.00	97.78

Figure 7.20   The %SWPWT field indicates the percentage of time a VM spends waiting for the VMkernel to swap memory from disk.

MEMORY CONFIGURATION TIPS

There are also memory performance considerations relating to the server on which ESX/ESXi is running. The following two sections cover a couple of the more common areas that can be overlooked, thereby potentially impacting the memory performance achievable by the host.

Server BIOS Settings

After purchasing a new server, ensure that you are getting the maximum performance benefits from its installed memory by checking its memory-related BIOS settings. For example, on an HP ProLiant G6 server, you can set the Maximum Memory Bus Frequency to a fixed setting, but it's best to leave it set to Auto unless you have a definite requirement to change it. Another example is

Memory Interleaving, which you should set to Full Interleaving for maximum performance, unless you are using NUMA, in which case you should use No Interleaving. Other server manufacturers should also have similar memory settings in their server BIOS.

Physical Memory Placement

The placement of physical memory in your server is very important, as incorrect placement can lead to degraded memory performance or an imbalance on SMP servers. This is particularly relevant to new Intel Nehalem and recent AMD servers; if they are configured for NUMA, separate memory is allocated to an individual processor to form a NUMA node. For more information on correct memory placement, check the server manufacturer's website or documentation.

DISK/STORAGE TROUBLESHOOTING

Troubleshooting storage issues, both local and, especially, remote, can often prove to be more complicated than troubleshooting CPU or memory issues, as with storage, more external variables are at play. There are three disk-related views within esxtop/resxtop:

- **Storage Adapter (press the d key)**—Displays the aggregated statistics per storage adapter (default) or storage path
- **Storage Device (press the u key)**—Shows utilization statistics host-wide and can be grouped by storage device (default), per path, per world, or per partition
- **Virtual Machine Storage (press the v key)**—Provides a VM-centric view of aggregated storage statistics, which can also be used to provide a view on a per-vSCSI-device basis

The counters between these three storage-related views are very similar, with the main difference being where the statistics are aggregated: at the adapter, device, or VM level. As there are these commonalities in metrics between all three views, the information in the following section can generally be applied to all views depending on the level at which you wish to troubleshoot an issue. The first three fields we will look at have to do with determining latency at the storage device driver, VMkernel, and VM guest OS levels. These three fields are toward the far right-hand side of the screen by default, so don't forget to expand your esxtop/resxtop view horizontally if you cannot see them initially.

DEVICE AVERAGE (DAVG/CMD)

DAVG/cmd (ms) is the amount of latency at the device driver and it indicates how long, on average and in milliseconds (ms), it takes for an I/O request to travel from the HBA to the storage device and back again. This counter is useful for identifying any storage issues involving, for example, the storage controller or fabric switch which is located outside the host. Although there are no hard and fast rules regarding what is an acceptable level of latency for DAVG, it is generally thought that a latency of more than 15ms indicates that there is a potential performance issue with the shared storage device.

VMKERNEL AVERAGE (KAVG/CMD)

KAVG/cmd shows the average latency (ms) experienced as a result of the VMkernel issuing the I/O command. As you would expect, this figure should be as close to 0.00 as possible, and a figure of 2.00 or greater provides a strong indication that queuing is occurring at the kernel in the host, which should be investigated.

GUEST AVERAGE (GAVG/CMD)

GAVG/cmd is the latency (ms) as seen by the guest OS and is the sum of both DAVG and KAVG, which indicates the round-trip latency experienced, as shown in Figure 7.21

```
11:53:19pm up 38 min, 127 worlds; CPU load average: 0.07, 0.08, 0.08
```

ADAPTR PATH	NPTH	CMDS/s	READS/s	WRITES/s	MBREAD/s	MBWRTN/s	DAVG/cmd	KAVG/cmd	GAVG/cmd	QAVG/cmd
vmhba0 -	0	0.00	0.00	0.00	0.00	0.00	0.00	0.00	0.00	0.00
vmhba1 -	1	0.00	0.00	0.00	0.00	0.00	0.00	0.00	0.00	0.00
vmhba32 -	0	0.00	0.00	0.00	0.00	0.00	0.00	0.00	0.00	0.00
vmhba33 -	0	0.00	0.00	0.00	0.00	0.00	0.00	0.00	0.00	0.00
vmhba34 -	1	2.18	0.00	2.18	0.00	0.03	10.38	0.01	10.39	0.00
vmhba35 -	0	0.00	0.00	0.00	0.00	0.00	0.00	0.00	0.00	0.00

Figure 7.21   DAVG, KAVG, and GAVG are three useful metrics when determining storage latency.

There is no one set of rules when it comes to determining what each of these values should be for your particular vSphere implementation, though as a rule of thumb, latency times of more than 20ms to 25ms for DAVG and GAVG, and of 2ms for KAVG, would indicate a storage latency issue.

QUEUE DEPTHS (QUED)

Queue depths are another important factor to consider when troubleshooting storage issues, as these indicate the number of storage commands which are backed up and waiting to be processed. As with queue lengths in the everyday world—for example, a queue of cars at a traffic intersection—the deeper the queue, the greater the chance of a slow response, thereby indicating the possibility of a bottleneck. We will now take a look at a couple of key metrics that will help to indicate the length of storage-related queues.

The following queue length metrics are only available via the storage device view, which you can obtain by pressing the u key.

The value provided in the QUED field indicates the number of commands that are actively queued at the VMkernel. Once again, there is no definitive value on what the maximum acceptable queue length is, as it can vary depending on factors such as the model of HBA or the storage manufacturer used. The optimal value, however, is 0, which indicates that there are currently no commands in the queue, though it is advisable to check with your storage vendor for the optimal queue depth value as the allowable queue depth may just need to be increased.

A common cause of excessive queue depths is too many VMs or an I/O-intensive VM connecting to a particular LUN. In such a situation, consider moving some of the VMs off the LUN and try to balance the VMs more evenly, taking into account the overall loading on the LUN. If you have an I/O-intensive VM that causes queuing at the LUN or HBA level, you could consider increasing the allowable queue depth within ESX/ESXi. As mentioned earlier, find out from your storage vendor what this value should be. This setting determines the number of commands which an HBA is prepared to accept for processing on a particular LUN.

The final two esxtop/resxtop metrics which we will discuss in this section are the error statistics, which are strong indicators of a storage issue.

STORAGE COMMAND ABORTS (ABRT/S)

The ABRT/s value, found by enabling the ERRSTATS/s field, indicates the number of storage commands which are aborted per second. The aborts are issued by a VM's guest OS when the attached storage it is trying to access hasn't responded within a predefined period of time; for a Windows guest OS this is 60 seconds. A value greater than 0 here is usually a sign that something between the guest OS and the actual storage device is not responding or is unable to meet the demands placed on it.

STORAGE COMMAND RESETS (RESETS/S)

RESETS/s is the number of storage-related commands which are reset per second. Anything consistently greater than 0 is also a strong indicator of an underlying storage-related issue.

STORAGE CONFIGURATION TIPS

There are a number of storage configuration "tweaks" which can benefit your host and the VMs running on it. The following are some recommendations which can assist in achieving improved storage-related performance.

- **Partition alignment**—When a new Virtual Machine File System (VMFS) volume is created from within vCenter the partition is automatically aligned along the 64KB boundary, which will be the most efficient for most storage solutions. However, if the underlying stripe size of the storage LUN is not aligned to 64KB, this will cause an inefficiency and almost certainly a reduction in storage performance on that VMFS volume. Check with your storage administrator or vendor to determine the offset of the LUN before creating the VMFS, as once it is created and data is added there is no easy way to realign it without the use of a third-party utility such as Vizioncore's vOptimizer Pro.

- **VM disk types**—When creating a VM disk for a VM, you have three types from which to choose, as detailed in Chapter 3. Of these, Eager-Zeroed disks offer the best disk performance on the first write to a disk block. Eager-Zeroed disks are allocated and zeroed when the virtual disk is created, resulting in one less step that the VM needs to wait on (albeit a very slight delay) during runtime, thereby offering the best performance. Thin disks have the highest I/O penalty because space is both allocated and zeroed on demand on the first write. For subsequent writes, there is no I/O penalty. It ultimately becomes a trade-off between provisioned storage capacity and optimal first-write performance.

- **VMFS or Raw Device Mappings (RDMs)**—There has been extensive debate around the subject of which of these two disk types offers the best performance and in which scenarios they should be applied. Often, virtualization administrators will lean toward using RDMs for VMs running heavy disk I/O workloads as are found with databases and the like, though the differences in performance between the two have been shown to be negligible for most average and even heavy workloads. Random reads and writes and >32KB block size I/O sequential reads and writes on both VMFS and RDMs offer comparable performance, with the smaller (i.e., <32KB) block size sequential reads and writes seeing RDMs providing slightly better performance. Also, under some read and write situations, the RDM disk type does use fewer CPU cycles, though as mentioned before, these differences in performance are unlikely to impact the vast majority of VM workloads.

- **VM placement**—Carefully consider where you place each of your VMs based on the predicted levels of storage I/O the VM will require. Try to keep VMs with high storage I/O utilization requirements spread evenly across multiple paths—for example, the LUNs, ESX/ESXi hosts, and their storage controllers. Mix VMs with both high and low storage I/O requirements. Databases and email servers are two typical examples where you will likely see high levels of I/O utilization.

- **Dedicated network**—Always ensure that any network-based storage traffic—for example, iSCSI and NFS—runs on their own dedicated network uplinks. This is also highly advisable for Storage VMotion traffic which can be particularly bandwidth-intensive.

- **VM swap file location**—Relocate the VM swap file away from the VMFS volume which hosts the VM's vmdk files. The purpose of this is to reduce any potential impact from VMs that regularly swap memory out to disk and are located on the same VMFS volume as those that don't.

- **PVSCSI controller**—The best performance gains are seen from the PVSCSI adapter when used with VMs which have a significant storage I/O requirement and are connected to a high-performance storage system generally providing more than 2,000 IOPS. For more information on PVSCSI, see Chapter 5.

- **HBA placement**—To realize the maximum speeds achievable by an HBA in the host, ensure that the HBA is placed in an expansion slot on the system board that can handle the throughput. Take care when adding an HBA to a new or existing server; if it is intended for an x8 PCIe slot make sure it does, in fact, get inserted into an x16 or x8 PCIe expansion slot, as inserting it into an x4 PCIe slot will only limit the available bandwidth to the HBA.

NETWORK TROUBLESHOOTING

Fewer esxtop/resxtop metrics are available for the networking resource utilization view, with the two fields shown in Figure 7.22 providing you with the main information you will need to conduct basic troubleshooting on a networking issue.

- **%DRPTX**—This field indicates the percentage of dropped transmit packets.
- **%DRPRX**—This field indicates the percentage of dropped received packets.

```
2:25:15am up  3:10, 156 worlds; CPU load average: 0.08, 0.08, 0.08

  PORT-ID           USED-BY  TEAM-PNIC DTYP DNAME      PKTTX/s  PKTRX/s  MbRX/s  %DRPTX  %DRPRX
16777217         Management       n/a  H vSwitch0        0.00     0.00    0.00    0.00    0.00
16777218             vmnic2         -  H vSwitch0        8.89     8.89    0.03    0.00    0.00
16777219               vmk1    vmnic2  H vSwitch0        0.00     2.37    0.00    0.00    0.00
16777220        4096:vswif0    vmnic2  H vSwitch0        7.51     8.50    0.02    0.00    0.00
16777221 4247:W2K8_x86_Manage  vmnic2  H vSwitch0        0.00     0.59    0.00    0.00   78.57
16777222        4299:W2K8R2    vmnic2  H vSwitch0        0.00     1.38    0.00    0.00   41.67
16777223 4349:vSphere Managem  vmnic2  H vSwitch0        0.20     0.59    0.00    0.00   72.73
16777224       4303:W2K8_DC01  vmnic2  H vSwitch0        0.00     1.98    0.00    0.00   33.33
16777225      4300:W2K8_Test01 vmnic2  H vSwitch0        0.20     2.17    0.00    0.00    0.00
16777226     4320:W2K8R2-DC01  vmnic2  H vSwitch0        0.00     2.37    0.00    0.00    0.00
16777227      4421:W2K3_SQL01  vmnic2  H vSwitch0        0.20     2.17    0.00    0.00    0.00
33554433         Management       n/a  H vSwitch1        0.00     0.00    0.00    0.00    0.00
33554434             vmnic0         -  H vSwitch1     1118.84  1743.47   18.78    0.00    0.00
33554435               vmk0    vmnic0  H vSwitch1     1118.84   658.62   18.24    0.00    0.00
```

Figure 7.22   High volumes of dropped transmit or receive network packets are a good indication that the physical network cards aren't coping with the required load.

On a healthy host, you would expect to see both of these metrics remain at 0, though if either of these statistics reaches a higher value, this indicates a definite problem which should be investigated further. If you see dropped network packets in the %DRPTX field, the associated network port or VM will almost certainly be experiencing impaired network transmit performance. The likely cause of this is that the underlying physical network adapter in the host is nearing its performance capacity; a solution for resolving this would be either to upgrade the network card or to distribute the network load across multiple network cards using NIC teaming.

If there are dropped receive packets (%DRPRX), as seen in four of the VMs in Figure 7.22, rather than it being a physical NIC issue this could in fact be an indication that the VM needs additional CPU resources allocating to it, as the VM's vCPU cannot keep up with the rate of incoming packets.

NETWORK CONFIGURATION TIPS

Although there are fewer metrics within esxtop/resxtop to review when performance-troubleshooting a network-related issue, there are a number of other hardware and configuration considerations that can assist in improving the network performance of a host or VM. The following items outline some of the more popular configurations or technologies used to achieve an increase in network performance at both the host and VM levels.

- **Jumbo frames**—Jumbo frames for iSCSI or NAS storage traffic can offer a significant improvement in performance between the VM, the ESX/ESXi host, and the storage appliance. However, an MTU mismatch on one or more of the network devices between any network end points can impact performance. In a typical network configuration, you should have jumbo frames and the MTU size matching on the following items:
  - VM
  - ESX/ESXi host's vSwitch
  - Switch or router
  - End device (e.g., physical server, NAS, or SAN storage device)
- **Enhanced network card features**—An increasing number of network cards are now being produced with a number of performance enhancement features, such as:
  - **Offloading**—TCP segmentation and checksum offload on a host can be achieved by using a VMware-approved iSCSI HBA. Although there are approved network cards that have offload features on their chipsets, they won't necessarily work with ESX/ESXi; hence, an approved iSCSI HBA is required. The benefit of using an iSCSI HBA is that the TCP, IP, and iSCSI processes are performed (offloaded) on the chipsets found on the HBA rather than by the host CPUs, thereby freeing up valuable CPU cycles that can be allocated to something else.
  - **NetQueue support**—Modern network cards have network queues built in which handle the processing of networking packets. This is particularly important in modern networks as the volume of packets which can potentially be transferred to achieve, for example, 10Gb speeds, would seriously impact the performance or even saturate a single CPU on the ESX/ESXi host. ESX/ESXi utilizes the multiple network queues found on the hardware of modern NICs to distribute the queues in parallel across multiple

CPU cores, thereby spreading the load more evenly and ensuring that a single CPU isn't saturated. The multiple-queue feature in ESX/ESXi is driver-specific, so make sure that ESX/ESXi has the multiqueue driver for your particular NIC.

- **PCIe v2.0 support**—These network or HBA cards provide double the bandwidth per channel of v1.0 cards, which will ensure that you can achieve the maximum throughput of your network cards—in particular, those running at higher network speeds such as 10GbE.

- **Unused vNIC removal**—Reclaim valuable CPU cycles by removing any unused vNICs due to the guest OS regularly polling every NIC to detect its status. This is also one of the reasons it is recommended that you detach the CD drive from the VM.

- **NIC placement**—Make sure you put your network card in an expansion slot with sufficient bandwidth to meet the demands of the card. This is becoming more important with the increased mainstream adoption of high-throughput PCIe-based cards (e.g., 8Gb FC HBA and 10GbE Ethernet cards). As mentioned above, the new PCIe 2.0 standard doubles the available bandwidth per channel, which will address any such bandwidth concerns.

- **VMXNET drivers**—For a VM, the best network performance in a driver can be found using a paravirtualized VMXNET driver, which is built by VMware with performance in mind. See Chapter 6 for more information on this.

ADDITIONAL TROUBLESHOOTING TIPS

We have now covered the four core resource types found in both a host and a VM, and have looked at some of the basic troubleshooting and configuration techniques which can assist you in maintaining the performance of your vSphere environment. Here are some additional tips that don't fall into any of the previous four resource categories.

- **VMware Tools**—Ensure that VMware Tools has been installed on all the VMs in your environment and that the VM hardware level is at level 7.

- **Correct guest OS type**—When creating a VM ensure that you select the correct guest OS when prompted during the VM creation process so that the correct optimal devices and their associated settings are automatically selected for that particular guest OS.

- **Disabling of unused devices**—Leaving devices such as CD-ROMs connected to a VM consumes valuable CPU cycles, as the guest OS will periodically poll the CD-ROM device to see if it is still present. If it's not attached, it won't be polled and these valuable CPU cycles will not be consumed.

- **Application performance**—The end-to-end performance of an application running on a VM's guest OS can be comprehensively monitored and any bottlenecks detected using another product in VMware's vSphere suite, called AppSpeed.

SUMMARY

vSphere provides the administrator with some comprehensive and effective methods for monitoring, alerting, and troubleshooting the performance of both hosts and VMs. In this chapter, we looked at the various methods and discussed the new performance enhancements found in vSphere. Effective troubleshooting of vSphere issues is a valuable skill for an administrator to have, though it is definitely a topic with many deeper levels. For additional information on performance, refer to the following vSphere performance resources:

- Scott Drummond's blog, http://vpivot.com/
- VMware performance community, http://communities.vmware.com/community/vmtn/general/performance
- VROOM!—The VMware performance team's blog, http://blogs.vmware.com/performance/
- esxtop Performance Counters, http://communities.vmware.com/docs/DOC-5240
- Interpreting esxtop Statistics, http://communities.vmware.com/docs/DOC-9279

BACKUPS IN vSPHERE

Having good backups is a must for any environment, physical or virtual. Traditional backup methods that are used in physical environments can still be used in virtual environments, but alternatives are available that can make the process of backing up your virtual machines (VM) faster and more efficient. VMware introduced a product called VMware Consolidated Backup (VCB) in VI3 that was a new approach to backing up ESX VMs. VCB leverages a proxy server to back up virtual disks, thus offloading the burden from the VM. VCB also provides network-less backups by backing up the VM's virtual disks over the storage area network (SAN) fabric. In vSphere, VMware introduced the vStorage APIs for Data Protection as the successor to VCB that allows backup applications to use APIs to connect to hosts and VMs. In this chapter, we will cover some different methods for backing up VMs in vSphere, what data you will want to back up, and VMware's new backup product, VMware Data Recovery.

BACKUP METHODS

There are several methods that you can use to back up your VMs, and each has advantages and disadvantages. The simplest and least efficient method is to use traditional backup agents running inside the guest operating system. Another method is to use backup scripts which run inside the Service Console that take a snapshot of a VM and make a copy of its virtual disk file to an alternate storage device. You can also use one of the many third-party backup solutions that are available. Let's take a look at some of these methods so that you can decide which one will work best in your environment.

TRADITIONAL BACKUPS

With a traditional backup, a backup agent is installed on the guest OS and the backup system communicates with the agent to back up the files on the server. This method can cause high disk and network I/O as well as high CPU utilization on the servers that are being backed up. Although this may be okay on a physical server, when done in a virtual environment it can affect other VMs running on the same host, as they are all competing for the host's resources and a backup on one VM can leave fewer resources for the other VMs.

Advantages of traditional backups include the following.

- They are easy to deploy, as most environments are already using this method.
- They make it easier to restore individual files than other methods.
- No additional software is needed and no process changes are required if you are already using this method.

Disadvantages of traditional backups include the following.

- They cause excessive resource usage on hosts.
- They are slower than other methods.
- You cannot do bare metal restores as they require the OS and the backup agent to be installed first.
- Without careful scheduling of backups, they can have a significant negative impact on the overall virtual infrastructure, as all VMs try to back up at the same time.

If your VMs do not see that much usage during your backup windows and increased resource utilization is not a problem in your environment, you may consider this method. If you do use this method, be sure to monitor your host, network, and storage performance during backups to ensure that you are not encountering resource bottlenecks that could be affecting other VMs on the host. Also try to ensure that you only back up a single VM concurrently on a particular host, if possible, to avoid bottlenecks, or stagger your backups so that you are not backing up too many VMs on the same host and/or LUN at the same time.

BACKUP SCRIPTS

Backup scripts typically work by taking a snapshot of a VM and then copying its large .vmdk file to another storage device, where it can be backed up to tape or just left there to use in case a file or the VM needs to be restored. These scripts run inside the ESX Service Console and can use the Perl language or other scripting methods such as bash that are supported by ESX. This method can be slow and inefficient and is useful as a complementary method to another backup method. Because the .vmdk file as a whole is being backed up, individual file restores are more difficult with this method. To restore individual files, the .vmdk file needs to be mounted by another VM or utility and then the file needs to be copied to the original server. This method is best suited for restoring a whole VM image and is useful for disaster recovery scenarios.

Advantages of backup scripts include the following.

- They are easy to set up and use.
- No additional software is needed.
- They are good for whole VM image restores (bare metal).

Disadvantages of backup scripts include the following.

- Individual file restores are difficult.
- They require access to the ESX Service Console.
- They may not work with ESXi.
- They can be slower than other methods.

If you choose to use this method either as your primary backup solution or in conjunction with another method, you might want to check out some of the user-developed scripts, such as vGhetto from William Lam (http://communities.vmware.com/docs/DOC-9852).

THIRD-PARTY vSPHERE-SPECIFIC BACKUP PRODUCTS

Several third-party backup products were developed specifically for backing up vSphere environments, and they are a great alternative to traditional backup methods as they provide more options and greater flexibility when backing up and restoring your VMs. These products all work by copying VM virtual disks over the network or SAN fabric from a source datastore to a destination disk-based storage device (local, SAN, NFS, iSCSI, and CIFS). Additionally, most of these products leverage the vStorage APIs, and can do full and differential back-ups as well as both whole VM (bare metal) and individual file restores. The most popular of these products are

- Vizioncore vRanger Pro (www.vizioncore.com/products/vRangerPro/index.php)

- Veeam Backup & Replication (http://veeam.com/vmware-esx-backup.html)

- And PHD Virtual Backup for VMware ESX (www.phdvirtual.com/solutions /server_virtualization_vmESX.php)

These products all vary in price, performance, and features, and you should eval-uate each one to see which one integrates best into your environment and satis-fies your requirements. You should also make sure that any product you look at supports everything in your environment, including ESXi, guest OSs, and your storage devices. Before you purchase a backup product, request an evaluation copy and install and use it to ensure that it will work properly for you. Although disk-to-disk (D2D) backups are more efficient than tape backups, you can still utilize tape backups in most cases by backing up the target disk datasources, a process also known as disk-to-disk-to-tape (D2D2T). In addition to these prod-ucts, a number of traditional backup applications are available, such as Symantec NetBackup and EMC Avamar, which have evolved to support backing up virtual environments and support the use of the new vStorage APIs.

BACKUP TYPES

When it comes to backing up VMs you have two options: Back up the large .vmdk virtual disk file (known as an image-level backup) at the virtualization datastore level, or back up the individual files (known as a file-level backup) at the guest OS level. Both options have advantages and can be used jointly to pro-vide different restoration alternatives for your VMs.

File-level backups allow for easy individual file restores which are useful when you have only a few files to restore to a VM and you do not want to restore all the data just to restore the individual files. You can perform a file-level backup using traditional backup methods by running a backup agent inside the VM's guest OS. Additionally, many backup applications that support virtualization can perform file-level backups through nontraditional methods, such as VCB. File-level backups are great for restoring a small number of files, but restoring a whole VM can be more time-consuming because you typically need to install a guest OS and backup agent before you can restore the rest of the VM data.

Image-level backups allow for whole VM or bare metal restores and are useful when you need to quickly restore a VM to a previous state, or for disaster recovery purposes which require bare metal restores instead of individual file restores. To perform an image-level backup you need to use a product or method that supports it, rather than traditional backup agents which work inside the guest OS and do not have access to the virtualization layer and the .vmdk virtual disk file. You can still do individual file restores with image-level backups; it just typically takes a few more steps. Most backup applications that support image-level backups have individual file-level restore capabilities.

VMWARE DATA RECOVERY

With vSphere, VMware released a new product called VMware Data Recovery (VDR) which adds the capability to back up VMs right from vSphere. Unlike VCB, which is an enabling technology and not an actual backup product, VDR is a stand-alone product that creates hot backups of VMs to any virtual disk storage attached to an ESX/ESXi host or to any NFS/CIFS network storage server or device and is not meant as a replacement for VCB. An additional feature of VDR is its ability to provide data deduplication to reduce storage requirements using block-based in-line destination deduplication technology that VMware developed. This means duplicate data is found at the block level instead of at the file level while it is being streamed to the destination disk, and the deduplication process occurs as the data is stored on the destination disk. The deduplication feature cannot be disabled, so all backups done by VDR are deduplicated.

VDR takes full advantage of the new vStorage APIs in vSphere and is not compatible with VI3 hosts and VMs. VDR leverages the Changed Block Tracking (CBT) feature in the vStorage APIs for quicker incremental backups. VDR is integrated with vCenter Server and can back up VMs even when they are moved to other hosts by VMotion and the Distributed Resource Scheduler (DRS). VDR is available only in the Essentials Plus, Advanced, Enterprise, and Enterprise Plus vSphere editions. It comes packaged as a plug-in to vCenter Server and a prebuilt OVF format backup appliance that runs on your host servers (you can run multiple backup appliances).

VDR can only do backups at the VM level (VM image) and does not do file-level backups. Full backups are initially performed and subsequent backups are incremental. It does have individual file-level restore (FLR) capability and can restore files to VMs running a Windows guest OS. In 1.0.x versions of VDR, the

FLR was considered experimental and was done using a command-line application that mounted the virtual disk from a selected restore point to a Windows drive letter so that the files could be accessed and copied from it. In VDR 1.1, VMware added full support for FLR for Windows VMs and also included a new graphical application to replace the command-line utility.

VMware's VDR product directly competes with those of several third-party vendors, including those from Veeam (Backup & Replication), PHD (esXpress), and Vizioncore (vRanger). However, VDR is a pretty basic, first-generation backup product and is better suited for small and medium-size businesses. Although its basic functionality is similar to that of the other, more mature, products, it lacks the polish, advanced features, and scalability that the more robust third-party applications offer. Some of the limitations of VDR include

- Support for only vSphere ESX/ESXi hosts
- No support for multiple vCenter Servers or stand-alone hosts not managed by a vCenter Server
- Support for only 100 VMs per backup appliance and 2TB of source data
- Only basic backup scheduling capability
- And support for file-level recovery only on Windows systems

Because of the limitations with VDR, it may not be a good fit for organizations that have large numbers of VMs or large amounts of virtual data storage, or that predominantly run Linux VMs. Despite its limitations, VDR is still a good choice for small to medium-size organizations or those that want to augment their current backup solution or perform disaster recovery backups.

INSTALLING VMWARE DATA RECOVERY

The requirements for using VDR are pretty simple. You need to have a vSphere edition that supports it, a vCenter Server, and some storage to use for a target backup datastore. This can be any type of storage attached to an ESX/ESXi host (local, SAN, iSCSI, NFS) or any NFS/CIFS network storage server or device. One thing to note is that VDR only supports licensed versions of ESXi and not the free edition. To install VDR follow these steps.

1. Download VDR from VMware's website. It is available as a single ISO file that contains the VDR appliance as well as the FLR application. The ISO file contains the client plug-in install file, the Windows FLR install file, and the OVF/VMDK files for the VDR appliance.

2. Burn the ISO file to a physical DVD or mount it to a virtual CD-ROM. The autorun program will bring up an installer wizard that will install the VDR plug-in to the vSphere Client on the server/workstation that you run it on; it does not install the VDR appliance, which must be installed manually later on. Optionally, you can copy the VMwareDataRecoveryPlugin.msi file from the ISO/DVD and run it separately. The wizard is very simple; just click Next a few times and the plug-in will be installed. Once it is installed, start your vSphere Client and select Plug-ins from the top menu, and then Manage Plug-ins; you will see the new plug-in installed.

3. Enable the plug-in by right-clicking on it and choosing Enable. Once it is enabled, you will see a new option on the Home screen under Solutions and Applications, called VMware Data Recovery. Click on it and you will see a screen that will prompt you to connect to a VDR backup appliance. Since we don't have one installed yet, we will have to do that next. Note that the VDR plug-in connects to the backup appliance using port 22024, so be sure that port is open in any firewalls between the system running the vSphere client and the backup appliance.

4. To deploy the appliance, use the vSphere Client and the OVF template from the ISO/DVD file to create a new VM. Since the OVF template is on the ISO/DVD, you will need it to deploy the template. In the vSphere Client, select File from the top menu and then Deploy OVF Template. The wizard will load, and the first screen will ask you to select the source; click the Browse button and select the VMwareDataRecovery.ovf file located in the `\DataRecovery\VMwareDataRecovery-ovf` directory. Click Next, and you will see the template information; although the actual template is only about 400MB, the virtual disk size of the VM that is created on the specified host will be about 5GB. Click Next, and then give the VM a name or keep the default. Continue through the screens, selecting a destination Datacenter/Host/Resource pool and a storage volume, and click Finish at the final Summary screen to create the VDR appliance on your host server.

CONFIGURING VMWARE DATA RECOVERY

If you want to store your backups on a storage volume connected to the host on which the VM is located, you should edit the settings for the newly created VM and add an additional virtual disk to it to store your backups. This can be any storage type that is configured on your ESX host. One thing to keep in mind when creating the virtual disk is the block size of its VMFS volume. The default 1MB block size only allows for a maximum virtual disk size of 256GB. If you need a larger disk size, you will need to use a volume with a 2MB or larger block size so that you can create larger virtual disks on it. If you want to store your backups on a network storage device such as a CIFS share, you can skip this step and move on to the next one.

Before you power on the VDR appliance, edit the settings and make sure the NIC for the VM is connected to your desired network. The VDR appliance is configured to automatically obtain an IP address using DHCP, but if DHCP is unavailable you can change this when it first boots up. The appliance is built using the CentOS Release 5.2 Linux operating system, and when you power it on you will see the familiar Linux boot sequence. Select the Configure Network option and enter your IP address and network settings. Optionally, you can log in to the appliance using the default username of "root" and password of "vmwa@re", and change the password using the `passwd` command.

Once the appliance is powered on and the network is configured, connect to it using a web browser using the URL https://<ip address of appliance>:5480 (note the "https"). The login is the same as the console login. In the web interface, you can only do basic things, such as viewing system information, viewing/changing network settings, and rebooting/shutting down the appliance.

The main interface for managing the VDR appliance is the plug-in in the vSphere Client. Click the Home link and then click the VMware Data Recovery link, and you will be presented with a prompt to connect to a VDR appliance. Enter the IP address/host name of the VDR appliance and click the Connect button. You will be prompted to enter login credentials for the vCenter Server (not the VDR appliance). After your login credentials are verified, your backup destinations will be displayed; this includes any virtual disks that you added to the VDR appliance, and you can also add network shares. If you choose to add a network share you must use the IP address of the server (i.e., \\172.200.100.55\share) and not the host name (\\server\share); this is specified in the release notes. You can use the Refresh button to display any disks that you recently added to the VM that are not showing up. Before you can use a virtual disk (not a network share), you need to format it. Then it will show as a local volume instead of a physical disk and the name will change to scsi:x:y.

Once you are done with your backup destinations, click Next and you will be at the Configuration Complete screen. If you check the box to create a backup job and click the Close button, a new wizard will open that lets you create a backup job. In the Backup Job Wizard, you can specify the VMs/virtual disks to be backed up, the destination, the backup schedule, and the retention policy, as shown in Figure 8.1. The backup window is the most important setting, and you should know how it works. VDR will attempt to back up your VM in the specified window (not at a specific time), and if the backup does not complete in that window, the backup will stop and will restart when the window occurs again. So, if you specify many VMs to be backed up during a window, it's possible that some of them may not be backed up due to resource/time constraints. Only eight VMs can be backed up concurrently, and multiple backups will occur only if CPU utilization is less than 80%. VDR will give higher priority to the VMs that did not get backed up in subsequent backup windows.

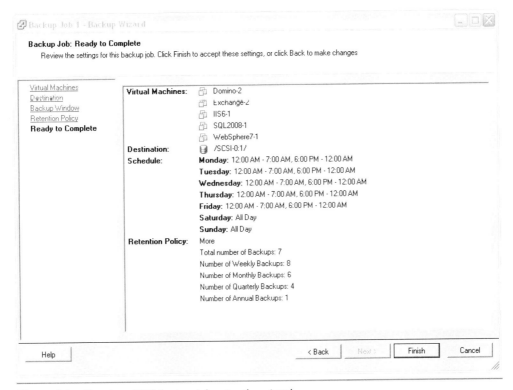

Figure 8.1   Creating a VDR backup job using the wizard

Once you are done with the wizard, you will be at the main VDR screen where you can choose from among four different tabs. The Backup tab will show all your jobs, including those which are not in compliance (i.e., have not run yet). You can start a backup immediately by selecting a job and choosing the Bring to Compliance option. The Restore tab will show all your completed backups and available restore points. You can choose to do either a restore which will replace the selected VM, or a restore rehearsal which will create another copy of the VM and will not replace the original. Restore rehearsals are a good way to test that your backups are working and that you can restore them if needed. The Reports tab shows you event and status data, as shown in Figure 8.2, and the Configuration tab lets you configure the appliance and manage backup destinations. Here you can also see the free space on your backup destinations, as well as mount/unmount them, extend them, and check their integrity.

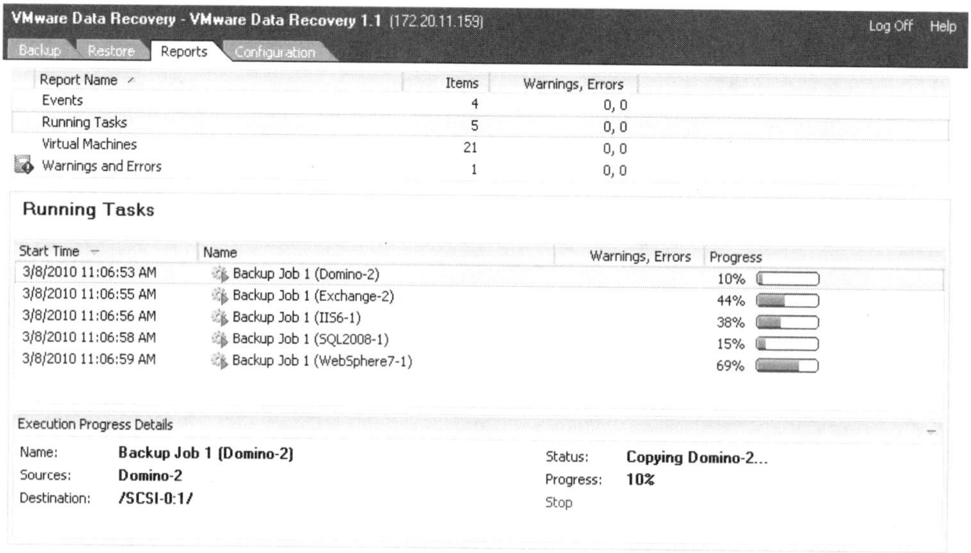

Figure 8.2   Reports tab in VDR showing tasks that are running

To use the Windows VDR Restore Client so that you can restore individual files instead of whole VMs, you need to first copy the VDR client file to a Windows workstation or server. The client file is located on the VDR ISO and is called VMwareRestoreClient.exe; this file does not need to be installed and is a self-contained application (ThinApp). When you run the Restore Client, you can select from two modes: The default standard mode only allows files to be restored for the VM you are logged in to, so you need to run it from inside the VM that you want to restore to. For standard mode, you connect directly to a VDR appliance. Advanced mode lets you restore files for any VM that has been backed up. For Advanced mode, you connect to a vCenter Server.

The Restore Client uses VMware's Virtual Disk Development Kit (VDDK) to access information about the contents of restore points. It uses the VDDK to mount the virtual disk from the VM backup that you select from the list of restore points. To mount the disk, you select a restore point and then click the Mount button, as shown in Figure 8.3.

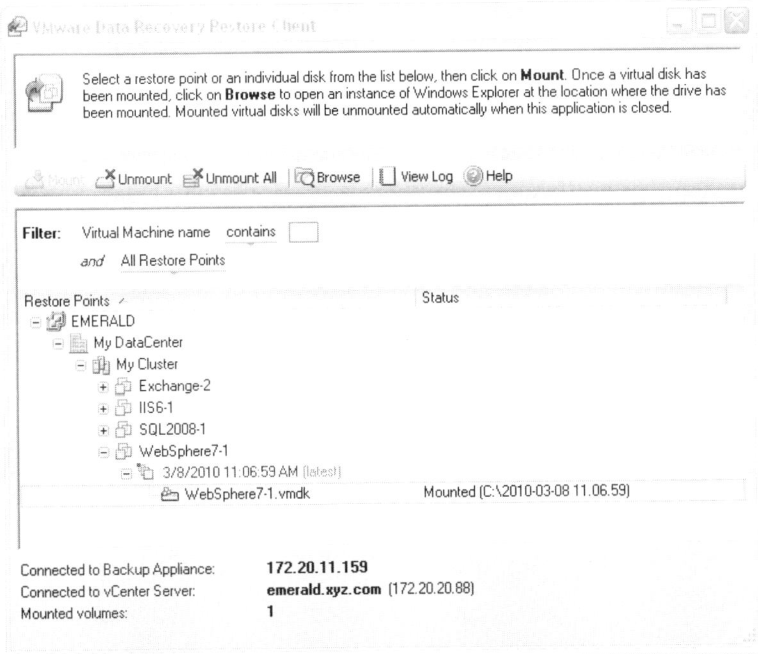

Figure 8.3   Using the Restore Client to restore individual files to a VM

Once the disk is mounted, a junction point is created on the PC that is running the Restore Client. The junction point is a directory that has the same name as the restore point and contains a directory for each mounted disk associated with that restore point. You can then browse the contents of the virtual disk using Windows Explorer for the restore point that you selected by clicking the Browse button. You can copy the files from the selected restore point to any location you desire. You can optionally run the Restore Client directly from the VM that you want to restore to so that the copy operation is easier. Once you are done, you can click the Unmount button to close the junction point, or close the Restore Client which will automatically unmount all restore points.

If you plan to use VDR, you should make sure you understand it thoroughly and read the administration guide (http://vmware.com/pdf/vdr_11_admin.pdf) and the release notes which contain many known issues that you may encounter. VDR is a pretty solid entry-level backup application that is great for organizations that want to add additional backup and recovery options to their virtual environment.

SUMMARY

Backups are important, so make sure you choose a solution that will work for the needs of your environment. A backup tool is like a good insurance policy; you pay your premium each month and you hope you never need to use it, but if something happens you are glad you have it. Restoring your data is even more important than backing it up. You need to make sure the solution you use can easily restore files as needed in your environment. You should also plan your backup strategy around your current or future disaster recovery strategy, as good backups are the foundation for any DR plan. If you plan to do disaster recovery, you should look for a backup strategy that supports your disaster recovery requirements for recovering from an event. Additionally, you may look into some of the products that can replicate your VMs from your production environment to a disaster recovery environment. Once you implement a backup solution in your virtual environment, make sure you test the restore ability so that you don't run into any surprises later on when trying to restore critical data.

ADVANCED FEATURES

Advanced features are what really add value to vSphere and help distinguish it from its competitors. The features covered in this chapter provide protection for virtual machines (VMs) running on ESX and ESXi hosts, as well as optimize resources and performance and simplify VM management. These features typically have many requirements, though, and they can be tricky to set up properly. So, make sure you understand how they work and how to configure them before using them.

HIGH AVAILABILITY (HA)

HA is one of ESX's best features and is a low-cost alternative to traditional server clustering. HA does not provide 100% availability of VMs, but rather provides higher availability by rapidly recovering VMs on failed hosts. The HA feature continuously monitors all ESX Server hosts in a cluster and detects failures, and will automatically restart VMs on other host servers in an ESX cluster in case of a host failure.

HOW HA WORKS

HA is based on a modified version of the EMC/Legato Automated Availability Manager (AAM) 5.1.2 product that VMware bought to use with VMware VI3. HA works by taking a cluster of ESX and ESXi hosts and placing an agent on each host to maintain a "heartbeat" with the other hosts in the cluster; loss of a heartbeat initiates a restart of all affected VMs on other hosts. vCenter Server does not provide a single point of failure for this feature, and the feature will continue to work even if the vCenter Server is unavailable. In fact, if the vCenter Server goes down, HA clusters can still restart VMs on other hosts; however, information regarding availability of extra resources will be based on the state of the cluster before the vCenter Server went down.

HA monitors whether sufficient resources are available in the cluster at all times in order to be able to restart VMs on different physical host machines in the event of host failure. Safe restart of VMs is made possible by the locking technology in the ESX Server storage stack, which allows multiple ESX Servers to have access to the same VM's file simultaneously. HA relies on what are called "primary" and "secondary" hosts; the first five hosts powered on in an HA cluster are designated as primary hosts, and the remaining hosts in the cluster are considered secondary hosts. The job of the primary hosts is to replicate and maintain the state of the cluster and to initiate failover actions. If a primary host fails, a new primary is chosen at random from the secondary hosts. Any host that joins the cluster must communicate with an existing primary host to complete its configuration (except when you are adding the first host to the cluster). At least one primary host must be functional for VMware HA to operate correctly. If all primary hosts are unavailable, no hosts can be successfully configured for VMware HA.

HA uses a failure detection interval that is set by default to 15 seconds (15000 milliseconds); you can modify this interval by using an advanced HA setting of `das.failuredetectiontime = 15000`. A host failure is detected after the HA service on a host has stopped sending heartbeats to the other hosts in the cluster. A host stops sending heartbeats if it is isolated from the network, it crashes, or it is completely down due to a hardware failure. Once a failure is detected, other hosts in the cluster treat the host as failed, while the host declares itself as isolated from the network. By default, the isolated host leaves its VMs powered on, but the isolation response for each VM is configurable on a per-VM basis. These VMs can then successfully fail over to other hosts in the cluster. HA also has a restart priority that can be set for each VM so that certain VMs are started before others. This priority can be set to either low, medium, or high, and also can be disabled so that VMs are not automatically restarted on other hosts. Here's what happens when a host failure occurs.

1. One of the primary hosts is selected to coordinate the failover actions, and one of the remaining hosts with spare capacity becomes the failover target.

2. VMs affected by the failure are sorted by priority, and are powered on until the failover target runs out of spare capacity, in which case another host with sufficient capacity is chosen for the remaining VMs.

3. If the host selected as coordinator fails, another primary continues the effort.

4. If one of the hosts that fails was a primary node, one of the remaining secondary nodes is promoted to being a primary.

The HA feature was enhanced starting with ESX 3.5, and now provides VM failure monitoring in case of operating system failures such as the Windows Blue Screen of Death (BSOD). If an OS failure is detected due to loss of a heartbeat from VMware Tools, the VM will automatically be reset on the same host so that its OS is restarted. This new functionality allows HA to also monitor VMs via a heartbeat that is sent every second when using VMware Tools, and further enhances HA's ability to recover from failures in your environment.

When this feature was first introduced, it was found that VMs that were functioning properly occasionally stopped sending heartbeats, which caused unnecessary VM resets. To avoid this scenario, the VM monitoring feature was enhanced to also check for network or disk I/O activity on the VM. Once heartbeats from the VM have stopped, the I/O stats for the VM are checked. If no activity has occurred in the preceding two minutes, the VM is restarted. You can change this interval using the HA advanced setting, `das.iostatsInterval`.

VMware enhanced this feature even further in version 4.1 by adding application monitoring to HA. With application monitoring, an application's heartbeat will also be monitored, and if it stops responding, the VM will be restarted. However, unlike VM monitoring, which relies on a heartbeat generated by VMware Tools, application monitoring requires that an application be specifically written to take advantage of this feature. To do this, VMware has provided an SDK that developers can use to modify their applications to take advantage of this feature.

CONFIGURING HA

HA may seem like a simple feature, but it's actually rather complex, as a lot is going on behind the scenes. You can set up the HA feature either during your initial cluster setup or afterward. To configure it, simply select the cluster on which you want to enable HA, right-click on it, and edit the settings for it. Put a checkmark next to the Turn On VMware HA field on the Cluster Features page, and HA will be enabled for the cluster. You can optionally configure some additional settings to change the way HA functions. To access these settings, click on the VMware HA item in the Cluster Settings window.

The Host Monitoring Status section is new to vSphere and is used to enable the exchange of heartbeats among hosts in the cluster. In VI3, hosts always exchanged heartbeats if HA was enabled, and if any network or host maintenance was being performed, HA could be triggered unnecessarily. The Enable Host Monitoring setting allows you to turn this on or off when needed. For HA to work, Host Monitoring must be enabled. If you are doing maintenance, you can temporarily disable it.

The Admission Control section allows you to enable or disable admission control, which determines whether VMs will be allowed to start if, by doing so, they will violate availability constraints. When Admission Control is enabled, any attempt to power on a VM when there is insufficient failover capacity within the cluster will fail. This is a safety mechanism to ensure that enough capacity is available to handle VMs from failed hosts. When Admission Control is disabled, VMs will be allowed to be powered on regardless of whether they decrease the resources needed to handle VMs from failed hosts. If you do disable Admission Control, HA will still work, but you may experience issues when recovering from a failure event if you do not have enough resources on the remaining hosts to handle the VMs that are being restarted.

The Admission Control Policy section allows you to select a type of policy to use. The three available policies are described in the sections that follow.

Host Failures Cluster Tolerates

This is used to ensure that there is sufficient capacity among the remaining host servers to be able to handle the additional load from the VMs on failed host servers. Setting the number of host failures allowed will cause the cluster to continuously monitor that sufficient resources are available to power on additional VMs on other hosts in case of a failure. Specifically, only CPU and memory resources are factored in when determining resource availability; disk and network resources are not. You should set the number of host failures allowed based on the total number of hosts in your cluster, their size, and how busy they are.

vCenter Server supports up to four host failures per cluster; if all five primaries were to fail simultaneously, HA would not function properly. For example, if you had four ESX hosts in your cluster, you would probably only want to allow for one host failure; if you had eight ESX hosts in your cluster, you might want to allow for two host failures; and if you had a larger cluster with 20 ESX hosts, you might want to allow for up to four host failures. This policy uses a slot size to determine the necessary spare resources to support the number of host failures that you select. A slot is a logical representation of the memory and CPU resources that satisfy the requirements for any powered-on VM in the cluster. HA automatically calculates slot sizes using CPU and memory reservations, and then the maximum number of slots that each host can support is determined. It does this by dividing the host's CPU resource amount by the CPU component of the slot size, and rounds down the result. The same calculation is made for the host's memory resource amount. The two numbers are then compared, and the lower number is the number of slots that the host can support. The failover capacity is computed by determining how many hosts (starting from the largest) can fail and still leave enough slots to satisfy the requirements of all powered-on VMs. Slot size calculations can be confusing and are affected by different things. For more information on slot sizes, see the vSphere Availability Guide at www.vmware.com/pdf/vsphere4/r40/vsp_40_availability.pdf.

Percentage of Cluster Resources Reserved As Failover Capacity

Instead of using slot sizes, HA uses calculations to ensure that a percentage of the cluster's resources are reserved for failover. It does this by calculating the total resource requirements for all powered-on VMs in the cluster. Next, it calculates the total number of host resources available for VMs. Finally, it calculates the current CPU failover capacity and current memory failover capacity for the cluster, and if they are less than the percentage that is specified for the configured failover capacity, admission control will be enforced. The resource requirements for powered-on VMs comprise two components, CPU and memory, and are calculated just like slot sizes are. The total number of host resources available for VMs is calculated by summing the host's CPU and memory resources. The current CPU failover capacity is computed by subtracting the total CPU resource requirements from the total host CPU resources and dividing the result by the total host CPU resources. The current memory failover capacity is calculated similarly. This method is a bit more balanced than specifying host failures, but it is not as automated because you have to manually specify a percentage.

Specify a Failover Host

This method is the simplest, as you are specifying a single host onto which to restart failed VMs. If the specified host has failed, or if it does not have enough resources, HA will restart the VMs on another host in the cluster. You can only specify one failover host, and HA will prevent VMs from being powered on or moved to the failover host during normal operations to ensure that it has sufficient capacity.

If you select a cluster in the vSphere Client and then choose the Summary tab, you can see the cluster's current capacity percentages. It is important to note that when a host fails, all of its VMs will be restarted on the single ESX host that has the lightest workload. This policy can quickly overload the host. When this occurs, the Distributed Resource Scheduler (DRS) kicks in to spread the load across the remaining hosts in the cluster. If you plan to use HA without DRS, you should ensure that you have plenty of extra capacity on your ESX hosts to handle the load from any one failed host. Additionally, you can set restart priorities so that you can specify which VMs are restarted first, and even prevent some VMs from being restarted in case of a failure.

The Virtual Machine Options section is for the cluster default settings that will apply to all VMs in the cluster by default, as well as individual VM settings. The cluster default settings apply to each VM created in or moved to the cluster, unless the VM is individually specified. The first setting is VM Restart Priority, which is the priority given to a VM when it is restarted on another host in case of a host failure. This can be set to High, Medium, Low, or Disabled. Any VM set to Disabled will not be restarted in case of a host failure.

The second setting is Host Isolation Response, which is used to determine what action the failed host that is isolated should take with the VMs that are running on it. This is used if a host is still running but has a failure in a particular subsystem (e.g., a NIC or host bus adapter [HBA] failure) or a connectivity problem (e.g., cable or switch) and is not completely down. When a host declares itself isolated and the VMs are restarted on other host, this setting dictates what happens on the failed host. The options include leaving the VM powered on, powering off the VM (hard shutdown), and shutting down the VM (graceful shutdown). If you choose to shut down the VM, HA will wait five minutes for the VM to shut down gracefully before it forcefully shuts it down. You can modify the time period that it waits for a graceful shutdown in the Advanced Configuration settings. It is usually desirable to have the VM on the failed host powered off or shut down so that it releases its lock on its disk file and also does not cause any conflicts with the new host that powers on the VM.

One reason you may choose to leave the VM powered on is if you do not have network redundancy or do not have a reliable network. In this case, you may experience false triggers to HA where the ESX host is okay but has just lost network connectivity. If you have proper network redundancy on your ESX hosts, HA events should be very rare. This setting will not come into play if the failed host experiences a disastrous event, such as completely losing power, because all the VMs will be immediately powered off anyway. In two-host configurations, you almost always want to set this to leave the VM powered on.

The last section is for Virtual Machine Monitoring (and Application Monitoring in vSphere 4.1), which restarts on the same host VMs that have OS failures. You can enable/disable this feature by checking the Enable VM Monitoring field and then using the slider to select a sensitivity from Low to High; if you want to customize your settings, you can click the Advanced Options button (vSphere 4.1) or check the Custom field (vSphere 4.0) and customize the settings on the screen that appears. In vSphere 4.1, instead of checking to enable VM monitoring, you can choose Disabled, VM Monitoring, or VM & Application Monitoring. Here are the VM monitoring advanced/custom options that you can set.

- **Failure Interval**—This declares a VM failure if no heartbeat is received for the specified number of seconds (default is 30).

- **Minimum Uptime**—After a VM has been powered on, its heartbeats are allowed to stabilize for the specified number of seconds. This time should include the guest OS boot time (default is 120).

- **Maximum per-VM Resets**—This is the maximum number of failures and automated resets allowed within the time that the maximum resets time window specifies. If no window is specified, then once the maximum is reached, automated reset is discontinued for the repeatedly failing VM and further investigation is necessary (default is 3).

- **Maximum Resets Time Window**—This is the amount of time for the specified maximum per-VM resets to occur before automated restarts stop (default is one hour).

You can also set individual VM settings that are different from the cluster defaults.

vSphere 4.1 added another new feature to HA that checks the cluster's operational status. Available on the cluster's Summary tab, this detail window, called Cluster Operational Status, displays more information about the current HA operational status, including the specific status and errors for each host in the HA cluster.

ADVANCED CONFIGURATION

Many advanced configuration options can be set to tweak how HA functions. You can set these options through the Advanced Options button in the HA settings, but you have to know the setting names and their values to be able to set them. These options are not displayed by default, except for the options that are set if you enable Virtual Machine Monitoring, and you must manually add them if you wish to use them. To see a list of the many HA advanced options that you can set, visit http://vsphere-land.com/vinfo/ha-advanced-options.

ADDITIONAL RESOURCES

Understanding the mechanics of HA can be confusing, but fortunately some good information is available on the Internet that can help you with this. Check out the following resources to find out more about the HA feature:

- vSphere Availability Guide
  (http://vmware.com/pdf/vsphere4/r40_u1/vsp_40_u1_availability.pdf)
- HA Deepdive (www.yellow-bricks.com/vmware-high-availability-deepdiv/)
- HA: Concepts, Implementation, and Best Practices
  (www.vmware.com/files/pdf/VMwareHA_twp.pdf)

DISTRIBUTED RESOURCE SCHEDULER (DRS)

DRS is a powerful feature that enables your virtual environment to automatically balance itself across your ESX host servers in an effort to eliminate resource contention. It utilizes the VMotion feature to provide automated resource optimization through automatic migration of VMs across hosts in a cluster. DRS also provides automatic initial VM placement on any of the hosts in the cluster, and makes automatic resource relocation and optimization decisions as hosts or VMs are added to or removed from the cluster. You can also configure DRS for manual control so that it only provides recommendations that you can review and carry out.

HOW DRS WORKS

DRS works by utilizing resource pools and clusters that combine the resources of multiple hosts into a single entity. Multiple resource pools can also be created so that you can divide the resources of a single or multiple hosts into separate entities. Currently, DRS will only migrate VMs based on the availability and utilization of the CPU and memory resources. It does not take into account high disk or network utilization to load-balance VMs across hosts.

When a VM experiences increased load, DRS first evaluates its priority against the established resource allocation rules and then, if justified, redistributes VMs among the physical servers to try to eliminate contention for resources. VMotion will then handle the live migration of the VM to a different ESX host with complete transparency to end users. The dynamic resource allocation ensures that capacity is preferentially dedicated to the highest-priority applications, while at the same time maximizing overall resource utilization. Unlike the HA feature, which will still operate when vCenter Server is unavailable, DRS requires that vCenter Server be running for it to function.

CONFIGURING DRS

Similar to HA, the DRS feature can be set up in a cluster either during its initial setup or afterward. To configure DRS, simply select the cluster on which you want to enable DRS, right-click on it, and edit its settings, or select the cluster and in the Summary pane click the Edit Settings link. Put a checkmark next to the Enable VMware DRS field on the General page, and DRS will be enabled for the cluster. You can optionally configure some additional settings to change the way DRS functions. To access these settings, click on the VMware DRS item in the Cluster Settings window.

Once you enable DRS, you must select an automation level that controls how DRS will function. You can choose from the following three levels.

- **Manual**—Initial placement is the host on which DRS was last located; migration recommendations require approval.
- **Partially Automated**—Initial placement is automated; migration recommendations require approval.
- **Fully Automated**—Initial placement is automated; migration recommendations are automatically executed.

When considering an automation level, it is usually best to choose Fully Automated and let DRS handle everything. However, when first enabling DRS, you might want to set the automation level to Manual or Partially Automated so that you can observe its recommendations for a while before turning it loose on Fully Automated. Even when selecting Fully Automated, you can still configure individual VM automation levels, so you can specify certain VMs to not be migrated at all (disabled) or to be set to Manual or Partially Automated. To configure individual VM automation levels, click on Virtual Machine Options, located under DRS. Usually, the default three-star level is a good starting point and works well for most environments. You should be careful when choosing more aggressive levels, as you could have VMs moving very frequently between hosts (i.e., VM pong), which can create performance issues because of the constant VMotions which cause an entire LUN to be locked during the operation (i.e., SCSI reservations).

DRS makes its recommendations by applying stars to indicate how much the recommendation would improve the cluster's performance. One star indicates a slight improvement, and four stars indicates significant improvement. Five stars, the maximum, indicates a mandatory move because of a host entering maintenance mode or affinity rule violations. If DRS is set to work in Fully Automated mode, you have the option to set a migration threshold based on how much it would improve the cluster's performance. The lowest threshold, which is the most conservative, only applies five-star recommendations; the highest threshold, which is very aggressive, applies all recommendations. There are also settings in between to only apply two-, three-, or four-star recommendations.

You can configure affinity rules in DRS to keep certain VMs either on the same host or on separate hosts when DRS migrates VMs from host to host. These affinity rules (not to be confused with CPU affinity) are useful for ensuring that when DRS moves VMs around, it has some limits on where it can place the VMs. You might want to keep VMs on the same host if they are part of a tiered application that runs on multiple VMs, such as a web, application, or database server. You might want to keep VMs on different hosts for servers that are clustered or redundant, such as Active Directory (AD), DNS, or web servers, so that a single ESX failure does not affect both servers at the same time. Doing this ensures that at least one will stay up and remain available while the other recovers from a host failure. Also, you might want to separate servers that have high I/O workloads so that you do not overburden a specific host with too many high-workload servers.

Because DRS does not take into account network and disk workloads when moving VMs, creating a rule for servers that are known to have high workloads in those areas can help you to avoid disk and network I/O bottlenecks on your hosts. In general, try to limit the number of rules you create, and only create ones that are necessary. Having too many rules makes it more difficult for DRS to try to place VMs on hosts to balance the resource load. Also watch out for conflicts between multiple rules which can cause problems.

Once you have DRS enabled, you can monitor it by selecting the cluster in vCenter Server and choosing the Summary tab. Here you can see load deviations, the number of faults and recommendations, and the automation level. By clicking the resource distribution chart you can also see CPU and memory utilization on a per-VM basis, grouped by host. Additionally, you can select the DRS tab in vCenter Server to display any pending recommendations, faults, and the DRS action history. By default, DRS recommendations are generated every five minutes; you can click the Run DRS link to generate them immediately if you do not want to wait. You can also click the Apply Recommendations button to automatically apply the pending recommendations.

DISTRIBUTED POWER MANAGEMENT (DPM)

DPM is a subcomponent of DRS and is a green feature that was introduced in VI 3.5 that will power down hosts during periods of inactivity to help save power. All the VMs on a host that will be powered down are relocated to other hosts before the initial host is powered down. When activity increases on the other hosts and DPM deems that additional capacity is needed, it will automatically power the host back on and move VMs back onto it using DRS. DPM requires that the host has a supported power management protocol that automatically powers it on after it has been powered off. You can configure DPM in either manual or automatic mode. In manual mode, it will simply make recommendations similar to DRS, and you will have to manually approve them so that they are applied. You can also configure DPM so that certain host servers are excluded from DPM, as well as specify that certain hosts are always automatic or always manual.

How DPM Works

Although DPM existed in VI3, it was not officially supported and was considered experimental. This was because it relied on Wake On LAN (WOL) technology that exists in certain network adapters but was not always a reliable means for powering a server on. Being able to power up servers when needed is critical when workloads increase, so a more reliable technology was needed for DPM to be fully supported. For this, VMware turned to two technologies in vSphere: Intelligent Platform Management Interface (IPMI) and HP's Integrated Lights-Out (iLO).

IPMI is a standard that was started by Intel and is supported by most major computer manufacturers. It defines a common set of interfaces that can be used to manage and monitor server hardware health. Since IPMI works at the hardware layer and does not depend on an operating system, it works with any software or operating system that is designed to access it. IPMI relies on a Baseboard Management Controller (BMC) that is a component in server motherboards and monitors many different sensors on the server, including temperature, drive status, fan speed, power status, and much more. IPMI works even when a server is powered off, as long as it is connected to a power source. The BMC is connected to many other controllers on the server and administration can be done using a variety of methods. For instance, out-of-band management can be done using a LAN connection via the network controller interconnects to the BMC. Other out-of-band management options include remote management boards and serial connections.

For HP servers, DPM uses HP's proprietary iLO remote, out-of-band management controllers that are built into every HP server. HP has used its iLO technology under several different names for years, and has only recently begun to also embrace the IPMI standard. Dell's Remote Access Card (DRAC) remote management controllers provide the same functionality as HP's iLO, but Dell fully supports IPMI. Typically on Dell DRAC boards you need to enable IPMI via the server BIOS to be able to use it.

In addition to the IPMI and iLO power management protocols, vSphere also now fully supports WOL. However, if multiple protocols exist in a server, they are used in the following order: IPMI, iLO, WOL.

CONFIGURING DPM

DPM requires that the host be a member of a DRS-enabled cluster. Before you can configure DPM in vSphere, you typically have to enable the power management protocol on whatever method you are using. If you are using WOL, this is usually enabled in your host server's BIOS. Depending on the server for IPMI, you can usually enable this also in the server BIOS or in the web-based configuration utility for the server out-of-band management board (e.g., Dell DRAC). This setting is usually referred to as IPMI over LAN. For HP's iLOs, make sure the Lights-Out functionality is enabled in the iLO web-based configuration utility; it usually is by default. Both IPMI and iLO require authentication to be able to access any of their functionality; WOL does not.

You can determine whether a NIC supports the WOL feature and that it is enabled in the vSphere client by selecting a host, choosing the Configuration tab, and then, under Hardware, selecting Network Adapters. All of the host's NICs will be displayed and one of the columns will show whether WOL is supported. Once you have configured the protocol that you will use with DPM, you can configure it in vSphere by following these steps.

- For IPMI/iLO, select the host in the vSphere Client, and on the Configuration tab under Software, select Power Management. Click Properties and enter the username/password of a user account that can log in to the management board, as well as the IP address and MAC address of the board. You can usually find the MAC address for iLO boards on the NIC tab of the System Information screen on the iLO web page.

- For WOL, there is nothing to configure, but you must make sure the NIC that DPM uses is the one assigned to the VMkernel virtual switch (vSwitch). You may need to rearrange your NICs so that you have one that supports WOL in the VMkernel vSwitch. Additionally, the switch port that the NIC is connected to must be set to Auto-negotiate, as many NICs support WOL only if they can switch to 100MBps or less when the host is powered off.

Once DPM is enabled and configured properly, you will want to test it before you use it. To test it, simply select the host in the vSphere Client, right-click on it, and select Enter Standby Mode, which will power down the host. You will be prompted if you want to move powered-off/suspended VMs to other hosts. Powered-on VMs will automatically be migrated using VMotion; if they are not capable of using VMotion, they will be powered off. Your host will begin to shut down and should power off after a few minutes. Verify that your host has powered off, and then, in the vSphere Client, right-click on the host and select Power On. If the feature is working, the host should power back on automatically.

Once you have verified that DPM works properly, you need to enable DPM. To do this, edit the settings for your cluster; next, under the DRS category, select Power

Management. You can then select either the Off, Manual, or Automatic option. The Manual option will only make recommendations for powering off hosts; the Automatic option will enable vCenter Server to automatically execute power management-related recommendations. You can also set a threshold for DPM, as you can with DRS, which will determine how aggressive it gets with powering off hosts. The DRS threshold and the DPM threshold are essentially independent. You can differentiate the aggressiveness of the migration and host power state recommendations they respectively provide. The threshold priority ratings are based on the amount of over- or underutilization found in the DRS cluster and the improvement that is expected from the intended host power state change. Priority-one recommendations are the biggest improvement, and priority-five the least. The threshold ranges from conservative, which only applies priority-one recommendations, to aggressive, which applies priority-five recommendations.

If you select Host Options, you can change the Power Management settings on individual hosts to have them use the cluster default, always use Manual, or always use Automatic; you can also disable the feature for them.

DPM CONSIDERATIONS

Although DPM is a great technology that can save you money and that every large datacenter should take advantage of, you should be aware of the following considerations before you use it.

- If you are using a monitoring system to monitor that your ESX servers are up or down, you will trigger an alert whenever a host is shut down. Having servers going up and down automatically can generate a lot of confusion and false alarms. In addition, many datacenters measure uptime statistics on all the servers. Having hosts going down during periods of inactivity can significantly skew those numbers. If you use DPM, you should consider adjusting your operational procedures to exclude the ESX hosts from monitoring and instead only monitor the VMs.

- If you are using HA in your cluster, be aware that DRS and DPM maintain excess powered-on capacity to meet the HA settings. Therefore, the cluster may not allow additional VMs to be powered on and/or some hosts may not be powered down, even though the cluster may appear to be sufficiently idle. Additionally, if HA strict admission control is enabled, DPM will not power off hosts if doing so would violate failover requirements. If HA strict admission control is disabled, DPM will power off hosts even if doing so violates failover requirements.

- Similar to DRS, the DPM feature works best if all hosts are in Automatic mode, which gives DPM more flexibility in selecting hosts to power on and off. If hosts are in Manual DPM mode, DPM must wait for approval to perform its action, which can limit its effectiveness. DPM is more biased toward hosts in Automatic mode than Manual mode because of this. Consider using Automatic mode whenever possible, and disabling DPM on hosts that you do not want to be powered off.

- DPM will consider historical demand when determining how much capacity to keep available, and keeps some extra capacity available for changes in demand.

- Having servers power off and on automatically requires a lot of trust in the technology. To protect against a situation in which a host is not powered on when necessary, set an alarm in vCenter Server to be alerted if this happens. You can create a host alarm for the event "DRS cannot exit the host out of standby mode" so that you can be alerted when this happens and can take care of the situation.

VMOTION

VMotion is a powerful feature that allows you to quickly move an entire running VM from one ESX host to another without any downtime or interruption to the VM. This is also known as a "hot" or "live" migration.

HOW VMOTION WORKS

The entire state of a VM is encapsulated and the VMFS filesystem allows both the source and the target ESX host to access the VM files concurrently. The active memory and precise execution state of a VM can then be rapidly transmitted over a high-speed network. The VM retains its network identity and connections, ensuring a seamless migration process as outlined in the following steps.

1. The migration request is made to move the VM from ESX1 to ESX2.

2. vCenter Server verifies that the VM is in a stable state on ESX1.

3. vCenter Server checks the compatibility of ESX2 (CPU/networking/etc.) to ensure that it matches that of ESX1.

4. The VM is registered on ESX2.

5. The VM state information (including memory, registers, and network connections) is copied to ESX2. Additional changes are copied to a memory bitmap on ESX1.

6. The VM is quiesced on ESX1 and the memory bitmap is copied to ESX2.

7. The VM is started on ESX2 and all requests for the VM are now directed to ESX2.

8. A final copy of the VM's memory is made from ESX1 to ESX2.

9. The VM is unregistered from ESX1.

10. The VM resumes operation on ESX2.

CONFIGURING VMOTION

VMotion requires shared storage for it to function (Fibre Channel [FC], iSCSI, or NFS), and also has some strict requirements to ensure compatibility of a VM moving from one ESX host to another, as outlined in the following list.

- Both the source ESX host and the destination ESX host must be able to access the same shared storage on which the VM is located; the shared storage can be either FC, iSCSI, or NFS. VMotion will also work with Raw Device Mappings (RDMs) as long as they are configured to work in virtual compatibility mode.

- ESX hosts must have a Gigabit Ethernet network adapter or higher to be configured on the VMkernel vSwitch used by VMotion; slower NICs will work, but they are not recommended. For best results, and because VMotion traffic is sent as clear text, it is best to have an isolated network for VMotion traffic.

- ESX hosts must have processors that are able to execute each other's instructions. Processor clock speeds, cache sizes, and number of cores can differ among ESX hosts, but they must have the same processor vendor class (Intel or AMD) and compatible feature sets. It is possible to override these restrictions for CPUs from the same vendor, but doing so can cause a VM to crash because it must access a CPU feature or instruction that the new ESX host does not support.

Here are some additional requirements for VMotion to function properly.

- vSwitch network labels (port groups) must match exactly (including case) on each ESX host.

- A VM cannot be using CPU affinity, which pins a VM to run on a specific processor(s) on an ESX host.

- A VM cannot be connected to an internal-only (no NICs assigned to it) vSwitch.

- Using jumbo frames is recommended for best performance.
- The source and destination hosts must be licensed for VMotion.
- A VM cannot have its virtual CD-ROM and floppy drives mapped to either a host device or a local datastore ISO file.

Before configuring VMotion on your host servers, you should make sure they meet the requirements for using it. Configuring VMotion is fairly simple; you must first set up the VMkernel networking stack on a vSwitch which is used for VMotion by creating a port group on the vSwitch. You can do this by editing the vSwitch that you want to use for VMotion, clicking the Add button, and selecting VMkernel. You then configure the port group properties and set the IP address for the VMotion interface. You can verify the network connectivity of the VMotion interface by using the vmkping Service Console utility to ping the VMkernel interface of other hosts.

VMOTION CONSIDERATIONS

Configuring VMotion is easy, but there are requirements and compatibility issues that you need to be aware of. Here are some considerations that you should know about when using and configuring VMotion.

- In versions prior to ESX 3.5, VMs that had their swap file (.vswp file) not located on shared storage could not be moved with VMotion. This was because the destination host would not be able to access the .vswp file that was located on the source host's local disk. Beginning with ESX 3.5, support for using VMotion on VMs that have local .vswp files was added. If a VM with a local .vswp file is VMotioned, the .vswp file is re-created on the destination host and the nonzero contents of the .vswp file are copied over as part of the VMotion operation. This can cause the VMotion operation to take slightly longer than normal due to the added .vswp copy operation in addition to the normal CPU and memory state copy operation. Using a local swap file datastore can be advantageous, as it frees up valuable and expensive shared disk space to be used for other things, such as snapshots and virtual disks.
- If your VMs have their CD-ROM drive mapped to either a host device or a local ISO datastore, they cannot be VMotioned, as the destination server will not have access to the drive. Additionally, if the CD-ROM is mapped to a shared ISO datastore, make sure all ESX hosts can see that shared ISO datastore. Consider using a shared ISO datastore on a VMFS volume, or alternately, on an NFS or Samba share instead.

- Using VMotion with VMs with running snapshots is supported, as long as the VM is being migrated to a new host without moving its configuration file or disks.

- It's very important to ensure that vSwitch network labels are identical (case-sensitive) across all hosts. If they are not, you cannot VMotion a VM between two hosts that do not have the same Network Labels configured on their vSwitches.

- CPU compatibility is one of the biggest headaches when dealing with VMotion because VMotion transfers the running architectural state of a VM between host systems. To ensure a successful migration, the processor of the destination host must be able to execute the equivalent instructions as that of the source host. Processor speeds, cache sizes, and number of cores can vary between the source and destination hosts, but the processors must come from the same vendor (either Intel or AMD) and use compatible feature sets to be compatible with VMotion. When a VM is first powered on, it determines its available CPU feature set based on the host's CPU feature set. It is possible to mask some of the host's CPU features using a CPU compatibility mask in order to allow VMotions between hosts that have slightly dissimilar feature sets. See VMware Knowledge Base articles 1991 (http://kb.vmware.com/kb/1991), 1992 (http://kb.vmware.com/kb/1992), and 1993 (http://kb.vmware.com/kb/1993) for more information on how to set up these masks. Additionally, you can use the Enhanced VMotion feature to help deal with CPU incompatibilities between hosts.

- It is a recommended security practice to put your VMotion network traffic onto its own isolated network so that it is only accessible to the host servers. The reason for this is twofold. First, VMotion traffic is sent as clear text and is not encrypted, so isolating it ensures that sensitive data cannot be sniffed out on the network. Second, it ensures that VMotion traffic experiences minimal latency and is not affected by other network traffic as a VMotion operation is a time-sensitive operation.

ENHANCED VMOTION COMPATIBILITY (EVC)

Enhanced VMotion Compatibility (EVC) is designed to further ensure compatibility between ESX hosts. EVC leverages the Intel FlexMigration technology as well as the AMD-V Extended Migration technology to present the same feature set as the baseline processors. EVC ensures that all hosts in a cluster present the same CPU feature set to every VM, even if the actual CPUs differ on the host servers. This feature will still not allow you to migrate VMs from an Intel CPU host to an AMD host. Therefore, you should only create clusters with ESX hosts of the same processor family, or choose a processor vendor and stick with it. Before you enable EVC, make sure your hosts meet the following requirements.

- All hosts in the cluster must have CPUs from the same vendor (either Intel or AMD).
- All VMs in the cluster must be powered off or migrated out of the cluster when EVC is being enabled.
- All hosts in the cluster must either have hardware live migration support (Intel FlexMigration or AMD-V Extended Migration), or have the CPU whose baseline feature set you intend to enable for the cluster. See VMware Knowledge Base article 1003212 (http://kb.vmware.com/kb/1003212) for a list of supported processors.
- Host servers must have the following enabled in their BIOS settings: For AMD systems, enable AMD-V and No Execute (NX); for Intel systems, enable Intel VT and Execute Disable (XD).

Once you are sure your hosts meet the requirements, you are ready to enable EVC by editing the cluster settings. There are two methods that you can use for doing this, as EVC cannot be enabled on existing clusters unless all VMs are shut down. The first method is to create a new cluster that is enabled for EVC, and then to move your ESX hosts into the cluster. The second method is to shut down all the VMs in your current cluster or migrate them out of the cluster to enable it.

The first method tends to be easier, as it does not require any VM downtime. If you choose the first method, you can simply create a new cluster and then move your hosts one by one to the cluster by first putting it in maintenance mode to migrate the VMs to other hosts. Then, once the host is moved to the new cluster, you can VMotion the VMs back to the host from the old cluster to the new one. The downside to this method is that you have to once again set up your cluster HA and DRS settings on the new cluster, which means you'll lose your cluster performance and migration history.

STORAGE VMOTION

Storage VMotion (SVMotion) allows you to migrate a running VM's disk files from one datastore to another on the same ESX host. The difference between

VMotion and SVMotion is that VMotion simply moves a VM from one ESX host to another, but keeps the storage location of the VM the same. SVMotion changes the storage location of the VM while it is running and moves it to another datastore on the same ESX host, but the VM remains on the same host. The VM's data files can be moved to any datastore on the ESX host which includes local and shared storage.

How SVMotion Works

The SVMotion process is as follows.

1. A new VM directory is created on the target datastore, and VM data files and virtual disk files are copied to the target directory.

2. The ESX host does a "self" VMotion to the target directory.

3. The Changed Block Tracking (CBT) feature keeps track of blocks that change during the copy process.

4. VM disk files are copied to the target directory.

5. Disk blocks that changed before the copy completed are copied to the target disk file.

6. The source disk files and directory are deleted.

SVMotion does more than just copy disk files from one datastore to another; it can also convert thick disks to thin disks, and vice versa, as part of the copy process. SVMotion can also be used to shrink a thin disk after it has grown and data has been deleted from it. Typically when you perform an SVMotion, you are moving the VM location to another storage device; however, you can also leave the VM on its current storage device when performing a disk conversion. SVMotion can be an invaluable tool when performing storage maintenance, as VMs can be easily moved to other storage devices while they are running.

Configuring SVMotion

You should be aware of the following requirements for using SVMotion.

- VM disks must be in persistent mode or be an RDM that is in virtual compatibility mode. For virtual compatibility mode RDMs, you can migrate the mapping file or convert them to thick-provisioned or thin-provisioned disks during migration, as long as the destination is not an NFS datastore. For physical compatibility mode RDMs, you can migrate the mapping file only.

- The VM must have no snapshots. If it does, it cannot be migrated.
- ESX/ESXi 3.5 hosts must be licensed and configured for VMotion. ESX/ESXi 4.0 and later hosts do not require VMotion configuration in order to perform migration with SVMotion. ESX/ESXi 4.0 hosts must be licensed for SVMotion (Enterprise and Enterprise Plus only).
- The host that the VM is running on must have access to the source and target datastores and must have enough resources available to support two instances of the VM running at the same time.
- A single host can be involved in up to two migrations with VMotion or SVMotion at one time.

In vSphere, SVMotion is no longer tied to VMotion; it is licensed separately and does not require that VMotion be configured to use it. No extra configuration is required to configure SVMotion, and it can be used right away as long as you meet the requirements outlined in the preceding list. In VI3, you needed to use a remote command-line utility (svmotion.pl) to perform an SVMotion; in vSphere, this is now integrated into the vSphere Client. To perform an SVMotion, you select a VM and choose the Migrate option; however, you can still use svmotion.pl to perform an SVMotion using the vSphere CLI. When the Migration Wizard loads, you have the following three options from which to choose.

- **Change Host**—This performs a VMotion.
- **Change Datastore**—This performs an SVMotion.
- **Change Host and Datastore**—This performs a cold migration for which the VM must be powered off.

FAULT TOLERANCE (FT)

Fault Tolerance (FT) was introduced as a new feature in vSphere to provide something that was missing in VI3: continuous availability for a VM in case of a host failure. HA was introduced in VI3 to protect against host failures, but it caused the VM to be down for a short period of time while it was restarted on another host. FT takes that to the next level and guarantees that the VM stays operational during a host failure by keeping a secondary copy of it running on another host server; in case of a host failure, that VM then becomes the primary VM and a new secondary is created on another functional host. The primary VM and secondary VM stay in sync with each other by using a technology called Record/Replay that was first introduced with VMware Workstation. Record/Replay works by recording the computer execution on a VM and saving it into a logfile; it can then take that recorded information and replay it on another VM to have a copy that is a duplicate of the original VM.

The technology behind the Record/Replay functionality is built into certain models of Intel and AMD processors, and is called vLockstep by VMware. This technology required Intel and AMD to make changes to both the performance counter architecture and virtualization hardware assists (Intel VT and AMD-V) that are inside their physical processors. Because of this, only newer processors support the FT feature; this includes the third-generation AMD Opteron based on the AMD Barcelona, Budapest, and Shanghai processor families; and Intel Xeon processors based on the Core 2 and Core i7 micro architectures and their successors. VMware has published a Knowledge Base article (http://kb.vmware.com/kb/1008027) that provides more details on this.

HOW FT WORKS

FT works by creating a secondary VM on another ESX host that shares the same virtual disk file as the primary VM, and then transfers the CPU and virtual device inputs from the primary VM (record) to the secondary VM (replay) via an FT logging NIC so that it is in sync with the primary and ready to take over in case of a failure. Although both the primary and secondary VMs receive the same inputs, only the primary VM produces output such as disk writes and network transmits. The secondary VM's output is suppressed by the hypervisor and is not on the network until it becomes a primary VM, so essentially both VMs function as a single VM. It's important to note that not everything that happens on the primary VM is copied to the secondary; certain actions and instructions are not relevant to the secondary VM, and to record everything would take up a huge amount of disk space and processing power. Instead, only nondeterministic events which include inputs to the VM (disk reads, received network traffic, keystrokes, mouse clicks, etc.) and certain CPU events (RDTSC, interrupts, etc.) are recorded. Inputs are then fed to the secondary VM at the same execution point so that it is in exactly the same state as the primary VM.

The information from the primary VM is copied to the secondary VM using a special logging network that is configured on each host server. It is highly recommended that you use a dedicated gigabit or higher NIC for the FT logging traffic; using slower-speed NICs is not recommended. You could use a shared NIC for FT logging for small or dev/test environments and for testing the feature. The information that is sent over the FT logging network between the two hosts can be very intensive depending on the operation of the VM. VMware has a formula that you can use to determine the FT Logging bandwidth requirements:

VMware FT logging bandwidth = (Avg disk reads (MB/s) × 8 + Avg network input (Mbps)) × 1.2 [20% headroom]

To get the VM statistics needed for this formula you must use the performance metrics that are supplied in the vSphere Client. The 20% headroom is to allow for CPU events that also need to be transmitted and are not included in the formula. Note that disk or network writes are not used by FT, as these do not factor into the state of the VM. As you can see, disk reads will typically take up the most bandwidth, and if you have a VM that does a lot of disk reading, you can reduce the amount of disk read traffic across the FT logging network by adding a special VM parameter, `replay.logReadData = checksum`, to the VMX file of the VM; this will cause the secondary VM to read data directly from the shared disk instead of having it transmitted over the FT logging network. For more information on this, see the Knowledge Base article at http://kb.vmware.com/kb/1011965.

It is important to note that if you experience an OS failure on the primary VM, such as a Windows BSOD, the secondary VM will also experience the failure, as it is an identical copy of the primary. However, the HA VM monitor feature will detect this, and will restart the primary VM and then respawn a new secondary VM. Also note that FT does not protect against a storage failure; since the VMs on both hosts use the same storage and virtual disk file, it is a single point of failure. Therefore, it's important to have as much redundancy as possible, such as dual storage adapters in your host servers attached to separate switches (multipathing), to prevent this. If a path to the SAN fails on the primary host, the FT feature will detect this and switch over to the secondary VM, but this is not a desirable situation. Furthermore, if there was a complete SAN failure or problem with the LUN that the VM was on, the FT feature would not protect against this.

Because of the high overhead and limitations of FT, you will want to use it sparingly. FT could be used in some cases to replace existing Microsoft Cluster Server (MSCS) implementations, but it's important to note what FT does not do, which is to protect against application failure on a VM; it only protects against a host failure. If protection for application failure is something you need, a solution such as MSCS would be better for you. FT is only meant to keep a VM running if there is a problem with the underlying host hardware. If you want to protect against an operating system failure, the VMware HA feature can provide this also, as it can detect unresponsive VMs and restart them on the same host server. You can use FT and HA together to provide maximum protection; if both the primary and secondary hosts failed at the same time, HA would restart the VM on another operable host and respawn a new secondary VM.

CONFIGURING FT

Although FT is a great feature, it does have many requirements and limitations that you should be aware of. Perhaps the biggest is that it currently only supports single vCPU VMs, which is unfortunate, as many big enterprise applications that would benefit from FT usually need multiple vCPUs (e.g., vSMP). But don't let this discourage you from running FT, as you may find that some applications will run just fine with one vCPU on some of the newer, faster processors that are available. VMware has mentioned that support for vSMP will come in a future release. Trying to keep a single vCPU in lockstep between hosts is no easy task, and VMware needs more time to develop methods to try to keep multiple vCPUs in lockstep between hosts.

Here are the requirements for the host.

- The vLockstep technology used by FT requires the physical processor extensions added to the latest processors from Intel and AMD. In order to run FT, a host must have an FT-capable processor, and both hosts running an FT VM pair must be in the same processor family.
- CPU clock speeds between the two hosts must be within 400MHz of each other to ensure that the hosts can stay in sync.
- All hosts must be running the same build of ESX or ESXi and be licensed for FT, which is only included in the Advanced, Enterprise, and Enterprise Plus editions of vSphere.
- Hosts used together as an FT cluster must share storage for the protected VMs (FC, iSCSI, or NAS).
- Hosts must be in an HA-enabled cluster.
- Network and storage redundancy is recommended to improve reliability; use NIC teaming and storage multipathing for maximum reliability.
- Each host must have a dedicated NIC for FT logging and one for VMotion with speeds of at least 1Gbps. Each NIC must also be on the same network.
- Host certificate checking must be enabled in vCenter Server (configured in vCenter Server Settings→SSL Settings).

Here are the requirements for the VMs.

- The VMs must be single-processor (no vSMPs).
- All VM disks must be "thick" (fully allocated) and not "thin." If a VM has a thin disk, it will be converted to thick when FT is enabled.
- There can be no nonreplayable devices (USB devices, serial/parallel ports, sound cards, a physical CD-ROM, a physical floppy drive, physical RDMs) on the VM.
- Most guest OSs are supported, with the following exceptions that apply only to hosts with third-generation AMD Opteron processors (i.e., Barcelona, Budapest, Shanghai): Windows XP (32-bit), Windows 2000, and Solaris 10 (32-bit). See VMware Knowledge Base article 1008027 (http://kb.vmware.com/kb/1008027) for more details.

In addition to these requirements, there are also many limitations when using FT, and they are as follows.

- Snapshots must be removed before FT can be enabled on a VM. In addition, it is not possible to take snapshots of VMs on which FT is enabled.
- N_Port ID Virtualization (NPIV) is not supported with FT. To use FT with a VM you must disable the NPIV configuration.
- Paravirtualized adapters are not supported with FT.
- Physical RDM is not supported with FT. You may only use virtual RDMs.
- FT is not supported with VMs that have CD-ROM or floppy virtual devices connected to a physical or remote device. To use FT with a VM with this issue, remove the CD-ROM or floppy virtual device or reconfigure the backing with an ISO installed on shared storage.
- The hot-plug feature is automatically disabled for fault tolerant VMs. To hot-plug devices (when either adding or removing them), you must momentarily turn off FT, perform the hot plug, and then turn FT back on.
- EPT/RVI is automatically disabled for VMs with FT turned on.
- IPv6 is not supported; you must use IPv4 addresses with FT.
- You can only use FT on a vCenter Server running as a VM if it is running with a single vCPU.
- VMotion is supported on FT-enabled VMs, but you cannot VMotion both the primary and secondary VMs at the same time. SVMotion is not supported on FT-enabled VMs.

- In vSphere 4.0, FT was compatible with DRS, but the automation level was disabled for FT-enabled VMs. Starting in vSphere 4.1, you can use FT with DRS when the EVC feature is enabled. DRS will perform initial placement on FT-enabled VMs and also will include them in the cluster's load-balancing calculations. If EVC in the cluster is disabled, the FT-enabled VMs are given a DRS automation level of "disabled". When a primary VM is powered on, its secondary VM is automatically placed, and neither VM is moved for load-balancing purposes.

You might be wondering whether you meet the many requirements to use FT in your own environment. Fortunately, VMware has made this easy for you to determine by providing a utility called SiteSurvey (www.vmware.com/download/shared_utilities.html) that will look at your infrastructure and see if it is capable of running FT. It is available as either a Windows or a Linux download, and once you install and run it, you will be prompted to connect to a vCenter Server. Once it connects to the vCenter Server, you can choose from your available clusters to generate a SiteSurvey report that shows whether your hosts support FT and if the hosts and VMs meet the individual prerequisites to use the feature. You can also click on links in the report that will give you detailed information about all the prerequisites along with compatible CPU charts. These links go to VMware's website and display the help document for the SiteSurvey utility, which is full of great information about the prerequisites for FT. In vSphere 4.1, you can also click the blue caption icon next to the Host Configured for FT field on the Host Summary tab to see a list of FT requirements that the host does not meet. If you do this in vSphere 4.0, it shows general requirements that are not specific to the host.

Another method for checking to see if your hosts meet the FT requirements is to use the vCenter Server Profile Compliance tool. To check using this method just select your cluster in the left pane of the vSphere Client, and then in the right pane select the Profile Compliance tab. Click the Check Compliance Now link and it will check your hosts for compliance, including FT. Before you enable FT, be aware of one important limitation: VMware currently recommends that you do not use FT in a cluster that consists of a mix of ESX and ESXi hosts. This is because ESX hosts might become incompatible with ESXi hosts for FT purposes after they are patched, even when patched to the same level. This is a result of the patching process and will be resolved in a future release so that compatible ESX and ESXi versions are able to interoperate with FT even though patch numbers do not match exactly. Until this is resolved, you will need to take this into consideration if you plan to use FT, and make sure you adjust your clusters that will have FT-enabled VMs so that they consist of only ESX or ESXi hosts and not both. See VMware Knowledge Base article 1013637 (http://kb.vmware.com/kb/1013637) for more information on this.

Implementing FT is fairly simple and straightforward once you meet the requirements for using it. The first step is to configure the networking needed for FT on the host servers. You must configure two separate vSwitches on each host: one for VMotion and one for FT logging. Each vSwitch must have at least one 1Gbps NIC, but at least two are recommended for redundancy. The VMotion and FT logging NICs must be on different network subnets. You can do this by creating a VMkernel interface on each vSwitch, and selecting "Use this port group for VMotion" on one of them and "Use this port group for Fault Tolerance logging" on the other. You can confirm that the networking is configured by selecting the Summary tab for the host; the VMotion Enabled and Fault Tolerance Enabled fields should both say Yes. Once the networking is configured, you can enable FT on a VM by right-clicking on it and choosing the Fault Tolerance item, and then Turn On Fault Tolerance.

Once enabled, a secondary VM will be created on another host; at that point, you will see a new Fault Tolerance section on the Summary tab of the VM that will display information including the FT status, secondary VM location (host), CPU and memory in use by the secondary VM, secondary VM lag time (how far behind it is from the primary, in seconds), and bandwidth in use for FT logging. Once you have enabled FT, alarms are available that you can use to check for specific conditions such as FT state, latency, secondary VM status, and more.

FT CONSIDERATIONS

Here is some additional information that will help you understand and implement FT.

- VMware spent a lot of time working with Intel and AMD to refine their physical processors so that VMware could implement its vLockstep technology, which replicates nondeterministic transactions between the processors by reproducing their CPU instructions. All data is synchronized, so there is no loss of data or transactions between the two systems. In the event of a hardware failure, you may have an IP packet retransmitted, but there is no interruption in service or data loss, as the secondary VM can always reproduce execution of the primary VM up to its last output.

- FT does not use a specific CPU feature, but requires specific CPU families to function. vLockstep is more of a software solution that relies on some of the underlying functionality of the processors. The software level records the CPU instructions at the VM level and relies on the processor to do so; it has to be very accurate in terms of timing, and VMware needed the processors to be modified by Intel and AMD to ensure complete accuracy. The SiteSurvey utility simply looks for certain CPU models and families, but not specific CPU features, to determine whether a CPU is compatible with FT. In the future, VMware may update its CPU ID utility to also report whether a CPU is FT-capable.

- In the case of split-brain scenarios (i.e., loss of network connectivity between hosts), the secondary VM may try to become the primary, resulting in two primary VMs running at the same time. This is prevented by using a lock on a special FT file; once a failure is detected, both VMs will try to rename this file, and if the secondary succeeds it becomes the primary and spawns a new secondary. If the secondary fails because the primary is still running and already has the file locked, the secondary VM is killed and a new secondary is spawned on another host.

- There is no limit to the number of FT-enabled hosts in a cluster, but you cannot have FT-enabled VMs span clusters. A future release may support FT-enabled VMs spanning clusters.

- There is an API for FT that provides the ability to script certain actions, such as disabling/enabling FT using PowerShell.

- There is a limit of four FT-enabled VMs per host (not per cluster); this is not a hard limit, but is recommended for optimal performance.

- The current version of FT is designed to be used between hosts in the same datacenter, and is not designed to work over WAN links between datacenters due to latency issues and failover complications between sites. Future versions may be engineered to allow for FT usage between external datacenters.

- Be aware that the secondary VM can slow down the primary VM if it is not getting enough CPU resources to keep up. This is noticeable by a lag time of several seconds or more. To resolve this, try setting a CPU reservation on the primary VM which will also be applied to the secondary VM and will ensure that both VMs will run at the same CPU speed. If the secondary VM slows down to the point that it is severely impacting the performance of the primary VM, FT between the two will cease and a new secondary will be created on another host.

- Patching hosts can be tricky when using the FT feature because of the requirement that the hosts have the same build level, but it is doable, and you can choose between two methods to accomplish this. The simplest method is to temporarily disable FT on any VMs that are using it, update all the hosts in the cluster to the same build level, and then reenable FT on the VMs. This method requires FT to be disabled for a longer period of time; a workaround if you have four or more hosts in your cluster is to VMotion your FT-enabled VMs so that they are all on half of your ESX hosts. Then update the hosts without the FT VMs so that they are the same build levels; once that is complete, disable FT on the VMs, VMotion the primary VMs to one of the updated hosts, reenable FT, and a new secondary will be spawned on one of the updated hosts that has the same build level. Once all the FT VMs are moved and reenabled, update the remaining hosts so that they are the same build level and then VMotion the VMs around so that they are balanced among all the hosts.

- FT can be enabled and disabled easily at any time; often this is necessary when you need to do something that is not supported when using FT, such as an SVMotion, snapshot, or hot-add of hardware to the VM. In addition, if there are specific time periods when VM availability is critical, such as when a monthly process is running, you can enable it for that time frame to ensure that it stays up while the process is running, and disable it afterward.

- When FT is enabled, any memory limits on the primary VM will be removed and a memory reservation will be set equal to the amount of RAM assigned to the VM. You will be unable to change memory limits, shares, or reservations on the primary VM while FT is enabled.

For more information on FT, check out VMware's Availability Guide that is included as part of the vSphere documentation (http://vmware.com/pdf/vsphere4/r40_u1/vsp_40_u1_availability.pdf).

SUMMARY

In this chapter, we covered some of the more popular advanced features in vSphere. There is a lot to learn about these features, so make sure you read through the documentation and get as much hands-on experience with them as you can before implementing them in a production environment. VMware's Knowledge Base has a great deal of articles specifically about these features, so make sure you look there for any gotchas or compatibility issues as well tips for troubleshooting problems.

MANAGEMENT OF vSPHERE

10

You can manage vSphere using a variety of applications and scripting tools. The main management tool is the vSphere Client, which is a Windows application, but there are additional methods that include web browsers, command-line consoles, PowerShell, and the vSphere Management Assistant. In this chapter, we will cover the various methods for managing vSphere and discuss when you would use each one.

vSPHERE CLIENT

The vSphere Client is a Windows-only application. It requires that the Microsoft .NET Framework be installed, and it is the tool that is mainly used to manage vSphere. You can use the vSphere Client to manage both individual ESX and ESXi hosts as well as multiple hosts by connecting to a vCenter Server. You can have multiple instances of the vSphere Client open on one workstation, and each can be connected to different hosts and/or vCenter Servers. The vSphere Client is backward-compatible with older hosts and vCenter Servers, but not forward-compatible. If you try to connect to a newer host or vCenter Server from an older version of the vSphere Client, you will receive a message that will require you to download a newer client to continue.

The vSphere Client was previously known as the VI Client in VI3, and is mostly unchanged in vSphere. One enhancement in vSphere is the option at the vSphere Client login screen to pass the Windows credentials that you use to log in to your workstation to vCenter Server so that you are automatically logged in. The layout of the various views is more organized, with the different areas being categorized under Inventory, Administration, Management, and Solutions and Applications headings.

You can download the vSphere Client installer from VMware's website, and it is also available from the Home page when accessing a vCenter Server using a web browser. In vSphere 4.0, you can also download it from ESX hosts if the web service is enabled on them, but in vSphere 4.1, the vSphere Client was removed from the ESX installation.

You can enhance the vSphere Client with plug-ins that have been developed by both VMware and third-party vendors. Some of the plug-ins that come with vSphere include Converter, Update Manager, Guided Consolidation, and VMware Data Recovery. Plug-ins sometimes work in conjunction with an application extension that is installed on the vCenter Server or a stand-alone server. For example, Update Manager has an application extension that must be installed first before you can install the plug-in in the vSphere Client. There are also some plug-ins that are integrated into vCenter Server, such as the Hardware Status and Service Status plug-ins. These plug-ins do not need to be installed; they are available for use immediately when the vSphere Client is connected to the vCenter Server.

You can manage the plug-ins in the Plug-in Manager that is launched from the top menu of the vSphere Client. Here you can download and install plug-ins on your vSphere Client as well as enable and disable them. Plug-ins must be installed on each individual vSphere Client instance on which you wish to use them. Once installed in the vSphere Client, most plug-ins will appear in the Solutions and Applications view in the vSphere Client.

The vSphere Client also comes bundled with the Host Update Utility which is an optional component that can be installed. The Host Update Utility is a simple patch management application that is used to patch and update ESXi hosts. In vSphere, you can also use this utility to upgrade (not patch) ESX hosts as well. The Host Update Utility does not have a lot of features, like Update Manager does, but it is an easy-to-use tool that simplifies patch management in vSphere.

Web Access

You can also manage vCenter Servers and ESX hosts in a limited manner using a web browser; ESXi hosts do not support this feature. In vSphere, this web access is now disabled by default, though, and you must enable it on each host if you wish to use it. The web access interface is very limited and you cannot use it to manage host operations; it is only intended for virtual machine (VM) management. With the web access interface, you can do the following with VMs.

- Change the power state.
- Add/remove/edit hardware.
- Take/manage snapshots.
- Change VM settings.
- Open a console session.
- View tasks and events.
- View VM information and resource usage.

The web access interface is useful for doing basic VM administration on non-Windows workstations. It supports both Microsoft Internet Explorer and Mozilla Firefox web browsers. It is also useful when VM owners need access to a VM but you do not want to install the vSphere Client on their workstation. For more information on the web access interface, check out VMware's Web Access Administrator's Guide that is published in the Documentation section of its website (http://vmware.com/pdf/vsphere4/r40_u1/vsp_40_u1_web_access.pdf).

vSphere CLI

The vSphere CLI is a remote administration CLI that you can use to manage ESX and ESXi hosts. The CLI was originally developed for ESXi because it lacks the Service Console that ESX has, which enables remote administration using SSH. In VI3, it was referred to as the RCLI, and you can install it on either Linux or Windows workstations. The CLI installs a Perl environment on your workstation as all the CLI commands are Perl scripts that connect to hosts using the SDK to execute the commands that you specify.

You can download the CLI from VMware's website; it is listed under vSphere Downloads in the Drivers & Tools section. Once you install the CLI, it is listed in the VMware folder and the only option is a command prompt that puts you in the installed directory of the CLI. All the commands are Perl scripts and are located in the /bin subdirectory of the CLI install directory. Once you are in that directory, you can execute the commands by typing the command name with the .pl extension (e.g., `vmkfstools.pl`). The commands listed are based on the ESX Service Console commands, but there are some syntax differences. In addition, not all of the ESX Service Console commands are available in the CLI. You will notice that there are duplicate commands, with some starting with `vicfg-` and others with `esxcfg-`. This is because the `esxcfg-` commands are meant for VI3 hosts and will eventually be phased out. Both commands do the same thing, but the `esxcfg-` commands have better compatibility with VI3; for vSphere hosts, you should use the `vicfg-` commands.

Because the CLI is a remote utility, you need to specify a host name when using the commands with the `--server` parameter. You can optionally specify `--username` and `--password` parameters, but if you omit them you will be prompted for them. The syntax for running commands is as follows:

```
<command name.pl> -- server (host name/IP) --username (local host
username) --password (password for specified username) <command
parameters>
```

The following code snippet is an example of a command to list a host's NICs. It is based on the `esxcfg-nics` command in the Service Console. The `-l` parameter will list the NICs of a host.

```
vicfg-nic.pl --server onyx.xyz.com --username root --password
12345 -l
```

You must specify the host name and authentication information every time you run a CLI command. You can optionally put this information into a configuration file that you can reference with the `--config` parameter, but this is not recommended as your host authentication information is stored in plain text on your workstation. You can also use a `--sessionfile` parameter that you can create using the `save_session.pl` command located in the \Perl\apps\session subdirectory of the CLI directory. This file stores your session information but does not reveal password information and is automatically expired if not used in 30 minutes. One final option is to use a `--passthroughout` parameter that uses Microsoft SSPI to connect to a vCenter Server. Once connected and authenticated with vCenter Server, you no longer have to authenticate with any hosts.

For more information on using the CLI and the syntaxes for each command, reference the CLI documentation on VMware's website (www.vmware.com/support/developer/vcli/).

VSPHERE MANAGEMENT ASSISTANT

The vSphere Management Assistant (vMA) is a prebuilt Linux virtual appliance that comes packaged with the vSphere CLI and the vSphere SDK for Perl. It was originally released in VI3 and was called the Virtual Infrastructure Management Assistant (VIMA). The vMA was created because many users had requirements for running scripts and agents on their hosts, and the vMA can act as a remote Service Console for both ESX and ESXi hosts. The vMA allows administrators to run scripts or agents that interact with ESX and ESXi hosts and vCenter Server systems without having to explicitly authenticate each time. The vMA is essentially a centralized Service Console that you can use for your whole environment. In addition, the vMA can also collect logging information from ESX and ESXi hosts and vCenter Server and store it for analysis.

To deploy the vMA follow these steps.

1. Download the vMA ZIP file from VMware's website (it is located under the Tools and Drivers section of the vSphere download page), and extract the two files.
2. In the vSphere Client, select File and then Deploy OVF Template.
3. Select Deploy from File and browse to the .ovf file that was extracted from the ZIP file.
4. Continue through the wizard, selecting a host and datastore for the new VM.

Once the vMA is created, you will need to configure it by following these steps.

1. Open a console session to the VM and power it on.
2. You will be prompted for IP address information; enter the requested information.
3. You will be prompted for a new password for the vi-admin user, which is used as the admin account for the vMA; enter the requested information. The vMA will then start and you will be at a login prompt.

Once the vMA is configured, you need to add the hosts and vCenter Servers that you want to manage to it. To do this, follow these steps.

1. Log in to the vMA either using the console or via SSH as the vi-admin user.

2. To add a server, type `sudo vifp addserver <server name>` (e.g., `sudo vifp addserver emerald.xyz.com`) at the vMA command line. You will be prompted for the credentials for that server. For vCenter Servers enter a vCenter Server login, and for ESX and ESXi hosts enter a local host login.

3. You can continue adding servers; once you are done, you can display them by typing `vifp listservers` at the vMA command line.

4. To connect to a server, type `vifpinit <server name>` (e.g., `vifpinit onyx.xyz.com`) at the vMA command line. If you have added only one server you can omit the server name.

5. Once connected, you can begin to issue commands to that server using the same syntax as the vSphere CLI. To direct the command to a particular server use the `--server` parameter; for example, `vicfg-nics --server onyx.xyz.com -l`.

To learn more about using the vMA, check out the documentation on VMware's website (www.vmware.com/support/developer/vima/).

POWERSHELL AND POWERCLI

PowerShell is an extensible command-line shell and associated scripting language developed by Microsoft that you can use to help automate common administration tasks and provide information about your VMware environment. You can use PowerShell for many different things in Windows environments, but you can also use it with VMware environments since VMware released its PowerCLI (formerly known as the VI Toolkit for Windows in VI3), which provides PowerShell with access to the VMware API. PowerShell is fairly easy to install and use, and many great scripts have been written that work with VMware environments.

Once you download PowerShell from Microsoft's website at www.microsoft.com/windowsserver2003/technologies/management/power-shell/download.mspx and install it, you need to download and install VMware's PowerCLI from www.vmware.com/support/developer/windowstoolkit/. PowerCLI contains many VMware-specific PowerShell cmdlets that you can use. You can run the individual cmdlets from the special PowerShell command prompt, or put them together into a script to perform multiple tasks. PowerShell scripts typically have a .ps1 extension and can be written with any text editor.

You can also add a graphical interface to PowerShell using Quest Software's PowerGUI and PowerPack for VMware, which makes PowerShell easier to use and adds additional functionality. These are available at www.powergui.org/downloads.jspa and www.powergui.org/entry.jspa?externalID=2551&categoryID=290.

An even better environment for using PowerShell with vSphere is the free vEcoShell from Quest Software. vEcoShell provides a simple, consistent, and integrated management user interface for creating, debugging, and simplifying the management of Windows PowerShell scripts with robust scripting capabilities through an Integrated Development Environment (IDE). For downloads and information on installing the vEcoShell, visit http://thevesi.org/.

For a good step-by-step tutorial on setting up PowerShell and PowerGUI, check out my two-part article on Searchvmware.com:

- **Installing and using the PowerShell tool (Part 1)**—
  http://searchvmware.techtarget.com/tip/0,289483,sid179_gci1347396,00.html
- **Using Quest's PowerGUI PowerPack script editor (Part 2)**—
  http://searchvmware.techtarget.com/tip/0,289483,sid179_gci1352704_mem 1,00.html

Using PowerShell with VMware has grown in popularity, and there are currently many freely available scripts written by other users that you can use in your environment. For more information on using PowerShell and sample scripts check out these resources:

- **Using PowerShell for virtually everything (Hugo Peeters)**—
  www.peetersonline.nl
- **Virtu-al (Alan Renouf)**—www.virtu-al.net
- **LucD Notes (Luc Dekens)**—http://lucd.info/
- **TechProsaic (Hal Rottenberg)**—http://halr9000.com/
- **vSphere PowerCLI blog**—http://blogs.vmware.com/vipowershell/
- **VMware Community Sample Code**—
  http://communities.vmware.com/community/developer/codecentral
- **Managing VMware with PowerShell FAQ**—
  http://communities.vmware.com/docs/DOC-4210

- **PowerCLI Quick Reference Guide**—www.virtu-al.net/2009/12/04/powercli-quick-reference-guide/
- **PowerCLI Developer Community**—http://communities.vmware.com/community/vmtn/vsphere/automationtools/powercli

Looking at sample code is often the best way to learn how to script, so be sure to check out the many scripts that other users have written to get you started writing your own. Additionally, check out VMware's Developer Community at http://communities.vmware.com/community/developer for more scripting resources and to post any questions you may have.

ESX SERVICE CONSOLE

Although you can manage VMware ESX hosts using the vSphere Client that is included with every component of vSphere, many times you will need to log in to the Service Console and use the ESX command line to perform certain actions and to troubleshoot problems. In some cases, using the GUI client is not even possible (e.g., network configuration problems) and you must use the ESX command line to troubleshoot and reconfigure your host. Therefore, it's a good idea to get familiar with the many commands that are available so that you know how to use them when necessary. Many of the ESX Service Console commands are also available in the PowerCLI that can be used to manage both ESX and ESXi hosts.

The ESX Service Console is based on Red Hat Linux, and therefore many Linux commands can be used inside it. You can access the Service Console either at the physical server console or by using an SSH utility. By default, you cannot use the root account to log in remotely using SSH; you can enable this (see http://kb.vmware.com/kb/8375637), but it is recommended that you create a separate account instead. Once you log in to the ESX Service Console, you can use most traditional Linux commands as well as a number of commands that perform ESX and VM-specific functions. You may not use these commands that often, but they are good to know for when you do need to use them, so you should become familiar with them.

As mentioned, most Linux commands work in the ESX Service Console and you can use them for troubleshooting and configuration purposes. Many new VMware administrators without Linux experience might be intimidated by the ESX Service Console which is based on Red Hat Linux. The reality is that unless you want to do a lot of the configuration and administration of ESX the hard way, you will not have to log in to the Service Console and use the CLI that much. Almost all the configuration and administration of the ESX server can also be done using the vSphere Client that is provided with ESX. If you do want to get your hands dirty and use the CLI, it's best to learn some basic Linux commands. There are certain situations where using the CLI is necessary, such as restarting some of the ESX services, reconfiguring networking, or killing a stuck VM.

For a list and description of the top 25 ESX Service Console commands, check out the article at http://searchservervirtualization.techtarget.com/tip/ 0,289483,sid94_gci1379075_mem1,00.html.

Also, remember that unlike Windows, all Linux commands are case-sensitive (and are usually lowercase), so make sure you get the case right when typing them or they will not work. This is also true about directory names and filenames on the filesystem. You can get a list of all the commands for the ESX Service Console as well as their syntaxes in the Appendix of the vSphere Server Configuration Guide, which is located on VMware's website (www.vmware.com/pdf/vsphere4/r40_u1/vsp_40_u1_esx_server_config.pdf).

ESXi MANAGEMENT CONSOLE

ESXi has a very simple management interface that you can access at the physical server console by pressing F2; it is known as the Direct Console User Interface (DCUI). With it you can do some basic configuration and administration of the ESXi host, such as set the management interface IP information, restart management agents, and view system logs, as shown in Figure 10.1.

You can also access a hidden console that is a BusyBox shell to troubleshoot and diagnose an ESXi host. VMware refers to this as Tech Support mode. This mode is enabled by default, but you can disable it for security purposes using the Advanced Settings configuration. Using this console is generally not recommended, unless you know what you are doing and are advised by VMware support to use it to resolve a problem. However, if you want to access it, be aware of the following caveats.

- The console is neither audited nor logged, so any commands issued inside it are not recorded. When Tech Support mode is activated it is noted in the system logs.
- Some of the commands, if used incorrectly, can result in an unusable system.
- You can only log in to the console using the root account.

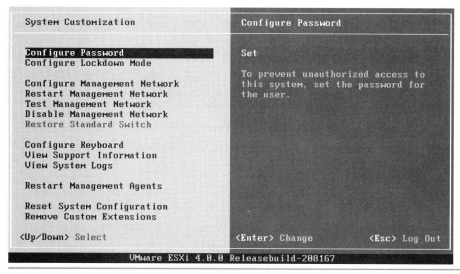

Figure 10.1   The ESXi Direct Console User Interface

To access Tech Support mode, follow these steps.

1. At the local ESXi console, press Alt-F1; it does not matter if you are at the main screen or in the Customize System screen. This will display a screen that shows various system messages.

2. You will not receive a prompt, and anything you type on this screen will not be displayed. Type the word unsupported to enter Tech Support mode.

3. You will be prompted for the root password. Once you enter the root password, you will be at a prompt where you can enter commands.

A limited number of Linux commands work in the console. Commands such as cd, ls, vi, reboot, and cp will work, but others will not. In addition, you can use many of the esxcfg commands to view or change configurations as well as use the esxtop application to view performance statistics. These commands are all located in the /sbin directory, and you can view a list of them all using the ls command.

Another useful command is vim-cmd, which is kind of a super command that can do many things. If you type vim-cmd vmsvc you will get a list of all the commands that you can use with vim-cmd, such as vim-cmd vmsvc/getallvms which will return a list of all VMs on the host. You need to use vim-cmd vmsvc/ as the prefix to any commands that you enter.

Another (unsupported) feature for the Tech Support mode console is the ability to enable SSH so that it can be access remotely. To do this, follow these steps.

1. Access Tech Support mode as described earlier.

2. Type `vi /etc/inetd.conf`.

3. Scroll down until you see the lines that start with `#ssh`. There are two lines, one for IPv4 and one for IPv6. Remove the # from the appropriate line by pressing x when the cursor is on it.

4. Type `:wq!` to save and quit.

5. Restart the management service by typing `/sbin/services.sh restart`; you may need to restart the ESXi host for the change to take effect.

Once you are done using Tech Support mode, you can log out by typing the `exit` command. To get back to the regular ESXi console at any time simply press Alt-F2.

FREE THIRD-PARTY TOOLS

In addition to the management utilities provided by VMware, there are also many third-party utilities to help you administer your virtual environment. Often these utilities make up for shortcomings in VMware's product and make for easier administration of your hosts and VMs. A few of the most commonly used tools are mentioned in the following sections. For a more complete list, see http://vsphere-land.com/vinfo/free-tools.

SSH CONSOLE UTILITIES

SSH console utilities allow you to remotely connect to your ESX host Service Console using the secure SSH protocol for remote administration. Almost every admin has the PuTTY utility installed on his workstation, as it is one of the best utilities that you can use to connect to your ESX hosts remotely using SSH. It is available for free at www.chiark.greenend.org.uk/~sgtatham/putty/download.html.

SCP FILE TRANSFER UTILITIES

SCP file transfer utilities allow you to transfer files to and from ESX hosts using Secure Copy Protocol (SCP). Following are a couple of these utilities.

- **Veeam FastSCP**—This is one of the fastest file transfer utilities, as it does not encrypt data as it is copied. It is available for free at http://veeam.com/vmware-esx-fastscp.html.

- **WinSCP**—This is a good file transfer utility that has a Windows Explorer-like interface. It is available for free at http://winscp.net/eng/index.php.

SUMMARY

As you can see, there are many management tools for your vSphere environment. You will most likely use many of these, as they all have their strengths and the situation may sometimes require using a specific tool. In addition, scripting with PowerShell can be a great timesaver when you need to automate repetitive tasks and change configuration information. So, get used to using all the tools and gain some experience using them, as they are also very helpful in troubleshooting problems in your vSphere environment.

INSTALLING vSPHERE

11

In this chapter, you will learn how to install the main components of vSphere which include ESX, ESXi, and vCenter Server. Before you start installing vSphere, you should prepare everything you will need to install and configure all of the various components discussed in this chapter. Doing this ahead of time will help to ensure that your installation goes smoothly. It's always a good idea to read through the documentation before you install the software so that you can get a good idea of what to expect when installing it. Here are some steps that you should take to prepare for building your virtual environment.

1. Download the latest version of the ESX or ESXi ISO files from VMware's website.
2. Download the latest version of the vCenter Server installation application from VMware's website.
3. Generate your license keys from the VMware licensing website.
4. Make sure you have a database server set up to be used with vCenter Server.
5. Download the Release Notes and Installation documentation from VMware's website for the version of ESX or ESXi and vCenter Server that you are installing.

INSTALLING vCENTER SERVER

You can install vCenter Server before or after you install ESX and ESXi, but it is generally recommended that you install it first, as it provides centralized management for all your hosts. Before installing vCenter Server, you need to make some important decisions, such as whether you'll run it on a physical server or inside a virtual machine (VM), as well as the operating system and database platform to use with it. Understanding and making the right choices before installing it is very important, because changing them later can be difficult.

CHOOSING A DATABASE FOR vCENTER SERVER

The vCenter Server database contains a variety of information, including host and VM configurations, alarm and event data, historical performance data, High Availability (HA)/Distributed Resource Scheduler (DRS)/resource pool/cluster data, and task information. When ESX hosts are added to vCenter Server the host and VM configuration is automatically imported into the database. vCenter Server continually updates its database from data that is pushed to it from the ESX and ESXi hosts, so if changes are made to the hosts directly, vCenter Server stays up-to-date.

The database is not critical to the operation of ESX servers or their VMs; they would continue to function normally if vCenter Server or its database were unavailable (except for some advanced features, such as Distributed Power Management [DPM], DRS, and vMotion, which would not work; however, HA would still work, but you would not be able to make HA configuration changes to it). If the database were to crash and a new one was created, you could add your ESX servers back in and the database would repopulate the configuration information. The only data unique to the database that would be lost if the database were rebuilt is data pertaining to performance statistics, alarms, events, tasks, clusters, HA and DRS configurations, host profiles, resource pools, roles, permissions, and custom attributes.

The size of the database will vary based on the number of hosts and VMs that are managed by the vCenter Server and the level and interval of performance statistics that are being collected. Most of the tables in the database are relatively small and do not grow that much, with the exception of the tasks, events, and performance statistics tables, which can grow quite large over time. The database will initially start out small and will grow as more and more performance statistics are collected. Therefore, it is important to plan to have adequate disk space available on your database server for your database to grow. You can change the amount, interval, and level of statistics that are collected in the vCenter Server configuration settings.

As the settings are decreased or increased, the total size of the database will change also. A database size estimator is built into vCenter Server that displays the total projected database size based on the current settings. Table 11.1 shows some database size estimates based on the default Level 1 statistics settings; these may vary depending on the database type you are using.

Table 11.1   Estimated vCenter Server Database Size

Number of Hosts	Number of VMs	Estimated Database Size
5	200	2GB
25	1,000	7GB
50	2,000	14GB
75	3,000	21GB

Choosing between the supported databases will depend primarily on what already exists in your environment and what you have expertise administering. If you do not have a database currently running in your environment, SQL Server is recommended because it costs less and is easier to set up, configure, and maintain than Oracle or DB2. It's possible to install the database server on the same server as vCenter Server, but this is not recommended due to resource contention between the two applications. You can also consider installing your database server on a VM if you do not have a physical server available for it.

For medium to large production environments, it is recommended that you install either the Standard or Enterprise version of SQL Server 2005 or 2008, IBM DB2 9.5, or an Oracle Standard or Enterprise 10g or 11g database. SQL Server 2005 Express is only recommended for small installations of up to five ESX hosts and 50 VMs. The database requirements for vCenter Server can change, so it is best to check the installation documentation and release notes for the version of vCenter Server that you are installing.

One final database consideration concerns Update Manager. If you choose to use Update Manager to patch your hosts and VMs, you should be aware that it requires a database also. It's possible to share the database that vCenter Server uses with Update Manager, but for maximum performance of your vCenter

Server, it is recommended that you install it to a separate database on the database server. Additionally, it is also recommended that you install the Update Manager plug-in/service on a separate server from the vCenter Server. If you have a smaller environment (fewer than five hosts), you can get away with running them on the same server as long as your vCenter Server has enough resources to handle them both.

Once you have chosen your database platform, you should read through the latest release notes and installation guide for the version of vCenter Server that you are installing for specific information on setting up a database to be used with vCenter Server. If you are going to be running your database on a server that is separate from your vCenter Server, which is recommended, you will need to set up an ODBC connection on the vCenter Server with information to connect to the database server.

Before setting up your ODBC connection, you should first make sure the new database and user account are created on your database server. The information you will need are the database name, database username and password, and database host name or IP address. If you are using Oracle for your database, you should also install the Oracle client, which also installs the Oracle ODBC driver. If you are using SQL Server 2005 or 2008 as your database server, you should first download the SQL Server Native Client (sql-ncli.msi) from the Microsoft website or from the SQL Server install CD and install it. If you will be using the SQL Server 2005 Express database that comes with vCenter Server, there is no need to perform this step, as the vCenter Server installation will automatically install the database, configure it, and create the ODBC data source.

If you are installing vCenter Server 4.0, be aware that a 32-bit ODBC DSN is required, even on 64-bit operating systems. This requirement applies to all supported databases. By default, any DSN created on a 64-bit system is 64-bit, so you will need to manually create a 32-bit DSN. If you're using Microsoft SQL Server, it automatically installs both the 32-bit and 64-bit drivers; for Oracle, you need to install the specific 32-bit drivers. Once you do that, you need to run the 32-bit ODBC Administrator application which is located at <WindowsDir>\SysWOW64\odbcad32.exe. Be aware that there are two odbcad32.exe files in different directories, the other being the 64-bit version located in <WindowsDir>\System32\odbcad32.exe. Even though it is named odbcad32.exe, the one in the System32 folder is the 64-bit version. You can find more information on this at http://support.microsoft.com/kb/942976.

If you are installing vCenter Server 4.1, this is not a requirement, as vCenter Server is now a 64-bit application. So, make sure you are using 64-bit ODBC drivers and create a 64-bit DSN. To create a 64-bit DSN you can use the ODBC Administrator tool from the Control Panel or run odbcad32.exe located in the System32 folder. Be sure to read the ESX/ESXi and vCenter Server installation guide for information on how to correctly set up the database that you will use for vCenter Server.

PHYSICAL SERVER OR VIRTUAL MACHINE?

Before you install vCenter Server, you need to decide whether you want to run it on a physical server or on a VM. VMware fully supports both options, but there are definite advantages and disadvantages to running vCenter Server on a VM.

Here are some of the advantages to running VCenter Server on a VM.

- **High availability**—Using the HA feature on your ESX host servers provides high availability for the vCenter Server. A hardware failure on a physical server normally would make vCenter Server unavailable until it was repaired or reinstalled on another server. Setting up HA when vCenter Server is on a physical server requires either Microsoft Cluster Server or vCenter Server Heartbeat, both expensive options. Optionally, you can use the Fault Tolerance (FT) feature if your environment is small enough to only use one vCPU in your vCenter Server.

- **Cost savings**—You will need one less physical server to dedicate to vCenter Server. This can be particularly advantageous for small installations that have very few physical servers.

- **Snapshots**—The snapshot feature can be useful when patching or installing upgrades to the vCenter Server.

Here are some of the disadvantages of running vCenter Server on a VM.

- **Cold migration**—Because cold migration is a vCenter Server function, you cannot cold-migrate the vCenter Server because it has to be down to perform a cold migration to another ESX host (you can use a manual command-line process to accomplish this, though).

- **Recovery**—If a major outage strikes that affects all ESX hosts (e.g., a storage area network [SAN] failure), you will lose the centralized management capabilities of ESX hosts while vCenter Server is down. When it comes time to restart the VMs, you will need to log in to each host individually to locate which host the vCenter Server VM is on so that you can start it.

Neither of these disadvantages is a big concern and should not stop you from considering virtualizing vCenter Server. Many administrators are not comfortable with virtualizing vCenter Server and stick to running it on a physical server. However, as noted in the previous list, there are some advantages to virtualizing vCenter Server, and you should consider them before making your choice.

OPERATING SYSTEM AND HARDWARE

vCenter Server requires a Windows operating system, such as Server 2003 or Server 2008; you can use Windows XP 64-bit, but that is not recommended since Microsoft is no longer supporting it. If you are installing vSphere 4.0, you can use either a 32-bit or a 64-bit version of Windows. Be aware, though, that 64-bit operating systems are recommended and should be considered required if your vCenter Server is managing more than 200 hosts. If you are installing vSphere 4.1, you can only use a 64-bit operating system with vCenter Server. If you attempt to install it on a 32-bit operating system, it will give you an error message and will not install.

Whether you are running vCenter Server as a VM or as a physical server, there are some recommended hardware configurations for vCenter Server which are listed in Table 11.2.

Table 11.2   vCenter Server Recommended Hardware Configurations

Number of Hosts	Number of VMs	Recommended Hardware
50	250	2 CPUs, 4GB memory
200	2,000	4 CPUs, 4GB memory
300	3,000	4 CPUs, 8GB memory

The minimum hardware requirements for vCenter Server are two CPUs (2GHz or faster) and 3GB of memory; a gigabit network connection is also recommended. Minimum required disk space is 2GB, but this is only for vCenter Server and does not take into account the database or Update Manager on the same server.

PREREQUISITES

There are a few prerequisites for installing vCenter Server, and they include the following.

- You must create a supported database if you are not using the included SQL Server 2005 Express. Look at the vCenter Server installation documentation for how to do this, as it is specific to each database.

- The server that vCenter Server runs on should be a member of an Active Directory (AD) domain. If it is not, you will not be able to use AD groups/users for roles and must configure local accounts. You should also not install vCenter Server on a domain controller.

- The Windows computer name of the server that vCenter Server runs on cannot be more than 15 characters long.

- The server that vCenter Server runs on should have a fixed IP address or a DHCP reservation and a DNS host name that must match the computer name. It's very important to also have a reverse DNS record.

- If you are using a domain user account to install vCenter Server, make sure it is a member of the local Administrators group and also has the Act as part of the Operating System and Log On as a Service permissions.

vCENTER SERVER INSTALLATION STEPS

Once you have everything prepared, install vCenter Server by following these steps.

1. Launch autorun from the vCenter Server installation media. Under Product Installers, select vCenter Server; the other companion products can all be installed afterward.

2. Once the wizard launches, accept the EULA and at the Customer Information screen, enter a name, an organization, and optionally a license key. If you don't enter a license key, vCenter Server will still be fully functional at the Enterprise Plus level for 60 days and you can set up licensing anytime during that period.

3. At the Database Options screen, select to either install SQL Server 2005 Express or use an existing database that you already have set up. If you select an existing database, you need to select a 32-bit ODBC system DSN (pre-vCenter Server 4.1 only) that must already be configured on the

vCenter Server. If you use the built-in SQL Server 2005 Express database, you can skip to step 5.

4. If you chose to use an existing database in the preceding step, the next window will prompt you for a database username and password that vCenter Server uses to connect to the database. This username/password must already be set up on the database server. You may receive a warning message on this step after it connects to the database, saying that it is set to Full Recovery Model. This isn't necessarily a problem, but it can cause the SQL transaction logs to get quite large. Therefore, it is recommended that you change this to Simple Recovery Model, which keeps the size of the transaction log down. The trade-off here is that you could lose some recent data if there was a problem with the database and you had to recover it. In most cases, though, this is only historical performance data, which may be an acceptable loss. You can read more about the recovery models in VMware's Knowledge Base article 1001046 (http://kb.vmware.com/kb/1001046).

5. At the vCenter Server Service screen, choose the account that the vCenter Server will run as. The default is the built-in SYSTEM account which is recommended in most cases. You can choose another local or domain account instead; just make sure it is a member of the local Administrators group.

6. At the Destination folder screen, either accept the default folder or choose another one.

7. At the Linked Mode Options screen, choose to create a stand-alone vCenter Server instance or join an existing Linked Mode group. If you do not choose to join a Linked Mode group now, you can do so later, after vCenter Server is installed.

8. At the Configure Ports screen, specify which ports vCenter Server uses for its services and connections to other servers. It's recommended that you leave these at the defaults, unless you have changed the ports on your other servers because of a conflict. Be aware that if you are running another web server on the vCenter Server, such as Microsoft Internet Information Services (IIS), ports 80 and 443 will conflict with vCenter Server's built-in Tomcat web server.

9. Finally, at the Ready to Install screen, click Install to begin the installation or go back to update information on previous screens.

Once the installation finishes, the vCenter Server services will automatically be started and the vCenter Server will be ready for use. Be aware that the vSphere Client and plug-ins, such as Update Manager, Converter, and Guided

Consolidation, are not installed automatically and must be installed manually either on the vCenter Server or on another Windows server.

INSTALLING **ESX** AND **ESXI**

Before you install ESX or ESXi, you should download the ISO file from VMware's website for the version you wish to install, and burn the ISO to a CD that you can mount on the server. Optionally, if you are using a remote console utility such as HP's Integrated Lights-Out (iLO) or Dell's Remote Access Card (DRAC), you can mount the ISO or map a workstation CD-ROM as a virtual CD-ROM on the server from a remote workstation. This is not the preferred method, though, as data corruption can occur if the server encounters too much load while the installation is running. In addition, the installation will be very slow. If you do choose this method, it is recommended that you run the media test that is built into the ESX installer and that you are on the same network LAN segment as the target host to ensure adequate bandwidth and lower latency.

If you are not using the Boot from SAN feature, it is best to disconnect the server on which you are installing ESX from the SAN fabric before installing; once the install completes, you can reconnect it before you reboot the server.

PREPARING THE SERVER FOR INSTALLATION

Before you proceed with installing ESX or ESXi on your server hardware, you should always test or "burn in" the memory to ensure that there are no defects with it. Defective memory will usually not be noticeable when you first deploy a new server, and it may be months before you see signs of defective memory which can cause hard server crashes or the dreaded Purple Screen of Death (PSOD).

Most servers perform a brief memory test when they first start up as part of their POST procedure. This is not a very good test and will only detect the most obvious of memory problems. A much more thorough test checks the interaction of adjacent memory cells to ensure that writing to one cell does not overwrite an adjacent cell. A good free memory test utility is available, called Memtest86+, which performs many different tests to thoroughly test your server's memory. You can download it from www.memtest.org as a small 2MB ISO file that you can burn to a CD, and then boot from it on your new server and let the memory burn in for at least 24 hours, or at least until one complete pass finishes. However, it is best to let it run for several passes and for at least 72 hours to more thoroughly test your server's memory.

Memtest86+ will run indefinitely and the pass counter will increment as all of the tests are run. The more RAM you have in your system, the longer it will take to complete one pass. A system with 32GB will generally take about one day to complete. Memtest86+ not only tests your system's RAM, but also tests the CPU L1 and L2 caches. If it detects an error, the easiest way to identify the memory module that caused it is to simply remove a DIMM and run the test again, repeating the test until it passes. The Memtest86+ documentation is very good, and includes troubleshooting methods, detailed test descriptions, and the causes of errors. Performing this extra step ahead of time is worthwhile insurance to ensure that your server is not affected by memory defects later on.

IMPORTANCE OF THE HARDWARE COMPATIBILITY GUIDE

VMware publishes a guide called the Hardware Compatibility Guide that lists all the various hardware components that are supported by each version of ESX and ESXi. This very important guide is split into different subguides which include systems (server makes/models), storage devices (SAN/iSCSI/NFS), and I/O devices (NICs/storage controllers) and is updated frequently with new hardware being added and older hardware removed.

You might wonder why this guide is important. There are two reasons. The first is that ESX/ESXi has a limited set of hardware device drivers that are installed and loaded into the VMkernel, and while it is possible to install additional non-supported device drivers, doing so is not recommended or supported. Consequently, if you use a network or storage adapter that is not in the guide, there is a very good chance that it might not work because the driver for it is not included.

The second reason is that VMware only provides support for server hardware that is listed in the guide. Just because server hardware is not listed on the Hardware Compatibility Guide doesn't mean it will not work with ESX/ESXi, though. A lot of older hardware and other hardware brands/models are not listed on the Hardware Compatibility Guide and work just fine but are unsupported by VMware. So, if you are using hardware that is not listed in the guide and you call VMware's Global Support Services (GSS) for assistance with an issue, you might be wondering if they will help you at all. What VMware will do is assist customers in problem analysis to determine whether the issue is related to the unsupported hardware. If the hardware is suspected to be related to the issue, VMware reserves the right to request that the unsupported hardware be removed from the server. If VMware does suspect that the problem is related to the unsupported hardware, it will request that you open a support request with the hardware vendor instead.

So, you might be wondering how the hardware in the guide is selected. Hardware vendors have to test and certify that their hardware works properly with the latest versions of ESX and ESXi. Once this has been completed, VMware will add them to the guide. VMware works with hardware vendors as part of its Technology Alliance Partner (TAP) program, and any vendor can apply to have its hardware added to the guide. Once an application is received, the vendor is responsible for completing the certification criteria and submitting the results to VMware for review and approval. The first step of this process requires vendors to submit a VMware Compatibility Analysis for the hardware that they intend to certify. After VMware reviews the analysis and approves it, the next step is for the vendor to engage with a third-party testing lab to certify that their hardware works properly with ESX/ESXi. VMware will not disclose the specific testing criteria that are used for certifying hardware for the guide, but it does use the same certification criteria for all vendors that apply.

You'll probably notice that the guide contains mostly newer hardware and that older hardware is periodically removed. VMware does not enforce an expiration period for hardware added to the guide, but it is up to each vendor to certify their hardware for the most current VMware product releases. Vendors are free to initiate the certification process anytime they need to have new hardware added to the guide. Additionally, each vendor can choose to remove older hardware from the guide as they release newer hardware versions.

So, although using hardware that is not listed on the guide may be okay for labs, it is highly recommended that you only use hardware in the guide for production use. Be sure to check the guide periodically, especially if you plan to upgrade to a newer ESX/ESXi version, as you will want to make sure your hardware is listed before upgrading. You should check this guide before you purchase any server hardware to use with ESX/ESXi. Do not make any assumptions that all newer big-name (i.e., HP, IBM, Dell) hardware will be in the guide, as this can come back to bite you. Also be sure that all your server components are listed in the guide, including NICs and storage adapters. Often, it may take a short period of time before newer hardware is added to the Hardware Compatibility Guide. If you have newer hardware and it is not yet listed in the guide, contact the vendor to see where they are in terms of getting their hardware certified by VMware.

The guide is available via an interactive website; additionally, you can download the full guide in PDF format for each of the different hardware components. So, make sure you bookmark the guide (www.vmware.com/resources/compatibility/) and periodically check it as you don't want to find out when you call VMware support that you are using unsupported hardware.

BOOT FROM SAN CONSIDERATIONS

If you are installing ESX to a LUN to utilize the Boot from SAN feature, there are several considerations that you should be aware of.

- ESX does not support booting from a shared LUN. If you want an ESX Server host to boot from a SAN, you must allocate an entire LUN to each ESX Server host. Make sure that other boot LUNs for other ESX servers are masked so that each ESX host only sees its own boot LUN.

- It is best to present only the LUN onto which ESX is being installed until after the installation is complete. Do not present any data LUNs for VMFS storage until after ESX is correctly installed.

- Configure the host bus adapter (HBA) BIOS to enable the Boot from SAN option, and select the LUN to be used for booting before installing ESX.

- Make note of the World Wide Name (WWN; the SAN equivalent of a network MAC address which consists of 16 hexadecimal digits grouped into eight pairs) for the HBA adapter, as you will need it when configuring the SAN.

If you are using ESXi, be aware that it currently does not support Boot from SAN. Although it does work, VMware lists this feature as experimental, meaning that you can test it but that you should not use it in a production environment. In a future release, VMware will surely support this feature with ESXi, as it considers ESXi to be its future platform and will eventually phase out ESX.

ESX PARTITION CONSIDERATIONS

Partitions let you segment a physical drive into separate logical drives. Partitions are treated as independent disks with their own defined sizes and are assigned mount points so that they can be accessed from the default root partition. Partitions are used to ensure that unchecked log growth does not affect other critical operating system partitions. The default partitions on a Linux system are the /boot partition which stores files used to boot the computer, and the / partition which is the root partition from which all mount points derive. The additional partitions that ESX uses are set to mount automatically when the server boots up, so they are accessible from the root partition.

When you install ESX you have the option to use the default partition sizes or specify your own partitions. The default sizes will typically work for many environments, but there are changes you can make to ensure that you do not run into problems later if your partitions run out of space or you try to increase the memory allocated to the Service Console. First, let's cover what partitions are created by default. ESX hosts have required and optional partitions: /boot and vmkcore are physical partitions; /, swap, /var/log, and all the optional partitions are stored on a virtual disk called esxconsole-<system-uuid>/esxconsole.vmdk. The virtual disk is stored in a VMFS volume. The following partitions are required.

- **/boot**—This is the boot partition that contains files used to boot the ESX server. The ESX boot disk requires 1.25GB of free space and includes the /boot and vmkcore partitions. The /boot partition alone requires 1100MB; the extra space is used for the vmkcore partition.

- **/**—This is the root partition that contains the ESX server operating system files. It is calculated dynamically based on the size of the /usr partition. By default, the minimum size is 5GB and no /usr partition is defined.

- **swap**—This partition does not have a mount point and is used by the Service Console as swap space for virtual memory. By default, this partition is 600MB.

- **/var/log**—This partition is where the ESX server logfiles are stored. By default, this partition is 2GB.

- **vmkcore**—This partition serves as a repository for vmkernel core dump files in the event that a core dump occurs. By default, this partition is 100MB and is part of the /boot partition.

- **vmfs**—The remaining free space after all the other partitions are created on the drive on which ESX is installed is used to create a VMFS volume. The VMFS volume also holds the esxconsole.vmdk file.

With the default partition sizes, the total Service Console size is 7.6GB. You cannot define the sizes of the /boot, vmkcore, and /vmfs partitions when you use the graphical or text installation modes. The following changes are recommended for the default partitions.

- **/boot**—This partition cannot be changed.

- **/**—It is okay to leave the root partition at 5GB.

- **swap**—Change this from 600MB to 1600MB. This should be twice the amount of memory that is dedicated to the Service Console. The default amount of memory typically devoted to the Service Console is 358MB. However, if the host has limited physical memory, the memory devoted to the Service Console is 300MB, which is why the default swap size is 600MB. The recommended amount of memory for the Service Console is a maximum of 800MB, which would require a 1600MB swap partition.

- **/var/log**—Change this from 2GB to 5GB to allow for extra space for log-files.

- **vmkcore**—This partition cannot be changed.

- **vmfs**—This will be created using the remaining disk space on the physical disk and cannot be changed.

The extra /home, /tmp, /var, and /opt partitions are normally folders created in the / partition. By creating separate partitions for them, you ensure that they will not fill up and negatively impact the critical / partition.

- **/home**—Create a partition of 2GB for any home directories that are created for local users on the ESX host.

- **/tmp**—Create a partition of 2GB for the directory that is used to store temporary files.

- **/var**—Create a partition of 4GB for the directory that is used to hold administrative log and configuration files.

- **/opt**—Create a partition of 2GB for the directory that is used for logging of the HA feature.

Using these custom partition sizes, the total disk space used by the Service Console is about 19GB. It is highly recommended that you use custom partitions, as once you install ESX with the default partition sizes, it is very difficult to change them later on. Taking a little bit of extra time and disk space when doing your initial configuration can help you avoid problems that you might experience later. We will cover how to make these changes during the ESX installation steps momentarily. Table 11.3 provides a summary of the default sizes compared to the recommended partition size changes.

Table 11.3   ESX Default and Recommended Partition Size Comparison

Partition Name	Default Size	Recommended Size
/boot	1100MB	Can't be changed
/ (root)	5120MB	5120MB
swap	600MB	1600MB
/var/log	2048MB	2048MB
vmkcore	100MB	Can't be changed
/home	N/A	2048MB
/tmp	N/A	2048MB
/var	N/A	4096MB
/opt	N/A	2048MB

One important note is that when the VMFS partition is created with the ESX installer, it is created with a 1MB block size, which only supports a maximum size of 256GB for individual virtual disk files. There is no way to change this in the installer or afterward, as the VMFS volume cannot be deleted because the Service Console resides on it. Some workarounds for this are documented in VMware Knowledge Base article 1012683 (http://kb.vmware.com/kb/1012683).

ESX INSTALLATION STEPS

Once you are ready to install ESX, just follow these steps to complete the installation.

1. When you boot from the ESX installation CD or ISO file, the ESX installer loads and you will be presented with a Welcome screen that provides you with the option of using the graphical installer or a text-based installer, plus additional options for scripted installations. If you do not choose an option, the graphical installer will automatically start after a period of time. You can use the text-based installer if you experience mouse or video problems when using the graphical installer. These instructions are based on the graphical installer, but most of the options are similar with the text-based installer. If you press F2 at this screen, you can enter some additional install options. A line of text will appear at the bottom of the screen with various

default boot options. One boot option that you might add to the end of the line is `askmedia`, which will cause the installer to prompt for a location (e.g., FTP, HTTP, DVD, NFS) for the unpacked ESX ISO installer.

2. Click Next on the Welcome screen, and at the License Agreement screen, accept the agreement and click Next.

3. On the Select Keyboard screen, select a keyboard type and click Next.

4. The Custom Drivers screen allows you to install custom network or storage adapter drivers that are not included by default in ESX. Drivers that were not originally compatible with ESX sometimes get released after the build of ESX is published, and custom drivers allow you to use them without waiting until they are included in the next ESX build. VMware publishes custom driver CD images on the vSphere download page at http://downloads.vmware.com/d/info/datacenter_downloads/vmware_vsphere_4/4#drivers_tools. In most cases, you will not need custom drivers and can click Next and continue. You will receive a prompt asking if you want to load the system drivers; click Yes. If you do need to install custom drivers, select Yes, click the Add button, insert your custom driver CD, and select the appropriate driver. You can also install custom drivers after ESX is installed using the CLI or vSphere Client.

5. At the next screen, the default system drivers will load as well as any custom drivers that you may have specified. Once they are loaded, click Next.

6. At the License screen, enter a license key for the ESX host or choose to enter one later. If you choose to enter one later, the server will run using an evaluation license for 60 days and you can license it later on. If the host will be managed by vCenter Server, you should do all your licensing in vCenter Server instead. Once you select a license option, click Next.

7. At the Network Configuration screen, select one of the available network adapters to use for the Service Console management network. All available network adapters will be shown, and you can choose one from the drop-down list. The type of adapter, the MAC address, and the connection state will be displayed, so you can choose the correct adapter. To make it easier to match up the correct physical adapter, you can unplug the network cables from all the other adapters so that only the one you want shows as connected. Optionally, you can specify a VLAN ID if the port that your adapter is plugged into is set up for 802.1Q VLAN tagging. Once you select a network adapter, click Next.

8. At the second Network Configuration screen, you can choose to use DHCP to automatically assign IP information to the network adapter that you

selected in the preceding step, or to manually specify it. This network configuration is for Service Console networking. It is recommended that you not use DHCP for this, because if the IP address of the ESX Service Console were to change later on, it can cause problems. If you do need to use DHCP, make sure you set an IP address reservation for the ESX host on the DHCP server. This information is used to create a virtual switch (vSwitch) for the Service Console network and also to set up a vswif interface for it with the IP address you enter. The Service Console vswif interface uses a generated MAC address and not the default MAC address of the physical NIC (pNIC). If you do use a DHCP reservation to obtain an IP address for the Service Console interface, you have to do it after the ESX host is installed because you will not know the MAC address of the vswif interface until after ESX has booted the first time. You can find the MAC address once ESX has booted by connecting to the ESX host with the vSphere Client and selecting Configuration, and then Networking, and then click the Properties link for the vSwitch with the vswif interface (usually vSwitch0). Next, in the Port List, select the Service Console, and the MAC address that has been assigned to it will be displayed on the right. You can change all of these settings after the ESX host is started. Optionally, you can click the "Test these settings" button to ensure that your network connectivity works. Once you are finished, click Next to continue.

9. If you added the `askmedia` boot option in step 1, you will get an Install Media screen where you will be able to choose a location to unpack your ESX installation files.

10. At the Setup Type screen, choose either a standard setup, which uses default partition sizes, or an advanced setup, which allows you to customize partition sizes. These partitions are the ones that are used by the Service Console. For the standard setup, default partitions are created and the remaining disk space is used to create a VMFS volume for your VMs. If you wish to use the recommended partition sizes that were covered earlier in this chapter, you should select the advanced setup type, and click Next to continue.

11. At the ESX Storage Device screen, choose the disk on which to install ESX. This is the location of the `/boot` and `vmkcore` partitions. For the advanced setup, you can choose separate disks for ESX (`/boot` and `vmkcore`) and the VMFS volume which also contains the Service Console. If you only have a single physical disk in your host, they will both be installed on the same disk. For the standard setup, you can only choose a single disk for both ESX and the VMFS volume. Once you select a disk, click Next to continue. You

will receive a warning message that all existing data on the selected disk will be erased. If you chose the standard setup type, you can skip to step 14.

12. If you chose the advanced setup type, the next screen will let you specify a VMFS datastore. Choose to create a new datastore or use an existing datastore. The default for creating a new datastore is to create it on the same disk on which the ESX /boot and vmkcore partitions are created. If you uncheck that option, you can specify a separate disk instead. In most cases, you will want to keep them together to avoid complications. You can also choose a name for your VMFS volume. It's recommended that you not use the default name of storage1 and instead use a more descriptive name such as <hostname>-local (e.g., diamond-local). Click Next to continue.

13. If you chose the advanced setup type, in the next screen you can specify your custom partition sizes that were covered earlier in this chapter. You will see three default partitions that can be created or edited, as shown in Figure 11.1.

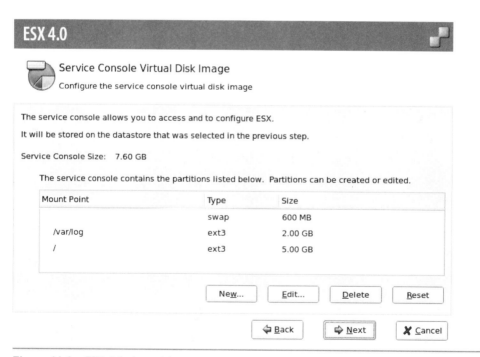

Figure 11.1   ESX default partitions

If you to choose the use the custom partition sizes, follow these steps.

1. Edit swap and change it from 600MB to 1600MB.

2. Create a new /home partition of type EXT3 and size 2GB.

3. Create a new /tmp partition of type EXT3 and size 2GB.

4. Create a new /var partition of type EXT3 and size 4GB.

5. Create a new /opt partition of type EXT3 and size 2GB.

Once you are done, your partitions should like Figure 11.2. Click Next to continue.

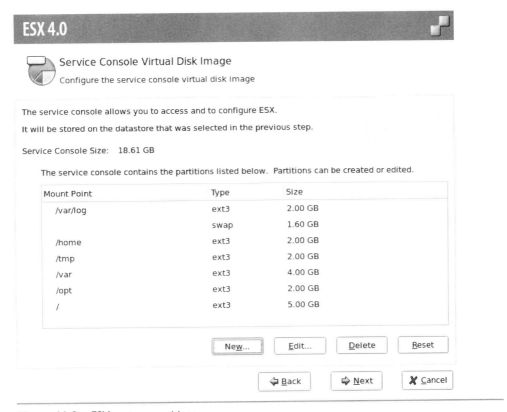

Figure 11.2   ESX custom partitions

14. At the Time Zone Settings screen, choose a time zone and click Next.

15. At the Date and Time screen, choose to automatically or manually set the time of the ESX host server. If you choose the automatic option, you can

specify an NTP time server (e.g., time.nist.gov) with which the ESX host server can synchronize. Once you set this, click the Synchronize button to have it synchronize immediately. If you choose the manual option, you can enter your own date and time. You can always configure NTP after the ESX host is created using the vSphere Client.

16. At the Set Administrator Password screen, enter at least a six-character password for the default root account. Optionally, you can add additional user accounts which can also be added later, after the ESX host is started. It is recommended that you create at least one nonroot user account which can be used to remotely connect to the host using SSH, and then using the su – command to elevate access to it so that you can perform administration commands. Once you are finished, click Next to continue.

17. A Summary screen will be displayed, listing all the options that you selected. Review the options; if necessary, go back and make changes, and then click Next to begin the installation.

18. The installation will begin and will display a status as it completes. Once the installation is 100% complete, click Next. You will see an Installation Complete screen; click Finish to reboot your host and start the ESX server. When the ESX host reboots, you can log in to the physical console using the root username and password that you set.

INSTALLING ESXi

The ESXi installation process is much simpler than the ESX installation process due to the lack of a full Service Console in ESXi. ESXi comes in two versions: the embedded version which is built into some new servers, and the installable version which can be installed on any server that meets the ESXi requirements. In most cases, you install ESXi to the local hard disk of a server, but it is possible to install it to a USB flash drive as well.

INSTALLING ESXi ON A LOCAL HARD DISK

Installing ESXi is pretty straightforward, as you have far fewer decisions to make than when installing ESX, and subsequently you have fewer installation screens to work through. Once you are ready to install ESXi, follow these steps.

1. When you boot from the ESXi installation CD or ISO file, a Welcome screen will be displayed. Press Enter to begin the installation.

2. At the EULA screen, press F11 to accept the licensing agreement.

3. At the Disk Selection screen, select a disk on which to install ESXi and press Enter to continue. You may receive a warning message that the disk contains an existing partition and will be overwritten; if so, make sure you have selected the correct disk and press Enter to continue.

4. Press F11 to confirm the installation of ESXi and the installation will begin.

5. Once the installation completes, a screen will be displayed confirming that the installation was successful. Remove the CD from the server and press Enter to reboot.

When the server reboots, it will display its login screen with options for configuring it from the console (F2) or for shutting it down and restarting the server (F12). The server will initially attempt to use DHCP to get an IP address for the Management network. If you are not using DHCP, it will fail and you can manually configure it. Once you have the Management network configured, you will be able to connect to the ESXi host using the vSphere Client.

INSTALLING ESXI ON A USB FLASH DRIVE

The Embedded edition of ESXi is only available on servers from manufacturers that support that option. It is typically provided on a vendor USB flash drive that contains the ESXi image and simply plugs into an internal port built into the server's motherboard. Many people don't order this option, though, and want to install ESXi on USB flash drives themselves. Fortunately, it is a fairly simple process to create your own USB flash drive that you can use in any server that supports booting from removable USB drives. And if you're concerned about support, be aware that VMware fully supports installing ESXi onto a flash drive, as documented in the ESXi hardware requirements. However, VMware may require that you use a flash drive that is approved by the server vendor. Before we go over how to do this, let's cover why you would want to do this.

Pros and Cons

The primary reason you would want to install ESXi on a USB flash drive is so that you do not have to install hard drives in your host servers. This adds cost to the server, and in some cases (e.g., blades) it is desirable to not have internal hard drives. Most ESX and ESXi hosts utilize shared storage because of features such as VMotion, FT, DRS, and HA that require it. As a result, local storage goes mostly unused in host servers and serves mainly as a place to install ESX/ESXi. Not having to order hard drives in your servers can save you hundreds of dollars per server. Another reason is that many people today are using headless computing, where nothing is stored directly on a server, and if there is a failure the server can easily be replaced without having to reinstall any operating systems or applications. Having ESXi on a removable flash drive supports this model. A server can simply be replaced and the flash drive removed from the old server and plugged into the new server. A final reason which may not apply to many people is that you can dual-boot with ESXi installed on a USB flash drive; simply remove the flash drive and you can boot from a partition on your local hard disk.

Despite the many reasons why you might want to boot from a flash drive for ESXi, there are a few reasons that you may choose not to do this. The first is that having local disks on a host can be very handy, so you can create local VMFS volumes to use for both noncritical VMs and redundant VMs such as DNS servers that could keep running if your shared storage was unavailable. Additionally, local storage is good for making backup copies of your VMs and for using Storage VMotion (SVMotion) to copy VMs to it when doing maintenance on shared storage. The second is reliability; you cannot use RAID with flash drives, so if your flash drive fails or has a problem, your ESXi host will be down until you replace it with a new flash drive and reconfigure it. If you use the local disk in a RAID group, your server can continue running if a drive fails. The final reason concerns performance. Be aware that USB flash drives are much slower than SCSI or SAS hard drives. USB 2.0, which is common in most servers, has a maximum data speed of 480Mbps (60 MBps), but transfer rates are typically much slower than that. In contrast, SAS controllers typically transfer data at 3Gbps. Also, reads (average 30MBps) from a USB flash drive are much faster than writes (average 5MBps). The slower speed will not have much of an effect on your ESXi host, though, and should not deter you from using USB. The boot time of the host will be a bit slower, but only by a minute or two. Additionally, some of the reads/writes that are done afterward to configuration and logfiles will be slightly slower, but this is minimal and will not affect the performance of any VMs running on the host.

Requirements

The requirements to install ESXi on a USB flash drive are quite simple; all you need is an ISO image of ESXi installable and a 1GB or larger flash drive. Despite being only 60MB in size, the actual install size of ESXi is closer to 1GB because of some extra files and partitions that are created when it is installed. These are not directly part of ESXi, but are used for things such as the installation of VMware Tools onto guest operating systems and storage of a backup image of ESXi whenever it is updated. Because this device is going to be the heart of your server, I recommend that you get a quality name-brand USB flash drive; avoid novelty and cheap, generic flash drives which may have high failure rates. Be aware that all flash drives are not created equal, and performance can widely vary between brands, models, and sizes. Again, getting a brand-name flash drive will help to ensure that yours performs well. You can test the speed of your flash drives using many freeware hard disk utilities, such as HD_Speed (www.steel-bytes.com/?mid=20). In comparing two different model/size flash drives, I had one drive average 31MBps for reads and 6MBps for writes, and the other average 23MBps for reads and 8MBps for writes.

Another important requirement is that your server supports booting from a removable USB device. Most modern servers do support this, but sometimes you need to enable it in the server's BIOS. You can also specify the load order for boot devices; USB is usually above hard drives and network PXE boot, but below CD-ROM and floppy drives. In addition, some server BIOSs allow you to choose USB 1.1 or 2.0 for your ports; be sure this is set to 2.0 as it is much faster than 1.1. You should try to use an internal USB slot for your ESXi flash drive. Most modern servers have at least one internal USB slot, so open the cover and look around for it. Also ensure that the flash drive will fit inside your server with the cover closed. Although you can install it externally, doing so is not recommended as it can be easily removed or bumped and broken.

Installation Steps

The process to create the bootable flash drive is to boot from the ESXi installation CD as you would normally do when installing it to a new server, but instead of installing it to the hard drive of the server you will be installing it to the USB drive. You can use any server or workstation that supports ESXi to create the flash drive; once it's created, you can use the drive in the server on which you want to install ESXi. Follow these steps to install ESXi to a flash drive.

1. Download the ESXi installable ISO file from VMware's website.

2. When you've downloaded the ISO file, burn it to a CD/DVD to use in a server/workstation.

3. Make sure your flash drive is installed into a USB port in the server; then boot from the CD/DVD that you created and choose to run the ESXi installer.

4. When prompted to select a drive to install to, choose the USB flash drive instead of any local disk partitions that may appear, as shown in Figure 11.3.

5. Once the installation of ESXi completes, remove the CD/DVD and reboot, and ESXi will load from the flash drive.

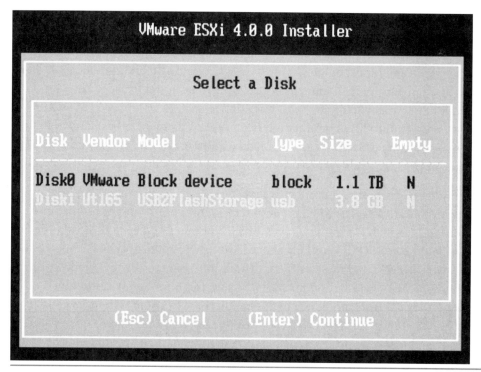

Figure 11.3   Selecting a USB flash drive onto which to install ESXi

An alternative method is to use VMware Workstation, which makes the process even easier. Once you have VMware Workstation installed, follow these steps to create an ESXi USB flash drive.

1. Create a new VM in VMware Workstation. Make sure it can run ESXi (you'll need at least 2GB of memory); Workstation 7 can do this natively, and Workstation 6.5 can do this with a few modifications to the .vmx file. Customize the hardware and add a USB controller to it.

2. Connect your USB flash drive directly to the VM using the VM→Removable Devices menu. You will notice it is removed from the host PC when it is connected to the VM.

3. When the ESXi installer loads, go through the screens and select the USB flash drive to install it on instead of the hard drive for the VM. You'll know it's the right one because it's the same size as your flash drive.

4. Once the install completes, power off the VM, pull out the flash drive, plug it into a server, and you're ready to go.

Additional Considerations

After you create the flash drive for ESXi using Workstation, you might try to boot from it using the VM that you created to do so. However, this will not work, as booting from a flash drive for ESXi on VMware Workstation is not supported. Once ESXi has been installed to your flash drive, if you insert it into a Windows PC you will see that the volume label has been changed to Hypervisor0 and there are only four small files on it. You will also see that the size of the drive is now showing as 4MB instead of the actual size of the flash drive; this is because there is a 4MB FAT partition on the disk and the other partitions are only readable by ESXi. Examining the layout of the flash drive in detail, you will see that there is one 4MB primary partition on the disk that is the bootloader that runs when the host boots up. There is also an 896MB extended partition with four logical disks that are used for the following.

- A 250MB logical disk contains the core hypervisor code (VMkernel) which is packaged into several files that total 60MB. Any server manufacturer customizations (i.e., HP, Dell, IBM) are also stored here.

- A 250MB logical disk is used to hold a backup copy of the hypervisor code whenever any updates are applied to ESXi. This disk is initially empty, except for one 150-byte boot.cfg file, until an update to ESXi is applied. Once an update is applied, all the files from logical disk 1 are copied to logical disk 2 before the new ESXi image is copied to logical disk 1.

- A 110MB logical disk is initially empty, but it can be used to hold diagnostic core dumps.

- A 286MB logical disk contains VMware Tools ISO files, the vSphere Client installer, other tools and drivers, and runtime storage. These files are not part of the VMkernel, but are mostly auxiliary files.

If you ever want to reuse the flash drive with Windows, you must low-level-format it first to delete all the partitions. You won't be able to do this with the Disk Management utility that comes with Windows. There are a few ways to do this, but the easiest is to use the HDD Low Level Format Tool (www.softpedia.com/get/System/Hard-Disk-Utils/HDD-Low-Level-Format-Tool.shtml). Simply download, install, and run it, and select your USB flash drive (make absolutely sure you choose the correct drive!), select Continue, and then on the Low-level Format tab select Format This Device. Once the format completes, you can select the drive in Windows Explorer and format to its full capacity.

You might wonder how long a flash drive will last and if you should worry about it wearing out, which would cause your server to stop working. Flash drives usually have limited write cycles, meaning they can only be written to so many times before they no longer work and you experience errors. Quality flash drives can last many years and go through at least 10,000 write cycles before they experience problems, and ESXi is mostly reading from its flash drive, which does not cause wear on it. Subsequently, your flash drive should last for many years; however, it is a good idea to have a backup one just in case something happens.

Creating a backup copy of a USB flash drive is easy to do. You cannot simply copy the contents of the drive to another drive, however; you must create a disk image of the flash drive and then use that image to write to another flash drive of the same size. USB Image Tool (www.alexpage.de/usb-image-tool/download/) is a freeware tool that you can use to do this. Simply insert your flash drive into a Windows workstation, run the tool, select your flash drive, and click the Backup button. This will create an image of the flash drive in an .img format file. You can then remove the flash drive, insert a new one that is the same size, and click the Restore button to copy the image to the new drive. Although this method is good for periodically backing up your ESXi flash drive, you can also use it to quickly make multiple copies of a new ESXi flash drive for use in multiple servers.

Installing ESXi on a flash drive is a great way to save money when purchasing server hardware and to get new servers up and running very quickly and easily. If you're already using ESXi installed on local disks, it's probably not worth switching, but for new servers you should definitely consider it.

SUMMARY

In this chapter, we covered how to install ESX, ESXi, and vCenter Server. If you make a mistake while installing something or want to configure something different afterward (e.g., ESX partitions), you can easily reinstall it later. Run through the installations several times before you install to your production environment so that you can gain experience with it and also play around with the various configuration options that are part of the installation. Once you have your installation down pat, make sure you document it so that your other hosts are consistent and so that others who may be installing hosts in your environment choose the same options that you do.

UPGRADING TO VSPHERE 12

If you have an existing VI3 environment, at some point you'll probably want to upgrade it to vSphere. Before jumping right into the upgrade process, though, there are many considerations and requirements that you should be aware of. Once you are aware of everything you need to know, you should then put together a plan for how you are going to proceed. Upgrading to vSphere is fairly straightforward, but there are many gotchas that can make the process more difficult. To avoid surprises during the upgrade, you should properly prepare and know all the steps so that your upgrade is trouble-free and uneventful. In this chapter, we will cover considerations and steps for upgrading your existing virtual environment to vSphere.

COMPATIBILITY CONSIDERATIONS

There are many things to consider when upgrading your VI3 environment to vSphere, such as hardware and software compatibility and upgrade methods. You should spend some time researching this to ensure that you have all your bases covered beforehand. Finding out after you upgrade that some of your management tools are not compatible with vSphere can make things very difficult. Upgrading is a much simpler process than downgrading, so make sure you consider everything before beginning your upgrade.

HARDWARE COMPATIBILITY

Your server and storage hardware may be supported in VI3, but don't assume that it's supported in vSphere. Check VMware's online Hardware Compatibility Guide to make sure all your hardware components are supported in vSphere. This includes servers, I/O adapters, and storage devices. You may be able to get away with using servers that are not listed in the guide, but it's critical that your I/O adapters and storage are listed. Refer to the Importance of the Hardware Compatibility Guide section in Chapter 11 for more information on this. The other consideration that you need to be aware of in regard to hardware is the requirement for 64-bit hardware. See the section Selecting Physical Host Hardware to Use with vSphere in Chapter 2 for more information on this.

You should also be aware that the following features in vSphere require very specific hardware.

- **Hardware iSCSI**—Very few hardware iSCSI initiators are supported, and most of them are based on the QLogic adapters. Be sure to check the Hardware Compatibility Guide before using one, because if it is not listed, vSphere will see it as a network adapter instead of a storage adapter.

- **Fault Tolerance (FT)**—This requires very specific CPU families from Intel and AMD. See VMware Knowledge Base article 1008027 (http://kb.vmware.com/kb/1008027) for a list of supported CPUs. You can read more about the FT feature in Chapter 10.

- **VMDirectPath**—This requires specific chipset technology from Intel and AMD that supports Intel VT-d or the AMD I/O Memory Management Unit (IOMMU). You can read more about VMDirectPath in Chapter 2. Intel VT-d has been available for some time, but AMD finally released IOMMU in the HP ProLiant G7 servers.

SOFTWARE AND DATABASE COMPATIBILITY

When upgrading vCenter Server you should be aware that the requirements have changed in vSphere and some older operating systems and databases are no longer supported. vCenter Server 4.0 no longer supports SQL Server 2000 and requires either SQL Server 2005 or 2008. Consequently, if your vCenter Server 2.5 is using a SQL Server 2000 database, it will complicate the upgrade process.

Migrating the database to SQL Server 2005, which is supported with both vCenter Server 2.5 and 4.0, is the easiest method. If you plan to use SQL Server

2008, though, because vCenter Server 2.5 does not support SQL Server 2008 you will have to shut down the vCenter Server, migrate the database to SQL Server 2008, change the ODBC data sources, and then install vCenter Server 4.0. If you are using the built-in MSDE database with vCenter Server 2.x, it will automatically be upgraded to SQL Server 2005 Express. Optionally, you can migrate it to another supported database format before upgrading.

In addition, beginning with vSphere 4.1, vCenter Server is only supported on a 64-bit Windows operating system. So, if you do not have a 64-bit Windows OS, you must use vSphere 4.0 instead. See Chapter 11 for more information on this. Also be sure to look at VMware's Compatibility Matrix (www.vmware.com/pdf/vsphere4/r40/vsp_compatibility_matrix.pdf) to learn more regarding compatibility of the various vSphere components.

THIRD-PARTY APPLICATION COMPATIBILITY

If you are using any third-party applications (e.g., backup, management) with vSphere, make sure you check to see if they are supported in vSphere. A newer version may be available that is supported in vSphere. Also, if you are using vendor-supplied hardware management agents running inside your ESX Service Console, check for a newer version of them that supports vSphere. Using older versions can cause hard crashes of your ESX server.

VMWARE PRODUCT COMPATIBILITY

When vSphere first came out many of the VMware companion products did not support it yet. Products such as Lab Manager, View, and SRM only worked with VI3 and required newer releases before they supported vSphere. Most of those products now support vSphere, but it's always best to check first, especially if you are using a newer version of vSphere, such as 4.1. VMware publishes a Software Compatibility Matrix (http://partner-web.vmware.com/comp_guide/docs/vSphere_Comp_Matrix.pdf) that you can use as a reference.

PLANNING AN UPGRADE

Careful planning will make your upgrade go much more smoothly; without a solid plan your upgrade could turn into a nightmare. There are several methods that you can use to upgrade your environment, and the one you use will depend on several factors, such as acceptable downtime and disruption to the environment, how much extra capacity you have, and whether you are using new hardware. The upgrade to vSphere has three main phases that are done in sequential order, so you need to keep this in mind when planning your upgrade.

UPGRADE PHASES

There is a definite order to follow when upgrading your environment. Think of the upgrade process as a pyramid, with vCenter Server being at the top, ESX and ESXi hosts in the middle, and virtual machines (VMs) at the bottom, as shown in Figure 12.1.

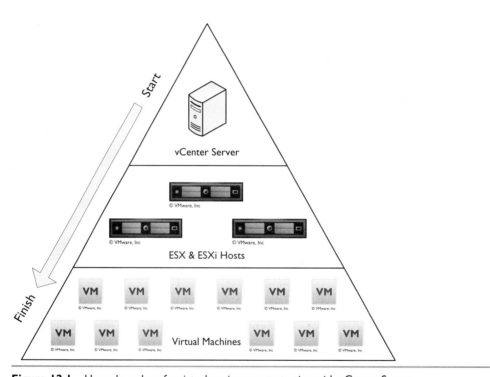

Figure 12.1 Upgrade order of a virtual environment, starting with vCenter Server

As a precursor, though, you should ensure that you identify and plan on any hardware upgrades that you may need to make to support vSphere. This could include memory upgrades, adding supported NICs and storage controllers, and upgrading hardware firmware levels. Additionally, you should plan to upgrade any third-party tools and agents at whatever point makes sense depending on their backward-compatibility support. VI3 and vSphere are backward-compatible, but not forward-compatible. For example, a vSphere 4 vCenter Server can manage VI3 VMs, but a VI3 vCenter Server cannot manage vSphere 4 hosts. The same holds true with the client: The vSphere Client 4 can be used with the VI3 vCenter Server and host, but the VI3 Client cannot be used with vSphere 4. All of these compatibilities are listed in VMware's Compatibility Matrix (www.vmware.com/pdf/vsphere4/r40/vsp_compatibility_matrix.pdf). Here is more information on each upgrade phase.

- **Upgrade Phase 1, vCenter Server**—This is where you should start your upgrade, as vCenter Server is at the top of the compatibility pyramid. Once you upgrade your vCenter Server to vSphere, you must upgrade your VI3 Clients to the new vSphere Client. If you try to access a vSphere host or vCenter Server with a VI3 Client, you will be prompted that you must upgrade it first. Once you upgrade your vCenter Server, you can proceed with upgrading the rest of your environment.

- **Upgrade Phase 2, ESX and ESXi hosts**—You will most likely not be upgrading all your hosts at once, unless you have a small environment. vSphere hosts and VI3 hosts can coexist in the same cluster, and features such as VMotion and High Availability (HA) will still work. But although they can coexist, you should try to minimize the amount of time in which you have a mixed environment, because there are more risks of issues occurring due to differences between the versions.

- **Upgrade Phase 3, Virtual Machines**—Upgrading VMs consists of upgrading the virtual hardware from version 4 that is used in VI3 to version 7 that is used in vSphere. In addition, you should upgrade VMware Tools on each VM to whatever vSphere version you are running on your host. However, if you are running a mixed environment of hosts and there is a possibility of a VM moving from a vSphere host to a VI3 host due to a Distributed Resource Scheduler (DRS) or HA event, you should not upgrade the virtual hardware and VMware Tools to version 7. You should instead wait until all your hosts are upgraded to vSphere, because although a vSphere host can support either version, a VI3 host can support only the VI3 version of virtual hardware and VMware Tools.

UPGRADE METHODS

There are several ways you can upgrade your environment. Which one you use will depend on the following factors:

- **Downtime**—How much VM downtime you are willing to experience
- **Capacity**—Whether you have enough extra host capacity to move VMs around on hosts so that you can shut hosts down
- **Hardware**—Whether you are using new hardware for your vSphere hosts or reusing your current VI3 hardware

These factors will help determine whether you should do a fresh install or an in-place or migration upgrade when upgrading to vSphere.

Upgrade or Fresh Install

One decision you will have to make is whether to upgrade your existing hosts and vCenter Server or start fresh with a new installation. There are pros and cons to each method. For instance, a fresh install ensures that your hosts and vCenter Server are cleaner, with no residual files that you may have collected from the previous version. However, a fresh install requires that you reconfigure settings and other things that may have been wiped out. For ESX and ESXi hosts, you must reconfigure such things as your virtual networking, local user accounts, and DNS, time, security, and advanced settings. If you have any scripts or agents in the ESX Service Console, you must also reinstall them. Your VMFS datastores will not get overwritten unless you choose to do so, so all your VMs will remain intact once the host is upgraded. Optionally, if you have hosts with spare capacity, you can cold-migrate or VMotion the VMs to those hosts while you perform the upgrade. If you have simple virtual networks and are mostly using default settings on your hosts, a fresh install might make more sense.

For vCenter Server, if you perform a fresh install you will lose all the configuration settings that are unique to vCenter Server, such as clusters, DRS, HA, roles, and permissions, as well as all historical performance statistics for hosts and VMs. This information is stored in the vCenter Server database, which can get quite large over time. For this reason, many people like to start with a fresh database so that all the old data in the database does not carry over to the new server. As part of the upgrade, the vCenter Server database schema is modified and elements such as tables, views, and stored procedures are updated. Again, if your environment is smaller and you don't mind losing your old performance data and reconfiguring things, a fresh install might be the way to go.

The process for this is fairly straightforward. You just remove your hosts from vCenter Server, shut down vCenter Server and install a fresh copy with a fresh database, and then add your hosts back into vCenter Server and reconfigure your settings. Optionally, you can also build a new vCenter Server and leave your existing vCenter Server in place, and then migrate hosts to it one by one.

The disadvantage of fresh installs is that you have more downtime and disruption in your virtual environment and you have to reconfigure all your settings. There are typically a lot more settings in vCenter Server than in ESX and ESXi, and many people do not want to lose their performance data, so many will do fresh installs for ESX and ESXi hosts but not for vCenter Server. If you've upgraded your hosts and vCenter Servers several times in the past, you might want to take advantage of fresh installs to get rid of all the crud that may have carried over each time and was never cleaned up. If you do choose to do a fresh install, make sure you document all your settings so that you know what to reconfigure afterward.

In-Place Upgrade or Migration Upgrade

There are two methods for upgrading hosts and vCenter Servers. You can choose to upgrade them in-place, or build a new environment and migrate your VMs to it. The decision here is highly dependent on whether you have extra hardware available, or if you have enough spare capacity on your hosts to hold your VMs while you shut down the hosts. If you run vCenter Server as a VM, you don't have to worry about extra hardware for that, but you'll need extra host hardware or enough spare capacity.

There are two ways to do a migration: with a new vCenter Server or using an existing vCenter Server. To migrate with a new vCenter Server, you set up a new vSphere environment with a new vCenter Server, and then configure clusters and other settings and move hosts from the old vCenter Server to the new one. You can do all of this while the host is running, without incurring any downtime for the VMs. To upgrade the hosts, you will need to move the VMs off of them or shut them down while you perform the upgrade. Here are some methods you can use to migrate to a new environment with a new vCenter Server. These methods all require shared storage that all hosts can access.

The following method moves 3.x hosts with VMs to vCenter Server 4.0.

1. Build a new vCenter Server 4.0.
2. Disable HA and DRS on the 2.x vCenter Server (unless you have plenty of spare capacity).
3. Configure clusters and settings on the new vCenter Server 4.0.

4. Disconnect a 3.x host from the vCenter Server 2.x.

5. Add the 3.x host to the new vCenter Server 4.0.

6. Continue the process until all 3.x hosts are moved to the new vCenter Server 4.0.

7. Shut down the 3.x hosts and upgrade them to vSphere 4.0. If you have enough capacity, you can do this as a rolling upgrade to reduce or eliminate VM downtime.

The following method moves 3.x hosts without VMs to vCenter Server 4.0.

1. Build a new vCenter Server 4.0.

2. Disable HA and DRS on the vCenter Server 2.x (unless you have plenty of spare capacity).

3. Configure clusters and settings on the new vCenter Server 4.0.

4. Move all VMs from the 3.x host to other hosts in the cluster and disconnect the 3.x host from the 2.x vCenter Server.

5. Rebuild the 3.x host with vSphere 4.0.

6. Add the new 4.0 host to the 4.0 vCenter Server.

7. Remove VMs from inventory (you don't need to shut them down) on 3.x hosts managed by the vCenter Server 2.x.

8. Add VMs to 4.0 hosts managed by the vCenter Server 4.0.

9. Repeat until all 3.x hosts have been upgraded.

These methods become easier if you have new or unused existing server hardware onto which you can install ESX or ESXi 4.0. You would then add the new hosts to the new vCenter Server 4.0 and just move the VMs to the new hosts without shutting down the 3.x hosts in the old environment. The other methods involve having only one environment with only one vCenter Server and are considered an in-place migration. These methods use a single vCenter Server that has been upgraded to vSphere 4.0.

The following method moves VMs to other hosts while upgrading.

1. Move VMs from a 3.x host to other 3.x hosts in the same cluster.

2. Shut down the vacated 3.x host and upgrade it to vSphere 4.0.

3. Power on the new 4.x host.

4. Move VMs from the 3.x host to the new 4.0 host.

5. Continue the process until all hosts are upgraded to vSphere 4.0.

The following method shuts down VMs on the hosts while upgrading.

1. Shut down the VMs on the 3.x host.

2. Shut down the 3.x host and upgrade it to vSphere 4.0.

3. Power on the new 4.0 host.

4. Continue the process until all the hosts are upgraded to vSphere 4.0.

To move VMs from one host to another while they are powered on, you can use the VMotion feature if the VMs are on shared storage. For VMs on local storage you can either shut them down and cold-migrate them, or use Storage VMotion (SVMotion) and VMotion together if you have shared storage to move them to other hosts. Using SVMotion to move VMs on local storage to other hosts is a multistep process, but it does avoid downtime. Here's how to do it.

1. Use SVMotion to move the VM from local storage on Host A to shared storage on Host A.

2. Use VMotion to move the VM from Host A to Host B on the same shared storage.

3. Use SVMotion to move the VM from shared storage on Host B to local storage on Host B (or keep it on shared storage).

Once you decide on a method that meets your requirements, you can begin the upgrade of your virtual environment to vSphere.

UPGRADE TECHNIQUES

Once you are ready to begin upgrading your environment, you should try to test the upgrade process first so that you are comfortable with it. If you have a dedicated test virtual environment, that is the perfect place to start. If not, and you have some extra hardware, try downloading an evaluation copy of VI3, installing it, and then upgrading it to vSphere. Even if you don't do this, you can install vCenter Server 2.x on a VM and practice upgrading it to vSphere. Otherwise, you might try the upgrade first on noncritical hosts that you can afford to have more downtime with in case you run into problems with the upgrade. Read the vSphere Upgrade Guide on VMware's website for the version that you are using; for 4.0 Update 1 the guide is located at http://vmware.com/pdf/vsphere4/r40_u1/vsp_40_u1_upgrade_guide.pdf. Pay very careful attention to the database steps when upgrading vCenter Server as this can be the trickiest part of the upgrade.

ROLLING BACK TO PREVIOUS VERSIONS

It is possible, but not easy, to roll back to previous versions once you have upgraded them. Therefore, before you upgrade a host, vCenter Server, or VM, be absolutely sure you are ready to do it.

Rolling Back vCenter Server

For vCenter Server, it is critical to back up the SQL database before you upgrade; otherwise, once you upgrade it, you cannot go back to the old database schema. Here are the steps for rolling back vCenter Server to a previous version.

1. Completely uninstall vCenter Server 4.0.
2. Restore the vCenter Server 2.x SQL database.
3. Install vCenter Server 2.x and tell it to use an existing database, and select your restored 2.x SQL database.
4. Reconfigure your license server with your 3.x license files.

Rolling Back ESX Hosts

Rolling back to a previous ESX version can be tricky, but it is possible. In most cases, it is easier to just reinstall ESX 3.x. Otherwise, if you want to roll back, here are the steps.

1. In the ESX Service Console, run the `/usr/sbin/rollback-to-esx3` command which reconfigures the bootloader to boot the previous ESX 3.x version. The `-f` parameter forces the rollback and suppresses the confirmation message. Once you run the command, you can no longer boot to ESX 4.0.
2. Reboot the host and it will boot to ESX 3.x.
3. Once the host boots to ESX 3.x, delete the ESX 4.0 Service Console VM folder (`esxconsole-<UUID>`) from the VMFS datastore.

Rolling Back ESXi Hosts

Rolling back to a previous ESXi version is much simpler because it is stored as a single image and ESXi always saves a copy of the previous version image whenever upgrading. Only one previous build is ever stored, and once you revert back to a previous version, it is irreversible; to go to a newer version you must reinstall it. The steps for reverting back to a previous ESXi version are as follows.

1. Reboot the ESXi 4.0 host.

2. When you see the page that displays the current boot build, press Shift-r to select the standby build.

3. Press Shift-y to confirm the selection, and press Enter.

Rolling Back VMs

For VMs, if you upgrade their virtual hardware from version 4 that is used by VI3 to version 7 that is used by vSphere, be aware that this is irreversible. If you snapshot the VM before upgrading it, it is possible to roll back if you revert to the snapshot. There is also a workaround to go back to version 4 using vCenter Converter, as outlined in the following steps.

1. Install vCenter Converter on a workstation and run it.

2. Run the Convert Machine Wizard. For the source, specify a VM type and a vCenter Server/host to connect to on which the VM is located.

3. For the destination type, select a VM and choose the same vCenter Server/host.

4. On the Host/Resource page, give the VM a different name and choose the VM hardware 4 version.

5. Once the process completes, power on the new VM, verify that it works, and then delete the original VM. Once you delete the original VM, rename the new VM to the original VM's name.

PRE-UPGRADE CHECKLIST

Before you upgrade any part of your virtual environment there is a pre-upgrade checklist that you should use to ensure that you are ready and have covered all your bases. VMware has published the complete checklist on its website (www.vmware.com/files/pdf/vsphere-migration-prerequisites-checklist.pdf), but here are some of the most important items.

Prerequisites:

- Be sure all your other VMware products and third-party products are compatible with the vSphere version that you are installing.

- Be sure all your server hardware, I/O devices, and storage devices are listed in the Hardware Compatibility Guide for the version of vSphere that you are installing.

vCenter Server:

- Ensure that the physical or virtual hardware for vCenter Server is sufficient. Although vCenter Server 2.x could get away with one CPU and 1GB of RAM, vCenter 4.0 requires two CPUs and at least 2GB of RAM (preferably 3GB) as the Tomcat service in vCenter Server 4.0 uses much more RAM than in 2.x.

- Ensure that your database is supported; MSDE, SQL Server 2000, and Oracle 9i are no longer supported in vCenter Server 4.0. Upgrade the database to a supported version before upgrading vCenter Server.

- For vCenter Server 4.0, make sure you use a 32-bit ODBC data source; for vCenter Server 4.1, you must use a 64-bit data source.

- If the database is 64-bit Oracle, make sure the default installation path of C:\Program Files(x86) is changed to remove the parentheses ().

- Ensure that for the Microsoft SQL database, the system DSN is using the SQL Native Client driver. You may have to manually install this.

- Ensure that the Oracle and Microsoft SQL databases have the appropriate permissions (MS SQL requires the db_owner privilege on the MSDB and vCenter database).

- Confirm that the vCenter Server system name is no more than 15 characters long.

- Ensure that ports 80, 443, 389, and 686 are not used by any existing application on the vCenter Server system and that there are no firewalls (including Windows firewalls) preventing these ports from/to the vCenter Server system.

- Ensure that you have taken a complete backup of vCenter Server, the vCenter database, templates in the vCenter repository, license files, and SSL certificate files before the install or upgrade.

ESX/ESXi hosts:

- Ensure that there is either a local VMFS or a shared VMFS volume with at least 10GB of free space to store the ESX 4 Service Console .vmdk file.

- Ensure that you have backed up your ESX host (service console files, .vmx files, custom scripts, host configuration files, and local VMFS filesystem).

- Ensure that you have backed up your ESXi host (using VI CLI and the `vicfg-cfgbackup` command).

- For ESX hosts, if you are using any hardware management agents inside the Service Console, make sure you upgrade to the latest version. Also ensure that any third-party agents, scripts, or software is upgraded to the latest version.

Virtual machines:

- Ensure that there are no suspend files for a VM in order to do the VM hardware upgrade.
- Ensure that the VM has a CD-ROM device configured in order for VMware Tools to mount the virtual ISO and install/upgrade VMware Tools.
- Ensure that it is okay to upgrade the VM hardware from version 4 to version 7. Once upgraded, you cannot revert back to an earlier VM format unless you have created a snapshot of the VM prior to the changes.
- Ensure that the VMs are backed up before upgrading them.

Licensing:

- Ensure that you have the necessary licenses for the required features of VMware vSphere. The evaluation license is valid for 60 days after you power on the ESX/ESXi host.
- Ensure that you have a backup copy of the existing VI3 License Server license files.

Once you are sure you meet all the necessary prerequisites, you're ready to begin upgrading your environment.

PHASE 1: UPGRADING vCENTER SERVER

Before you upgrade vCenter Server, you need to make sure you have a good backup of the SQL database and that the SQL database you are using is supported by vCenter Server 4.0. Also make sure you have downloaded the vCenter Server installer and generated your license keys. Upgrading your vCenter Server does not require any host or VM downtime.

BACKING UP KEY FILES

In addition to a database backup, you should also back up the following key files in case you need to roll back to the previous version.

- Back up the SSL certificate folder under `%ALLUSERSPROFILE%\Application Data\VMware\VMware VirtualCenter` or `%ALLUSERSPROFILE%\VMware\VMware VirtualCenter\`.

- Back up the vpxd.cfg file which is located in `%ALLUSERSPROFILE%\Application Data\VMware\VMware VirtualCenter` or `%ALLUSERSPROFILE%\VMware\VMware VirtualCenter\`.

- Back up the license server .lic key file which is usually located in `C:\Program Files\VMware\VMware License Server\Licenses`.

- Make note of your ODBC DSN, username, and password.

AGENT PRE-UPGRADE CHECK TOOL

As part of the upgrade to vCenter Server, all of the hosts that are managed by it must have their vCenter Server agent (vpxa) that is running on them upgraded as well. It is fairly common to have this process fail on some hosts for various reasons, and as a result, they become disconnected from vCenter Server after the upgrade. When this happens you can manually get the agent to install, but the Agent Pre-upgrade Check tool is available that is designed to prevent the failure from happening. The tool checks each host for some of the usual things that cause the agent installation to fail. This includes making sure the host has sufficient disk space on the Service Console partitions, the host is reachable, the filesystem is intact, and any required patches are applied.

You can launch the tool from the vCenter Server installer; it is listed under Utility. Once you run the tool, it goes out to VMware's website and downloads any new updates that are available for it. When the wizard launches follow these steps to complete it.

1. At the Database Connect screen, choose your ODBC DSN to connect to, and enter a username and password for it as well as the credential type. If you are using the built-in database, you can select Use VirtualCenter credentials.

2. At the Select Mode screen, choose to scan all hosts or select custom mode to select the hosts; if you select custom mode, the next screen will let you choose the hosts.

3. At the Run Test screen, click the "Run precheck" button to begin checking the hosts. This will not cause any disruption to your hosts or to the VMs

running on them. Once the scan completes, click the Next button to see the results.

4. At the Pre-check screen, you will see your hosts listed as the results of the test. Click the links to see each host's individual report, or click the Run Report button for the full results.

If any of the hosts fail, read the results and resolve any issues with them. When you're finished, you're ready to upgrade vCenter Server.

RUNNING THE vCENTER SERVER INSTALLER

When you are ready to begin the upgrade, run the vCenter Server 4.0 installer by running the autorun.exe file on the install media. From the vSphere vCenter Server installer menu, choose the vCenter Server product installer and follow these steps.

1. At the Welcome screen, the installer will detect a previous vCenter Server version. Click Next to begin the upgrade.

2. At the License Agreement screen, accept the agreement and click Next.

3. At the Customer Information screen, enter your information and optionally enter a vCenter Server 4.0 license key. If you do not enter one, you can always enter one later, as it will use a 60-day evaluation key instead. Click Next to continue.

4. At the Database Options screen, the ODBC DSN that is already used by vCenter Server will be selected and you must provide a username/password if you are using SQL authentication; if you are using Windows authentication, you can leave this field blank. If you are using the built-in database, you can leave those fields blank also. Click Next to continue.

5. You may receive a message that some of the existing extensions (e.g., Update Manager, Converter) will not be compatible after the upgrade. You can upgrade them manually afterward using the vCenter Server product installer. Click OK to continue.

6. At the Database Upgrade screen, you have an option to upgrade the existing vCenter Server database. If you choose not to upgrade, you cannot continue, as the database upgrade is required. You also must check the box confirming that you have backed up your database and SSL certificates before you can continue. This screen is meant as a final warning to let you know your database will be upgraded, and if you do not have a backup, you cannot roll back to vCenter Server 2.x. Click Next to continue.

7. At the vCenter Server Service screen, either accept the default to use the built-in SYSTEM account or specify a user domain account instead. Click Next to continue.

8. At the Configure Ports screen, you have the option to change any of the default port numbers that are used by vCenter Server. It's recommended that you leave these at the defaults, unless you have changed the ports on your other servers because of a conflict. Be aware that if you are running another web server on the vCenter Server, such as Microsoft Internet Information Services (IIS), ports 80 and 443 will conflict with vCenter Server's built-in Tomcat web server. Click Next to continue.

9. At the Ready to Install screen, click the Install button to begin the upgrade. Your database will be upgraded as part of the vCenter Server installation. If you are upgrading from vCenter Server 2.5, the Database Upgrade Wizard runs in the background and requires no interaction. If you are upgrading from vCenter Server 2.0.x, the Database Upgrade Wizard appears and you must complete the wizard. If the Database Upgrade Wizard does display, you will have the option to keep the existing performance data, discard it, or keep only the last 12 months of it. If you keep the data, the upgrade will take quite a while if there is a lot of old performance data in the database.

10. The installer will run and will install and configure various components as well as upgrade the database. Once it completes, click Finish and the wizard will close. You will need to restart the system next.

POST-INSTALLATION STEPS

Once the vCenter Server restarts, you will need to connect to it using the vSphere Client. If you try to connect with the VI3 Client, you will get an error message stating that the required client support files need to be retrieved from the server and installed. You can run the vSphere Client installer by choosing the Run the Installer option; you can also download it and run it manually. In addition, you can access the vSphere Client installer from the vCenter Server install image or by accessing the vCenter Server with a web browser. When you run the vSphere Client installer you will also have the option to install the Host Update utility which you can use to upgrade hosts from VI3 to vSphere.

Once you install the vSphere Client and connect to the vCenter Server, the first thing you will want to do is set up the legacy licensing for your VI3 hosts. The hosts will be okay for 14 days if a licensing server is not available, but it is best to do this right away. If you did an in-place upgrade, you will not have to do anything, as this is taken care of automatically, even if your license server is on another server. You should verify, though, that your VMware License Server service is running.

If you uninstalled vCenter Server or did a clean installation, you will need to configure the legacy licensing support. To do this select vCenter Server Settings under the Administration section and then select Licensing in the left pane. In the right pane, you can enter the IP address/host name of a new or existing VI3 licensing server and check the option to Reconfigure ESX 3 hosts. You can verify that the VI3 licenses are being read by selecting Licensing under the Administration section. All your VI3 licenses should be displayed in the Product view.

After the installation, if you are using an Oracle database, you should copy the Oracle JDBC Driver (ojdbc14.jar) to the <VMware vCenter Server>\tomcat\lib folder. For SQL Server databases, if you enabled bulk logging for the upgrade, disable it after the upgrade is complete.

Finally, you will want to upgrade your extensions to the new vSphere versions. To do this, run the vCenter Server 4.0 installer and select each extension. You can install the Update Manager, Converter, and Guided Consolidation extensions. When you run the installation, the installer will detect the old version of each extension and automatically upgrade it. After you upgrade the extensions, you must also upgrade the plug-in component in each vSphere Client instance by going to the Plug-in Manager and installing the new plug-ins.

PHASE 2: UPGRADING ESX AND ESXi

You have several options for upgrading your ESX and ESXi hosts to vSphere. The first option is to use the Update Manager plug-in that comes with vCenter Server. The second is to use the Host Update utility that installs with the vSphere Client that is normally used to patch/upgrade ESXi hosts. The Host Update utility is typically used to patch stand-alone hosts when vCenter Server is not being used, but in vSphere, it can now upgrade VI3 ESX hosts to vSphere as well. The final option is to simply burn the vSphere install ISO to a DVD, boot the host from it, and run through the installer.

Update Manager is much more robust than the Host Update utility, and you can orchestrate upgrades so that both hosts and VMs are updated. You can schedule upgrades via Update Manager, and automation and workflow are built into it to make the process much easier. The Host Update utility provides an easy way to upgrade hosts from a remote location, without a CD, and with minimal down time. The utility upgrades the VMkernel and the service console on ESX hosts, and upgrades the image of ESXi hosts. It does not upgrade VMFS datastores, VM hardware, or VMware Tools, as Update Manager does.

USING THE HOST UPDATE UTILITY

The Host Update utility is an optional add-on when installing the vSphere Client. If you do not have it, you can simply reinstall the vSphere Client to install it.[1] Once you are ready to use it to upgrade your host, follow these steps.

1. Launch the Host Update utility and you will first be prompted that the utility needs to download patches from the VMware patch repository. Click No for this, as we are using the utility to upgrade hosts and not patch them.

2. From the top menu, select Host and then select Add Host and enter the IP address/host name of the host you wish to update. The host information will be displayed; note that patching is supported only for ESXi hosts and not for ESX hosts, but you can use the utility to upgrade ESX hosts.

3. You will need to put the host in maintenance mode before you can upgrade it, so shut down the VMs on the host or move them to other hosts before proceeding.

4. To begin the upgrade, click the Upgrade Host button and the Upgrade Wizard will launch.

5. At the Image Location screen, select the ISO or ZIP file of the ESX/ESXi 4.0 image that you wish to use to upgrade the host to, and click Next to continue.

6. The ISO will be validated. At the EULA screen, accept the licensing agreement and click Next to continue.

7. At the Host Credentials screen, enter the host user credentials (root) and click Next. If you have not placed the host in maintenance mode yet, you will be warned that you need to before proceeding. At the Host Compatibility Check screen, the host will be checked and any problems will be noted; if there are no problems, it will automatically go to the next screen.

8. At the Console OS Settings screen, select a datastore and size for the Service Console virtual disk file. You must choose either a local or a storage area network (SAN) datastore, as neither software iSCSI nor NFS datastores are

---

[1] Beginning with vSphere 4.1 the Host Update utility was dropped and the only update methods available are using Update Manager and the vihostupdate/esxupdate command line utilities.

supported for this. If you are using a SAN datastore, it cannot be shared with other hosts and it must be zoned to only that host. The minimum size for the virtual disk is 7.82GB; however, if you want to create additional partitions inside the Service Console per the recommendations in Chapter 11, you should increase this to at least 18GB. Once you select a datastore and size, click Next to continue.

9. At the Post-Upgrade Options screen, choose whether a rollback will be attempted in case the upgrade fails. In addition, you can choose to run a post-upgrade script and also select to roll back the upgrade if the script fails. Click Next to continue.

10. At the Ready to Complete screen, click Finish to begin the upgrade. The upgrade will proceed and the status will be displayed. First the ISO image will be copied to the host, and then the host will be shut down and restarted and the upgrade will begin. The new Service Console VM will be created and partitioned, and the packages will be installed inside it; then it will reboot again once it is complete.

When the host restarts you will get a message that the upgrade has succeeded. If the upgrade failed for whatever reason, you should restart the Host Update utility before trying again. You can also view the log located on the host in the `/var/log/vmware/vua.log` file. If the host shows Disconnected in vCenter Server afterward, right-click on it and select Connect. Finally, exit maintenance mode, and the upgrade will be complete and your host will be ready to use.

USING UPDATE MANAGER

Update Manager uses baselines that are created and then used to determine if a host is compliant with the specification of the baseline. If it is not, the host is remediated to bring it into compliance with the baseline. To upgrade hosts to vSphere with Update Manager, you need to first create a new upgrade baseline for vSphere 4.0. Once you create the baseline, you attach it to the host and then the upgrade begins. To create a new baseline, follow these steps.

1. Launch Update Manager from the vSphere Client, select the Baseline and Groups tab, and then select the Upgrade Baselines tab below it.

2. Click the Create link to create an Upgrade Baseline.

3. At the Baseline Name & Type screen, enter a name for the baseline and choose the Host Upgrade baseline type; click Next to continue.

4. At the Upgrade Version screen, select an upgrade ISO file to use for ESX hosts and an upgrade ZIP file to use for ESXi hosts. These files are available on the vSphere download page on VMware's website. Once you click Next, the files will be uploaded to the Update Manager server and imported.

5. At the COS VMDK Location screen, choose to automatically use a datastore which will use a local datastore, or manually choose a datastore instead. Click Next to continue.

6. At the Post-upgrade Options screen, choose whether a rollback will be attempted in case the upgrade fails. In addition, you can choose to run a post-upgrade script and select to roll back the upgrade if the script fails. Click Next to continue.

7. At the Ready to Complete screen, click Finish to create the baseline.

Now that you have a baseline created, you can attach it to your VI3 hosts to bring them into compliance with the baseline. When you attach the baseline to your hosts, your hosts will be evaluated, and if they are not in compliance with the baseline, they will be upgraded to bring them into compliance. Follow these steps to attach the baseline to a host.

1. In the Hosts and Clusters tab, select the VI3 host that you want to upgrade to vSphere, and in the right pane select the Update Manager tab.

2. Click the link to Attach the vSphere upgrade baseline to the host.

3. Once the baseline is attached, click the Remediate button to begin the process of upgrading the host to make it compliant.

4. The Remediation Wizard will launch; at the Remediation Selection screen, select the Upgrade baseline and click Next to continue.

5. At the EULA screen, accept the licensing agreement and click Next to continue.

6. At the ESX 4.0 Upgrade screen, you have the option to change the COS VMDK Location, Rollback on Failure, and Post-upgrade Script settings. These settings will display even if you are upgrading an ESXi host, in which case you can ignore them. Click Next to continue.

7. At the Host Remediation Options screen, choose to have the remediation occur immediately, or scheduled for a later time. In addition, you can specify failure options for when the host is placed in maintenance mode. If VMs cannot be powered off or VMotioned to other hosts, you can specify to retry, fail the task, power them off, or suspend them. Click Next to continue.

8. At the Ready to Complete screen, click Finish to begin the remediation. The host will automatically enter maintenance mode and restart, and the upgrade will begin.

Once the remediation completes, the host will show as compliant and will automatically exit maintenance mode. If the upgrade fails, you can check the logs to try to find out why. On ESXi hosts, you can use the vSphere Client to export the logs, which are located in `/esx3-installation/esx4-upgrade/` and `/var/log/vmware/`. For ESX hosts, the logs are located in `/esx4-upgrade/` and `/var/log/vmware/` on the host server.

POST-UPGRADE CONSIDERATIONS

Once you upgrade your hosts, there are some steps you may need to perform afterward to clean them up.

- If vCenter Server manages the host, you must reconnect the host to vCenter Server by right-clicking the host in the vCenter Server inventory and selecting Connect.

- When the upgrade is complete, ESX/ESXi is in evaluation mode. Evaluation mode lasts for 60 days. You must assign an upgraded license to your product within 60 days of the upgrade.

- After the ESX/ESXi upgrade, third-party agents are disabled but remain on the disk. To reenable them, you must reinstall them. You can use the `vihostupdate` vSphere CLI command to install third-party extensions.

- For ESX hosts only, the web access service is disabled by default in vSphere as a security measure. If you want to enable it, follow these steps.

   1. Log in to the ESX Service Console.

   2. Type `service vmware-webAccess status` to check the status of the service.

   3. Type `service vmware-webAccess start` to start the service. The service will run only until the host is restarted.

   4. To have the service start each time the host boots, type `chkconfig --level 345 vmware-webAccess on`.

- Once you have determined the upgrade is stable, you can remove the ESX3 instance from the bootloader menu that displays when the host starts up. This removes the ability to roll back to ESX3 and deletes the ESX3 files from the /boot directory, deletes the ESX3 references from the /etc/fstab directory, and deletes the /usr/sbin/rollback-to-esx3 script. To remove ESX3 from the bootloader menu, follow these steps.

1. Log in to the ESX Service Console.

2. Type `cleanup-esx3`; optionally, you can use the `-f` parameter to suppress the confirmation message.

3. Reboot the host. The ESX3 option will be gone from the bootloader menu.

- Once you have upgraded all your VI3 hosts to vSphere, you can uninstall the VMware License Server application from the vCenter Server.

PHASE 3: UPGRADING VIRTUAL MACHINES

After you upgrade your hosts to vSphere, you need to upgrade your VMs as well. This includes upgrading the virtual hardware from version 4 that is used in VI3 to version 7 that is used in vSphere, and also upgrading VMware Tools to the latest version. However, if there is a possibility that the VMs will be migrated to a VI3 host due to a VMotion, HA, or DRS event, you should wait as the version 7 VM hardware is not supported on VI3 hosts. There are two ways you can upgrade both the virtual hardware and VMware Tools. You can use the vSphere Client and upgrade VMs one by one, or you can use Update Manager and update many VMs at once. You must first power off the VMs to upgrade their virtual hardware. VMware Tools upgrades can be done while the VM is powered on, but Windows VMs must be restarted afterward. The process for upgrading Windows VMs is as follows.

1. Power on the VM.

2. Upgrade VMware Tools.

3. Reboot the VM at the end of the VMware Tools upgrade.

4. Power off the VM.

5. Upgrade the virtual hardware.

6. Power on the VM. Windows detects new devices and prompts you to reboot the VM.

7. Reboot the VM to make the devices work properly.

UPGRADING VMWARE TOOLS

To upgrade VMware Tools on a VM using the vSphere Client, follow these steps.

1. Make sure the VMs are powered on, open the console for the VM, and log in to the guest OS.

2. Select the VM in the vSphere Client, right-click on it, and select Guest and then Install/Upgrade VMware Tools.

3. Choose either an Interactive or Automatic upgrade. The Interactive option allows you to select which components to install. The Automatic option will install VMware Tools without prompts and automatically restart the VM afterward.

To upgrade VMware Tools on multiple VMs at once, follow these steps.

1. Select a host in the left pane, and then select the Virtual Machine tab.

2. Hold the Ctrl key while clicking on multiple powered-on VMs.

3. Once you have selected them all, right-click and select Guest→Install/Upgrade VMware Tools.

To configure VMs to automatically upgrade VMware Tools when they boot, follow these steps.

1. Power off the VM.

2. Edit the settings of the VM.

3. On the Options tab, select VMware Tools in the left pane, and in the right pane under Advanced, put a checkmark by the "Check and upgrade Tools before each power-on" field.

The next time the VM is powered on it will install or upgrade VMware Tools automatically and restart if necessary.

UPGRADING VIRTUAL MACHINE HARDWARE

Upgrading virtual hardware from version 4 to version 7 is reversible if you take a VM backup or snapshot before performing the upgrade. If you do not take a snapshot before upgrading, you must use vCenter Converter to create a new VM with version 4 hardware. VMs must be powered off when their virtual hardware is upgraded. Also make sure you upgrade VMware Tools before upgrading virtual hardware. To upgrade the virtual hardware of a VM, follow these steps.

1. Power off the VM.

2. Select the VM in the vSphere Client, right-click on it, and select Upgrade Virtual Hardware.

3. Choose Yes at the confirmation message and the upgrade will proceed.

4. Power on the VM.

5. Log in to Windows. Restart once the new devices are detected.

To upgrade virtual hardware on multiple VMs at once, follow these steps.

1. Select a host in the left pane, and then select the Virtual Machine tab.

2. Hold the Ctrl key while clicking on multiple powered-off VMs.

3. Once you have selected them all, right-click and select Upgrade Virtual Hardware.

Using Update Manager to Upgrade VMware Tools and Virtual Hardware

You can also use Update Manager to upgrade VMware Tools on VMs. Baselines have already been created for VMs to upgrade their VMware Tools and virtual hardware version to match the host, as shown in Figure 12.2.

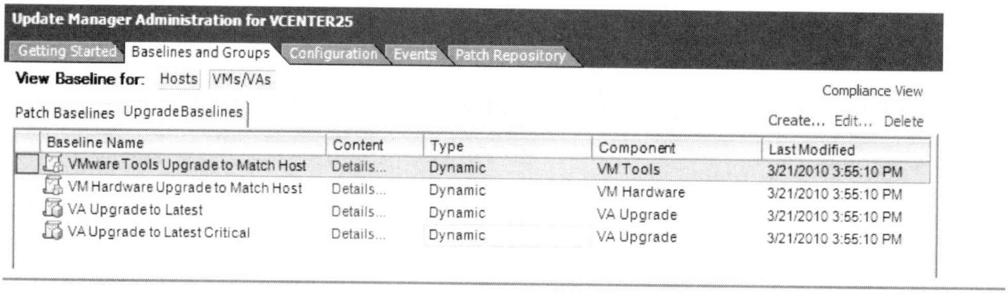

Figure 12.2 Upgrading virtual hardware and VMware Tools using baselines

To upgrade VMs using Update Manager, just attach those baselines to the VMs and remediate them, and they will automatically be upgraded.

Once you upgrade your VM hardware, you can take advantage of the features in vSphere that require the new hardware. One new feature in particular that you may want to take advantage of is the new VMXNET3 virtual NIC (vNIC) type that offers more features and better performance than the VMXNET2 vNIC.

SUMMARY

Upgrading your virtual environment to vSphere is exciting, as you can finally start using the many new features that are available in vSphere. It is best to get some experience using vSphere before upgrading so that you are better prepared to use it. Read through the documentation, set up a test lab if you can, and look through the Upgrade Center web page (www.vmware.com/products/vsphere/upgrade-center/) on VMware's website. There are many great guides, tools, and videos that can help prepare you for your upgrade to vSphere. The more prepared and experienced you are beforehand the smoother your upgrade will be when you go to do it.

CREATING AND CONFIGURING VIRTUAL MACHINES

Virtual machines (VMs) in vSphere are different from the previous VI3 release, and there are many changes that you need to be aware of when creating them. It's very easy to create a VM in vSphere using the default settings, but there are many configuration options and virtual hardware choices that you can change that can make a huge impact on how your VM functions. Making the wrong choices can degrade your VM's performance and cause it to not function properly, which can affect the applications running on it. In this chapter, we will cover the various options and settings that you will need to consider when creating a VM to help ensure that you make the right choices.

CREATING A VIRTUAL MACHINE IN VSPHERE

In this section, we will step through the process of creating a VM in vSphere and discuss what you will need to know to create and configure it properly.

CREATING A VIRTUAL MACHINE

There are various methods for creating VMs. You can use prebuilt templates, clone an existing VM, import a VM from an OVF file, use Converter to turn a physical server into a VM, or create a VM from scratch. Here we will discuss how to create a new VM from scratch. To get started you first need to open the vSphere Client and connect to your vCenter Server (or individual host). Then follow these steps.

1. Select an object in the left pane. This can be a datacenter, host, cluster, resource pool, and so on. Right-click on the object and select New Virtual Machine. This loads the Create New Virtual Machine Wizard.

2. The first screen of the wizard prompts you for the configuration type for creating the VM, and the options are either Typical or Custom. If you choose Typical, the wizard will not display some of the more advanced configuration options, such as choosing the VM hardware version, number of vCPUs, amount of RAM, number/types of NICs, and advanced disk options. For this example, choose the Custom configuration option.

3. At the Name and Location screen, enter a unique name for your VM. Note that this does not have to match the name defined in the VM operating system, but it's usually a good idea that they match to avoid confusion. The name supplied here is used to create the VM's directory on the datastore you select, and is also used to name all the files that make up the VM. You can also choose an inventory location here from any datacenter objects that you have configured. If you did not select a host object in step 1, you will also be prompted to select a host on which your VM will reside.

4. Depending on whether you have any resource pools configured, in the next screen choose a resource pool in which your VM will reside. If you have none, you will not see this screen.

5. At the Datastore screen, choose the datastore on which your VM will reside. Any local and shared datastores that are available to that host will be displayed. Make sure that whatever datastore you choose has sufficient storage space available for the size of the VM disk you want to create.

6. Next, choose the VM hardware version. The default is version 7, which is new to vSphere; you can also choose version 4, which was used in VI3. If the VM is in a mixed environment of vSphere and VI3 hosts, and has the chance of being migrated to a VI3 host due to a High Availability (HA), Distributed Resource Scheduler (DRS), or VMotion event, you should choose version 4; otherwise, stick with version 7, as it is required for some of the features that are new to vSphere to work.

7. At the Guest Operating System screen, choose the guest OS that your VM will be running. It's important to note that this does not automatically install whatever OS you choose. Although you can install an OS other than what is specified by this selection (e.g., you can choose Red Hat Linux and

install Windows Server 2003), it is important that you not do this. Many people often do not understand what this setting does, and the importance of setting this correctly is understated in the wizard. The guest OS selection does several important things.

- It determines whether features such as CPU Hot Plug and Memory Hot Add will be allowed based on whether the OS supports them.
- It determines what VMware Tools install ISO to mount when installing on a VM.
- It determines the defaults for other configuration screens in the VM creation wizard.
- It determines which virtual hardware devices will be made available to the VM.
- It enables the host to better handle specific hardware quirks that may be unique to the OS chosen.

Setting this incorrectly can negatively affect the performance of your VM and occasionally can cause high CPU utilization, so it's important to set this correctly. Make absolutely sure you choose the correct OS, edition, version, and 32/64-bit release to match the guest OS to be installed on the VM.

8. At the CPU screen, choose the number of vCPUs to assign to your VM. This will be between one and eight or between one and the maximum number of combined physical CPUs/cores in your host. For example, if your host has two dual-core CPUs, the most vCPUs that you can assign to a VM is four; you cannot overcommit CPU resources, like you can with memory and disk resources. Resist assigning more vCPUs than necessary to the VM, as you can actually slow the VM down in some situations when you have too many vSMP VMs running on a host and the CPU scheduler has trouble scheduling them all. Many applications will run just fine with one vCPU, but you should test to find out how many work best for your application.

9. At the Memory screen, select the amount of memory to assign to the VM. You can assign from 4MB to 255GB to a VM, regardless of the amount of RAM a host physically has; this is called memory overcommitment, and it is possible thanks to a virtual swap file (.vswp) that is created for the VM when it is powered on in its home directory. The .vswp file is the size of the amount of memory that is assigned to the VM minus the size of any memory reservations. Take care to only assign the amount of memory to a VM that it actually needs to support the applications running on it. You can easily increase this later if needed.

10. At the Network screen, select the number of virtual NICs (vNICs), their type, and the network to which they are assigned. Note that although a VM supports up to ten NICs in vSphere, only four can be assigned to it while it is created; you can add additional NICs later by editing the VM's settings. The networks shown will be whatever networks are configured on the virtual switch (vSwitch) port groups of the host on which the VM is being created. The adapter types shown will vary based on the guest OS that was selected in step 7, as some adapters are not supported by certain operating systems. The vNIC adapter types are covered in more detail in Chapter 6.

11. At the SCSI Controller screen, select the type of SCSI controller to use with your VM's hard disk. If you want to use an Integrated Development Environment (IDE) adapter instead, the process to select it is not straightforward. You first have to select a SCSI controller, and then, in the Advanced Options screen for creating a disk, you need to switch the virtual device node from SCSI to IDE. Even though the Summary screen will show that a SCSI adapter will be used when creating the VM, if you edit the settings of the VM after it is created the SCSI adapter will not be present. Instead, a hidden IDE adapter is used, which is also used by the VM's CD/DVD drive. Be aware that some operating systems (e.g., Windows Server 2003) do not have drivers for the newer controller types, such as the new LSI Logic SAS. You will need to download the driver and mount it to the VM's CD/DVD or floppy drive during the operating system installation. Additionally, vSphere 4.0 did not support the use of VMware paravirtualization controllers for boot disks; it is supported beginning in vSphere 4.0 Update 1. The SCSI controller types are covered in more detail in Chapter 5.

12. At the Select a Disk screen, choose a virtual disk option for the VM. There are four options from which to choose.

   • **Create a new virtual disk**—This option simply creates a new virtual disk to be used with the VM. If you choose this option and click Next, you will get a Create a Disk screen that lets you choose the size of the virtual disk to create, provisioning options, and a location for the virtual disk. The default disk created will be Lazy-Zeroed thick; you can change this using the Disk Provisioning options. You can create thin disks by choosing the "Allocate and commit space on demand" option, and you can create Eager-Zeroed thick disks by choosing the "Support clustering features such as Fault Tolerance" option. The different virtual disk types are discussed in Chapter 3. You can also specify a separate datastore for your virtual disk other than the one chosen in step 5 for the VM.

- **Use an existing virtual disk**—This option lets you choose an existing virtual disk file to use with the VM. If you choose this option and click Next, you will get a Select an Existing Disk screen where you can browse through datastores and directories to select an existing virtual disk file.

- **Raw Device Mappings**—This option lets you choose to use a Raw Device Mapping (RDM, covered in Chapter 3) as your virtual disk file. If you choose this option, you will be presented with several different screens to select an RDM. The first screen is the Select Target LUN screen, which displays a list of all unused LUNs from which to choose. Next, a Select Datastore screen is displayed which gives you two options for storing the LUN mapping file: You can choose to store it on the datastore that you selected for the VM in step 5, or you can store it on an alternate datastore. Next, a Compatibility Mode screen is displayed that lets you choose between physical and virtual compatibility modes. Physical mode will allow the guest to access the LUN directly, but does not allow snapshots to be taken of the RDM, if you choose virtual snapshots are allowed.

- **Do not create disk**—This option will not create a virtual disk for your VM. If you choose this option, you can always create a virtual disk later on if needed. You can use this option when booting your VM from Live CDs.

13. If you chose to create a new disk or use an existing disk, an Advanced Option screen will be displayed. In this screen, choose a virtual device node and the disk mode. The virtual device node is the SCSI ID of the disk which consists of the controller number and device number (e.g., 0:0). Here you can also select an IDE device node. If you select this type, the SCSI controller you chose earlier will be removed from the VM and a hidden IDE controller will be used instead. The IDE controller has two channels, each supporting a master and slave device (hence the 0-0, 0-1, 1-0, 1-1 node numbers), and is also used for CD-DVD drives assigned to the VM. You can set the disk mode to Independent, which means it will not be included in snapshots. Here you also can choose whether the disk is Persistent or Nonpersistent; you would typically want to use Persistent disks, as all changes to Nonpersistent disks are discarded when a VM is powered off. Once you select the virtual device node and disk mode, click Next.

14. At the Ready to Complete screen, a summary of all the VM options that you selected is displayed. If necessary, select the checkbox to edit the VM settings before you continue, which allows you to edit the settings and remove or add devices as needed. Click Continue to edit the VM's settings or click Finish to create the VM.

Once you click Finish, if you did not choose to edit the VM's settings, you will see the Create Virtual Machine task in the vSphere Client. When it completes, your VM will be ready to be powered on and you will be able to install an operating system on it.

INSTALLING VMWARE TOOLS

VMware Tools is a suite of utilities that you can install on VMs. It contains drivers and applications that help optimize the guest operating system to run on a VMware host. VMware Tools is bundled with all ESX/ESXi hosts, and there are different versions of it that are specific to different operating system types. VMware Tools is not required for a VM to run, but it is highly recommended that you install it for the added functionality (e.g., time synchronization) and benefits that it provides. VMware Tools contains the following components:

- Enhanced and optimized device drivers, including video, network, SCSI, memory, VMCI, and mouse drivers, as well as a sync driver designed to work with Consolidated Backup

- A control panel inside the guest operating system from which you can change certain settings and connect/disconnect virtual drives

- A memory balloon driver that inflates and deflates to optimize the memory management of the host server

- A service that can synchronize the guest's clock with the host server's clock and also controls the seamless grab and release of the mouse cursor on Windows VMs

- A set of scripts that run when a VM's power state changes that can help automate operations on the guest operating system

- And a user process that controls copying and pasting between a VM and a remote console session

Installing VMware Tools is pretty straightforward and simple on Windows operating systems, as outlined in the following steps.

1. Open a remote console session to the VM with the vSphere Client and power the VM on.

2. Once the VM boots up, log in to the operating system.

3. From the top menu of the remote console, choose Guest and then select the Install/Upgrade VMware Tools option. Optionally, you can select this option by right-clicking on the VM in the vSphere Client view.

4. Click OK on the initial message that is displayed, and then the Installation Wizard will be launched. Click Next on the Welcome screen to continue.

5. Choose from one of the three setup types (Typical, Complete, or Custom). In most cases, you will want to select Typical. Custom lets you choose from the various components, device drivers, and SDKs to install, and Complete installs some additional components that are not included with Typical and are not used that often, such as Shared Folders. Click Next once you select a setup type.

6. Click Install to begin the installation. When the installation completes a window may appear on Windows systems stating that hardware acceleration is not enabled and asking if you want to enable it. It is recommended that you do this to improve mouse and video performance. If you select Yes, a Display Properties window will be opened as well as a Notepad window containing instructions on how to enable hardware acceleration. To enable it click the Advanced button in the Settings tab of the Display Properties window. A new window will be opened; click on the Troubleshoot tab of that window. Next, move the Hardware Acceleration slider from None to Full, and click OK when completed. Then click OK again to close the Display Properties window.

7. Once you click Finish on the VMware Tools installation, you will be prompted to reboot the guest VM, which you can choose to do immediately or later on. A few of the drivers take effect without a reboot, but it is recommended that you reboot the VM so that all of the new drivers will be loaded.

Installing VMware Tools on other operating systems (Linux, Solaris, and Netware) is a bit more complicated. For detailed information on installing VMware Tools on non-Windows operating systems, see the Basic System Administration documentation on VMware's website, or the following VMware Knowledge Base articles:

- http://kb.vmware.com/kb/1018392
- http://kb.vmware.com/kb/1018414
- And http://kb.vmware.com/kb/340

Once VMware Tools is installed, you can launch a control panel application that lets you configure a few options, such as time synchronization, connecting virtual devices, and setting script options for power events. To open the application on Windows systems just double-click on the icon that appears in the system tray; if the icon has been hidden, you can access it using the Windows control panel. To open the application on Linux and Solaris guests, open a terminal window and enter the command /usr/bin/vmware-toolbox &.

You can use the vSphere Client to keep track of your VMs and of whether VMware Tools is installed and up-to-date. Just select the Virtual Machine tab on any object (e.g., host, cluster, datacenter) to see a list of all VMs in that object and you will see a VMware Tools status column. If you don't see the VMware Tools column, right-click on the column headings and a selection menu will appear where you can select which columns are displayed.

VM HARDWARE, OPTIONS, AND RESOURCE CONTROLS

You have many configuration options to choose from when setting up your VMs. It's important that you understand these settings so that you can set them correctly and not cause problems with your VMs. These settings are available when you edit the VM's settings. The settings fall into three categories: Hardware, Options, and Resources, which appear in tabs of the same names in the Virtual Machine Properties window.

VM HARDWARE

The Hardware tab of the Virtual Machine Properties window lets you add and remove virtual hardware to and from your VMs, as well as configure some of the various hardware components that are installed in your VM, as shown in Figure 13.1.

There is a new option in vSphere to show all hardware devices of a VM. This displays additional hardware that is normally hidden, such as PCI and IDE controllers. However, there are no settings for these devices that you can change, and it is purely informational. Here are the various hardware components that you can use with your VM.

- **Memory**—You can set this in 4MB intervals from 4MB up to 255GB. The upper limit is not defined by the amount of memory a host physically has, but rather by how much is supported by ESX. It's possible to assign more

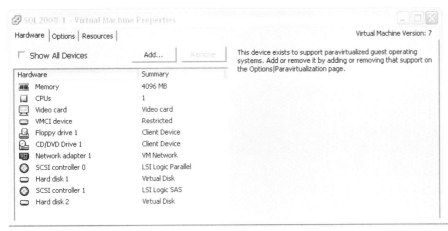

Figure 13.1   Editing a VM's hardware

memory than a host physically has because of the .vswp file that is created and used if a host runs out of physical memory. You can change the amount of memory a VM is assigned only when the VM is powered off.

- **CPUs**—You can set this from one to eight depending on the number of physical CPUs and cores that your host server has present and whether it supports hyperthreading. The amount you can select will change based on your host server. For example, you will only be able to select one or two on a host that has only two physical single-core, nonhyperthreading processors. You can change the number of CPUs only when a VM is powered off.

- **Video card**—A VM will always have one video card, which cannot be removed. You can configure the number of displays (from one to ten) and the amount of memory (from 1.17MB to 128MB) that the video card will have. You cannot enable 3D support on ESX hosts, as it is meant for use with VMware Workstation VMs. You can change the video card settings only when the VM is powered off.

- **VMCI device**—A VM will always have one VMCI device, which cannot be removed. If enabled, it will allow high-speed communication between the VM and other VMs that have it enabled, as well as the host. You can enable/disable the VMCI device only while the VM is powered off. VMCI is covered in detail in Chapter 3.

- **Floppy drive**—A VM can have up to two floppy drives, and you can only add or remove them when the VM is powered off. Configurable settings include the device status (connected or not) and device type (use client/host device or an image), which you can change while the VM is either powered off or on.

- **CD/DVD drive**—A VM can have up to four CD/DVD drives that you can add or remove only when the VM is powered off. Configurable settings include the device status (connected or not), device type (use client/host device or an image), and mode (Pass-through or Emulate IDE), which you can change while the VM is either powered off or on. Additionally, you can change the virtual device node (either 0:0, 0:1, 1:0, or 1:1) only while the VM is powered off.

- **Network adapter**—A VM can have up to ten network adapters that you can add or remove only when the VM is powered off. Configurable settings include device status (connected or not) and network label, which you can configure while the VM is either powered on or off. You can change the MAC address of the network adapter while the VM is powered off. You cannot change the adapter type at all; if you want to change the type, you need to remove the adapter and add a new one with the desired type.

- **SCSI controller**—A VM can have up to four SCSI controllers that you can add or remove only when the VM is powered off. You cannot manually add a SCSI controller to a VM, as they are automatically added or removed when you add hard disks and assign them a virtual device node ID. When you add hard disks to a VM, they will default to use the existing SCSI controller unless you select a virtual device node on another SCSI controller. Additionally, you can change the SCSI controller type (BusLogic or LSI Logic) and the SCSI bus sharing option only while the VM is powered off. SCSI bus sharing allows for the sharing of a disk between VMs (although only one VM can be powered on and used it at any given time).

- **Hard disk**—A VM can have up to 60 hard disks, 15 per SCSI controller. The virtual device node ID (e.g., 0:0) that you can set is a combination of the controller number followed by the hard disk device number. The device number will be incremented when new hard disks are added, until all the devices are used up on it (up to 15). It will then add another SCSI controller (from one to three) as needed for additional disks. Optionally, you can choose to manually set a virtual device node ID to force it to add another controller. You do this in the Advanced Options section when adding a hard disk. If you choose a virtual device node ID that is not on an existing controller (e.g., 1:0), a new controller will be added. You can add hard disks while a VM is either powered on or off, but you can remove them only while the VM is powered off. You can increase the size of a hard disk while a VM is powered on, but you cannot decrease it. You can change virtual device node IDs on existing drives only when a VM is powered off; take care, though, as doing this may change your disks around in your operating system and cause the VM to fail to boot. An additional option that you can change when the VM is powered off is the disk mode (Independent, Persistent or Independent, Nonpersistent).

- **Serial port**—A VM can have up to four serial ports that you can add or remove only when the VM is powered off. You can change the device status (connected or not), connection (host physical port, output file, or named pipe), and I/O mode while the VM is powered on or off.

- **Parallel port**—A VM can have up to three parallel ports that you can add or remove only when the VM is powered off. You can change the device status (connected or not) and connection (host physical port or output file) while the VM is powered on or off.

- **USB controller**—You can add a single USB controller to a VM while the VM is powered on or off. This device has no configurable options and is not officially supported in vSphere.

- **SCSI device**—This allows you to add to the VM SCSI devices that are connected to the host. If you add a SCSI device, you will be able to select from the SCSI devices connected to the host (e.g., tape drives, CD-ROM). You can add these while a VM is powered off or on, and you can assign them any free SCSI ID.

This comprises all the virtual hardware that you can assign to a VM that the guest operating system will see. These virtual hardware devices are all emulated by the VMkernel and exist solely in the memory of the host server.

VM Options

The Options tab of the Virtual Machine Properties window lets you set advanced configuration options that affect the operation of the VM, such as power and boot options, as shown in Figure 13.2.

Here are the various options and settings that you can use with your VM.

- **General Options**—This section contains the VM name, configuration file name, working directory location, and guest operating system. The VM name is the display name for the VM, and if this is changed, be aware that the VM's files whose names begin with the VM's name are not updated (e.g., .vmx and .vmdk files). Having the names not match is okay and does

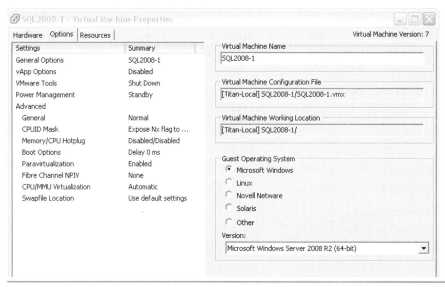

Figure 13.2   Setting VM options

not cause any problems, but it can be confusing. If you want the VM name and filenames to match, you can perform a Storage VMotion (SVMotion) of the VM to the same datastore, which will sync the names back up. You cannot change the working directory location and configuration filename in the vSphere Client. However, you can change the VM name and guest operating system whether the VM is powered off or on.

- **vApp Options**—You can enable vApp options on a VM and set individual options on a VM that may differ from your default vApp objects. Once enabled, additional options will be displayed that will allow you to configure the vApp properties.

- **VMware Tools**—This section contains various settings that affect the VMware Tools application that is installed on the VM's guest operating system. In the first part of this section, you can set the behavior of the various VM power controls, such as the Power Off button, which you can configure to perform either a hard power off or a graceful operating system shutdown. In the second part of this section, you can run VMware Tools scripts when a VM changes certain power states. These scripts are located on the guest operating system (typically in C:\Program Files\VMware\VMware Tools) where they can be modified as needed. You can also set script options inside the VMware Tools application that runs on the VM. In the last part of this section, you can access advanced settings which control whether a VM checks for the latest version of VMware Tools and automatically updates it if needed, as well as whether the VM syncs its time from the host server. You can also set these options on the VMware Tools application on the VM. You can change these settings only when the VM is powered off.

- **Power Management**—This section controls the VM's behavior when the guest OS is placed in standby mode. The default is to leave the VM powered on, but you can change this to suspend the VM instead. Additionally, you can set the vNIC used for Wake on LAN (WOL) traffic. You can change these settings only when the VM is powered off.

- **Advanced, General**—This section contains settings to enable or disable video hardware acceleration and logging to the vmware.log file, which you can change while the VM is powered on or off. The debugging and statistics option allows you to change the amount of information logged regarding the VM, which can be useful for troubleshooting purposes and can be changed only while the VM is powered off. The Configuration Parameters button, which you can select only while the VM is powered off, opens a new window where you can set advanced configuration parameters that are written to the VM's .vmx configuration file. Many of the VM options (e.g., CPU IDs, VMware Tools options, etc.) that you set are displayed in this area in their actual setting form. It's best to not add, remove, or modify these settings unless you are sure you know what you are doing.

- **Advanced, CPUID Mask**—This section allows you to control what specific CPU features are presented to the VM. You can choose to either hide or expose the NX flag to the VM, and also set advanced CPU masks to hide certain CPU capabilities. The NX flag is an advanced CPU feature used by both Intel and AMD processors that stands for No Execute and provides the ability to segregate areas of memory so that any code in them is not allowed to execute. Intel refers to this feature as XD (Execute Disabled). By hiding this flag from the VM and preventing it from using this feature, you can increase VMotion compatibility between hosts that may not support certain CPU features. The Advanced button lets you set CPU identification masks on your VM to further mask CPU features and increase compatibility. CPU masks can be fairly complicated to figure out and set properly; for more information on how to set them, see VMware Knowledge Base articles 1991, 1992, and 1993 (http://kb.vmware.com/kb/1991, http://kb.vmware.com/kb/1992, http://kb.vmware.com/kb/1993). You can change these settings only when a VM is powered off.

- **Advanced, Memory/CPU Hotplug**—This section will appear only if you have a guest OS selected in the General options that supports this feature. It allows you to enable/disable either the Memory Hot Add or CPU Hot Plug feature and is disabled by default. If your guest OS supports only one feature (e.g., Memory Hot Add), the nonsupported feature will be grayed out. You can change these settings only when a VM is powered off.

- **Advanced, Boot Options**—This section allows you to set the length of time the BIOS screen will be displayed when a VM is powered on or rebooted. The default is 0, which causes the BIOS screen to be only briefly displayed; setting this to a value in milliseconds will increase the delay (e.g., 5000ms = 5 seconds). Setting this to a higher value can be useful if you are trying to get to the boot option menu to boot from a CD-ROM and need more time to press the Esc key. In addition, you can force the VM to go to the BIOS setup screen at the next boot by checking the Force BIOS Setup field. You can change these settings while the VM is either powered on or off.

- **Advanced, Paravirtualization**—This section is for enabling or disabling paravirtualization support for the VM if the guest operating system supports it. Paravirtualization allows the operating system to communicate directly with the virtualization layer hypervisor (VMware Tools is a form of paravirtualization) for certain instructions. Enabling this feature will limit the VMotion of a VM, as it cannot be moved while running to a host that does not support paravirtualization. You can change this setting only while the VM is powered off; it is enabled by default.

- **Advanced, Fibre Channel NPIV**—This section is for assigning world-wide names (WWNs) to VMs running on hosts with Fibre Channel (FC) adapters that support N-Port ID Virtualization (NPIV). NPIV allows for sharing a single physical FC port among multiple virtual ports using unique identifiers. NPIV is supported only for VMs that have Raw Device Mappings (RDMs); otherwise, VMs use the WWNs of the host's physical FC adapters. You can change this setting while the VM is either powered on or off.

- **Advanced, CPU/MMU Virtualization**—This section controls whether CPU hardware virtualization (VT-x/AMD-v) or the memory management unit (MMU) is virtualized or not. Newer CPUs support these features and can improve the performance of a VM by decreasing latencies of certain memory operations. By default, the host will automatically determine if this feature can be used, but you can also choose whether software or hardware for instruction set and MMU virtualization is used. You can change this setting while the VM is either powered on or off.

- **Advanced, Swapfile Location**—This section controls where the VM's swap file (.vswp) is stored. By default, it is stored based on the setting of the cluster or host that the VM is on, which is typically in the same directory as the VM. If you do not want to use the default setting for a particular VM, you can change this setting to force the VM to store it either in its home directory or on a separate host swap file datastore. If you choose to store it on a separate datastore, this can greatly increase the length of time that it takes to VMotion a VM between hosts if both hosts do not have access to the datastore on which it is located (e.g., a local datastore). Because swap files can take up a lot of valuable disk space, it is sometimes desirable to store them on alternative cheaper storage locations.

Take care when changing these options, as they can affect the behavior and performance of your VMs in both positive and negative ways. Make sure you understand each setting and what the affect will be on your VMs before you change them.

VM RESOURCES

The Resources tab of the Virtual Machine Properties window lets you control the hardware resource settings (CPU, memory, and disk) for your VMs. These settings can both limit and guarantee the amount of resources that each VM will have available to it, as well as prioritize a VM's access to resources against other VMs. It is often better to manage resource allocations on resource pools rather than individual VMs. Here are the various resource settings that you can use with your VM.

- **CPU**—This section allows you to set shares, reservations, and limits for a VM to control the amount of host CPU resources that the VM has access to, as shown in Figure 13.3. You can use one of these settings, or use them together to specifically tailor the amount of CPU resources that a VM can utilize (e.g., set a reservation of 500MHz and a limit of 1GHz). It is generally easier to configure and use shares than it is to set up individual reservations and limits on your VMs.
  - **Shares**—Defines a VM's priority (low, normal, high, or custom) to access CPU resources compared to other VMs.
  - **Reservations**—Guarantees that a VM has access to a certain amount of CPU resources and can be set between 0 and the total amount of CPU megahertz that a host has. This can be misleading, however, as a VM can never use more CPU megahertz than the number of vCPUs assigned to

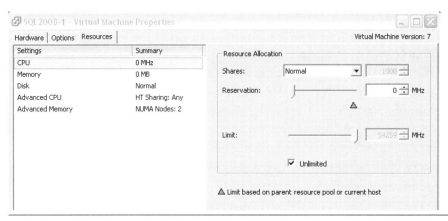

Figure 13.3   VM CPU resource settings

it. For example, a host with two dual-core 2.6GHz processors will have a total of 9768MHz; a VM with a single vCPU can only ever use 2.6GHz and not the full 9768MHz, even if you set a reservation higher than 2.6GHz. Unused reserved CPU capacity is available for use as an unreserved resource for other VMs.

- **Limit**—Controls the maximum amount of CPU resources that a VM can use regardless of how much is available. By default, this is set to Unlimited, but you can set it between 0 and the total amount of CPU megahertz that a host has. Again, similar to reservations, this setting can be misleading, as a VM can never use more CPU megahertz than the number of vCPUs assigned to it.

- **Memory**—This section allows you to set shares, reservations, and limits for a VM to control the amount of host memory resources that the VM has access to. You can use one of these settings, or use them together to specifically tailor the amount of memory resources that a VM can utilize (e.g., set a reservation of 512MB and a limit of 1GB). Similar to CPUs, it is generally easier to configure and use shares than it is to set up individual reservations and limits on your VMs.

  - **Shares**—Defines a VM's priority (low, normal, high, or custom) to access a host's physical host memory compared to other VMs.

  - **Reservations**—Guarantees that a VM has access to a set amount of physical host memory, and can be set between 0 and the total amount of memory that has been assigned to a VM. If a memory reservation is set on a VM and the host server does not have enough free physical memory to meet that reservation, the VM will not be allowed to be powered on. When memory reservations are set on a VM the size of a VM's disk swap file (.vswp) is reduced by the amount of RAM that is reserved for the VM. Reserved RAM, once touched, is not available for use by other VMs. It becomes locked by the reservation holder. This can have a significant negative impact on overall consolidation density.

- **Limit**—Controls the maximum amount of physical host memory that a VM can use regardless of how much is available. By default, this is set to Unlimited, but you can set it between 0 and the total amount of physical host memory that a host has. The Unlimited setting is also misleading, as a VM can never use more memory than it has been assigned, regardless of the limit that is set. When a VM reaches the limit of physical host memory that has been set on it, it begins to use its disk swap file (.vswp) for additional memory.

- **Disk**—This section allows you allocate disk I/O bandwidth used by a VM for its virtual disks. Since disk I/O is a different type of resource than CPU and memory, you can only set a priority to a VM using shares to control the I/O bandwidth that it has available compared to other VMs. By default, all VMs have equal priority, but you can change the priority of individual VMs to low, normal, high, or a custom priority.

- **Advanced CPU**—This section allows you to set some additional CPU options, such as hyperthreaded core sharing and CPU affinity. This section will not show up if you are using DRS or if a host has only one processor and does not support hyperthreading. Be careful with these settings, as the host CPU scheduler does a very good job of scheduling CPU resources among VMs, and these settings can disrupt that and slow down your VMs if not set properly. Use these settings only if you must fine-tune CPU control for critical VMs. If you set affinity and then join a cluster with DRS, the option to change it goes away and is no longer shown, but affinity is still set.

  - **Hyperthreaded core sharing**—This controls whether a VM can share a physical processor core or not and is applicable only if the host server supports hyperthreading. The default option of Any allows a VM to freely share CPU cores with vCPUs within the VM or with other VMs. Changing this to None will ensure that the vCPUs of the VM have exclusive use of a processor core when they schedule it and the other hyperthread of the core is halted so that nothing else can use it while the VM is using it, which essentially wastes CPU resources. You can also set this to

Internal whereby a VM can share a core with another vCPU assigned to a VM if a VM has only two vCPUs. Otherwise, the VM will never share a core with any other VM; if a VM has one or four vCPUs instead of two, this setting is treated the same as the None setting.

- **CPU affinity**—Setting a CPU scheduled affinity defines which CPU core a VM is forced to always use. By default, affinity is not defined and VMs are free to use any CPU core that is available as controlled by the host CPU scheduler. If you enable this, you can select specific CPU cores that a VM can use; you can select more than one core even for a single vCPU VM, but it can access only a single core at any given time. VI3 had checkboxes for selecting CPUs; in vSphere, you enter the information in a text box using dashes for ranges and commas to separate values (e.g., 2,3,4). The available CPUs listed are based on CPU cores and not sockets, so a host with two quad-core CPUs will have eight available CPUs; likewise, a host with two CPUs that support hyperthreading will have four available CPUs. If you select the full range, it is the same as not using affinity at all, as the VM can access all CPU cores. If you enable this option, you must select at least one CPU per the number of vCPUs that a VM has been assigned. You cannot set affinity if a VM resides on a host in a DRS cluster, and affinity is specific to a single host and cleared if the VM is migrated to a new host. For this reason, it is not recommended that you use affinity unless you have a situation that requires it.

- Advanced Memory—This section lets you select whether to use NUMA memory affinity for your VM. NUMA is a way of linking several small memory nodes together as a single larger node and can offer some performance benefits in certain situations. For more information on the NUMA architecture and how it relates to VMware, read the VMware Resource Management Guide that is located in the Documentation section of the company's website. This section is not displayed if your host does not utilize a NUMA memory architecture. In most situations, you should not change this; instead, let ESX manage this. Some exceptions to this are if you have a small number of VMs that use a large amount of memory, or if your VMs run applications that have memory-intensive workloads. Just like CPU affinity, this section is also not displayed if a VM resides on a host in a DRS, and the affinity is specific to a single host and cleared if the VM is migrated to a new host. Checking all the checkboxes displayed is the same as running no affinity.

That covers all the various options that you can set on your VMs to customize how they operate and function. Before you try changing these options, make sure you understand their effects and try them out on noncritical systems so that you can become more familiar with them.

SUMMARY

Properly creating and configuring your VMs will ensure that the guest operating systems and applications running on them are operating at peak efficiency. To make VM creation even easier you should look into making VM templates that allow you to create new VMs with just a few mouse clicks. By doing this, you can create a gold image that is standardized in whatever manner you want it to ensure that your operating systems are configured consistently.

BUILDING YOUR OWN vSPHERE LAB

Building your own VMware vSphere lab environment for use at home or at work can be an exciting and rewarding experience. There are plenty of good reasons you may be considering building your own VMware vSphere lab—for example, you may be studying for your VMware VCP accreditation, you may need a highly flexible and scalable IT environment from which to perform tests on a particular application, or you may want to familiarize yourself with vSphere to enable you to be more efficient in your job. The lab will provide you with an excellent platform on which to learn more about vSphere, its features, and the underlying hardware on which it runs and operates.

This chapter provides information on key areas you should consider, and points out the main considerations when building your own lab. To help you overcome this potential minefield and to provide you with a better understanding of what makes a successful vSphere lab, this chapter will guide you through the process of determining why you should build a VMware vSphere lab in the first place, and what you will need to consider when designing and building the lab—including both hardware and software requirements.

WHY BUILD A vSPHERE LAB?

What better way to learn about and test a product than to have your own sandbox in which to play, without fear of affecting live production systems. It is a common trait of those involved in IT to enjoy getting "under the hood" of a product to achieve a better understanding of how it ticks. The knowledge gained in doing this can, in most cases, be directly applied in the workplace.

Those of us who have been in IT for some time usually learn the real inner workings of a product when something breaks and we have to fix it, with the entire company and the CTO waiting for us to resolve the issue. These learning conditions are far from ideal, as who wants to deep dive into a potentially complex product under such circumstances?

By building your own vSphere lab, you not only have an excellent environment in which to install, use, and learn about VMware vSphere, but you can also use the lab as a platform on which to install, run, and test various operating systems, applications, and utilities. Through the use of VM templates, you can quickly deploy server environments that match all or part of your existing or proposed production IT infrastructure.

When you first consider building your own vSphere lab, ask yourself: "Why do I want to build and run my own vSphere lab?" Of course, there are many reasons people would want to build and run their own virtualization lab, but here are some of the more common ones.

- **Exam study**—In your own vSphere lab, you can easily build a mock production environment to follow examples in any study material you may have, and to confirm that what you have read in your study material actually works as described in practice.

- **Hands-on learning**—Probably the most common reason for putting together your own virtualization lab is to explore the hardware and software, wrestle with it, and get your hands dirty—breaking it, fixing it, and then breaking it again in the process. This is the preferred method of learning for many people, although it does require the luxury of time with very few of us in IT having access to the necessary non-production hardware and software during the workday to learn through this hands-on approach. In addition, the often-hefty price tags for attending training courses means that many people don't have the luxury of learning from a trained instructor, making a lab environment a popular choice.

- **Centralized home infrastructure**—Perhaps you are running a home office or need a centralized IT environment from which to run your home PCs for things such as centralized monitoring, management of your kid's Internet access, or management of the family file, music, and photo repository.

- **Because it's there**—Some of you, like myself, love to play with new enterprise IT products and technologies, even if they don't have direct application to your personal or work life. A virtualized lab environment provides an excellent platform from which to do this.

Whatever your reason, running your own vSphere lab will provide you with a platform and means to increase your product and technology understanding that will most likely assist you in your job, whether you work at a service desk, or whether you are a second- or third-line engineer, a technical architect, or professional presales consultant.

WHAT DO YOU WANT FROM A VSPHERE LAB?

You should now have a better understanding of why you want to build your own vSphere lab, but unfortunately, those thought-provoking questions found in the previous section don't end there. You now have a couple of new questions to ask yourself which are more closely related to the actual lab hardware and what you want from it.

So, before starting to design or build a vSphere lab, you should take some time to think about what you want to get out of the lab, not only now, but also in the future. Ask yourself a few basic questions such as the following.

- Where will I be running my vSphere lab; at home or at work?
- What is my budget for purchasing the hardware and software for the lab?
- Do I already have any existing hardware that I could utilize to build the lab?
- Am I building my vSphere lab to learn more about vSphere, or just to have a lab platform on which to run and test various operating systems, applications, or utilities?
- Will I want to use some of vSphere's more enterprise-level features, such as vMotion, Fault Tolerance (FT), or High Availability (HA)?
- Approximately how many VMs will I want to run at one time?
- Will I be running the vSphere lab 24/7, or will I run it only when required?
- Will I want to run x64 operating systems, such as Microsoft Windows Server 2008 R2, which is available only as an x64 distribution?

After answering these questions, you should now have a better idea of what you want to achieve with your vSphere lab, and from this we can now discuss the various building blocks that'll make up your new lab environment.

WHAT YOU NEED TO BUILD YOUR OWN vSPHERE LAB

vSphere labs can come in all shapes and sizes, depending on the requirement for the lab and the budget allocated. The lab's hardware can be as small as a single PC, laptop, or server and as large as a rack of spare servers located in your basement, garage, or employer's server room, complete with shared storage and resilient network switches.

As you can see, there are some real extremes in the actual hardware from which you can run VMware vSphere. You could use a laptop running VMware Workstation 7.1 which in turn is running VMware ESX/ESXi with nested virtual machines (VMs). Or you could use old server kit that you saved from the trash bin after it was discarded during a recent server hardware refresh. Whatever the size of your initial vSphere lab, you will have an excellent platform on which to learn more about the product and "kick the tires" of some of vSphere's more exciting and powerful features.

The key areas that make up your vSphere lab fall into three distinct categories: hardware, software, and environmental. The type, number, and complexity of the components that make up a vSphere lab will vary depending on the size of the lab you wish to build, though at the core of even the most basic vSphere lab you will find the required components listed in the following sections.

HARDWARE

The following are the various hardware components that make up the central framework of your vSphere lab.

- **Server**—The physical ESX/ESXi host in your vSphere lab could be a laptop, PC, or actual server. White-box PCs/servers are popular among home lab enthusiasts, as on a cost versus performance basis you generally get better value for your money when you build and run an ESX/ESXi white-box solution than when you buy an entry-level or second-hand enterprise server.

- **Storage**—vSphere and the lab VMs need a home. Local, direct attached, storage area network (SAN), or NAS-based storage provides just this. Each storage type comes with its own advantages and disadvantages, some more than others. A summary of these is provided later in this chapter, in the Shared Storage section.

- **Networking**—Your vSphere lab will need to talk to the outside world, even if only to provide management connectivity to the ESX/ESXi host via the vSphere Client.

SOFTWARE

The software you'll be running in your vSphere lab will likely be a combination of free and trial licensed products. Here are the main areas where your software usage in the lab will fall:

- **VMware**—The ESX/ESXi and vCenter Server installation media
- **Operating system (OS)**—Required by the guest OS of the VMs running in the vSphere lab
- **Third-party utilities**—Generally a mixture of both free and paid utilities for guest OS management, monitoring or anti-virus to name a few

ENVIRONMENT

A vSphere lab needs to reside somewhere, and this is often overlooked during the planning phase of building a lab. The following list provides some of the key environmental considerations:

- Minimizing the dust and keeping your lab free from water damage
- Keeping your lab at an acceptable temperature with sufficient cooling
- Determine how much power you lab equipment will consume
- Pay some thought to how much noise your lab equipment will generate

We will look at the hardware, software and environment categories in more detail and will discuss their various subcomponents, but first let's discuss the issue of VMware support for your vSphere lab.

SUPPORT: THE "OFFICIAL" LINE

To gain "official" vSphere support from VMware, whether it is in a production or lab environment, you need to pay for it. For many, purchasing official VMware product support isn't necessary for a vSphere lab environment, and as we will discuss shortly, you probably can't obtain such support in most lab instances anyway due to the hardware you'll be running it on.

For VMware vSphere to be officially supported in your lab or production environment, the underlying hardware needs to have undergone strict compliance testing and be included in VMware's vSphere Hardware Compatibility Guide (www.vmware.com/resources/compatibility/search.php). In reality, it is unlikely that your lab server, network, and storage hardware will be officially approved to run vSphere, but don't let this stop you, as vSphere will often still work despite your hardware not being in the compatibility guide.

With every new version of vSphere that comes out, the list of compatible devices and components, officially supported or otherwise, generally increases; the only exception to this are systems with 32-bit CPUs which are unable to run the new 64-bit-only VMkernel found in vSphere. This more expansive list of compatible devices and components found in vSphere is good news for those of us running our own vSphere lab on unapproved hardware. It wasn't uncommon with the previous version, VMware VI3, for the majority of an unapproved lab server's components to work without issue, though often, either the disk controller, network controller, or both would not be successfully detected by ESX/ESXi.

To get around this issue would usually involve some (unsupported) tweaking of the ESX/ESXi ISO build to modify or inject unsupported drivers. With the release of vSphere, it is more common than not for server-based components to be successfully detected and work without the need for any undesirable modification to the build.

HARDWARE

By using small-business, domestic-level, or second-hand enterprise-level server hardware for a vSphere lab, you can achieve considerable cost savings. However, using existing or purchasing non-VMware vSphere-approved hardware with the intention of running a vSphere lab on it does mean that there is a risk that some or all of this hardware will not work when you go to install and then subsequently run ESX/ESXi.

Though the risk of purchasing vSphere non-Hardware Compatibility Guide hardware and finding that it doesn't work has been reduced, thanks to a couple of excellent online resources which keep a list of nonapproved VMware vSphere hardware (systems, motherboards, memory, network adapters, I/O adapters) that the community has found will work successfully with VMware VI3 and/or vSphere. These resources are well worth a visit before taking the plunge and laying out your hard-earned money on hardware which may not otherwise work:

- **Ultimate Whitebox**—www.ultimatewhitebox.com
- **VM-Help**—www.vm-help.com/esx40i/esx40_whitebox_HCL.php

Let's take a look now at one of the most integral pieces of hardware that makes up a vSphere lab: the server.

SERVER

The term "server" is often used quite loosely when referring to an ESX/ESXi host running in a vSphere lab, as the host, as mentioned previously, could just as easily be found running on a PC or laptop (e.g., under VMware Workstation) as it could on an enterprise-level server such as an HP ProLiant, Dell PowcrEdge, or Cisco UCS. When looking at building your vSphere lab, the server(s) you use will generally fall into one of the following three categories, any of which could be new or used.

- **White box**—This can be a PC or a server constructed from off-the-shelf parts either laying around in your storeroom or purchased from an online or brick and mortar computer component reseller, or even a combination of both. Needless to say, the end product generally doesn't have a main stream enterprise level brand name associated with it, and would definitely not be in VMware's official compatibility guide. A white-box solution, however, will often be the most cost-effective way to purchase an ESX/ESXi host and can often offer the best bang for the buck with regard to performance.

- **Branded PC or laptop**—These factory-assembled machines have generally been produced en mass by a PC or laptop manufacturer such as Dell, HP, Lenovo, or Apple. As with a white-box solution, none of these PCs or laptops would be in VMware vSphere's official compatibility guide.

- **Branded server**—Similar to branded PCs and laptops, these servers would have been produced in high volumes but to a clearly defined build specification (at least, they should have been). Popular server manufacturers include HP, Dell, IBM, and Fujitsu. Many of the mid-level and high-end enterprise-level servers from these manufacturers will be found in the compatibility guide and come with enterprise-level features such a redundant components, higher memory capacity, and more CPU sockets. It is advisable that you check that the server is in the compatibility guide before purchasing.

Whatever the category your vSphere lab server(s) falls into, there are four key component areas that can determine the compatibility and effectiveness of a vSphere lab server for your requirements. These are

- CPU
- Memory

- Network controller
- Disk Storage/Array controller

In the following sections, we will take a more in-depth look at the considerations behind each component area.

CPU

A CPU is probably the most important component that you will select for your lab servers as it will determine what OS versions and vSphere advanced features you will be able to run in your lab. Let's first take a look at the process of selecting a CPU with virtualization extension capabilities.

Intel VT and AMD-V

With the mainstream use of Microsoft Windows Server and the fact that all versions from the recently released Windows Server 2008 R2 onward will now be 64-bit only, you should be looking at a server which has a 64-bit CPU with either Intel VT (Intel CPUs) or AMD-V (AMD CPUs) virtualization extensions installed on the die. This is because Intel VT or AMD-V (on some revisions of CPUs) is required on the CPU to run x64-based VMs under vSphere. These virtualization extensions are hardware-based enhancements that assist a software-based virtualization technology such as VMware ESX/ESXi, which leads to improved resource use and increased VM performance. Take a look at the VMware Knowledge Base article at http://kb.vmware.com/kb/1003945 for more details regarding the prerequisites for running x64-based VMs.

You can obtain the latest list of Intel CPUs which have Virtualization Technology (VT) on the die from http://ark.intel.com/VTList.aspx. For an outline of which AMD CPUs come with the AMD-V extensions, visit www.amd.com/us/products/technologies/virtualization/Pages/amd-v.aspx.

Intel VT and AMD-V are often turned off by default in the server BIOS, so it is always important to check that they are enabled in your lab server's BIOS. This is a common cause for x64 VMs failing to run on a server, and catches a fair few people out.

If you are looking at purchasing a second-hand server to use as a vSphere lab server, always ensure that you know the exact model of CPU installed in the server. Server manufacturers often offer servers with various models of CPU so as to provide customers with the choice of an entry-level specification through to a high-end performance model. Take the time to find out the exact model of CPU in the server and cross-check this with the server manufacturer's quick specification guide. If you are unsure as to the capabilities of a CPU in a server, you can run a free utility from VMware called the CPU Identification Utility which provides valuable information about the server's CPU and its capabilities. Of course, this is assuming that you have physical access to the server. The VMware CPU Identification Utility can be downloaded from http://www.vmware.com/download/shared_utilities.html

Matching Make and Model

If you intend to run more than one host in your vSphere lab, either initially or sometime in the future, there are some additional CPU considerations which you should be mindful of when first designing your vSphere lab environment. If you plan to only ever run a single host in your vSphere lab, then unless you run nested instances of ESX/ESXi on this physical ESX/ESXi host, you probably will not be looking at running any of the vSphere advanced features such as Fault Tolerance (FT) or High Availability (HA). Once you get a taste for and experience the benefits of running your own vSphere lab, you'll probably want to add an additional vSphere host so that you can get to use some of these "fun" features available with the product.

So, if you think you may run more than one vSphere lab server, the first thing you will want to decide is what make and model of processor to use in your vSphere lab. Sure, you can have both Intel and AMD in the same vSphere environment, but unfortunately, you won't be able to add them to the same cluster and use any of the features, such as VMotion, Distributed Resource Scheduler (DRS), and Fault Tolerance (FT), that can be found in the higher end editions of VMware vSphere. Matching the make of CPU between your vSphere lab servers is a straightforward process, though the next part of matching the model of CPU can prove to be a little trickier and can be an area of some confusion. Before I go on to describe how to match your model of CPU, let's examine why you would need to go through this process in the first place.

The primary reason you would want to match the model of CPU between ESX/ESXi hosts is so that VMotion, DRS, and FT will work successfully. For many businesses, these features hold much of the value in running vSphere. When a VM is first started, it detects the underlying physical CPU of the host on which it is running. When moving a VM from one host to another via VMotion or DRS, you want the VM to remain online without any disruption of service which could impact other systems or end users. With the VM effectively staying online the entire time, the target host will need to have the same underlying CPU instruction set. For example, if a VM is running on a host with an AMD Opteron CPU, and if it is allowed to be transferred while still running to another host with an Intel P4-based CPU, the VM will experience problems due to the difference in instructions presented from the Intel P4 CPU. You can also apply this example to different models of CPUs by the same manufacturer, as these can also have differences in on-board CPU instructions.

The good news is that because ESX/ESXi can mask particular CPU instructions, CPUs can have some minor differences in instructions between them. VMotion and DRS compatibility is further maximized with the introduction of Enhanced VMotion Compatibility (EVC) in vSphere, which is discussed in more detail in Chapter 9. Table 14.1 and Table 14.2 provide a summary of the models of server-grade CPUs that you can include together in a VM cluster using EVC.

Table 14.1 AMD CPUs That Are Compatible with EVC

AMD Opteron Generation 1	AMD Opteron Generation 2	AMD Opteron Generation 3
AMD Opteron Gen 1 (Rev E)	–	–
AMD Opteron Gen 2 (Rev F)	AMD Opteron Gen 1 (Rev F)	–
AMD Opteron Gen 3 (Greyhound)	AMD Opteron Gen 3 (Greyhound)	AMD Opteron Gen 3 (Greyhound)

Table 14.2 Intel CPUs That Are Compatible with EVC

Intel Xeon Core 2	Intel Xeon 45nm Core 2	Intel Xeon Core i7 (Nehalem)	Intel Xeon 32nm Core i7 (Westmere)
Intel Xeon Core 2 (Merom)	–	–	–
Intel Xeon 45nm Core 2 (Penryn)	Intel Xeon 45nm Core 2 (Penryn)	–	–
Intel Xeon Core i7 (Nehalem)	Intel Xeon Core i7 (Nehalem)	Intel Xeon Core i7 (Nehalem)	–
Intel Xeon 32nm Core i7 (Westmere)	Intel Xeon 32nm Core i7 (Westmere)	Intel Xeon 32nm Core i7 (Westmere)	Intel Xeon 32nm Core i7 (Westmere)

Each new generation of CPU, both AMD and Intel, exposes new CPU features. However, running a more recent CPU in a lower EVC mode for compatibility will mean you won't necessarily get the full benefit of these newer CPU features.

When it comes to non-server-grade CPUs such as the AMD Athlon x4, Phenom II, or Intel Core 2 (Quad Core), your best bet is to take the cautious approach and match your vSphere lab server CPUs as closely as possible so that they are at least from the same family or CPU release. This will minimize your chances of them being incompatible for inclusion into an ESX/ESXi cluster and will mean you will be making the most of any CPU features and enhancements that they may have.

Fault Tolerance (FT)

As covered in Chapter 9, FT is a new feature introduced with VMware vSphere. The vLockstep technology used in FT makes use of some CPU extensions found in more recent CPUs. If you'd like to use FT in your vSphere lab, ensure that the CPUs of your lab servers are compatible. For an up-to-date list of CPUs which can use FT, see the VMware Knowledge Base article at http://kb.vmware.com/kb/1008027.

MEMORY

Virtualization likes memory. In fact, it likes memory so much that your lab server will almost certainly make a great attempt at consuming as much memory as you can physically give it. The reason for this isn't that the ESX/ESXi is memory-inefficient (far from it, with features such as transparent page sharing [TPS]); it has more to do with the human factor. The ease at which you can provision VMs, especially from templates, is a double-edged sword. The speed and convenience are great, though this does tend to mean you end up with a significant number of VMs running in your vSphere lab in no time at all. In most instances, the number of VMs in your vSphere lab won't decrease as you start to install and configure more complex environments, with each VM consuming a portion of the host's physical memory. As you can probably gather, out of all your vSphere lab server's resources, the memory is going to be used the most.

The following are some memory-related considerations when looking to build or obtain a second-hand server for your vSphere lab.

- **Maximum memory**—Look at your potential lab server's maximum memory capacity. It's a good idea to ensure that your lab server can take at least 8GB of memory. I have 8GB in my lab servers and can usually run between six and eight average Windows-based VMs comfortably. Even if you are not initially going to fully populate all of the memory DIMM sockets in your lab server, try to have a server with as much potential maximum memory capacity as your budget will allow, as it is good to know you have spare DIMM sockets in reserve for when requirements and/or budget allow.

- **Lower-capacity older memory**—Buying or obtaining a free older enterprise-level server such as an HP ProLiant DL360 G3 or G4 or a Dell PowerEdge 1850 may seem like a good idea, though it can end up costing you more than anticipated. As well as the probable lack of CPU-based virtualization enhancements of Intel VT and AMD-V, older servers generally use smaller-capacity memory DIMMs compared to their modern-day counterparts. Online auction and shopping websites such as eBay are a good source for finding enterprise-level server memory, though enterprise level memory does tend to hold its value quite well, especially the larger 1GB+ capacity DIMMs. These enterprise-level servers do have more memory DIMM sockets than an entry-level or white-box server, but populating them with 4GB to 8GB of memory by using more DIMMs can prove to be an expensive task. It pays to do your homework: For the same as or less than it would cost you to buy this additional memory, you could purchase a higher CPU specification entry-level branded server or build your own white-box server, both of which would take cheaper, higher-capacity memory DIMMs.

- **ECC or non-ECC**—If you are looking at using an entry-level branded server such as an HP ProLiant ML110 or ML115, Dell PowerEdge T110, or Lenovo TS200 in your vSphere lab, you will find that the default memory, usually 1GB to 2GB, that comes with the server has Error Correction Code (ECC) memory. This type of memory is often found in servers, as it is able to detect multiple-bit and correct single-bit errors during the transmission and storage of data on the DIMM. On ECC memory DIMMs, there are extra modules that store parity or ECC information. A memory DIMM with ECC is easy to spot, as the number of memory modules will be divisible by 3 or 5 (e.g., 9). This is not the case with non-ECC DIMMs (e.g., 8). With servers being designed to run 24/7 and usually with large amounts of memory, especially with the introduction of server virtualization, the risk of memory errors is much greater compared to that of a desktop PC or laptop. The result of uncorrected memory errors is usually system instability or, more likely, a system crash. That being said, modern branded memory is quite reliable, so it will be unusual for you to actually experience memory errors. As you'd expect, ECC memory is usually more expensive than non-ECC memory, meaning that for a lab environment where you won't be running business-critical systems and where budget is more likely an issue, the use of non-ECC memory is often preferable. Although it is sometimes possible to mix ECC and non-ECC memory in a server, this is not recommended, as it can cause problems. However, you can put ECC memory in a non-ECC server, as it will work, just without the ECC capabilities.

- **Registered and unregistered memory**—Registered memory, also known as buffered memory, contains a register on the DIMM that operates as a temporary holding area (buffer) for address and command signals moving between the memory module and CPU. Registered memory is responsible for holding data in the register for a single clock cycle before releasing it, which increases the reliability of the data flow to and from the DIMM. This type of memory is only really seen in enterprise-level servers where a high density of memory can be found. Registered DIMMs cannot be used in most branded entry-level and white-box servers, and shouldn't be confused with ECC memory, although it is common for registered memory to also have ECC. So, those 1GB DIMMs you had left over from the recent memory upgrade of your HP ProLiant DL360 or DL380 G7 servers unfortunately won't work in your branded entry-level or white-box server; in fact, they won't even fit due to different key (notch) positions..

NETWORK CONTROLLER

Having sufficient network ports for your vSphere lab is another must-have. Most servers, including enterprise-level servers, until recently would usually come with only a maximum of two network ports. Although this would be sufficient for a very basic vSphere lab (e.g., ESX host, VM, and Service Console traffic), if you would like to use some of the more advanced vSphere features mentioned previously in this chapter (VMotion, DRS, or FT) you'll have to provide a way to accommodate the requirement for extra network ports. Table 14.3 provides a quick tally to see how many ports a lab server running most of the vSphere features along with iSCSI or NFS-based shared storage may require following VMware's recommended best practices.

Table 14.3 Total Required Network Ports to Use All Features, iSCSI Storage, and Redundancy

Description	Ports Required	Redundancy	Total
Service Console (ESX)	1	1	2
VM traffic	1	1	2

Continues

Table 14.3 Total Required Network Ports to Use All Features, iSCSI Storage, and Redundancy *(Continued)*

Description	Ports Required	Redundancy	Total
VMotion	1	1	2
Fault Tolerance (FT)	1	1	2
iSCSI/NFS	1	1	2
		Total per ESX/ESXi host	10

By simply adding a couple of extra ESX/ESXi hosts to your lab, you'll see a significant requirement for network ports in your lab's network switch. For example, three hosts using the fully featured configuration outlined in Table 14.3 would require 30 physical network ports! Before we go any further, let's not forget that this is a lab environment, so unless you have a definite requirement for resilience, you can instantly cut the number of ports in half. Add to this the use of VLANs which we discussed in Chapter 6, and once again the number of physical network ports for your vSphere lab suddenly doesn't seem as daunting.

Depending on the size and complexity of your lab, you will almost certainly want your networking traffic, with the possible exception of the Service Console, to be running at gigabit (Gb) speeds. Fortunately, the vast majority of modern Ethernet network cards and onboard network ports found on motherboards run at gigabit speeds.

Even if you are using VLANs, you should ideally be looking at splitting your lab's network traffic out onto at least two physical gigabit network ports on your host. If you require additional network ports in your host, you should consider purchasing a second-hand single-, dual-, or quad-port VMware vSphere-approved PCI, PCI-X, or PCIe network card, depending on the expansion port types on your lab server's system board, which you can pick up relatively cheaply from an online marketplace such as eBay. Quad-port cards are ideal, as the extra ports can come in useful, so it is often worth spending that little bit extra, if possible, for this added flexibility. It is also well worth the time researching what network card to purchase by looking at the official vSphere Hardware Compatibility Guide or at one of the white-box sites mentioned earlier in this chapter.

Two popular, VMware-approved network cards in vSphere lab environments are the PCIe-based Intel Pro 1000 PT and the HP NC380T. Network cards such as the HP NC380T come with TCP/IP Offload Engine (TOE) functionality, but it should be pointed out that because the card has this ability does not necessarily mean it will work with vSphere. The use of TOE for iSCSI traffic makes perfect sense, but when viewing the VMware Hardware Compatibility Guide's list of approved cards for the purpose of iSCSI, the HP NC380T is not listed. Consequently, the HP NC380T can be used as a network adapter in vSphere, but not as an iSCSI storage adapter. So, be careful when selecting your network card, and don't make any assumptions.

When selecting a network card, also look to see whether it supports jumbo frames, as this is now supported in vSphere for both iSCSI and NFS network traffic. You'll almost certainly want to implement this at some point in your new lab.

DISK ARRAY CONTROLLER

The importance of a disk array controller in your vSphere lab server will vary depending on whether you intend to run ESX/ESXi and/or VMs from locally attached disk storage or ESXi from USB memory stick storage and the VMs from shared SAN or NAS-based storage.

The disk type (e.g., SCSI, SAS, or SATA) and chosen RAID levels, if available on the controller, combined with the specification of the disk controller will have a significant impact on the disk I/O performance you can expect from your vSphere lab server. The specification of the disk or array controller, array level, and disk type will once again be largely determined by the budget you have to invest in your lab environment, along with any available server hardware you may already have for use in your lab.

On non-enterprise-level or white-box server solutions, the features and overall performance of the onboard disk or array controller can vary greatly between the model of the server and motherboard. Enterprise-level array controller features such as hot-pluggable disks and RAID 6 are not commonly found on entry-level systems, though as the server is intended for a lab environment, these features (in particular, hot-pluggable disks) are not essential. However, one enterprise-level array controller feature that is a definite nice-to-have if you are running your VMs on local disk is a cache, usually the bigger the better with it being battery backed, for added resilience, a bonus. It is not uncommon to find enterprise level array controllers with caches of 128MB, 256MB or greater which can provide a noticeable improvement to disk I/O performance..

The disk controller is almost always the most problematic component with regard to compatibility on non-VMware-approved hardware. If your vSphere lab server is a branded entry-level or white-box server, chances are your disk controller won't be in the vSphere Hardware Compatibility Guide, so there is a possibility that ESX/ESXi will not detect your disk controller. As mentioned earlier in this chapter, both the Ultimate Whitebox and VM-Help websites are useful sources of information when researching non-vSphere-approved disk controllers known to work with vSphere.

If you find that your lab server's disk controller is not detected by ESX/ESXi, all is not lost, as you could run ESXi off a USB memory stick (you cannot do this with ESX, as this is not supported from USB) and present VMDK-based storage for the VMs via iSCSI, NFS, or Fibre Channel (FC) shared storage. However, for many, especially those of you wishing to run ESX and not ESXi, this is not an ideal arrangement, in which case you could consider using a PCIe-based array controller such as an HP E200, HP P212 Smart Array, or Dell PERC 5i or 6i. All of these entry-level array controllers are approved for use with vSphere and can often be found at a reasonable price on eBay or similar.

When looking for a disk array controller for your lab server, give some thought to the type of disk you'll be want to connect and run from it. Many modern array controllers allow you to run either SAS or SATA disk types, giving you options to best fit your budget or any spare hard disks that you may have available. If you'll be running VMs from the local disk and your server's disk controller supports RAID, you will also want to think about the RAID level(s) you should run. Typically for performance you would want to consider RAID 1 (or 1+0,0+1), or if disk space is more of an issue, RAID 5. Of course, this is an extremely rough guide, and there many other influencing factors such as the disk speed, the number of disks, and the intended workload types. In any case, you should ideally always use some level of hardware-based RAID disk resilience, as even in a lab environment, valuable time can be wasted rebuilding VMs should your lab server experience a disk failure.

If you're building a white box or using a server with SATA connectivity, you may want to consider using a solid state drive (SSD). These solid-state memory storage devices are becoming increasingly popular in the desktop consumer space with their prices dropping and available storage capacities increasing. Despite their relatively high cost of storage per gigabyte (GB) compared to traditional SATA-based disks, SSDs can provide you with highly responsive read and write I/O performance. When combined with thin provisioned VMs, even a 64GB or 128GB SSD can meet the requirements of most small vSphere labs' VM requirements. Enterprise-level SSDs are also beginning to emerge in enterprise servers, NAS, and SAN-based storage appliances, but these are still seen as something of a premium product due to their relative high cost, although expect this to change over the coming year or two.

Although not directly related to array controllers, this seemed to be an appropriate place to mention the usefulness of having an internal USB port in your lab server if you plan to run USB-based ESXi (see Figure 14.1). Older servers don't usually have an internal USB port, so although it is not essential, it is nice to have, as you don't need to have your USB memory stick inserted into the front or rear of the server to run USB-based ESXi, where it can get knocked out or damaged.

Figure 14.1 An internal USB port located in the bottom-right corner of a motherboard

SHARED STORAGE

Although shared storage is not essential for running a successful vSphere lab, it does present an opportunity to use the more enterprise-level functions and features mentioned already, such as VMotion, DRS, and FT. Running shared storage in your lab also provides an excellent platform for learning and increasing your understanding of the concepts and technologies used in shared storage, such as FC switching, iSCSI, or LUN creation and presentation, to name a few.

The shared storage you'll be looking at using in your vSphere lab can take on the form of a physical device such as a SAN or NAS appliance, or it can be software-based and running on and utilizing the local disk and array controller resources of one or more standard servers. These shared storage solutions all have varying degrees of functionality, capacity, and performance, which is usually reflected in the solution's price tag.

If your vSphere lab is based at your work or datacenter, you may have the option of utilizing some of the shared storage on a dedicated LUN located on an existing production SAN or NAS appliance. If you don't have this luxury or you don't want to run dedicated shared storage specific to your vSphere lab on your production storage system, many other lower-cost options are available. For the purpose of this chapter, let's assume that you want to be mindful of cost by reprovisioning any old hardware you may have lying about, or that you are looking for a cost-effective non-enterprise-level shared storage solution. Let's first take a look at a few physical storage appliance options that would be well suited to a basic vSphere lab scenario.

Physical Storage Appliances

A physical storage appliance for your lab could be a decommissioned HP, NetApp, or EMC storage appliance with iSCSI or FC connectivity, though it could just as easily be something more modest such as a small-business-targeted iomega IX4-200d NAS server. The balancing act in choosing a shared storage solution for your lab is to find one which meets your performance, capacity, and budgetary requirements. This can prove difficult with compromises having to be made in one or more of these three core areas. A used SAN appliance with FC connectivity may sound like a good idea, but unless you specifically want FC-based storage in your lab, you should remember that you will require an additional switch (or two for resilience) which will consume valuable space and power.

That being said, having an FC switch on which to practice and configure zoning can be useful. Adding extra FC disks to increase the amount of usable disk capacity can prove to be costly when compared to non-FC SAS or SCSI disks, as with most enterprise-level components they do hold their value well. iSCSI or NFS-based storage appliances are usually the preferred option for shared storage in lab environments, as they can utilize existing Ethernet network switches and don't require any additional FC host bus adapters (HBAs) to be installed into your lab servers or SAN fabric switches. Adding extra port capacity for Ethernet-based iSCSI or NFS storage solutions is much easier and cheaper through the use of commodity Ethernet network cards, cables, and switches.

Other than cost, the main areas of consideration when selecting a physical storage appliance are as follows.

- **Capacity**—How much disk space will you require to house your VMs and ISO images? This figure doesn't need to be accurate; just a rough estimate will do, though it pays to aim on the high side as disk space does have a habit of mysteriously disappearing once your lab is up and running. Also keep in mind that you can thin-provision disks within vSphere, thereby providing you with additional valuable disk space. The type of shared storage you will likely be looking at using in your lab, unless you are either extremely lucky or have a decent budget, won't have hardware-based thin provisioning; this type of functionality is usually found only on modern enterprise-level storage appliances.

- **Expansion**—Think ahead. What are your options for adding extra disks and increasing your physical storage appliance's capacity? Try not to limit your lab's shared storage expansion options if possible, as introducing an extra storage device or replacing your existing appliance can prove to be costly and time-consuming.

- **Disk types**—You will generally find three major disk types in SAN and NAS appliances: SCSI (including FC SCSI), SAS, and SATA. Both SCSI and SAS-based disks offer better performance than SATA in a per-spindle IOPS comparison, though they are significantly costlier and in most instances come with a smaller disk capacity. Depending on the requirements of your vSphere lab, you may find that using SATA disks will suffice, with extra I/Os per second (IOPS) able to be added if required by adding extra SATA disks. Once again, it is a matter of trying to hit that sweet spot between requirements and available budget, while being mindful of potential future requirements.

- **RAID levels**—Even in a lab environment, you should use RAID-based data protection, though when it comes to shared storage appliances, this isn't too much of a consideration, as nearly all such shared storage solutions from those intended for small businesses through to those targeted at enterprise-level businesses have some built-in RAID capability. As with the disk types mentioned earlier, the RAID level you select will have some impact on the performance versus disk capacity you can expect. Without going into detail, RAID 1,1+0,0+1 will provide you with better overall performance in a mixed sequential and nonsequential data read/write environment, with RAID 5 giving good sequential read access and higher levels of available disk space utilization.

- **Connectivity**—FC and Ethernet connectivity are the two current mainstream methods of connecting ESX/ESXi hosts to shared storage. With the more modern storage appliances, there is a shift to also using SAS or 10GbE (10 gigabit Ethernet) connectivity, though you probably won't see widespread adoption of this in the majority of vSphere labs anytime soon due to the higher costs associated with purchasing these newer data transfer technologies.

If you are looking at running a small vSphere lab environment where enterprise-level disk performance isn't a requirement, there are a couple of well-priced NAS server appliances on the market which will likely meet your requirements. The iomega ix4-200d, shown in Figure 14.2, with its four SATA disks, two gigabit network ports which can be teamed, choice of RAID levels, and ability to use jumbo frames and present NFS or iSCSI-based storage, provides some useful features for an affordable price.

It will meet the requirements for up to approximately a dozen average non-disk I/O-intensive VMs and is also VMware-approved, which contributes to making it an attractive NAS storage solution. The small-business-oriented NetGear ReadyNAS range of NAS appliances, also shown in Figure 14.2, offers

Figure 14.2 An iomega ix4-200d network storage device (left) and a NetGear ReadyNAS network storage device (right)

comparable features to the ix4-200d and is VMware-approved, though the adoption of these in the VMware community doesn't seem as broad, perhaps due to iomega now having the EMC name and perceived pedigree behind it.

Mid- or enterprise-level second-hand storage appliances can also provide good value for a vSphere lab, with devices such as an HP StorageWorks MSA (G1) storage appliance with FC connectivity often being found at a reasonable price on eBay and similar. Also, look for older second-hand EMC or NetApp products, though be prepared for a steeper learning curve in familiarizing yourself with and configuring these enterprise-level storage appliances. Also note that although having your own EMC, HP, or NetApp enterprise storage appliance running in your lab may sound like a nice idea, remember that such an appliance can generate a considerable amount of noise and heat, and can produce a hefty utility bill. This may be fine for a vSphere lab located at your place of work, but it can be less so if you're running it from home.

Software or Virtual Appliance-Based Shared Storage

There are two types of shared storage software. The first is storage software which runs directly on the physical server, and the second is storage software which runs from within a virtual appliance (VA) running on an ESX/ESXi host or a VMware Workstation VM. Both types of storage software can use any locally attached disk running on the server and leverage hardware or software based RAID for resilience. This disk is presented via NFS or iSCSI to the ESX/ESXi hosts in your lab. A storage VA can even present local storage back to VMs running on the same ESX/ESXi host on which it is running.

A wide range of software and VA-based shared storage solutions are available for permanent use or limited trial, most of which will run satisfactorily on commodity server hardware. For a small or medium-size vSphere lab environment, they can offer a good compromise between performance, capacity, and the all-important budget.

The same considerations regarding capacity, expansion, disk type, and RAID levels in physical storage appliances also apply to bare metal storage software and VA install products. Running a storage VA offers the following advantages over running a dedicated storage server or appliance.

- **Less hardware**—With the storage server running as a virtualized instance on an ESX/ESXi host, this is one less server you need to source and run in your lab. This has the usual power and cooling savings associated with it.

- **Ease of patching and management**—As it is running virtualized, you receive all the usual patching and management benefits, such as snapshots, when upgrading or patching the VA.

You can achieve adequate disk resource utilization regardless of whether you are running storage software directly on the server or via a VA by using local disk storage in a server and presenting it through to an ESX/ESXi host. You can divide the local disk into variously sized LUNs for running VMs and their associated .vmdk files along with hosting ISO images. Some of these software and VA-based products take this a step further and allow for the consolidation of local disk storage between physical servers, including ESX/ESXi hosts, which not only allows for the aggregation of local disk storage found on the hosts into a central pool of storage, but also provides increased throughput and levels of resilience over the more traditional single-server/VA presentation model. The HP StorageWorks P4000 Virtual SAN Appliance (VSA) is one such product.

The HP LeftHand VSA (http://h18000.www1.hp.com/products/storage/software/vsa) can aggregate the local disk found on multiple ESX/ESXi hosts and then present it out as a single or multiple pool of storage to VMs running on those ESX/ESXi hosts. The LeftHand VSA offers the same features and functionality found in the StorageWorks P4000 hardware appliance range, which shares similarities with Dell EqualLogic appliances.

Here is a list of some of the more popular storage VA offerings.

- **Openfiler (www.openfiler.com)**—This open source storage SAN/NAS appliance software can be deployed as a bare metal install or as a VMware VA. Openfiler is free to use and comes with a comprehensive set of features that will meet the shared storage requirements of most vSphere labs. For a step-by-step guide on how to install Openfiler and attach it to an ESX/ESXi host, see http://www.techhead.co.uk/how-to-configure-openfiler-v23-iscsi-storage-for-use-with-vmware-esx.

- **StarWind (www.starwindsoftware.com/)**—StarWind software offers a full commercial or a 2TB and two-iSCSI connection limited trial solution which turns a Windows server into a shared iSCSI SAN. As with Openfiler, it offers HA SAN functionality by replicating the data between one or more nodes.

- **FreeNAS (http://freenas.org/freenas)**—This is another open source NAS server which is based on the free UNIX-like operating system.

- **EMC Celerra VSA Uber (http://nickapedia.com/2010/05/19/besser-uber-celerra-vsa-uber-v2/)**—This increasingly popular VSA offering from EMC provides a full unrestricted set of features as is found on an EMC Celerra storage appliance (minus fibre channel connectivity). The thinking behind making this unrestricted Celerra VSA available to the masses is that it gets people using and familiar with it, from which subsequent EMC storage purchases may follow.

NETWORK SWITCHES

A common misconception is that all network switches are created equal, but as many of you know, this is not the case. Choosing the right network switch that will meet your vSphere lab's requirements and your budget is an important step, as the network switch is a component that you will hopefully not have to replace or upgrade too often. It is also integral to the smooth running of your vSphere lab, for both general network and, most likely, Ethernet-based storage traffic.

So, what should you look for in an Ethernet switch? The following six tips cover all the main areas that you should consider when choosing a network switch for your lab.

- **Managed, unmanaged, or smart network switch**—If you intend to have more than one ESX/ESXi lab server in your environment, you will want to look at using a managed or smart Layer 2 network switch. A fully managed switch offers a greater level of management and functionality than a smart switch, though this increased level of functionality is reflected in a higher price. Depending on your budget, a smart switch is often a good compromise and will provide the features you require for your lab environment. The features will vary slightly on the various models of Layer 2 switches available, though most should provide you with the ability via a management interface or command line to configure advanced settings such as IEEE 802.1Q VLAN tagging, Link Aggregation Control Protocol (LACP), and Quality of Service (QoS). An unmanaged switch, as you'd expect, offers no management ability, though it will sometimes offer support for jumbo frames and basic support for Layer 2 and Layer 3 priority tabs, which won't be sufficient if you want to use VLAN tagging in your vSphere lab.

- **Layer 2 or Layer 3 switch**—If you want to route traffic between different VLANs (subnets) configured on the switch (e.g., Server A with IP 192.168.1.10/24 to Server B with IP 192.168.2.20/24), you will want to look at getting a Layer 3 switch. If you are using a layer 2 switch in your lab you will need a router external to your Layer 2 switch to handle the routing, which just adds to the amount of equipment you have lying around in your lab and have to power. A Layer 3 switch which provides routing functionality makes things a lot neater, though are more expensive than Layer 2 switches. However, all is not lost, as if your budget doesn't stretch to a Layer 3 network switch, an alternative is to run a Layer 2 switch with VLANs and then use an appropriate VA on your ESX/ESXi host to handle the routing capabilities. One of the most popular VA routers is called Vyatta Core, which is easy to configure and can be downloaded for free from www.vyatta.com/downloads.

- **Speed**—If you are using iSCSI or NFS along with advanced vSphere features such as VMotion, Storage VMotion (SVMotion), DRS, or FT, you will need a switch with gigabit speed ports. The older 100 megabit (Mb) port

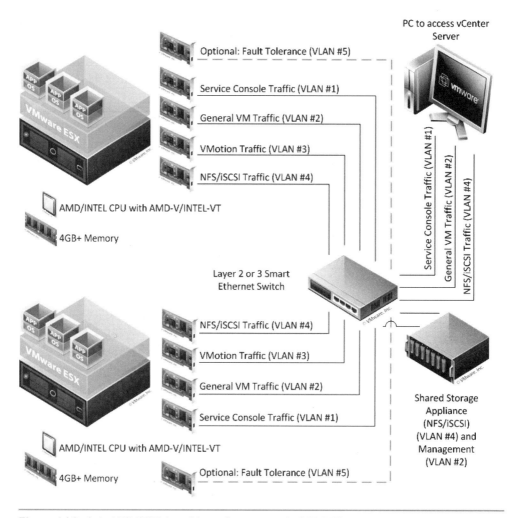

Figure 14.3 A dual ESX/ESXi host lab configuration with iSCSI/NFS shared storage to support some of vSphere's enterprise-level features, such as VMotion and FT

speeds found with Fast Ethernet won't be sufficient and will make most of these network-intensive features slow and unreliable.

- **Number of ports**—The number of ports you require on your lab's network switch will be determined by the number of ESX/ESXi lab servers you intend to run in your lab and how extensively you use VLAN tagging. Just remember that whatever you decide, you lose a least one port out of the total number for connecting your management PC or laptop. As shown in Figure 14.3, the number of required ports, if you don't intend to use VLAN tagging and routing, can soon add up, even in a small vSphere lab environment with two ESX/ESXi hosts and a single instance of shared storage.

- **Virtual LAN (VLAN) tagging**—To follow VMware best practices in keeping your various data traffic types (e.g., VMotion, FT) on separate networks and to avoid using multiple physical switches, the use of switches which support IEEE 802.1Q VLAN tagging is highly advisable. By using port or MAC address-based VLANs in your vSphere lab, you can easily implement the logical groupings of switch ports, thereby meeting the separate broadcast domain requirements. As you have probably guessed, by using VLAN tagging you can reduce the number of physical network ports required in your lab.

- **Jumbo frames**—With vSphere, jumbo frames are now officially supported. The increased packet sizes that jumbo frames allow means more data in fewer packet transmissions can be transferred between two network points. The most typical and recommended use for jumbo frames is for network-based storage traffic between ESX/ESXi hosts and a shared storage appliance. Most, but not all, gigabit networking switches and gigabit network cards you purchase these days will support jumbo frames, though don't expect the older Fast Ethernet switches and network cards to do so.

You will find switches that will meet your requirements from the following popular network switch manufacturers, all of which come with varying core feature sets and price tags: Cisco, HP, Linksys (Cisco), NetGear, DLink, and 3Com (HP). Commonly used switches in vSphere labs include the eight-port Linksys/Cisco SLM2008, as shown in Figure 14.4, and the eight-port HP ProCurve 1810G.

The HP ProCurve 1810G also comes in a larger 24-port model which would be better suited for larger vSphere labs. Both switches are Layer 2 and provide port-level VLAN tagging, QoS, and jumbo frames functionality. For subnet routing, I run the Vyatta router VA. If you'd rather use an external physical router, older end-of-life Cisco routers can be picked up quite cheaply on eBay.

Figure 14.4 An eight-port Linksys/Cisco SLM2008 gigabit switch

SOFTWARE COMPONENTS

In a vSphere lab, the software is where all the magic happens. For a very basic, single-host vSphere lab, you would only need a copy of VMware ESX/ESXi, with ESXi often being the more attractive option because it is free to download and use. This is fine if all you are after is some basic vSphere installation experience or you need a robust platform on which to run multiple VMs. However, the majority of you will probably be looking at doing much more with your new lab, which will involve using the "fun" stuff such as HA, DRS, and FT, along with other VMware products such as SRM, CapacityIQ, and AppSpeed. These are all available for download for time-limited evaluation.

As mentioned, you can download VMware ESXi and use it for free, with the full version of ESX and associated vSphere features available for download on a 60-day trial basis. At the end of the 60 days, you will need to have a full license for the edition of vSphere you wish to run. This means you will probably be looking at using multiple email accounts to download a fresh evaluation copy when your original copy expires. This can prove to be a hassle if you want to run a product for longer than the 30- or 60-day evaluation period for testing and so forth. In the absence of any Microsoft TechNet type of subscription but for VMware products, this is the only real option open to you and your lab.

Another consideration when planning your lab is that once your hosts are up and running, you are going to want to install VMs running an OS in your new lab. Unless you are using an open source OS such as Linux, you are most likely going to be looking at a Microsoft Server-based OS. By far, the most cost-effective (legal) way to gain access to your own Microsoft licenses for use in a lab environment is via a Microsoft TechNet subscription. For a few hundred pounds/dollars/euros, a TechNet subscription will gain you access to the vast majority of Microsoft's operating systems and applications with your own unique license keys—this is a bargain and a good investment, in my opinion. You can find TechNet discount codes on the Internet, so it can pay to spend a few minutes to search for them. If your budget won't stretch to a TechNet subscription, all is not lost, as Microsoft offers 180-day trials on many of its major operating system and server products.

ENVIRONMENTAL AND OTHER LAB CONSIDERATIONS

One aspect of running a vSphere lab that is often overlooked is the physical environment in which it is going to be run. The following points are less of an issue in data center or server room-based vSphere lab instances and more of a consideration for office or home-based setups.

- **Noise**—If you're using an enterprise-level server, you'll most likely find that the noise that one server generates, let alone two or more of them, is significant. This is fine if you are fortunate enough to have a server room, basement, or garage in which to run it, though you probably won't want to set one up in your family room or home office. White-box servers or smaller entry-level servers such as the HP ProLiant ML110 or ML115 run quietly enough that you can get away with having them run in most rooms without any disturbance.

- **Power**—Running a vSphere lab can be a costly affair, although it really does depend on whether you leave it on 24/7, as well as on the number of components and how much power they draw. For example, an ESX host running on an HP ProLiant ML110/ML115 G5 with 8GB of memory and 1 x SATA disk will consume, on average, 85W of power. Add your management PC, monitor, network switch, and any shared storage into the mix and you can consume 500W of power. If you are running your lab from home, check that you are getting the best deal for electricity from your electricity supplier. To help keep track of how much power your vSphere lab is consuming, consider using a power meter. These are inexpensive devices, and will give you a good appreciation for how much the lab is costing you to run; a good example is the Kill-A-Watt power meter from P3 International (www.p3international.com). An uninterruptible power supply (UPS) is also a useful addition to any lab, as it provides a clean power feed to your servers, network switches, and storage devices. As with using a UPS in a production environment, it will also protect you from any sudden power outages and provides a window to power down your lab VMs and hosts smoothly. A number of manufacturers produce small to medium-size UPSs. I always use APC, as I have worked with their UPS products in the enterprise for many years and have always found them to be reliable.

- **Time**—This is a variable that is often overlooked by many, but building and running your own lab can become something of a time-sink due to its flexibility and the large number of interesting things that you can discover and learn by running it. Be warned that you can get totally absorbed in running and trying out new applications or utilities, resulting in the hours just flying by. However, the outcome is positive, with an increase in your knowledge and understanding of these products, which can help fulfill your reasons for building the vSphere lab in the first place.

- **Financial**—Depending on the server, network, and storage hardware you decide to use in your lab, you can end up spending a significant amount of money. That being said, it is just as easy to put together a lab solution by keeping your ear to the ground for any appropriate hardware that your employer may be planning to dispose of during a hardware refresh cycle, which may end up costing you nothing or very little. At the end of the day, though, you can start as small as you want and slowly add extra pieces of hardware or upgrades over time. Just remember, you don't have to do it all at once!

RUNNING NESTED VMS

If space, portability, or budget is an issue or a serious consideration with your vSphere lab, you may want to consider one of the following lab solutions. In both of these methods of running virtualized instances of ESX/ESXi, you can use the more advanced vSphere features such as vMotion, HA, and DRS between virtual instances of ESX/ESXi or between physical and virtual instances. In my experience, the only advanced vSphere function that I have had difficulty running reliably on or between virtualized ESX/ESXi hosts is FT. As this feature is latency-sensitive in maintaining synchronization (vLockstep) between two hosts, it is more prone to failing in environments where solid and consistent performance is not present.

By running virtualized instances of ESX/ESXi on a physical ESX/ESXi host, you do receive the benefit of space, budget, and/or portability, though at the same time you are putting all your eggs in one basket in the event of a hardware failure. However, as this is a lab environment and no production VMs will ever be run from such an unsuitable production configuration, it may be deemed an acceptable risk to take in return for the benefits mentioned.

VMWARE ESX/ESXi ON VMWARE WORKSTATION 7

A useful way to run vSphere when you have access to limited lab hardware or you want to take ESX/ESXi on the road with you for demonstrations is to run it under VMware Workstation 7.x on a PC or laptop, as shown in Figure 14.5.

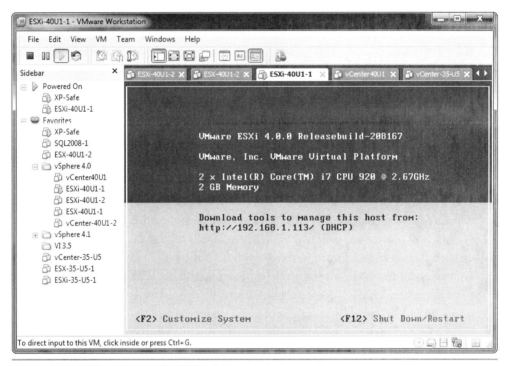

Figure 14.5 ESXi running inside a VM on VMware Workstation 7

VMware Workstation version 7.x now automatically detects the ESX/ESXi 4.0 install media and configures the VM within Workstation accordingly. This was possible with the previous version (6.5) of VMware Workstation, though some tweaking was required.

Don't expect the performance to be as good as running ESX/ESXi directly on a physical host; however, with sufficient CPU and memory resources combined with decent disk performance on the PC or laptop running VMware Workstaton, this can make for an adequate and convenient way to run a test instance of ESX/ESXi. If you have the luxury of being able to store and run your nested VMs from SSD storage, you will undoubtedly receive much better responsiveness and load times from them.

Of course, nothing is stopping you from running more than one instance of ESX/ESXi within VMware Workstation 7.x, though once again, don't expect lightning-fast performance due to the increased likelihood of resource contention (e.g., CPU, memory, and disk) on your PC or laptop, particularly once you start running a number of VMs. For this highly portable vSphere lab solution, it ultimately comes down to convenience and cost versus acceptable levels of performance.

VIRTUAL ESX/ESXi INSTANCES ON A PHYSICAL ESX/ESXi HOST

Running virtual instances of ESX/ESXi is one of the easiest ways to build a multiple-ESX/ESXi host environment. From a single physical ESX/ESXi host you can install and run multiple virtualized ESX/ESXi instances with nested VMs, providing you with a multihost vSphere lab in a single box. This has obvious appeal from a hardware outlay and running-cost perspective, though you may not get the level of performance you require from the VMs running on the nested instances of ESX/ESXi. As with running virtualized ESX/ESXi under VMware Workstation 7.x, you won't experience the same levels of performance. But for many labs, this trade-off between cost and performance may be acceptable, especially these days, with the increased power and number of cores found in most CPUs—in particular, Intel's Nehalem Xeon and i7 processors and AMD's 6 core Opteron and Phenom II processors. High-capacity (i.e., 2GB+ DIMMs) memory is now common, with 4GB DIMMs becoming more mainstream. Both of these server resources (CPU and memory) combined with the use of fast SSD disk storage can help you to overcome some of the performance degradation found with nesting VMs.

Unlike VMware Workstation 7.x, where installing virtualized instances of ESX/ESXi 4.0 is officially supported and possible without the requirement for any further tweaks or configuration changes, this is not the case with running virtualized instances of ESX/ESXi on a physical ESX/ESXi host. There are many gotchas when trying to install a virtual instance of ESX/ESXi on a physical ESX/ESXi host. There aren't any hard and fast rules regarding what works and what doesn't in all scenarios, so if you decide to try this, be prepared to spend some time reading through other people's findings and experiences on the VMware Community Forum and various VMware blog sites.

The following are examples and work arounds to some of the more common issues you may come across when running virtualized ESX/ESXi instances or nested VMs. When creating a VM from which to run a virtualized ESX/ESXi host, you will notice that there is no entry for VMware ESX/ESXi in the Guest Operating System section of the VM Creation Wizard. This is because it is not supported. To work around this, just make sure you select Linux—>Red Hat Enterprise Linux 5 (64 bit) and give the virtualized ESX/ESXi host enough memory, vCPUs, NICs, and access to disk space to meet the requirement of the nested VMs which you'll be running on it.

One important note is that you are unable to run 64-bit operating systems as nested VMs because these VMs are using the binary translation method, as the vCPU is running in legacy mode and not the x64 native long mode. See Chapter 2 for more details on these different modes of operation. This restriction will have implications if you want to run Microsoft Windows Server 2008 R2 which is only available as an x64 installation. If you try running an x64 OS as a nested VM, you will receive an error message saying that the host CPU is incompatible with the VM's requirements.

If you try to power on an x86 nested VM on a virtualized host, you will also get an error message saying that you cannot power on a VM in a VM. To get rid of this error, all you need to do is add an extra configuration parameter to your virtual ESX/ESXi host using the following steps.

1. Power down the VM on which you have installed your virtual ESX/ESXi instance and select Edit Settings either from the Summary tab within the vSphere Client or by right-clicking on the VM Name.

2. In the Virtual Machine Properties window, select the Options tab.

3. In the left pane, under Advanced, select General and then click the Configuration Parameters button. If this is grayed out, it means you haven't shut down your virtual ESX/ESXi host yet.

4. After you click the Configuration Parameters button, a new screen will open. From here, click the Add Row button and add the following new parameters:

   Name: `monitor_control.restrict_backdoor`

   Value: `True`

5. After entering these new parameters, click OK to apply the settings and then click OK to close the Virtual Machine Properties window.

One other thing you have to do before you start installing your x86 OS-based VMs is to change the Promiscuous Mode security setting on the vSwitches of the physical ESX/ESXi host that the virtualized ESX/ESXi is connected to, by following these steps.

1. Edit the vSwitch Properties on the physical host vSwitches that the virtualized ESX/ESXi host is connected to.

2. On the Ports tab, select vSwitch and click Edit.

3. On the Security tab, change Promiscuous Mode to Accept so that all three security Policy Exceptions are set to Accept, and then click OK to commit the changes.

This will now allow the VM and management traffic from your virtualized ESX/ESXi instances to travel out onto the physical network and to the physical ESX/ESXi host.

The last thing you should know is that if you intend to use your virtualized ESX/ESXi server hosts in a cluster, you will find that you will be unable to set the EVC mode to take advantage of maximized VMotion compatibility. This shouldn't pose an issue if you are only running a single, all-in-one-box vSphere lab solution with nested VMs, as the CPU types for all ESX/ESXi hosts, virtual or physical, will be the same. The reason you will be unable to enable EVC for your cluster is that the CPU which is presented through to the virtualized ESX/ESXi instance does not have the necessary Intel VT or AMD-V capabilities, even if the CPU of the underlying physical host does. This is similar to the reason mentioned earlier in this section that explained why you also can't run x64 OS nested VMs.

As you can see, it is relatively straightforward to install virtualized instances of ESX/ESXi and run nested VMs on them. Admittedly, it isn't as simple as dealing with physical ESX/ESXi hosts, though what you get in return is the requirement for less hardware and all the benefits that go along with that, such as reduced financial outlay, cooling, and power. Performance will almost certainly not be as good as running physical ESX/ESXi hosts, though what you want to achieve with your vSphere lab, including the number and types of VMs you will be running, will determine whether this is an acceptable compromise. When trying to install or run anything that is unsupported, don't forget to use the VMware Community Forum and the significant number of VMware-related blogs on the Internet. You can almost guarantee that someone else has come across the same or a similar issue before.

SUMMARY

Once you have your vSphere lab up and running, the possibilities of what you can install and run on it are almost endless, combined with the ability to expand it as and when needed to meet any requirements you may have. There is also no better way to learn about vSphere than to actually have your own stress-free environment in which to try things out without the fear of impacting anyone else. Your vSphere lab can be as large or as small as you require or what your budget will stretch to. Whatever it ends up looking like, as long as you've done your homework regarding what will and won't work and have followed some of the tips in this chapter, you will be well on your way toward building a successful lab. So, whatever your reason for building a vSphere lab, whether it is for studying for your VMware VCP accreditation, learning more to help you at work, or having a highly flexible platform on which to run multiple virtualized servers, the most important thing is to enjoy yourself and have fun!

INDEX

Numbers

2GB sparse disks, 63

64-bit VMkernels, ESX Service Consoles, 21–22

802.1Q VLAN tagging, support for, 137

A

AAM (Automated Availability Manager), 217

ability to hot-extend virtual disks, 4

ABRT/s (standard command aborts), 197–198

access

  DMA (direct memory access), 49

  ESX Service Console, 254

  Tech Support mode, 256

  vCenter Server, 11

  VMDirectPath, 49–53

  vSwitches, 11

  web

    clients, differences between ESX and ESXi, 34

    management, 249

Active Directory Application Mode (ADAM), 69

AD (Active Directory), vCenter Servers, 68, 81–82

ADAM (Active Directory Application Mode), 69

adapter

  displays, 46–47

  Flexible network, 133

adapters

  displays, 8

  Emulex PC, 118

  FC (Fibre Channel), 117

  HBAs (host bus adapters), 102

  IDE (integrated drive elctronics), 8, 44

  local storage, 117

  networks, 320

  PVSCSI (Paravirtualized SCSI), 94–97, 199

  SCSI, paravirtualization, 5, 44

I

FREE Online Edition

Your purchase of **Maximum vSphere™** includes access to a free online edition for 45 days through the Safari Books Online subscription service. Nearly every Prentice Hall book is available online through Safari Books Online, along with more than 5,000 other technical books and videos from publishers such as Addison-Wesley Professional, Cisco Press, Exam Cram, IBM Press, O'Reilly, Que, and Sams.

SAFARI BOOKS ONLINE allows you to search for a specific answer, cut and paste code, download chapters, and stay current with emerging technologies.

Activate your FREE Online Edition at
www.informit.com/safarifree

> **STEP 1:** Enter the coupon code: XNCUREH.

> **STEP 2:** New Safari users, complete the brief registration form.
> Safari subscribers, just log in.

If you have difficulty registering on Safari or accessing the online edition, please e-mail customer-service@safaribooksonline.com